TAXATION, ECONOMIC PROSPERITY, AND DISTRIBUTIVE JUSTICE

TAXATION, ECONOMIC PROSPERITY, AND DISTRIBUTIVE JUSTICE

Edited by

Ellen Frankel Paul, Fred D. Miller, Jr., and Jeffrey Paul

CAMBRIDGE
UNIVERSITY PRESS

University Printing House, Cambridge CB2 8BS, United Kingdom

One Liberty Plaza, 20th Floor, New York, NY 10006, USA

477 Williamstown Road, Port Melbourne, VIC 3207, Australia

314-321, 3rd Floor, Plot 3, Splendor Forum, Jasola District Centre, New Delhi - 110025, India

79 Anson Road, #06-04/06, Singapore 079906

Cambridge University Press is part of the University of Cambridge.

It furthers the University's mission by disseminating knowledge in the pursuit of education, learning and research at the highest international levels of excellence.

www.cambridge.org
Information on this title: www.cambridge.org/9780521685993

First published 2006

A catalogue record for this publication is available from the British Library

Library of Congress Cataloging in Publication data
Taxation, Economic Prosperity, and Distributive Justice /
edited by Ellen Frankel Paul, Fred D. Miller, Jr., and Jeffrey Paul. p. cm.
Includes bibliographical references and index.
ISBN 0-521-68599-0
1. Taxation—Moral and ethical aspects.
2. Fiscal policy—Moral and ethical aspects. 3. Distributive justice.
I. Paul, Ellen Frankel. II. Miller, Fred Dycus, 1944 III. Paul, Jeffrey.
HJ2321.T394 2006
174–dc22 2006044024

ISBN 978-0-521-68599-3 Paperback

The essays in this book have also been published, without introduction and index, in the semiannual journal *Social Philosophy & Policy*, Volume 23, Number 2, which is available by subscription.

CONTENTS

INTRODUCTION

What constitutes a just tax system, and what are its moral foundations? Should a society's tax regime be designed to achieve a just distribution of wealth among its citizens, or should such a regime be designed to promote economic growth, rising standards of living, and increasing levels of employment? Are these two goals—distributive justice and economic prosperity—compatible or incompatible? If they are incompatible, why should this be—that is, why should justice not require, or at least lead to, an increase in general prosperity?

The twelve essays in this volume—written by prominent philosophers, economists, political scientists, and legal theorists—address these questions and explore related issues. Some essays examine the history of tax policies and the normative principles that have informed the selection of various types of taxes and tax regimes. Some analyze economic data in order to discover which tax policies are most conducive to economic growth. Some look at particular theories of justice or property rights and seek to draw out their implications for the design of tax systems. Other essays propose specific tax reforms, such as revising the income tax to be more favorable to households with children, or replacing taxes on capital with taxes on consumption. Still others challenge traditional theories of taxation, offering new ways of understanding the fiscal relationship between governments and their citizens.

The collection's opening essay offers a brief history of federal tax policy in the United States. In "Social Philosophy and Tax Regimes in the United States, 1763 to the Present," W. Elliot Brownlee explores how ideas about social justice and economic performance have shaped the debates over taxation in the U.S. since the origins of the republic. He notes that these debates were most intense during major national emergencies: the American Revolution, the Civil War, World War I, the Great Depression, and World War II. Discussing each of these emergencies in turn, Brownlee shows how each produced a new tax regime—a tax system with its own characteristic tax base, rate structure, administrative apparatus, and social purpose. A system of tariffs and excise taxes financed the federal government in the early years of the republic, providing revenues that were used to repay debts incurred during the Revolutionary War. The Civil War required expanded revenues and led to higher tariffs on imports and rising excise taxes on alcohol and tobacco. The regressive nature of these consumption taxes led to concerns over equity and calls for a more progressive system designed to reduce economic inequality and to assign tax burdens according to a criterion of "ability to pay." The result was the system of progressive income taxation that emerged in the early twentieth century and was expanded and refined during the Depression and the two world wars. Brownlee concludes his essay by examining revisions of tax policy in the postwar period, focusing on efforts to reduce marginal tax rates in order to foster economic growth.

The next three essays take up the issue of taxation and its impact on economic growth, and explore this issue in greater detail. In "The Impact of Tax Policy on Economic Growth, Income Distribution, and Allocation of Taxes," James D. Gwartney and Robert A. Lawson analyze changes in tax policy during the 1980s and 1990s. Using a sample of seventy-seven countries, Gwartney and Lawson focus on marginal tax rates and the income thresholds at which they apply in order to examine how tax policy changes influenced economic growth, the distribution of income, and the share of taxes paid by various income groups. Many countries substantially reduced their highest marginal rates during the period from 1985 to 1995, and Gwartney and Lawson's analysis indicates that countries that reduced their highest marginal rates grew more rapidly than those that maintained high marginal rates. At the same time, the income distribution in several of the tax-cutting countries became more unequal, while there was little change or even a reduction in income inequality in most countries that maintained high marginal rates. Finally, the evidence suggests that there was a shift during the 1980s and 1990s in the payment of the personal income tax, a shift away from those with low and middle incomes and toward those with the highest incomes. Thus, there is reason to believe that cutting tax rates across all income brackets actually leads to an increase in the share of income taxes paid by the wealthiest taxpayers.

The relationship between a society's economic prosperity and the happiness or well-being of its citizens is the subject of Richard Vedder's essay, "Taxes, Growth, Equity, and Welfare." Vedder agrees with Gwartney and Lawson that high tax burdens tend to inhibit economic growth, and thus that reductions in tax rates can stimulate economic activity. Nevertheless, some economists argue that low taxes and high rates of economic growth can lead to greater inequalities in income distribution and to utility-reducing underconsumption of needed public goods—consequences that adversely affect the well-being of citizens. Vedder seeks to challenge these assertions, arguing that there is little reason to believe that increased governmental spending leads to greater equality and enhanced well-being. If such spending actually led to improvements in well-being, we would expect to see people migrating to (or remaining in) states and cities with higher tax burdens and more expansive governmental services. The evidence shows, however, that people tend to migrate to low-tax areas. Vedder also contends that inequality in the U.S. and other low-tax societies is actually less extensive than is typically claimed, at least if we measure inequality in terms of consumption spending rather than strictly in terms of income. Vedder concludes his essay with an examination of international income disparities and efforts aimed at poverty reduction.

He argues that governmental spending does not generally lead toward reductions in poverty or toward progress in income equalization between developing societies and developed ones. Rather, the evidence suggests that poverty is reduced and income increased largely as a result of private-sector activity—that is, as a result of market forces operating in societies that respect the rule of law and afford strong protections for private property rights.

In "The Consequences of Taxation," Joel Slemrod asks how a system of taxation might best be designed, given that any such system establishes incentives that can have profound effects on economic growth and prosperity. The consequences of taxation, Slemrod observes, depend on taxpayers' behavioral responses. These responses are embodied in the notion of the "elasticity" of taxable income: the idea that people seek to avoid paying taxes, especially when rates are progressive, by forgoing opportunities to earn more income or by shielding part of their income from taxation. It is generally acknowledged that the extent of this elasticity depends on people's preferences, especially the relative values they place on goods and leisure. Taxes on income can lead to a reduction in the supply of labor if individuals choose to forgo some of the goods they might have bought with their earnings, preferring instead to have more leisure time. Yet Slemrod argues that the elasticity of taxable income also depends on other factors: it depends on the availability of tax shelters and other "avoidance technologies," and on the response of government to taxpayers' use of such technologies. These factors are within the control of governments, and in the remainder of his essay Slemrod considers how government policies might be modified in order to achieve an optimal tax system and avoid the distorting effects that taxation can have on economic activity. He also examines a number of issues that complicate the quest for an optimal tax policy, including the existence of multiple taxing jurisdictions and the movement of people and capital across borders.

The next several essays explore the relationship between taxation and distributive justice. In "Justice: A Conservative View," John Kekes defends a view of justice based on desert, maintaining that justice prevails when people have what they deserve and do not have what they do not deserve. Kekes begins with an analysis of the requirements of successful human action: individuals must exercise sound judgment in the choice and pursuit of their goals; they must abide by the terms of cooperation set by their society; and, in many cases, they must engage in competition to achieve their goals. A just society, Kekes contends, is one that sets reasonable terms of cooperation. These terms fall into three broad categories: some concern relationships (e.g., with family members, friends, associates, etc.); some govern agreements, such as contracts or promises; and some prohibit actions that affect the security of others, such as negligence, assault, or homicide. Kekes offers a detailed discussion of these terms of cooperation and argues that they help to determine what individuals deserve.

He goes on to consider various objections to his view, including the egalitarian idea that individuals are (or should be presumed to be) equally deserving, because everyone has the same moral worth or is entitled to the same moral respect. He concludes by sketching the implications of his view with regard to policies on income taxation. Since individuals deserve to keep the income they earn, taxation can be justified only under limited circumstances, namely, when it is required for the provision of services that all citizens benefit from, such as national security, infrastructure, and the maintenance of a legal system. Taxation for the provision of benefits to the needy is not justified on this view, though Kekes suggests that we may have obligations to help others that are derived, not from justice, but from benevolence, decency, or other considerations.

Like Kekes, Eric Mack is concerned with the question of when, and for what purposes, taxation is justified. In "Non-Absolute Rights and Libertarian Taxation," Mack seeks to show that taxation for the purpose of providing a social safety-net is compatible with a rights-oriented libertarian theory. Such a theory asserts the existence of robust individual rights, including robust rights of property, and, if these property rights are absolute, then it seems that all taxation is theft. Yet when an individual finds himself in dire circumstances, through no fault of his own, it is generally thought to be permissible for him to seize or trespass upon another's property in order to escape from those circumstances. In this sense, Mack notes, property rights seem to be non-absolute. He presents a number of hypothetical cases designed to demonstrate the plausibility of this view of property rights, and then goes on to consider whether the non-absoluteness of rights can serve as a justification of taxation for the sake of rescuing individuals from dire need or poverty, by providing them with some minimal level of shelter, food, and basic medical care. In the course of the essay, Mack explores the issue of how dire an individual's circumstances have to be for him to have a dispensation from the normal obligation to respect property. Mack distinguishes among different dispensations that individuals in emergency situations may have, and among various obligations that property owners may have in these situations. In the end, he maintains that it is possible to argue from the premise that property rights are not absolute to the conclusion that taxation to provide a safety-net is justified, but he suggests that the path from the premise to the conclusion is a long and complex one.

Kevin A. Kordana and David H. Tabachnick are, like Mack, interested in exploring the nature of property rights and asking how these rights limit redistributive taxation. In "Taxation, the Private Law, and Distributive Justice," Kordana and Tabachnick begin by distinguishing two conceptions of property. On the one hand, pre-institutional theorists embrace the Lockean view that there is a natural right to property that exists prior to the establishment of any legal or political institutions. On the other hand, post-institutional theorists (e.g., Rawlsians) hold that private property is a matter of political convention. Given this distinction, Kordana and Tabachnick go on to examine the relationship between tax policy and the private law (that is, areas of law, such as tort and contract, that govern the interactions of private parties). The authors argue that for theorists with a post-institutional conception of property, there is no principled reason to limit the domain of distributive justice to tax and transfer policies: both tax policies *and* the rules of the private law can be constructed in service of distributive aims. Such theorists cannot maintain a commitment to a normative conception of private law that is independent of their overarching distributive principles. In contrast, theorists with a pre-institutional conception of property can derive the private law from sectors of morality that are independent of distributive justice. Nevertheless, Kordana and Tabachnick argue, this does not entail that the private law, for pre-institutional theorists, must be sanitized of equity-oriented values such as charity, beneficence, or the pursuit of equality. Pre-institutional theorists who hold principled commitments to equity-oriented values are free to invoke either tax and transfer programs or the rules of the private law to attain those values.

In "The Uneasy Case for Capital Taxation," Edward J. McCaffery examines the debate over whether income taxes or consumption taxes are preferable in terms of their justice or fairness. On the traditional view of taxation, the income tax has often been criticized as a "double tax" on capital, since individuals who invest their earnings rather than spending them must pay income taxes twice: on the initial earnings that they invest, and on the returns to their investments. In contrast, the traditional view holds that consumption taxes fail to tax the yield to capital at all. McCaffery contends, however, that the traditional view of consumption taxes is flawed. An alternative view would acknowledge that there are two kinds of consumption taxes. A prepaid consumption tax (which is equivalent to a tax on wages) does indeed ignore the yield to capital. However, a progressive postpaid consumption tax does not share this shortcoming. This tax would be paid at the time when consumption actually occurred, and would be paid according to a progressive rate scale so that those who consumed more would be subject to a higher rate. Thus, a progressive postpaid consumption tax would fall on the yield to capital, at the individual level, when (but only when) the returns to capital were used to enhance lifestyles in material terms. This type of tax would not penalize a person who used savings and investments to "smooth out" his or her consumption levels over time, that is, to shift labor earnings to different periods of the individual's life, such as retirement or periods of heightened medical or educational needs. McCaffery believes that considerations of fairness favor a progressive postpaid consumption tax, since it would fall on the yield to capital at precisely the right time, when such yield is used to finance a more costly lifestyle. He concludes that, for reasons of justice, a progressive postpaid consumption tax should be instituted, and that all other taxes on capital—such as capital gains taxes, gift and estate taxes, and corporate income taxes—should be repealed.

Daniel N. Shaviro's essay, "Households and the Fiscal System," explores one of the most difficult issues in income tax policy, asking how family or household status should affect tax liability. To what extent should marital status or family responsibilities affect the amount of income tax an individual is required to pay? Should a tax system be designed to achieve "marriage neutrality," so that couples who live together and pool their resources face the same tax liability whether they are married or not? Shaviro seeks to address these and similar questions by sketching out a general approach for thinking about the treatment of households in the fiscal system. He focuses on the fiscal rules currently in place in the United States, including not only the rules of the income tax code but also those that govern Social Security, Medicare, and various safety-net programs such as food stamps. He argues that these rules would be more just if they were to redefine the notion of household or couple status to include both married couples and "domestic partners" who live together and significantly pool their resources. Shaviro also notes that the fiscal system in the U.S. is currently biased in favor of one-earner couples and that it discourages work by secondary earners within households, and he suggests ways that these inequities could be mitigated. He concludes by considering the fiscal system's treatment of households with children. Here he finds a conflict between political rhetoric in the U.S., which is highly supportive of families with children, and actual U.S. policy, where the treatment of households with children is mixed. At the low end of the income scale, Shaviro observes, households with children do indeed receive far more favorable treatment than households with no children; yet these advantages tend to shrink or disappear as household income rises. He recommends revising the tax code to provide more favorable treatment to households with children, without restricting this treatment to relatively poor households.

The collection's final three essays examine different ways of understanding taxation and the relationship of government with its citizens. In "Taxation, the State, and the Community," Jeffrey Schoenblum offers a critique of traditional public finance theory, arguing that it fails to integrate the revenue-raising and revenue-spending functions of the state, and that it offers no convincing theory of the nature of the state itself or of communities within the state. Standard public finance theory views the state as an independent actor relying on the advice of experts to formulate policies designed to achieve gains in social welfare for the community. Yet, as Schoenblum observes, this standard view is tempered by a more cynical view of the state as an entity that, over time, accumulates more and more authority over the resources and property of its citizens. It is also possible to conceive of the state as a process by which various special-interest communities compete with one another for resources, or as a bureaucracy in which officials and politicians seek to pursue their own interests. A fully developed theory of the state, Schoenblum suggests, would take all these elements into account. Schoenblum goes on to discuss the emerging global community and the impact it is likely to have on the tax policies of individual states, focusing on the phenomena of tax competition among states and the movement of labor and capital across national borders. He maintains that understanding the role of subnational and supranational communities is essential for grasping how tax revenues are distributed in the real world. He concludes that the failure of public finance theory to come to grips with these realities is a result of the theory's powerful faith in bureaucratic expertise and in abstract models of social welfare, whether or not these models work in practice or would be agreed upon and implemented via the political process.

Like Schoenblum, Richard E. Wagner challenges some of the assumptions that underlie contemporary fiscal theory. In "Choice, Catallaxy, and Just Taxation: Contrasting Architectonics for Fiscal Theorizing," Wagner notes that contemporary theories of public finance tend to treat government as an agent, and tend to treat choices about taxation and spending as choices of that agent. This approach to political economy is a "disjunctive" one, since government is conceived as entirely separate from the market economy: citizens interact with one another in the marketplace, and the government intervenes in the marketplace in order to achieve certain desired ends. The alternative approach that Wagner offers is a "conjunctive" one, in which government is treated not as an agent that intervenes in a market economy but as an arena of organized participation within it. On this view, government is conceived of as a form of "catallaxy"—an adaptive system in which fiscal policies emerge through a process of complex interaction among citizens. This conjunctive approach can be traced back to the spontaneous-order theorists of the eighteenth-century Scottish Enlightenment, and Wagner contends that this approach is more appropriate to modern democratic societies, where policies on taxation and spending arise from within a society rather than being imposed on it from above by an autocratic ruler. After sketching the contours of this conjunctive approach, Wagner goes on to discuss the emergence of politically organized enterprises, such as public schools, hospitals, and parks, alongside their private-sector counterparts. He also explores the implications of his view with respect to tax policies, arguing that these policies should conform to principles of uniformity or generality if they are to be consistent with the democratic notion that taxes emerge from agreement among citizens rather than being forced on them from above. Thus, he concludes, broad-based taxes on income or consumption are preferable to narrow-based taxes that allow some groups of citizens to impose fiscal burdens on others.

The role of government in modern democratic societies is also the subject of the collection's final essay, Jonathan R. Macey's "Government as Investor: Tax Policy and the State." Macey conceives of government as analogous to an investor in the individuals and firms that fall under its authority. As an investor, government supplies goods and services that promote the development of human capital and the growth of businesses, such as police protection, enforcement of contracts, transportation infrastructure, subsidized education, and so on. In return, the government, like other investors, makes a residual claim on the earnings of people and firms that are subject to its taxing power. Macey acknowledges that the government-as-investor analogy is imperfect, since governments are able to exercise powers of coercion that are unavailable to ordinary investors. Nevertheless, he suggests that the acceptance of this view could actually strengthen the relationship between democratic governments and their citizens, since the view recognizes citizen-taxpayers as contracting partners with the state. Moreover, Macey argues that the government-as-investor framework he develops could lead to a number of tax policy improvements. Ordinary investors lack the power to unilaterally alter the agreements they reach with borrowers, and Macey contends that there should be similar limits on the government's ability to change people's tax status after they have already embarked on careers and made the sunken investments in human capital that career training requires. The government-as-investor framework also suggests that people should be able to make a once-in-a-lifetime payment in lieu of taxes to the state in order to discharge their tax liability. In the course of the essay, Macey compares his approach to other conceptions of the state's taxing authority, including Robert Nozick's view that income taxation is on a par with forced labor and thus violates people's natural rights. Macey finds this view unrealistic and concludes that the government-as-investor framework provides a superior alternative, one that does not jeopardize the state's ability to collect the revenues it needs to provide for the protection of its citizens.

The design of a society's system of taxation has a profound impact on its citizens' economic life and well-being. The essays in this volume offer valuable contributions to debates about the justice and economic consequences of various tax regimes.

ACKNOWLEDGMENTS

The editors wish to acknowledge several individuals at the Social Philosophy and Policy Center, Bowling Green State University, who provided invaluable assistance in the preparation of this volume. They include Program Manager Nicolás Maloberti, Mary Dilsaver, and Terrie Weaver.

The editors also extend special thanks to Assistant Managing Editor Tamara Sharp, for attending to innumerable day-to-day details of the book's preparation, and to Managing Editor Harry Dolan, for providing dedicated assistance throughout the editorial and production process.

CONTRIBUTORS

W. Elliot Brownlee is Professor Emeritus of History at the University of California, Santa Barbara. He is an economic historian who has written extensively on the history of taxation and public finance. His most recent books on this topic are *Funding the Modern American State: The Rise and Fall of the Era of Easy Finance, 1941–1995* (editor and principal contributor, 1996) and *Federal Taxation in America: A Short History* (2d ed., 2004). He is currently researching the history of taxation and public finance during the Reagan administration. In 2003, he published an essay on this subject in *The Reagan Presidency: Pragmatic Conservatism and Its Legacies,* which he and the late Hugh Davis Graham coedited. Brownlee is also writing a history of the financing of World War I and a comparative history of taxation in the United States and Japan since World War II.

James D. Gwartney is Professor of Economics and holder of the Gus A. Stavros Eminent Scholar Chair at Florida State University, where he directs the Stavros Center for the Advancement of Free Enterprise and Economic Education. He served as chief economist of the Joint Economic Committee of the U.S. Congress during 1999–2000. He is the coauthor of *Economics: Private and Public Choice* (2005), a widely used principles of economics text that is now in its eleventh edition. He is also coauthor of a primer on economics, *Common Sense Economics: What Everyone Should Know about Wealth and Prosperity* (2005), and of *Economic Freedom of the World,* an annual report that provides information on the institutions and policies of more than 120 countries. His publications have appeared both in professional journals and in popular media such as the *Wall Street Journal* and the *New York Times*. He holds a Ph.D. in economics from the University of Washington.

Robert A. Lawson is Professor of Economics and George H. Moor Chair in the School of Management at Capital University in Columbus, Ohio. He earned his B.S. in economics from the Honors Tutorial College at Ohio University and his M.S. and Ph.D. in economics from Florida State University. He has published numerous articles in journals such as *Public Choice, Cato Journal, Journal of Labor Research, Journal of Institutional and Theoretical Economics,* and *European Journal of Political Economy,* and is coauthor of the *Economic Freedom of the World* annual report. He is a senior fellow with the Buckeye Institute for Public Policy Solutions, for which he has written extensively on issues of state and local public finance.

Richard Vedder is Distinguished Professor of Economics at Ohio University. He is a graduate of Northwestern University and received his Ph.D.

from the University of Illinois. He is the author or editor of eight books and monographs, including *The American Economy in Historical Perspective* (1976), *Out of Work: Unemployment and Government in Twentieth-Century America* (with Lowell Gallaway, 1993), and *Going Broke by Degree: Why College Costs Too Much* (2004). He has written some two hundred scholarly papers published in academic journals and in edited volumes, and has also written extensively in the popular press, including the *Wall Street Journal, USA Today,* the *Washington Post,* the *Los Angeles Times, Investor's Business Daily,* the *Chicago Tribune,* and *Forbes Magazine.*

Joel Slemrod is Paul W. McCracken Collegiate Professor of Business Economics and Public Policy at the University of Michigan's Stephen M. Ross School of Business. He is also Professor of Economics in the University of Michigan's Department of Economics and director of the university's Office of Tax Policy Research. He received his A.B. degree from Princeton University in 1973 and his Ph.D. in economics from Harvard University in 1980. In 1983–84, he was a National Fellow at the Hoover Institution, and, in 1984–85, he served on the President's Council of Economic Advisers as the senior staff economist for tax policy. From 1992 to 1998, he was editor of the *National Tax Journal.* He is coauthor with Jon Bakija of *Taxing Ourselves: A Citizen's Guide to the Debate over Taxes* (3d ed., 2004).

John Kekes is Professor Emeritus of Philosophy of the State University of New York. He is the author of many books and articles on ethics and political thought. His books include *A Case for Conservatism* (1998), *The Illusions of Egalitarianism* (2003), and *The Roots of Evil* (2005). He welcomes comments on his work at jonkekes@nycap.rr.com.

Eric Mack is Professor of Philosophy at Tulane University and a faculty member of Tulane's Murphy Institute of Political Economy. His primary interests are in moral theory, legal and political philosophy, and the history of political philosophy. Among his recent publications are "Self-Ownership, Marxism, and Egalitarianism, Part I: Challenges to Historical Entitlement" and "Self-Ownership, Marxism, and Egalitarianism, Part II: Challenges to the Self-Ownership Thesis," in *Politics, Philosophy, and Economics* (2002); "Self-Ownership, Taxation, and Democracy: A Philosophical-Constitutional Perspective," in *Politics, Taxation, and the Rule of Law* (2002); "Libertarianism and Classical Liberalism" (with Gerald Gaus), in *A Handbook of Political Theory* (2004); and "Prerogatives, Restrictions, and Rights," in *Social Philosophy and Policy* (2005).

Kevin A. Kordana is Professor of Law at the University of Virginia School of Law, where he has taught since 1996. From 2002 to 2005, he was the Nicholas E. Chimicles Research Professor in Business Law and Regulation. He attended Yale Law School, where he was a symposium editor of

The Yale Law Journal and received the Olin Prize for the best paper in law and economics. Upon graduation, he clerked for Chief Judge Richard A. Posner of the U.S. Court of Appeals for the Seventh Circuit. He has been a visiting professor at the University of Southern California and George Washington University law schools.

David H. Tabachnick is a Ph.D. candidate in philosophy at the University of Virginia. His interests are in moral, political, and legal theory, and he teaches philosophy of law, ethics and international relations, and political philosophy. At the University of Virginia School of Law, he has co-taught public health law and ethics and has lectured on the philosophy of contract law. He has also taught in UVA's Social and Political Thought Program and has held predoctoral fellowships in philosophy, law, and ethics at UVA's Institute for Practical Ethics. His publications include "Tax and the Philosopher's Stone," in *Virginia Law Review* (2003), and "Rawls and Contract Law," in *George Washington Law Review* (2005), both coauthored with Kevin A. Kordana.

Edward J. McCaffery is Robert C. Packard Trustee Chair in Law and Political Science at the University of Southern California, and Visiting Professor of Law and Economics at the California Institute of Technology. He is the author of many articles and several books, including *Taxing Women* (1999) and *Fair Not Flat: How to Make the Tax System Better and Simpler* (2002). He is currently working on a book on property theory.

Daniel N. Shaviro is Wayne Perry Professor of Taxation at New York University School of Law. His research focuses on tax policy, governmental transfers, budgetary measures, social insurance, and entitlement reform. His books include *Do Deficits Matter?* (1997), *When Rules Change: An Economic and Political Analysis of Transition Relief and Retroactivity* (2000), *Making Sense of Social Security Reform* (2000), and *Who Should Pay for Medicare?* (2004).

Jeffrey Schoenblum is Centennial Professor of Law at Vanderbilt University Law School. He is the author of numerous books and articles, with a focus on issues of cross-border taxation of private wealth. His recent books include *Multistate and Multinational Estate Planning* (1999), *A Guide to International Estate Planning* (2000), and *Bilateral Transfer Tax Treaties* (2003). He has also delivered a number of endowed lectures, including the Norton Rose Lecture at Oxford University, the Paolo Fresco Lecture at the University of Genoa, and the Nottingham Lecture.

Richard E. Wagner is Holbert L. Harris Professor of Economics at George Mason University. He received his Ph.D. in economics from the University of Virginia in 1966. Prior to joining the faculty of George Mason

University in 1988, he held positions at the University of California at Irvine, Tulane University, Virginia Polytechnic Institute and State University, Auburn University, and Florida State University. His primary scholarly activities involve teaching and writing about public finance, economic sociology, and macroeconomics, all approached from within a generally emergent and evolutionary orientation. He is the author of over 150 professional articles and some thirty books and monographs.

Jonathan R. Macey is Sam Harris Professor of Corporate Law, Corporate Finance, and Securities Law at Yale University. He earned a B.A. (cum laude) from Harvard and a J.D. from Yale Law School, and received a Ph.D. *honoris causa* from the Stockholm School of Economics. He is a member of the Legal Advisory Committee to the Board of Directors of the New York Stock Exchange and a member of the Board of Editors of Thompson West Publishing Company. He is the author of more than 150 scholarly articles and several books, and his research interests include corporate governance, banking, public choice, and law and economics.

ACKNOWLEDGMENTS

The editors gratefully acknowledge the Pierre F. and Enid Goodrich Foundation for providing support for the essays in this volume, as well as Liberty Fund, Inc., for holding the conference at which these papers were discussed.

SOCIAL PHILOSOPHY AND TAX REGIMES IN THE UNITED STATES, 1763 TO THE PRESENT

By W. Elliot Brownlee

I. Introduction

Every major debate over tax policy in the United States since its origins has swept over a broad span of economic issues. Each of these debates has touched on all the central questions regarding the effect of taxation on the performance of the economy. Participants in the debates have asked: Will changes in tax policy encourage or discourage economic productivity? Will such changes promote economic expansion or perhaps cause unemployment? Will they dampen inflation or perhaps create inflationary pressures? What effect will changes in tax policy have on the distribution of income, wealth, or, more narrowly, the allocation of the tax burden among the members of society? What might the impact of these changes be on the distribution of economic power? Will they create a more just tax system, or contribute to a more just society? Will they do so at the cost of a less prosperous society? Or will they create more affluence at the cost of less justice? Discussions of such questions have been most intense during major national emergencies—the American Revolution, the Civil War, World War I, the Great Depression, and World War II. During each of these emergencies, passionate debates have yielded a new tax regime. This essay examines the debates and assesses how ideas about economic performance and tax justice have shaped their outcomes, especially the creation of new tax regimes.[1]

II. The Founding Regime

The fundamental structure of the federal tax system emerged from the revolutionary crisis that extended through the formation of the U.S. Constitution. At its heart, the crisis was a constitutional struggle to define the basic ideas underlying the federal government: ideas of representation and consent, constitutionality and rights, and sovereignty.[2] At the same

[1] I have defined a tax regime as a tax system with its own characteristic tax base, rate structure, administration apparatus, and social purpose. For a survey of U.S. regimes, see W. Elliot Brownlee, *Federal Taxation in America: A Short History* (Cambridge and Washington, DC: Cambridge University Press and the Wilson Center Press, 2004).

[2] The most powerful interpretation of the American Revolution as an intellectual movement remains Bernard Bailyn, *The Ideological Origins of the American Revolution* (Cambridge, MA: Harvard University Press, 1967).

time Americans forged their ideas of government, they struggled with an array of practical problems. Among the most pressing was to fund the foreign debts that the Confederation had inherited from the Revolutionary War, and to do so in a way that would win the confidence of the international financial markets to which the new nation would have to turn for capital. In the process of resolving problems that were both profound and mundane, the framers of the Constitution gave shape to the fiscal institutions they believed the new federal government—and a new nation—would need to survive and prosper.

The treatment of taxation in the Constitution reflected, first and foremost, a trust in republican government. To the architects of the Constitution, taxpaying was one of the normal obligations of a citizenry bound together in a republic by ties of affection and respect. In trying to provide the new republic with robust taxing powers, the founders revealed that they embraced a classical republicanism, perhaps best described as "civic humanism," that stressed communal responsibilities as well as private rights.[3] They believed that, in the process of taxing to fund the debts of the Revolutionary War, the new government would both nurture and demonstrate the fiscal virtue and economic capacity of the citizens of a republic.

Thus, the Constitution reflected the desire of Alexander Hamilton and its other architects to provide the new central government with far greater capacity to tax than had been possible under the Articles of Confederation. While the Confederation could only exhort the states to contribute voluntarily to the federal treasury, the Constitution gave the new government the fiscal authority that would reflect its sovereignty. Congress had the general power, in the words of Article I, Section 8, "to lay and collect taxes, duties, imposts, and excises."

In *The Federalist Papers*, Hamilton explained how the new nation would have the means to acquire the economic resources it needed to fulfill its promise. He emphasized that, in peacetime, customs duties and excises would provide the bulk of the republic's revenues, and would do so in a fashion that was just. His arguments on behalf of the fairness of customs duties and excises, however, were complicated and conflicted. He identified various aspects of tariffs and excises as just, or at least as promoting justice, and one such aspect was the predictable, sustainable flow of revenues from these taxes. Without access to such a flow, Hamilton argued in *The Federalist Papers*, the federal government risked degeneration into a tyranny, subjecting "the people ... to continual plunder," as in "the

[3] On the meaning and long-run influence of civic humanism, see Dorothy Ross, "The Liberal Tradition Revisited and the Republican Tradition Addressed," in John Higham and Paul K. Conkin, eds., *New Directions in American Intellectual History* (Baltimore, MD: Johns Hopkins University Press, 1979), 116–31.

Ottoman or Turkish empire."[4] Reliance on the taxation of commerce was also just, in Hamilton's view, because the "general Union" would be "conducive to the interests of commerce."[5]

This argument might seem to have been simply the invocation of the "benefit" theory of taxation that had originated with Thomas Hobbes. To Hobbes, taxation represented benefits received from "the commonwealth" (essentially for "defence"), and the best measure of those benefits was the value of consumption.[6] Hamilton, however, was an especially close reader of Adam Smith and had adopted Smith's broadening of the concept of benefit to encompass an "ability to pay" doctrine (Smith's first canon of taxation); in this way, Smith expressed his own civic humanism.[7] In this canon, Smith held: "The subjects of every state ought to contribute towards the support of the government, as nearly as possible, in proportion to their respective abilities." Smith defined "abilities" as "the revenues which they respectively enjoy under the protection of the state." Thus, he linked the "ability to pay" and "benefit" principles.[8]

Throughout Hamilton's discussion of taxation in *The Federalist Papers*, Hamilton wrestled with the "ability to pay" criterion. He acknowledged that consumers seemed likely to bear the burden of tariffs and excises, and advanced several arguments to offset this problem. First, he suggested that taxes on consumption might be the only practical way to tax personal property, and thus tax it according to "ability to pay."[9] Second, he suggested that merchants shared in carrying the burden of consumption taxation. "It is not always possible," Hamilton argued, "to raise the price of a commodity in exact proportion to every additional imposition laid upon it."[10] Third, he argued that consumers could adjust their spending to reduce their taxes. Hamilton likened "all duties upon articles of consumption" to "a fluid, which will, in time, find its level with the means of paying them." He noted, in particular: "The amount to be contributed by each citizen will in a degree be at his own option, and can be regulated by an attention to his resources."[11] Hamilton chose the

[4] Alexander Hamilton, *The Federalist No. 30*, in *The Federalist* (New York: The Modern Library, 1937), 183. At this point in *The Federalist No. 30*, Hamilton had not made it clear what taxes ought to replace requisitions of the Confederation, but in the pages that followed (183–84), Hamilton indicated that he was referring to both "external" taxes, like customs duties, and "internal" taxes, like excises.

[5] Hamilton, *The Federalist No. 12*, 72–73.

[6] Thomas Hobbes, *Leviathan*, with selected variants from the Latin edition of 1668, ed. Edwin Curley (Indianapolis: Hackett Publishing Company), 227–28.

[7] On Hamilton's reading of Adam Smith, see Ron Chernow, *Alexander Hamilton* (New York: The Penguin Press, 2004), 347 and 376–77. On Smith as a civic humanist, see Donald Winch, *Adam Smith's Politics: An Essay in Historiographic Revision* (Cambridge: Cambridge University Press, 1978).

[8] For the quotations from Smith, see his *An Inquiry into the Nature and Causes of the Wealth of Nations* (New York: Modern Library, 1937), 777 and 794.

[9] Hamilton, *The Federalist No. 12*, 72 and 75.

[10] Hamilton, *The Federalist No. 35*, 210–11.

[11] Hamilton, *The Federalist No. 21*, 129.

phrase "in a degree" carefully. He was well aware of Adam Smith's dislike of customs duties and excises on items of common consumption, and Hamilton wrote elsewhere in *The Federalist Papers* that consumption taxes were often "imperceptible," thus fooling consumers into paying more taxes than they realized.[12]

In recognition of the conflict with Smith's "ability to pay" criterion, Hamilton fell back on a practical argument: the burden of consumption taxes in the new republic would be slight. He based this argument on four claims. First, he asserted that the desire of the government for revenues would help keep consumption taxes low, confining them to "proper and moderate bounds." In other words, the need for revenue would form "a complete barrier against any material oppression of the citizens by taxes of this class"; the barrier was "a natural limitation of the power of imposing" such taxes.[13] Second, he claimed that popular hostility to excise taxation, in particular, would also limit the use of consumption taxes: "The genius of the people," he wrote, "will ill brook the inquisitive and preemptory spirit of excise laws."[14] Third, he proposed that the creation of an American customs-union would eliminate smuggling from one state of the Confederation to another and thus make more productive the duties that the various state governments currently levied on imports.[15] Fourth, he claimed that customs duties were relatively lower and less burdensome than in the competitor nations of France and Britain. Indeed, he went further to argue that the federal government could triple current customs duties "without prejudice to trade." Even so, he declared, customs duties in America would be substantially lower than in either France or Britain.[16]

Hamilton recognized, however, that wartime could bring more demanding fiscal requirements. The disruption of trade might reduce customs revenues, and, in any case, the demand for tax revenues might be huge. It was "wars and rebellions," the "two most mortal diseases of society," that had "occasioned that enormous accumulation of debts with which several of the European nations are oppressed."[17] Hamilton expected that excises were likely to be the most important source of wartime finance.

[12] Hamilton, *The Federalist No. 12*, 72. On Smith's criticisms of customs duties and excises on "the necessaries of life," see, for example, Smith, *An Inquiry into the Nature and Causes of the Wealth of Nations*, 821–39.

[13] Hamilton, *The Federalist No. 21*, 130.

[14] Hamilton, *The Federalist No. 12*, 72.

[15] Ibid., 73. Under the Articles of Confederation, the individual states could levy their own export duties. Some states set tariffs relatively low to attract imports; others set them relatively high to protect local industries.

[16] According to Hamilton's calculations, a trebling of American customs duties would establish a rate of 9 percent, contrasted with 15 percent in France and 20 percent in Britain. Hamilton, *The Federalist No. 12*, 75.

[17] Hamilton, *The Federalist No. 34*, 206.

Capitation taxes, or head taxes, were another possible major source.[18] With respect to the latter, there were no taxes more blatantly in conflict with an "ability to pay" doctrine, and no taxes more unpopular in America. Consequently, in *The Federalist Papers,* Hamilton discussed capitation taxes in a highly apologetic way. Hamilton wrote: "I should lament to see them introduced into practice under the national government." Nonetheless, he concluded, he could not rule out their use. "There may exist certain critical and tempestuous conjunctures of the State, in which a poll-tax may become an inestimable resource" on behalf of "the general defence and security."[19]

The third potential major source of wartime revenues was federal taxation of property *ad valorem* (according to its value). Such taxation of property was popular in the early republic. In an era when most wealth was in the form of real estate, the *ad valorem* tax on land offered the greatest potential for establishing a link between wealth and the responsibility to support government and public order. In addition, American republicans often saw such taxation as an attractive means of discouraging large, concentrated holdings of land. Hamilton, like Adam Smith, regarded taxation of land values as equitable and economically efficient. Thus, Hamilton wrote that after the settlement of the war debts of the states, "[a] small land-tax will answer the purpose of the States, and will be their most simple and most fit resource."[20]

Article I, Section 9 of the Constitution, however, severely limited the ability of the federal government to levy property taxes. It could tax property but only by allocating the property taxes among the states according to their relative populations, rather than the value of property in the states.[21] Thus, individuals in states with relatively low levels of wealth per

[18] Under a capitation tax, every taxpayer paid exactly the same amount of tax. Poll taxes, or taxes that all voters had to pay, were the most common form of capitation taxes.

[19] Hamilton, *The Federalist No. 36,* 223.

[20] Ibid., 221. For suggestions as to the connections between a Massachusetts tax policy of "communalism," which included high property taxes, and Federalist tax policies at the national level, see H. James Henderson, "Taxation and Political Culture: Massachusetts and Virginia, 1760–1800," *William and Mary Quarterly* 47 (January 1990): 90–114.

[21] Article I, Section 9 specified: "No capitation, or other direct tax shall be laid, unless in proportion to the census." As legal disputes over the meaning of this language have demonstrated, the writers of the Constitution did not have in mind a clear definition of a "direct" tax. However, they definitely regarded at least property taxes and capitation taxes as direct taxes, and they thought of excises and tariffs as "indirect" taxes. (The founders may have regarded a "direct" tax as one levied directly on an individual and an "indirect" tax as one that individuals—consumers, in the case of an excise tax—would pay through intermediaries.) In framing Article I, Section 9, the founders were not thinking about income taxes. At the time of the writing of the Constitution there were no income taxes, strictly defined, anywhere in America. The political leaders of the new nation never discussed income taxes until 1799, when Great Britain, to finance the wars against Napoleon, adopted an income tax. The best scholarly exploration of the meaning of direct and indirect taxation to the founders remains Edwin R. A. Seligman, *The Income Tax: A Study of the History, Theory, and Practice of Income Taxation at Home and Abroad,* 2d ed. (New York: The Macmillan Company, 1914), 535–71.

capita would have to pay relatively high rates of property taxation. The framers of the Constitution expected that the relatively poorer states would, consequently, never permit the enactment of significant property taxes by the federal government. This, in turn, would protect slave owners, who during the 1780s feared that the federal government might use *ad valorem* taxation of property in the form of slaves as a weapon to abolish slavery. In fact, Hamilton was personally hostile to slavery, and he may well have been interested in using the property tax in just that way. Nonetheless, creation of a strong Union was more important to him, and he supported Article I, Section 9 in order to keep the Southern states in the new republic.

Hamilton could live with the restriction of federal use of property taxation also because he recognized the administrative challenge of a federal property tax. He realized that obtaining a full and equitable assessment of property across the states of the new nation would be daunting. "In every country," he wrote, "it is a herculean task to obtain a valuation of the land; in a country imperfectly settled and progressive in improvement, the difficulties are increased almost to impracticability." Further, he did not think there was any way to measure, in a more general way, the "wealth of nations." Consequently, he saw "no general or stationary rule by which the ability of a state to pay taxes can be determined." In turn, he wrote, "the attempt . . . to regulate the contributions of the members of a confederacy by any such rule, cannot fail to be productive of glaring inequality and extreme oppression." Using population as the basis to distribute property taxes would reduce the risk of arbitrary assessments, and would have the advantages of "simplicity and certainty."[22]

Regardless of the reasons for including Article I, Section 9 in the Constitution, the provision had powerful implications for the long run. It had the practical effect of reserving for state and local governments the taxes that had the greatest potential for redistributing wealth. Allowing the federal government to impose a property tax would have enhanced, at least in principle, the power of the federal government to shape the distribution of income and wealth. With the advantage of hindsight, we know, for example, that it would have opened the door a century later to enacting at the national level the radical program of Henry George, who wanted to replace all taxes with a "single tax" on the site value of land.[23]

[22] Hamilton, *The Federalist No. 21*, 129–30.

[23] In his best-selling *Progress and Poverty* (1880), Henry George advocated shifting all taxation to a property tax on the monopoly profits embedded in the price of land (i.e., the true economic rent of land). He referred to these embedded profits as the "unearned increment," or site value, resulting from the location of a piece of land rather than its use. (In George's analysis, the price, or total value, of land equaled the sum of its site value and its use value.) See Henry George, *Progress and Poverty* (London: J.M. Dent and Sons, 1976). Article I, Section 9 of the Constitution meant that the federal government would have had to allocate a tax on site value to the states according to their shares of population, rather than their shares of total site value. Consequently, Henry George and his disciples had to pursue their "single-tax" reform at the state and local levels, rather than at the national level.

As the first secretary of the Treasury (1789–1795) of the new republic, Hamilton led in creating a peacetime tax regime based on customs duties and excises. In its first two sessions, the Congress adopted tariffs over a broad range of goods. It also adopted internal taxation in the form of an excise tax on distilled spirits.[24] The goal of the tariffs and excises was to pay off, in full, the loans foreign governments had made to the Continental Congress during the Revolution. In 1791, in his "Report on Manufactures," Hamilton declared that the development of modern manufacturing in America would be difficult because of "fear of want of success in untried enterprises" and competition from European manufacturers, who had reaped the benefits of the mercantilist policies of European governments. To stimulate new industries, he proposed selectively increasing tariffs on manufactured goods and raising exemptions on raw materials. In March 1792, Congress passed most of the protective tariffs Hamilton had proposed.[25]

Hamilton's tariff adjustments were too cautious to provide much protection, but otherwise the new tariff system worked much as Hamilton had predicted. The tariffs produced buoyant revenue in periods of expanding foreign trade, which began as early as the 1790s (when American merchants profited handsomely from the Napoleonic Wars), and these tariffs did not seem to impede trade significantly. Economic growth, which began to increase in a significant and sustained way during the 1820s, meant continuing increases in the per capita demand for imported goods and, in turn, increases in tariff revenues per capita. The flow of most ocean commerce through a few major ports, and a low level of smuggling, provided the setting for well-administered tariffs.

The most heated controversies over Hamilton's tax program concerned excise taxes rather than tariffs. The excise taxes on whiskey touched off the Whiskey Rebellion of 1794. Washington had to raise 15,000 troops to discourage the Pennsylvania farmers who had protested.[26] In the wake of the rebellion, the Federalist administrations of presidents George Washington (1789–1797) and John Adams (1797–1801) limited excise taxes almost exclusively to goods and services consumed by the affluent, and in 1802 the administration of Thomas Jefferson (1801–1809) abolished all excises.

[24] Hamilton regarded the excise tax on distilled spirits as consistent with his desire to keep excise taxes "within a narrow compass." It was also consistent with his view, expressed in *The Federalist No. 12*, that diminishing the consumption of "ardent spirits . . . would be equally favorable to the agriculture, to the economy, to the morals, and to the health of the society." There was, he wrote, "perhaps, nothing so much a subject of national extravagance as these spirits." Hamilton, *The Federalist No. 12*, 72 and 75.

[25] Alexander Hamilton, "Report on Manufactures," quoted in Jacob E. Cooke, ed., *The Reports of Alexander Hamilton* (New York: Harper and Row, 1964), 140. As Ron Chernow has recently pointed out, Hamilton carefully modulated his tax program. He wanted tariffs to be "moderate in scale, temporary in nature, and repealed as soon as possible." Chernow, *Alexander Hamilton*, 377.

[26] See Thomas P. Slaughter, *The Whiskey Rebellion: Frontier Epilogue to the American Revolution* (New York: Oxford University Press, 1986).

Hamilton's economic policies led to a fiscally strong federal government, just as he had planned. The revenue system not only serviced the nation's debt; it proved adequate for almost all the other needs of the new federal government. It used indirect taxes to finance an undeclared naval war with France in the late 1790s and Jefferson's war against the Barbary "pirates."[27] Tariff revenues, in combination with the borrowing that the general taxing power made possible, funded the Louisiana Purchase in 1803. Tariff revenues, along with subsidies in the form of grants of public lands, allowed presidents from Thomas Jefferson through John Quincy Adams (1825–1829) to implement the ambitious program of internal improvements (e.g., roads and canals) designed by Albert Gallatin, Jefferson's secretary of the Treasury. Tariff revenues allowed the federal government to eliminate the national debt in 1835. The next year Congress and President Andrew Jackson launched a major distribution of surplus revenues to the states. The states, in turn, used the funds largely for internal improvements and schools. Meanwhile, the federal government increasingly liberalized the terms by which it distributed its huge resources of land in the public domain. In 1820, Congress reduced the price of federal land to a level that was just enough to cover the cost to the federal government of survey and sale. Making enormous quantities of land available at cost to most migrating people represented a massive subsidy for agriculture and wealth-holding by lower- and middle-income groups. Hamilton's fiscal policies were an important part of a model of a central government that worked creatively, positively, and effectively to unleash the nation's economic energies.

Hamilton's revenue system held until the Civil War. In the undeclared naval war with France and the War of 1812, just as Hamilton had expected, the national government expanded excise taxation and levied property taxes (allocated among the states according to population, as the Constitution required). The only significant departure from Hamilton's program came during the 1820s with a dramatic expansion of protectionism—raising tariff rates far beyond those that Hamilton had proposed. The wave of protectionism was halted in the early 1830s, however, and was then reversed decisively in 1846, when Congress passed the Walker Tariff. This tariff legislation paralleled Britain's repeal of the Corn Laws in the same year, and it seemed to herald the adoption of free trade throughout the Anglo-American world. Nonetheless, customs revenues remained substantial because international trade thrived. In fact, the revenues were

[27] A shift of American foreign policy by Federalist presidents George Washington and John Adams in a pro-British direction led to French seizures of American merchant ships and retaliation by American privateers and naval forces in 1798. The Convention of 1800 ended the hostilities. Federalist foreign policy also included bribing the Barbary States of North Africa not to raid American shipping in the Mediterranean. In 1801, President Thomas Jefferson abandoned the payments and engaged in a war with Tripoli (one of the Barbary States) which lasted until 1805.

sufficiently ample to finance the Mexican War, which began in the same year that Congress adopted the Walker Tariff.

On the eve of the Civil War, the federal tax system seemed stable. It could fund future wars of territorial or imperial expansion—so long as those wars were not substantially larger in scope than the Mexican War and did not disrupt the federal government's ability to raise revenue through international trade. And, so long as Americans believed that local and state governments based their systems of property taxation on the principle of "ability to pay," the federal government would not have to consider reducing its reliance on regressive taxation of consumption.

III. The Civil War Regime and Its Challengers

One of those rebellions that Hamilton feared might seriously disrupt the fiscal system of the early republic erupted in 1861. While the American Civil War did not significantly diminish customs duties, its scale and capital intensity demanded a program of emergency taxation that was unprecedented in scope. The Republicans introduced a tax system composed primarily of high tariffs and excise taxes. During and after the war, their system of consumption taxation became the financial centerpiece for the Republicans' ambitious new program of nation-building and national economic policy.

Two new long-term components of federal taxation emerged during the Civil War (1861–1865). The first component was a system of high tariffs. Over the course of the war, tariffs had risen dramatically, to almost half the total value of all dutiable imports. The highest rates were imposed on manufactured goods—particularly metals and metal products, including iron and steel, cotton textiles, and certain woolen goods. On many manufactured items, the rate of taxation reached 100 percent. By 1872, tariff duties dominated federal revenues; except in a few years of severe depression and during the financing of the Spanish-American War, they would do so until 1911. Until the Underwood-Simmons Tariff Act of 1913 significantly reduced the Civil War rates, the ratio between tariff duties and the value of dutiable goods rarely dropped below 40 percent.

The second new long-term component of federal taxation was a system of excise taxes on alcohol and tobacco products. There was nothing new about excise taxation of alcohol and tobacco, but the new, permanent taxes were much higher than any enacted before the Civil War. Buoyant, price-inelastic demand for alcohol and tobacco products meant that taxes on them yielded substantial revenues, even after the federal government increased the tax rates. In the years before World War I, revenues from levies on alcohol and tobacco always produced at least one-third of all federal tax revenues, and by the mid-1890s they averaged close to one-half. During the period from 1911 to 1913, alcohol and tobacco taxes produced even more revenue than did the tariffs.

These new long-term components made the nation's tax system significantly more regressive, and potentially much more unpopular than the low tariffs of the early republic. During the Civil War, to compensate for damage that these taxes might do to the Republican Party and the war effort, Republicans looked for supplementary taxation that bore a closer relationship to the criterion of "ability to pay" than did the tariffs and excises. They imitated the way in which British Liberals had relieved property taxes during the Crimean War and adopted a modest tax on the net incomes of individuals. The new tax significantly increased the taxes on the wealthy, and in 1865 accounted for about 21 percent of federal tax revenues (versus about 50 percent for excise taxes, and 29 percent for tariffs). Nonetheless, Republicans generally viewed the income tax as purely an emergency measure and phased it out between 1867 and 1872.

After the war, Republicans emphasized the way in which the new fiscal system offset the regressivity of consumption taxes by funding programs or providing regulation that benefited a wide swath of the citizenry. Northern Republicans prized subsidies for agriculture, education, public works, and an increasingly generous pension system. Many workers believed that the tariffs protected them from lower-wage labor in Europe, Latin America, and Asia. Many manufacturers welcomed the protection they believed the tariffs afforded them against foreign competitors, and they praised the tendency of a favorable trade balance with Europe to reduce the cost of capital in America. Small manufacturers were most supportive, but large manufacturers, even those who had little to fear from foreign competition, joined them. During the 1880s and 1890s, some large manufacturers were especially enthusiastic about the high-tariff system because it allowed them to build national marketing organizations, free of worries about short-term disruptions caused by European competitors. Even many bankers and members of the financial community, who were more appreciative of the benefits of free trade, liked the way in which substantial taxes on consumption forced increases in the nation's rate of saving and facilitated the repayment of the wartime debt. By using consumption taxes to finance the war debt and interest payments, the Republican leadership transferred significant amounts of capital from consumers to holders of federal debt (Europeans as well as Americans), who tended to be wealthier than the average consumer and more likely to invest.[28] And creditors, especially the holders of the federal debt, appreciated the way in which the Republican taxes tended to produce budget surpluses in the

[28] The aspect of the Civil War program that most stimulated productivity and economic growth may well have been the system of debt retirement and interest payments. This system accounted for as much as half of the rise of the shares of national economic product devoted to capital formation between the 1850s and the 1870s. See Jeffrey G. Williamson, "Watersheds and Turning Points: Conjectures on the Long-Term Impact of Civil War Financing," *Journal of Economic History* 34 (September 1974): 636–61.

1870s, reduced the debt, helped to contract the money supply, and eased the return to the domestic gold standard in 1879.[29]

This Civil War tax system of consumption taxation remained in place, quite intact, until World War I. However, well before the war, critics of the system succeeded in moving it to the center stage of political drama. Previously, issues of tax justice had been salient largely during periods of war that required federal experiments with direct taxation. Now, they became significant in peacetime politics.

One issue was simply the regressivity of the tariff system. The Democratic Party emphasized this issue and made it part of an appeal to roll back tariffs. Doing so, Democrats argued, would apply the criterion of "ability to pay" and reduce the tax burden on American consumers.

A second issue was the way in which the tariff fueled the programs that Republicans had created, particularly during the years of the Civil War and Reconstruction, when they usually controlled all branches of the federal government. Reducing tariffs, Democrats argued, would not only make the tax system fairer, it would make the entire fabric of government more virtuous—and economically efficient. Reducing tariffs would, in their view, undermine the public corruption, special privilege, and monopoly power that they saw as the consequences of Republican power. Thus, the critique of the tariff became part of a more general attack on special privilege, monopoly power, and public corruption—an attack that drew on the ideals of the American Revolution. Important support for this criticism came from the radical idealism of Henry George. While he and his followers primarily sought to reform state and local taxes, their goal of breaking the influence of monopoly power led them to become critics of protective tariffs.[30]

During the 1880s, and especially during the depression of 1893–97, these two ideas for creating a more virtuous system of public finance became the foundation of proposals not only to eliminate protective tariffs but also to adopt a progressive income tax. That tax increasingly won support from Democrats, largely from the West and South, and from supporters of Henry George and his single-tax reform, who viewed income taxation as a step in the right direction for tax reform. Most of the Democratic and single-tax advocates of the progressive income tax wanted to shrink government and consequently proposed the tax only as a limited tax, one that would only partially replace tariff revenues.

These advocates of income taxation wanted primarily to reallocate fiscal burdens according to "ability to pay." During the 1890s, unemploy-

[29] During the Civil War, the federal government had gone off the gold standard, placing the Union on a fiduciary standard, or one founded on public confidence in the currency itself. This happened in 1862, when the federal government discontinued its offer to convert greenbacks, printed to help finance the war, into gold.

[30] See note 23 above. On the career and influence of George, see Charles A. Barker, *Henry George* (New York: Oxford University Press, 1955), and W. Elliot Brownlee, "Progress and Poverty: One Hundred Years Later," *National Tax Association Proceedings* (1979): 228–32.

ment increased and personal income declined. Deflation increased the real value of debts and interest payments, wiping out net incomes and bankrupting many farms and other small businesses. Moreover, incomes fell more rapidly than tax burdens. On the one hand, these trends increased popular pressure to reduce consumption taxation. On the other hand, they reduced any threat of an income tax to the incomes of ordinary working people. Consequently, the "ability to pay" criterion, already firmly grounded in republican ideology, became even more appealing.

Increasingly, the Democratic and single-tax advocates of income taxation sought another goal: restoration of a virtuous republic free of concentrations of economic power. They wanted to go beyond removing the protections to big business that the tariff, which they sometimes called "the mother of trusts," provided. And they wanted to do more than simply adjust tax burdens to make them easier for common people to bear. They wanted, as well, to use taxes to attack monopoly power. Aggressively taxing the largest incomes and corporate profits, they argued, would reduce the maldistribution of wealth and power that was responsible for the evils of industrialization. Income taxation that attacked monopoly would be not only just but economically efficient, stimulating economic growth by fostering opportunities for small businesses. On one level, the enthusiasm for antimonopoly taxation reflected a revival of the benefit theory of taxation. On another, it reflected the long-standing American struggle to limit the role of special privilege within a republic. The specific impetus for the antimonopoly campaign was the proliferation in the 1880s and 1890s of corporations that were technologically advanced, vertically integrated, geographically vast, bureaucratically complex, and sometimes monopolistic in their practices. Thus, support for a radical, progressive income tax had far more to do with the search for tax relief, social justice, and economic opportunity than with the quest for an elastic source of revenue. Until World War II, this search would play a major role in shaping the income tax.

In 1893, depression conditions enabled Democrats to take control of both houses of Congress. The next year, with the critical support of the surging Populist movement, they enacted an income tax as part of the Wilson-Gorman Tariff.[31] In making the case for the new tax, congressional Democrats emphasized both "ability to pay" and republican antimonopoly arguments. In the process, some of them refined arguments that had figured in the debates over the Civil War income tax. Most importantly, a few drew on Jeremy Bentham's and John Stuart Mill's revision of the "ability to pay" criterion to make "equal sacrifice" the basis for establish-

[31] President Grover Cleveland refused to sign the Wilson-Gorman Tariff, which included the income tax. Cleveland had supported modest taxation of investment income, but he objected to what he regarded as Wilson-Gorman's excessively high tariffs on raw materials. Under the provisions of Article I, Section 7 of the Constitution, the bill automatically became law.

ing equity. Mill had written: "Equality of taxation . . . means apportioning the contribution of each person towards the expenses of government, so that he shall feel neither more nor less inconvenience from his share of the payment than any other person experiences from his."[32] Drawing on Mill, Senator John Sharp Williams declared: "Government . . . has the right to demand from each citizen only an equal sacrifice, and nothing more." Williams went on: "Equality of taxation is impossible in any community without an income tax." In response, Republicans argued, among other things, that taxation according to "ability to pay" or "equal sacrifice" would penalize enterprise, initiative, savings, and investment; would pit rich against poor; and would create an invasive army of government officials. Opponents of progressive income taxation, down to the present day, would invoke similar arguments.[33]

The Republican leaders, reinforced by some northeastern Democrats, did succeed in limiting the progressivity of the new tax. Congress reproduced many of the technical features of the Civil War income tax and set a somewhat lower rate on incomes and profits (2 percent). But Congress also introduced several changes that reflected rising popular enthusiasm for taxing the rich. For example, Congress applied the 2 percent tax to the income of business corporations. This tax embodied the assumption that the federal government ought to tax corporations according to a "benefit" theory of taxation as well as the principle of ability to pay. Americans had begun to regard corporate taxation as an especially important vehicle for both taxing the rich and assaulting special privilege.

The 1894 tax was short-lived. In 1895 the Supreme Court, in *Pollock v. Farmers' Loan and Trust Co.*, declared that the income tax of the Wilson-Gorman Tariff was unconstitutional.[34] The Court viewed income taxation as direct taxation and then argued that the Wilson-Gorman income tax was unconstitutional because the federal government had failed to allocate the tax across the states according to population.

During the next fifteen years, however, support for income taxation grew, winning support even among Republicans, and in the urban Northeast. There, both Republican and Democratic leaders found that the tax had begun to appeal to their constituents as a means of making up for the failure of property taxation to reach intangible personal property such as stocks and bonds. The economist Richard T. Ely captured the essence of the new reform program at the state level: "Some way must be contrived

[32] John Stuart Mill, *Principles of Political Economy* (London: Longmans, Green and Co., 1886), 484.

[33] For the quotation by John Sharp Williams, see Richard J. Joseph, *The Origins of the American Income Tax: The Revenue Act of 1894 and Its Aftermath* (Syracuse, NY: Syracuse University Press, 2004), 91–92. Joseph has provided the best general discussion we have of the congressional debates and what he calls "the rationales" for and against the 1894 tax legislation. See ibid., 89–104.

[34] *Pollock v. Farmers' Loan and Trust Co.* (Rehearing), 158 U.S. 601, 15 S.Ct. 673, L.Ed. 1108 (1895).

to make owners of . . . new kinds of property, who include most of our wealthiest citizens, pay their fair share of taxes." His solution was for states to adopt the income tax, "the fairest tax ever devised."[35] As ferment over tax issues waxed at the state and local level, some defenders of the wealthiest property owners joined in support of federal income taxation. They concluded that the federal tax might help take the wind out of the sails of more radical tax measures at the state and local levels. The most influential among these conservatives was a group of urban economists and attorneys who were tax experts. Edwin R. A. Seligman, an economist at Columbia University, led them in promoting income taxation, on the one hand, and in moderating the rhetoric used to justify the tax, on the other. As early as 1894, Seligman had argued that the point of the tax was to "round out the existing tax system in the direction of greater justice." Such language helped shift the discourse over taxation away from one of its previous points of emphasis—the restructuring and salvation of industrial America—to an emphasis on a moderate redistribution of the tax burden.[36]

Presidents Theodore Roosevelt (1901–1909) and William Howard Taft (1909–1913) both recognized the growing support for progressive income taxation and made vague gestures on behalf of its adoption. By 1909, there were enough insurgent Republicans in Congress who supported a graduated income tax to force action. Congress enacted a modest corporate income tax, described as "a special excise tax," and submitted the Sixteenth Amendment, which legalized a federal income tax, to the states for ratification.

Ratification prevailed in 1913, in large part because of two other sets of campaigns, both of which redirected interest in income taxation toward economic restructuring. One set consisted of efforts to enact the "single tax" of Henry George. Beginning in 1909, soap magnate Joseph Fels, who had converted to George's faith, began to finance state and local campaigns for the tax. Although the campaigns won no significant electoral victories except in Oregon in 1910, they awakened the interest of the urban middle class in using the income tax to attack concentrated holdings of real estate.[37] The campaigns also convinced more wealthy property owners that they needed moderate reform as a defensive measure, and their support was important to the crucial victory of ratification of the Sixteenth Amendment in New York in 1911. The second set of campaigns consisted of those of the four major candidates in the presidential election of 1912. The Republican, Democratic, Progressive, and Socialist

[35] Richard T. Ely, *Taxation in American States and Cities* (New York: Thomas Y. Crowell, 1888), 140 and 288.

[36] Edwin R. A. Seligman, "The Income Tax," *Political Science Quarterly* (1894): 610.

[37] On Joseph Fels's campaigns, see Arthur P. Dudden, *Joseph Fels and the Single-Tax Movement* (Philadelphia: Temple University Press, 1971), 199–245; and Arthur N. Young, *The Single Tax Movement in the United States* (Princeton, NJ: Princeton University Press, 1916), 163–83.

candidates (William Howard Taft, Woodrow Wilson, Theodore Roosevelt, and Eugene Debs, respectively) all supported income taxation and, in some form, federal policy designed to attack monopoly power.

In 1913, bipartisan support for income taxation was broad, and the Democrats controlled Congress. Nonetheless, the income-tax measure they enacted was only modest. This was so largely because the nation's political leaders were unsure of how much redistribution they wanted the new tax instrument to accomplish. President Woodrow Wilson, for example, wanted a progressive rate structure, but he urged caution on Furnifold M. Simmons, chair of the Senate Finance Committee. "Individual judgments will naturally differ," Wilson wrote, "with regard to the burden it is fair to lay upon incomes which run above the usual levels."[38] In any case, virtually none of the income-tax proponents within the government believed that the income tax would become a major, let alone the dominant, permanent source of revenue within the consumption-based federal tax system. The Republicans who supported income taxation still generally adhered to protectionist orthodoxy and wanted to retain the tariff and "sin taxes" at the heart of federal taxation. The Democratic drafters of the 1913 legislation regarded the revenue capacity of the tax as far less interesting than its ability to advance economic justice, through both redistribution of the tax burden and attacking monopoly power.

Consequently, the Underwood-Simmons Tariff Act of 1913, which reestablished the income tax, was less progressive and less ambitious in its revenue goals than the Civil War legislation or even the legislation of 1894. In the first several years of the income tax, only about 2 percent of American households paid taxes. Meanwhile, the tariff and the taxation of tobacco and alcohol remained the most productive sources of revenue. The tariff, in fact, became even more productive because the 1913 reduction of tariff rates by the Wilson administration stimulated trade and increased revenues. If it had not been for World War I mobilization, the major consequence of the passage of the income tax in 1913 might have been the protection of the regime of consumption taxation inherited from the Civil War, and that regime might well have lasted another generation or more.

IV. The Wartime Wilsonian Regime

The United States did, however, intervene in World War I, in 1917. To do so amid the disruption of international trade meant that the United States, for the first time since the War of 1812, had to abandon its reliance on customs duties. Moreover, the huge scale of the financial requirements of the American war effort meant that the federal government had to find

[38] Woodrow Wilson to Furnifold M. Simmons, September 4, 1913, in Arthur S. Link, ed., *The Papers of Woodrow Wilson*, vol. 28 (Princeton, NJ: Princeton University Press, 1978), 254.

new taxes that did far more than just replace customs revenues. What were the options potentially available to the administration of Woodrow Wilson?

First, there was a set of consumption tax alternatives. In the realm of internal sales taxation, the only measures with which the federal government had recent experience were taxes on spirits and tobacco. To be sure, the resulting revenues were significant. In 1914, taxes on spirits, "fermented liquors," and tobacco produced over $300 million in revenue. In that year, these revenues exceeded tariff revenues, were more than four times as large as revenues from the income tax, and accounted for nearly one-half of all the nation's tax revenues. Transforming the systems for assessing and collecting "sin taxes" into a system for imposing general taxes on consumption, however, was virtually impossible, particularly because of the brief period of time (roughly a year and a half) the United States was at war. The assessment and collection of a general sales tax, assessed at the point of final transaction, would have required intervention in millions of transactions. The Treasury had no way to identify and monitor the hundreds of thousands of businesses that participated in such transactions. Consequently, no one within the federal government ever seriously considered a general consumption tax.

The second set of alternatives included ways of expanding income taxation that were progressive but collected large revenues from middle- and low-income Americans. Such taxes would have set personal exemptions at low levels and would have levied high rates on wages and salaries. During World War I, advocates of these "mass-based" income taxes had to face the reality that the federal government lacked the capacity to administer them. In levying such taxes, the Bureau of Internal Revenue would have had to face the facts, which the 1910 census revealed, that approximately one-third of American workers were employed as farmers, either as owner-operators of farms or as agricultural laborers, and at least another third owned or worked in small, usually unincorporated, nonfarm businesses. During World War I, the federal government did not know who these people were, and had no means of readily discovering their identities. Even more daunting would have been determining and analyzing their wages, salaries, rents, gross incomes, and capital gains, to say nothing of mobilizing an army of auditors and collectors.

The federal government learned the identities and earnings of a significant number of Americans only after it developed an administrative apparatus for the Social Security system, which was enacted in 1935. With Social Security's mechanisms in place for the collection of taxes at the source, the federal government was then able to introduce the mass-based taxation of incomes during World War II. Could such a system have been created during the first two decades of the century? Perhaps, but certainly not in time to finance the war effort, even if the war had dragged on into 1919. President Franklin D. Roosevelt signed the Social Security legislation into law in August of 1935, but it was over two years before the federal government could process employer reports of wages paid. Even then, the federal government did not identify the many Americans, such as farmers and other self-employed individuals, who were outside the system. By the late 1930s, the administrative capacity of the federal government had grown considerably beyond what it had been in 1917, as had that of the corporations that were part of the system for collecting Social Security taxes. It would have taken the federal government far longer than two years to create a comparable administrative apparatus in 1917. Even more time would have been necessary to adapt that infrastructure to tax assessment and collection. Mass-based income taxation was simply not a realistic option in 1917. No one in the Treasury seriously entertained its enactment, and the war did not go on long enough to initiate serious consideration.[39]

There was in place, however, a set of taxes that already identified most middle-class Americans, and assessed significant portions of their wealth-holdings. This third set of alternatives consisted of the various property taxes that were technically the responsibility of the states of the Union. Many members of the Wilson administration (including Wilson himself) and the House of Representatives found the single-tax ideas of Henry George appealing and wanted the federal government to take a hard look at property taxation as a means of war finance. Another possibility under consideration within the Treasury was adapting state and local systems of property taxation to help in assessing income taxes. Here, Britain's experience with its income tax was of interest. As historian Martin Daunton has written recently, "collection and assessment of the income tax" in Britain "were based on the existing machinery of the land and assessed taxes, which passed responsibility to the taxpaying class."[40] In the United States, assessment and collection of property taxes also relied heavily on voluntary compliance. In the last analysis, however, the Wilson administration had to acknowledge a number of obstacles to the creation of a federal property tax system: the formidable problem of overcoming the constitutional requirement that a direct tax be allocated to the states on the basis of population; the interest of states and localities in maintaining control over their powerful revenue engine; the likelihood that any federal takeover would meet popular resistance; and the extreme difficulty, identified more than a century before by Alexander Hamilton, of reconciling—that is to say, equalizing—the valuations of property that the

[39] On the early administrative problems of Social Security, see Arthur J. Altmeyer, *The Formative Years of Social Security: A Chronicle of Social Security Legislation and Administration, 1934–1954* (Madison: University of Wisconsin Press, 1968), 43–98.

[40] Martin Daunton, *Trusting Leviathan: The Politics of Taxation in Britain, 1799–1914* (Cambridge: Cambridge University Press, 2001), 188. The "assessed taxes" were special taxes directed at "signs of conspicuous wealth and display such as male servants, windows, carriages, and pleasure horses" (ibid., 33–34).

different, and diverse, state and county governments had made. In the early twentieth century, there were enormous variations in property tax systems across the states; and within any given state, property tax administration and assessment were highly decentralized.

The impossibility of developing mass-based systems of consumption, income, or property taxation meant that the federal government had to focus its wartime tax initiatives on the available targets of opportunity—the incomes of wealthy individuals and corporations. While mass-based income or consumption taxation would have required dramatically new administrative arrangements, taxing the rich allowed the Treasury and the Congress to conscript the information systems of corporations into the armies of tax assessment. In addition, in doing so, the federal government could take advantage of the experience of other nations.

Most compelling was the British experience. Experts within the federal government studied, in particular, how the British during the war had abandoned their earlier practice of treating "companies merely as withholding agents who forwarded tax to the Inland Revenue, rather than taxable entities in their own right," as Daunton has put the matter.[41] Instead, the British adopted a system of taxation of wartime profits—the EPD, or excess-profits duty. Americans closely studied the EPD, as well as a radical version of the tax that Canada had adopted. Treasury experts learned from that study and copied many elements of the British system in proposing legislation. Nevertheless, the Treasury did not embrace a crucial aspect of the British tax—the definition of excess profits as those above prewar profits. Instead, the Treasury experts followed the Canadian example and proposed defining excess corporate profits as profits above and beyond those that a reasonable rate of return would produce. But Treasury experts and many Democrats in Congress intended to go even a step further. As one Treasury staff member put it, the excess-profits tax had "the manifest advantage . . . of becoming a permanent part of the Government's revenue system, and can be used, if need be, as a check upon monopolies or trusts earning exorbitant profits."[42] Indeed, making the tax a permanent part of the tax code, as a means of controlling monopoly power, was exactly what both Claude Kitchin, chair of the House Ways and Means committee, and the Wilson administration had in mind. They wanted entry into World War I to open the door for a permanent assault on monopoly power. The choice of radical excess-profits taxation was one that had dramatic economic and political implications. It was this choice that demonstrated how serious American policymakers were in not only raising huge tax revenues but also exploiting the wartime mobilization to confront the power of monopoly capitalism. Overnight,

[41] Ibid., 211.

[42] I. J. Talbert, Head of Law Division, Commissioner of Internal Revenue, to George R. Cooksey, Assistant Secretary of the Treasury, August 8, 1917, Papers of William Gibbs McAdoo, Library of Congress.

the modest income tax of 1913, which had focused on rebalancing the tax system on behalf of "ability to pay" and providing tax relief, became a massive effort to redistribute social power and, in the process, expand economic opportunity.

Excess-profits taxation, which the Wilson administration enacted in the Revenue Act of 1916 as a preparedness measure and then expanded after the United States entered World War I, accounted for about two-thirds of all federal tax revenues during the war. Under the Revenue Act of 1918, the progressive rates of excess-profits taxation ranged from 30 to 65 percent on profits above a "normal" rate of return. Most of the remaining revenue came from a highly progressive income tax on the wealthiest individuals. In 1918, the wealthiest 1 percent of households paid marginal tax rates that ranged from 15 to 77 percent. The effective rates of taxation of the incomes of the wealthiest households averaged 15 percent. This was perhaps low by the standards of the late twentieth century, but the 15 percent level represented a major increase from the 3 percent level that prevailed before the war, in 1916. Moreover, this 15 percent did not include whatever additional taxes wealthy individuals paid through the taxation of corporate incomes.[43] The substantial tax revenues meant that the federal government managed to cover roughly 30 percent of wartime expenditures through taxes—a larger share of total revenues than in any of the other belligerent nations.

With the excess-profits tax and a highly progressive income tax on the wealthy, the Wilson administration was the first to discover the revenue potential of taxing the rich. The numbers clearly showed where the money was. In 1918, only about 15 percent of American households had to pay personal income taxes, and the tax payments of the wealthiest 1 percent of American households accounted for about 80 percent of the revenues from the personal income tax. One might reasonably describe this as "soak-the-rich" taxation. In other words, the Wilson administration discovered that a highly progressive income tax has great value as a tool for building the state—above and beyond whatever capability it might also have for redistributing the cost of government, regulating the scale of business, or demonstrating the commitment of the government to social justice. The revenue capacity of "soak-the-rich" is especially apparent during periods when the concentration of incomes increases at the top, and also during periods when inflation pushes taxpayers into higher tax brackets ("bracket-creep").

If the Republicans had been in a position to manage the financing of the war, what kind of tax system might they have put in place? If we take Republican criticism of the Wilson administration seriously, in the first

[43] W. Elliot Brownlee, "Historical Perspective on U.S. Tax Policy Toward the Rich," in Joel B. Slemrod, ed., *Does Atlas Shrug? The Economic Consequences of Taxing the Rich* (New York and Cambridge, MA: Russell Sage Foundation and Harvard University Press, 2000), 44–45.

place they would have raised less tax revenue and borrowed more heavily. In the second place, they would have also taxed the wealthy and corporations heavily, and at progressive rates. There was no other feasible option. In the third place, however, they would have followed the preference of most professional economists, as well as the most politically active business leaders, including significant supporters of the Wilson administration, for the adoption of the British model of excess-profits taxation. Economist Edwin R. A. Seligman, for example, urged the adoption of the British standard of taxing profits that exceeded prewar levels, arguing: "[E]xcessive taxes on industry will disarrange business, damp enthusiasm, and restrict the spirit of enterprise at the very time when the opposite was [*sic*] needed." He added that a fiscal policy "predicated primarily on principles of social reform will be likely to lose the war." He had launched his career in the public sphere by challenging the single-tax ideas of Henry George, and he correctly regarded the Treasury's approach to excess-profits taxation as based on the same kind of assumptions about the nature of profits that George and his followers had made in their effort to socialize economic rent.[44]

In short, in order to raise significant tax revenues, the federal government had to rely heavily on taxation of corporations. Even under a Republican regime, the transformation of the federal tax system during World War I would have been the most dramatic in the history of the republic. The Wilson administration made the wartime break even sharper, however, by consistently rejecting alternatives that were tested by experience, easier to administer, and more favorable to the interests of powerful forces within the business community, including Wilson's own business supporters. Instead, the Wilson administration and the Congress consistently chose radical forms of anticorporate taxation. They sought to use the wartime crisis as a means of advancing the cause of economic democracy.

The Wilson administration failed, however, to sustain the most radical of its fiscal reforms. In fact, these reforms contributed to its political downfall. During the congressional elections of 1918, in reaction to the administration's proposal to roughly double wartime tax revenues, the investment banking community and the leaders of the Republican Party launched a successful assault. They blamed the wartime tax program for causing serious inflation and pointed to the problem of "bracket-creep." The outcome was clear: the capture of both houses of Congress by the Republicans in the 1918 elections.

[44] Edwin R. A. Seligman, "Our Fiscal Policy," in *Financial Mobilization for War, Papers Presented at a Joint Conference of the Western Economic Society and the City Club of Chicago, June 21 and 22, 1917* (Chicago: privately printed, 1917), 10 and 12. Seligman and experts in the Wilson administration agreed that businesses could not pass on the excess-profits taxes to consumers or others in the economy. While the Wilson administration experts thought the tax would penalize monopoly power and promote competition, Seligman believed it would drive up the cost of capital, impeding investment and undermining business confidence.

The political backlash from wartime inflation continued to damage the Democrats, and the cause of progressive taxation, even after the electoral defeats of 1918. Many Americans continued to blame increases in cost of living, which continued well into 1920, on wartime taxes. Some also blamed the tax program for damaging business and business confidence, thereby causing the depression of 1920–21. Wealthy individuals and corporations took advantage of this analysis of economic performance, and the postwar political weakness of the Wilson administration, to win popular support in 1921 for repealing the excess-profits tax and reducing the top marginal rate of the individual income tax to 58 percent.

The progressive income tax itself survived, however. It did so in part because of the enormous revenue capacity of the tax, but also because Woodrow Wilson, through his handling of wartime finance, had reinforced and enhanced Americans' belief in the justice of taxing according to ability to pay. In deference to the power of this ideal, and to protect the important new source of revenue, Andrew Mellon, the secretary of the Treasury from 1921 to 1932, cast his support behind preservation of the progressive income tax, and thus the progressive income tax survived the Republican program of returning to "normalcy."[45] In 1932, it was a Republican president, Herbert Hoover, who initiated the largest peacetime tax increases in the nation's history. (He did so to close the federal budget deficit, reduce upward pressure on interest rates, and thus stimulate economic recovery.) The Revenue Act of 1932 raised personal and corporate income-tax rates across the board and restored the top marginal rate nearly to World War I levels. Under Republican "normalcy," a tax structured according to the principle of "ability to pay" had become, for the first time, the central feature of peacetime public finance.

V. The Regimes of Depression, War, and Franklin Roosevelt

The next two national emergencies, the Great Depression and World War II, ended Republican "normalcy." These back-to-back crises of social order and national survival both created huge demands for taxation that would produce new revenues, redistribute social power, and reallocate the tax burden according to the criterion of "ability to pay." In response, the New Deal and wartime mobilization of President Franklin D. Roosevelt produced three great tax initiatives.

The first initiative echoed the approach of the wartime Wilson administration to income taxation. On this front, Roosevelt initially moved slowly, partly because he feared a conservative counterattack of the kind that had defeated the Wilson administration. Worrisome too was the possibility

[45] At the same time, however, Mellon led in reducing the top marginal rate on the rich in 1926 and in 1928, bringing it down to 25 percent. One of his objectives in so doing was to reduce avoidance and evasion of the income tax by the wealthy.

that Roosevelt might worsen the economic depression by undermining business confidence and investment. Finally, however, in 1935, the growing "Thunder on the Left," particularly Huey Long's "Share Our Wealth" movement, pushed Roosevelt into action. He first proposed a tax program that included a graduated tax on corporations and an increase in the maximum income-tax rate on individuals. In a message to Congress, he explained that accumulations of wealth meant "real and undesirable concentration of control in relatively few individuals over the employment and welfare of many, many others." He went on: "Whether it be wealth achieved through the cooperation of the entire community or riches gained by speculation—in either case the ownership of such wealth or riches represents a great public interest and a great ability to pay." Later that year, he explained to a newspaper publisher that his purpose was "not to destroy wealth, but to create a broader range of opportunity, to restrain the growth of unwholesome and sterile accumulations and to lay the burdens of Government where they can best be carried." Thus, he justified his tax-reform program in terms of both its inherent equity and its ability to liberate the energies of individuals and small corporations, thereby advancing recovery. There was no trade-off, Roosevelt believed, between growth and progressiveness.[46]

Congress gave Roosevelt most of what he wanted, including his 1936 proposal of an undistributed profits tax—a graduated tax on the profits that corporations did not distribute to their stockholders. Roosevelt believed that the measure would fight the concentration of corporate power. He and his Treasury advisers were convinced that the largest corporations had the power to retain shares of surpluses greater than those retained by small companies. The surpluses, they were certain, gave large corporations an unfair competitive advantage by reducing the need to borrow new capital. The tax, they believed, would create opportunities for smaller corporations and provide a powerful incentive for corporations to distribute their profits to their shareholders. New opportunities and spending would, in turn, stimulate economic recovery.

More than any other New Deal measure, this tax aroused fear and hostility on the part of large corporations. They correctly viewed the tax as a threat to their control over capital and their latitude for financial planning. Despite Roosevelt's hope that the measure would stimulate recovery, the tax may well have contributed significantly to the exceptionally low level of private investment during the 1930s, and even, by depressing business expectations, to the severity of the recession of 1937–38. Antimonopolist New Dealers like Harold Ickes went so far as to charge that capitalists had conspired and gone "on strike" in response to

[46] For the Roosevelt quotations, see Arthur M. Schlesinger, Jr., *The Age of Roosevelt: The Politics of Upheaval* (Boston: Houghton Mifflin, 1960), 328; and Walter K. Lambert, "New Deal Revenue Acts: The Politics of Taxation" (Ph.D. dissertation, University of Texas, Austin, 1970), 259–60.

New Deal taxes.[47] There is no evidence of such a conspiracy, but business leaders did enter the political arena and search for support outside the business community. In 1938, they found Roosevelt vulnerable, weakened by two major errors: reinforcing the recession of 1937–38 and opening in 1937 the disastrous fight to restructure the Supreme Court. In 1938, a coalition of Republicans and conservative Democrats gutted the tax on undistributed profits; in 1939, the coalition abolished the tax.

The second Roosevelt tax initiative was the establishment in 1935 of payroll taxes to finance the new Social Security system. These taxes were regressive. The incongruity between this initiative and Roosevelt's reforms of income taxation might suggest that he was little more than a cynical manipulator of the powerful symbolism of taxation. But he conceived of Social Security as an insurance system. In his mind, taxpayers received the benefits for which they had paid. Roosevelt's concept was shared by much of the American public, and it lent the payroll tax a popularity that enabled it to win a narrow victory in 1935. In addition, the benefit formula of even the initial Social Security program had a progressive dimension. In 1939, Roosevelt and Congress firmly established a progressive benefit formula and introduced pay-as-you-go financing.[48]

The third great initiative came during World War II. Because of the creation of the information-gathering capability of the Social Security system, and the continued expansion of corporate employment, the federal government had more options available than in World War I. In particular, mass-based income and/or consumption taxes were now administratively feasible.[49]

As in World War I, the commitment of a Democratic president to economic democracy shaped the choice of options. Roosevelt resisted conventional consumption taxation as too regressive, although, at one point in negotiations with Congress, he proposed a progressive tax on "spendings." More serious were Roosevelt's proposals of various Wilsonian taxes on excess corporate profits. However, he lacked broad support for these

[47] Both Kenneth D. Roose and Joseph A. Schumpeter stressed the role of the tax in the recession of 1937–38. See Roose, *The Economics of Recession and Revival: An Interpretation of 1937–38* (New Haven, CT: Yale University Press, 1954), 10–12 and 209–16; and Schumpeter, *Business Cycles* (New York: McGraw-Hill, 1939), 1038–40. On the conspiracy charges, see Mark Leff, *The Limits of Symbolic Reform: The New Deal and Taxation* (Cambridge: Cambridge University Press, 1984), 212–13. On the intellectual sources of the undistributed profits tax, see Michael Bernstein, *The Great Depression: Delayed Recovery and Economic Change in America, 1929–1939* (Cambridge: Cambridge University Press, 1987), 190–92.

[48] This tax measure may also have impeded recovery from the Great Depression by offsetting the demand-side stimulus of fiscal policy. On the limitations of the New Deal's fiscal policy, see E. Cary Brown, "Fiscal Policy in the 'Thirties': A Reappraisal," *American Economic Review* 46 (December 1956): 857–79; and Herbert Stein, *The Fiscal Revolution in America* (Chicago: University of Chicago Press, 1969), 39–168.

[49] By mid-1940, the Bureau of Old-Age Benefits had processed more than 312 million individual wage reports forwarded by the Bureau of Internal Revenue and had posted over 99 percent of them to more than 50 million individual employee accounts. Altmeyer, *The Formative Years of Social Security*, 86–87.

taxes from Democrats in Congress. Many worried that such a tax program would weaken the financial ability of corporations to cope with the depression they thought would more than likely follow the war. Federal Reserve Chairman Marriner Eccles and Vice President Henry Wallace shared this concern and consequently supported a sales-taxation approach to war finance. In response, Secretary of the Treasury Henry Morgenthau Jr. complained that his opponents had forgotten about the "people in the lower one-third." In the face of defections of many Democrats, like Wallace, who had once supported anticorporate taxation, Morgenthau declared: "I can get all my New Dealers in the bathtub now."[50]

Roosevelt abandoned the World War I method of determining excess profits, thus ending twenty-five years of Democratic initiatives in using income taxation to attack monopoly power. But Roosevelt succeeded in defeating consumption taxation and advancing instead a highly progressive income tax. By the end of World War II, the marginal rate of taxation on personal income had risen to 94 percent (on dollars earned over $200,000), higher than at any other time in the history of American income taxation. In 1944, the effective rate on the rich reached an all-time high of nearly 60 percent, or almost four times the highest level achieved during World War I. The rates were high enough so that, even with the broad base of taxation, in 1945 the richest 1 percent of households produced 32 percent of the revenue yield of the personal income tax.[51]

Roosevelt and Congress agreed not only on highly progressive rates but also on an exceptionally broad base for the reformed income tax. As Americans prepared for entry into World War II, President Franklin Roosevelt and the congressional leadership assumed that mobilization would be on an even greater scale than during World War I and that the inflationary pressures would be correspondingly more severe. As a consequence, the nation's leadership quickly reached a bipartisan consensus favoring an income tax that would reach deep into the American middle class. This broad base of taxpayers would finance an even larger portion of the costs of the war than they had done in World War I. At the same time, the high taxes would discourage consumers from bidding up prices in competition with the government. Under the new tax system, the number of individual taxpayers grew from 3.9 million in 1939 to 42.6 million in 1945, and federal income-tax collections over the period leaped from $2.2 billion to $35.1 billion. By the end of the war, nearly 90 percent of the members of the labor force submitted income-tax returns, and about 60 percent of the labor force paid income taxes. In 1944 and 1945, individual income taxes accounted for roughly 40 percent of federal rev-

[50] John Morton Blum, *From the Morgenthau Diaries: Years of War, 1941–1945* (Boston: Houghton Mifflin, 1967), 35.

[51] See Brownlee, "Historical Perspective on U.S. Tax Policy," 60; and Bureau of Internal Revenue, U.S. Department of the Treasury, *Statistics of Income for 1945, Part I* (Washington, DC: Government Printing Office, 1951), 71.

enues, whereas corporate income taxes provided about one-third—only half their share during World War I. And current tax revenues paid for approximately half of the costs of the war. Mass taxation had returned as a central element of federal taxation.

Mass taxation succeeded partly because of the popularity of the war effort. It was not as important as during World War I to leverage popular support and sacrifice for the war by enacting a highly redistributional tax system. More than in World War I, Americans concluded that their nation's security was at stake and that victory required both personal sacrifice through taxation and indulgence of the profits that helped fuel the war machine. Nonetheless, the high progressivity of the income tax was important, as well as the popularity of the war. Middle-class Americans accepted the income taxes they now paid in part because the overall rate structure of the tax system was highly progressive, providing a financial sacrifice to match the sacrifice made by fighting men and women.

VI. Survival and Reform of the World War II Regime

In contrast with Wilson's tax program of World War I, Roosevelt's wartime tax regime survived the war's aftermath essentially intact and remains essentially intact in the first decade of the twenty-first century. On an important level, this was a consequence of a general agreement of the two major political parties on the need to maintain a large federal government and to keep the World War II revenue system as the means of financing it. For the first time since the early nineteenth century, the two political parties agreed on the essential elements of the nation's fiscal policy.

Having agreed on the need for big government, the two parties also agreed on the attractiveness of the revenue capability of the World War II system. Of particular political value was the fact that the new tax regime was generally able to fund the expansion of both domestic and foreign programs without requiring any legislated tax increases, thus avoiding the unpleasant task of picking losers. This was so because both economic growth and long-term inflation, working through the expansion of the tax base, provided an elastic source of new revenues. In fact, that elasticity enabled the federal government to make periodic, substantial tax cuts.

The convergence on tax policy involved restraint by Republicans in seeking consumption taxation, and an acceptance by them of greater taxation of large incomes than they had found palatable before World War II. Conversion to a tax system based on consumption, or on a hybrid of income and consumption, would have been administratively feasible. But Republican leaders recognized the political appeal of "ability to pay" and did not seriously entertain such a conversion until the 1990s. For their part, Democrats largely abandoned taxation as an instrument to mobilize class interests. Most dramatically, they abandoned the antimonopoly rhetoric of World War I and the New Deal and adopted instead a more benign view of corporate power.

Republican and Democratic leaders also agreed that there were two major problems with high marginal rates of taxation, and, at least through the Reagan era, they often lent bipartisan support to tax-rate reform. The first problem was that the rates created economic disincentives for wealthy Americans to save and invest, and to work. The Kennedy-Johnson tax cuts in 1964 began the work of reducing the high marginal rates, and then the Reagan tax reforms (both the Economic Recovery Act of 1981 and the Tax Reform Act of 1986) continued the reductions, bringing the top rate down to roughly 36 percent.[52]

The second problem was that the high marginal rates tended to undermine the goal of broadening the economic base for taxation. They created incentives for taxpayers to seek lucrative loopholes in the form of special deductions and exemptions. The loopholes in turn created economic distortions by favoring one form of income over another, made the tax code mind-numbingly complex, and weakened the public's faith in the fairness of the income tax. The most comprehensive and successful effort to close loopholes was the Tax Reform Act of 1986. In a concerted effort to promote this measure, President Ronald Reagan invoked the search for tax equity, defined as horizontal equity—equal treatment for taxpayers in similar economic circumstances. Reagan declared that he was seeking to "free us from the grip of special interests." There would be, he said, "one group of losers in our tax plan—those individuals and corporations who are not paying their fair share, or for that matter, any share."[53]

None of the Republican or Democratic reforms, however, challenged the fundamental progressiveness of the rate structure. In 1986, for example, the Reagan administration coupled rate reductions at the top with significant cuts for low-income Americans. At the end of the Reagan administration, the tax code, even including Social Security taxes, was more progressive than it had been when Reagan took office.

After 1986, bipartisan agreement on tax reform broke down. Both Republicans and Democrats abandoned any interest in ridding the tax code of "tax expenditures." In fact, each party developed a list of new tax loopholes and enacted many of them into law. On the one hand, President George H. W. Bush revived the idea of preferential taxation of capital gains. On the other hand, President Bill Clinton returned to a "soak-the-

[52] The impact that cutting the top marginal rates has had on productivity is an open issue. Economic analysis finds daunting the long-run world, where all significant variables, including capital stocks, change simultaneously. However, accelerations in productivity have often followed marked reductions in the taxes on the richest Americans. For example, the productivity surges during the 1920s, the late 1950s and early 1960s, and the late 1990s each followed reductions in taxes on the rich during the 1920s, the post–World War II years, and the 1980s.

[53] Ronald Reagan, "Address by the President to the Nation," May 28, 1985, folder Tax Reform (5), OA 17746, Beryl Sprinkel Files, Ronald Reagan Library.

rich" policy and in 1993 led in significantly raising rates on the wealthiest Americans. Meanwhile, he plumped for numerous tax preferences for middle-class Americans. The tax cuts of President George W. Bush further increased the complexity of the tax code. At the same time, he and congressional Republicans undertook what seemed to be an incremental program to transform the progressive income tax into a system of regressive consumption taxation. If the program succeeds, the federal government will have broken away sharply from traditional definitions of "ability to pay" and returned to a pattern of fiscal development that the great national crises disrupted.

VII. Conclusion

Without the crises that the nation has faced since the founding of the republic, needs for national security and the services of a welfare state would still have led the federal government to grow substantially. It might even have grown to roughly the same size that it had reached by the middle of the twentieth century. Without the crises, however, the path of growth probably would have been smoother, and the development of the federal tax system more incremental. Periodic demands for new revenues would have been less intense, and calls for social justice through the tax system—through both redistribution and economic reform—would have been less pressing. New tax regimes might have emerged, but they would have appeared gradually rather than springing full-blown out of national emergencies. Moreover, all these new regimes might have relied on consumption taxation, rather than shifting to income taxation, and kept tax rates flat. In other words, the federal government might have emphasized the flat-rate taxation of consumption down to the present day. If the federal government adopts a flat-tax, consumption-tax regime in the early twenty-first century, perhaps we should view the shift as a return to the path the nation had taken before the disruptive series of crises that began with the Civil War and ended with World War II. If the federal government retains the progressive income tax, we should conclude that the canon of "ability to pay" has retained much of its historic power in the United States.

History, University of California, Santa Barbara

THE IMPACT OF TAX POLICY ON ECONOMIC GROWTH, INCOME DISTRIBUTION, AND ALLOCATION OF TAXES

By James D. Gwartney and Robert A. Lawson

I. Introduction

There is considerable disagreement about how taxes, especially high marginal tax rates on those with high incomes, influence economic performance and the distribution of income. This essay uses cross-country data on changes in marginal tax rates since 1980 to examine this topic. Section II uses economic theory to analyze the linkage between marginal tax rates and economic performance and considers a number of factors that complicate the measurement of that impact. Section III presents data on the top marginal tax rates during 1980–2002 for seventy-seven countries with a personal income tax and analyzes how changes in these rates influenced economic growth during 1990–2002. Section IV focuses on how reductions in marginal tax rates, particularly the highest rates, influence income inequality and the share of the personal income tax paid by various income groups. The final section summarizes the findings of this study.

II. Marginal Tax Rates and Economic Performance

From an economic viewpoint, marginal tax rates are considered particularly important because they affect the incentives of individuals to earn additional income. As marginal tax rates rise, individuals get to keep less and less of their additional earnings.

High marginal tax rates influence economic performance in at least three major ways. First, high marginal rates discourage work effort. As taxes reduce the amount of additional earnings that one is permitted to keep, individuals tend to work and earn less. People will adjust in various ways. Some—for example, those with a working spouse—may drop out of the labor force. Others will respond by working fewer hours per week, perhaps by quitting a second job. Still others will decide to take more lengthy vacations, forgo overtime opportunities, retire earlier, or forget about pursuing that promising but risky business venture. In some cases, high tax rates will even drive highly productive citizens to other countries where taxes are lower. For example, when the incomes of athletes, skilled professionals, and business entrepreneurs are not country-dependent, such people often relocate from high-tax to low-tax countries.

Second, high marginal tax rates distort price signals and encourage individuals to substitute less-desired but tax-deductible goods for nondeductible ones that are more desired. Goods and services may be tax-deductible either as the result of the design of the tax structure or because they appear as a legitimate business expense. In both cases, the personal costs of purchasing the deductible items will be lower than both society's cost of supplying the items and the cost of purchasing nondeductible goods of similar price. The high marginal rates have an unintended secondary effect that is often overlooked: they make tax-deductible items cheap for those confronting the high rates. The higher an individual's effective marginal tax rate, the lower the personal cost of the deductible item. This incentive structure accompanying high marginal rates will induce persons in high-tax brackets to spend excessively on plush offices, professional conferences held in favorite vacation spots, business entertainment, luxury cars used for business purposes, and numerous other deductible items. Those in high tax brackets will often purchase such items even when they are valued less than their production costs. Scarce resources are wasted producing goods that are not valued as much as other things that could have been produced and, as a result, living standards will fall short of their potential.

Third, high tax rates will reduce the incentives of people to invest in both physical and human capital. When tax rates are high, foreign investors will look for other places to put their money, and domestic investors will look for investment projects abroad where taxes are lower. High marginal rates will also reduce the incentive to invest in education and skill development. After all, high tax rates mean that investors in human capital, like their physical-capital counterparts, are unable to capture a substantial share of the returns from their investment. Furthermore, domestic investors will direct more of their investments into hobby businesses (like collecting antiques, raising horses, or giving golf lessons) that may not earn much money but are enjoyable and have tax-shelter advantages. This too, will divert resources away from projects with higher rates of return but fewer tax-avoidance benefits. Again, scarce capital will be wasted and resources channeled away from their most productive uses.

In summary, theory indicates that high marginal tax rates will reduce the supply of both labor and capital, and will adversely affect the efficiency of resource use. These negative side-effects are likely to be particularly strong when marginal tax rates are exceedingly high. Thus, one would expect countries with high marginal tax rates to grow less rapidly and fail to realize their full potential. Similarly, one would expect that reductions in marginal tax rates would enhance economic growth. This is particularly true if the initial marginal rates are quite high, say 50 percent or more.

While theory predicts that there will be a negative relationship between marginal tax rates and the growth rate of an economy, it also suggests several factors that will complicate measurement of the linkage. First, there is the difference between the short-run and long-run response to a change in marginal rates. To the extent that an increase in marginal tax rates reduces the supply of labor and capital, it will tend to slow the growth of real gross domestic product (GDP). These responses will take time, however, and the short-run response may be a misleading indicator of what will happen in the long run. Clearly, the labor supply response will generally be smaller in the short run than in the long run. For example, most people who have previously trained and developed skills for a career of market work are likely to remain in the labor force even if higher marginal tax rates substantially reduce the return from their prior investment. Thus, the short-run labor supply response to a change in marginal tax rates is likely to be small. This is consistent with the empirical findings. Most studies of this topic estimate that the elasticity of labor supply is between 0.1 and 0.2.[1] This implies that higher marginal tax rates that reduced wages by 10 percent would reduce the quantity of labor supplied by between 1 percent and 2 percent.

In the long run, however, the labor supply response will be larger, perhaps substantially larger. As a result of the high marginal rates, future labor force participants have less incentive to invest and acquire the education and training required for high-paying jobs, particularly if those jobs are stressful and difficult to perform. In contrast, people have more incentive to prepare for jobs that are interesting and provide substantial nonpecuniary, and therefore untaxed, benefits. With time, adjustments of this type will tend to reduce the quality and productivity of the labor force by larger and larger amounts. But they are likely to take a decade or more and, as a result, a lengthy period will pass before the full labor supply response will be observed. The recent work of economist Edward Prescott, the 2004 Nobel Prize winner, indicates that the long-run negative impact of higher tax rates on labor supply is substantially greater than the short-run estimates. Prescott uses marginal tax differences between France and the United States to derive estimates for the labor supply response over lengthy periods. He finds

[1] The elasticity of labor supply is equal to the percent change in the number of hours worked divided by the percent change in the wage rate. Thus, if a 10 percent reduction in wages led to a 1 percent reduction in hours worked, the elasticity of labor supply would be 0.1 (1 percent divided by 10 percent). For empirical estimates of the elasticity of labor supply, see Thomas MaCurdy, David Green, and Harry Paarsch, "Assessing Empirical Approaches for Analyzing Taxes and Labor Supply," *Journal of Human Resources* 25 (Summer 1990): 415–490; Robert Triest, "The Effects of Income Tax Deductions on Labor Supply When Deductions are Endogenous," *Review of Economics and Statistics* 74 (January 1992): 91–99; and Thomas J. Kniesner and James P. Ziliak, *The Effects of Recent Tax Reforms on Labor Supply* (Washington, DC: American Enterprise Institute, 1998).

that differences in marginal tax rates between France and the United States explain nearly all of the 30 percent shortfall of labor inputs in France relative to the United States.[2] Given the potential difference between the short-run and long-run impact of changes in marginal tax rates, it is important to analyze the effects of rate changes on growth over periods of a decade or more.

Second, the linkage between marginal tax rates and GDP growth may be weakened because GDP figures will often fail to register the negative impact of the price distortions accompanying high marginal tax rates. GDP registers the expenditures and costs of the goods and services produced even if these costs exceed the value derived by the consumer. If taxpayers purchase deductible items that they value less than their cost because their personal cost is low, the full costs of such items will nonetheless be added to GDP. For example, if a business owner in a 60 percent marginal tax bracket purchases a $50,000 automobile for business-related use, the transaction will add $50,000 to GDP even if the purchaser values it at only $25,000. Because GDP records the costs of production rather than the value to the consumer, both GDP and its growth rate will understate the adverse side-effects of high marginal tax rates.

Third, the linkage between marginal tax rates and GDP growth may also be weakened by the pattern of government expenditures. Several countries impose high marginal tax rates in order to derive revenues that are utilized to subsidize child-care services, retirement benefits, and payments to persons not working. Suppose that a country increases its marginal tax rates in order to subsidize child-care services for working-age parents. While the higher marginal tax rates tend to reduce labor supply, subsidies for child-care services act as an offsetting factor by making it less costly for adults with children to engage in market work. The net effect on labor supply is likely to be small. Further, the policy change will increase the share of child-care services provided by the government (and market suppliers) relative to the share supplied within the household sector. Because the former adds to GDP but the latter does not, the higher taxes that subsidize and provide child-care services may actually increase income as measured by GDP.

Alternatively, suppose that taxes are increased in order to provide more generous benefits to retirees and/or unemployed workers. The more generous retirement benefits would encourage more workers to retire earlier,

[2] Prescott concludes: "I find it remarkable that virtually all of the large difference in labor supply between France and the United States is due to differences in tax systems. I expected institutional constraints on the operation of labor markets and the nature of the unemployment benefit system to be more important. I was surprised that the welfare gain from reducing the intratemporal tax wedge is so large." See Edward C. Prescott, "Richard T. Ely Lecture: Prosperity and Depression," *American Economic Review, Papers and Proceedings* 92, no. 2 (May 2002): 1–15, at p. 9.

and the more generous unemployment benefits would lead to more lengthy periods of job search and higher rates of unemployment. Both of these expenditures would tend to reduce the effective supply of labor and thereby reinforce the impact of the higher marginal tax rates. In contrast with the expenditures on child-care services, these expenditures would tend to amplify the negative relationship between higher marginal tax rates and the quantity of labor supplied. Thus, variations in the pattern of expenditures accompanying differences in marginal tax rates will also influence both labor supply and the expected impact on the growth rate of income as measured by real GDP.

The impact of marginal tax rates will be greatest in the highest tax brackets. It is in the high tax brackets where changes in tax rates will exert their largest effects on both labor supply and tax-avoidance activities. Furthermore, as the Laffer curve analysis indicates, marginal tax rates can be pushed so high that they will actually reduce the revenues derived from the tax.[3] Obviously, marginal tax rates above the level that generates maximum revenue are highly inefficient. They reduce both aggregate output and the revenue derived by the government. However, tax rates near the revenue maximum level are also extremely inefficient. As rates are increased toward the revenue maximum point, the higher tax rates will squeeze out large quantities of gains from trade relative to the additional revenue generated. Thus, measured in terms of lost output, these additional revenues are very costly. Because the most severe side-effects of taxes will be exerted by the highest marginal rates, our empirical analysis will focus on these rates.

III. Changes in Top Marginal Tax Rates and Economic Growth

A. Marginal tax rates, 1980–2002

We have collected data for seventy-seven countries that levied a personal income tax throughout 1980–2002.[4] As table 1 shows, there has been a dramatic change in the top marginal personal income tax rate during the last two decades. The average top marginal tax rate in 1980 was 61.3 percent, and the parallel figure in 1985 was only slightly lower. However,

[3] The Laffer curve is used to show that increases in tax rates will, after a point, result in reduced tax revenues. See James M. Buchanan and Dwight R. Lee, "Politics, Time, and the Laffer Curve," *Journal of Political Economy* 90, no. 4 (1982): 816–19; and James M. Buchanan and Dwight R. Lee, "Tax Rates and Tax Revenues in Political Equilibrium: Some Simple Analytics," *Economic Inquiry* 20, no. 3 (1982): 344–54.

[4] The original source of the marginal tax rate data is Price Waterhouse Coopers, *Individual Taxes: A Worldwide Summary* (Hoboken, NJ: John Wiley and Sons, various years). The top marginal tax rates reported here include rates that apply at the subnational level if applicable.

TABLE 1. *Average and Median Top Marginal Tax Rates among Seventy-Seven Countries, 1980–2002*

	Average tax rate	Median tax rate
1980*	61.3	60
1985	59.2	60
1990	48.5	50
1995	40.8	40
2000	38.6	39
2002	37.1	35

*The requisite data for 1980 were not available for all seventy-seven countries. 1980 data are based on sixty-eight observations.
Source: Authors' calculations. See table 3.

the average top rate declined to 48.5 percent in 1990 and to 40.8 percent in 1995. Thus, the average top marginal tax rate among the seventy-seven countries declined by almost 20 percentage points between 1985 and 1995. Moreover, the trend has continued; the average top rate receded to 37.1 percent in 2002. The median top marginal tax rate followed a similar path.

High marginal tax rates will exert less impact on economic performance if they apply only at extremely high levels of income.[5] In order to consider the potential importance of this factor, the rating matrix used in the Economic Freedom of the World (EFW) index was used to adjust for

[5] The data for the United States illustrate why it is important to consider both the top rate and the income threshold at which it applies. The top marginal tax rate and the income threshold at which it begins to apply (in both current and 2004 dollars) are shown below for the United States for various years since 1963. Note that in 1963 the top marginal rate in the U.S. was 91 percent, but that rate only applied to incomes in excess of $2.46 million (measured in terms of 2004 prices). Thus, very few people confronted this rate. The top rate was cut to 70 percent by 1965, where it remained until 1980. By 1980, the income threshold for the top rate was much lower (about $494,000 in terms of 2004 prices), and far more taxpayers faced the top rate than in the early 1960s. A lower top marginal rate can be more restrictive than a higher one if the lower rate begins to apply at a substantially lower income threshold.

Year	Top marginal tax rate	Income threshold (current dollars)	Income threshold (2004 dollars)
1963	91	$400,000	$2,468,219
1965	70	200,000	1,198,187
1980	70	215,400	493,812
1984	50	162,400	295,263
2000	39.6	288,350	316,320

TABLE 2. *Top Marginal Tax Rates, Income Thresholds, and EFW Ratings*

	Income Threshold Level (1982–84 US$)			
Top marginal tax rate	Less than $25,000	$25,000 to $50,000	$50,000 to $150,000	More than $150,000
Less than 20%	10	10	10	10
21 to 25	9	9	10	10
26 to 30	8	8	9	9
31 to 35	7	7	8	9
36 to 40	5	6	7	8
41 to 45	4	5	6	7
46 to 50	3	4	5	5
51 to 55	2	3	4	4
56 to 60	1	2	3	3
61 to 65	0	1	2	2
66 to 70	0	0	1	1
More than 70%	0	0	0	0

Note: Countries with higher marginal tax rates that take effect at lower income thresholds received lower ratings based on the matrix found above.
Source: James Gwartney and Robert Lawson, *Economic Freedom of the World, 2004 Annual Report* (Vancouver, BC: Fraser Institute, 2004).

the income level at which the top rate initially applies.[6] This matrix assigns ratings on a zero-to-ten scale based on both the top marginal tax rate and the level of income at which it initially takes effect. Countries with the lowest top marginal tax rates (or modest top rates that only apply at high income levels) are assigned the highest ratings, while countries with high top marginal tax rates that take effect at low levels of income are rated the lowest. This matrix showing the zero-to-ten ratings for the various top marginal tax rate categories and income level categories is presented in table 2. Table 3 presents both the top marginal income tax rates and the EFW ratings for the countries of our study for various years during 1980–2002.

B. Changes in tax rates and growth

The dramatic changes in the highest marginal tax rates during the last two decades provide something like a natural experiment. Some coun-

[6] James Gwartney and Robert Lawson, *Economic Freedom of the World, 2004 Annual Report* (Vancouver, BC: Fraser Institute, 2004). Initially published in 1995, this report presents data on thirty-eight different variables designed to measure the consistency of a nation's institutions and policies with economic freedom. The report covers over 120 countries.

TABLE 3. *Top Marginal Tax Rates on Personal Income (Excluding Payroll Taxes) and EFW Ratings, 1980–2002*

	1980		1985		1990		1995		2000		2002		Average 1980–2000	
Countries	Tax rate	Rating	Tax rate	Rating	Tax rate	Rating	Tax rate	Rating	Tax rate	Rating	Tax rate	Rating	Tax rate	Rating
Argentina	45	6	62	2	35	7	30	9	35	8	35	7	40.3	6.5
Australia	62	2	60	2	49	3	47	4	47	3	47	3	52.0	2.8
Austria	62	2	62	2	50	4	50	4	50	4	50	4	54.0	3.3
Bangladesh	60	1	60	1	25	9	25	9	25	9	25	9	36.7	6.3
Barbados	60	1	60	1	50	4	40	5	40	5	40	5	48.3	3.5
Belgium	76	0	76	0	58	2	61	1	60	2	52	2	63.9	1.2
Belize			50	4	45	4	45	5	45	5	45	5	46.0	4.6
Bolivia	48	3	30	8	10	10	13	10	13	10	13	10	21.2	8.5
Botswana	75	0	60	2	50	3	35	7	25	9	25	9	45.0	5.0
Brazil	55	4	60	1	25	9	35	8	28	8	28	8	38.4	6.3
Cameroon			60	2	60	1	66	0	69	0	65	0	64.0	0.6
Canada	64	2	57	2	49	4	49	4	48	3	34	5	50.1	3.3
Chile	58	2	56	2	50	4	45	6	45	5	40	5	49.0	4.0
China			45	6	45	5	45	6	45	6	45	4	45.0	5.4
Colombia	56	2	49	5	30	8	30	8	35	7	35	7	39.2	6.2
Congo, Dem. R.	60	1	60	1	60	1	60	1	60	1	50	3	58.3	1.3
Costa Rica	50	5	50	3	25	9	25	9	25	9	30	8	34.2	7.2
Côte d'Ivoire	45	5	45	5	45	4	49	3	49	3	49	3	47.0	3.8
Cyprus	60	1	60	1	60	1	40	5	40	5	30	8	48.3	3.5
Denmark	66	0	73	0	68	0	64	1	59	2	59	1	64.8	0.7
Dominican Rep.	73	0	73	0	73	0	25	9	25	9	25	9	49.0	4.5
Ecuador	50	5	58	2	25	9	25	9	25	9	25	9	34.7	7.2
Egypt	80	0	65	2	65	2	50	3	34	7	34	7	54.7	3.5
El Salvador	60	3	48	3	60	2	30	8	30	8	30	8	43.0	5.3
Fiji	53	2	50	3	50	3	35	7	34	7	32	7	42.3	4.8
Finland	68	1	67	1	60	2	57	2	54	3	54	3	60.0	2.0
France	60	3	65	1	53	3	51	4	54	2	53	2	56.0	2.5
Germany	65	2	65	1	53	4	57	3	56	3	51	4	57.8	2.8
Ghana	60	1	60	1	55	2	35	7	30	8	30	8	45.0	4.5

continued

TABLE 3. *Top Marginal Tax Rates on Personal Income (Excluding Payroll Taxes) and EFW Ratings, 1980–2002*

Countries	1980		1985		1990		1995		2000		2002		Average 1980–2000	
	Tax rate	Rating	Tax rate	Rating	Tax rate	Rating	Tax rate	Rating	Tax rate	Rating	Tax rate	Rating	Tax rate	Rating
Greece	60	3	63	1	50	4	45	5	43	5	40	5	50.1	3.8
Guatemala	40	8	48	5	34	7	25	9	31	7	31	7	34.8	7.2
Honduras	40	8	46	5	46	5	40	7	25	9	25	9	37.0	7.2
Hong Kong	15	10	25	9	25	9	20	10	17	10	17	10	19.8	9.7
Iceland	63	0	56	1	40	5	47	4	45	6	46	5	49.5	3.5
India	60	1	62	0	53	2	40	5	30	8	32	7	46.2	3.8
Indonesia	50	3	35	7	35	7	30	8	35	7	35	7	36.7	6.5
Iran			90	0	75	0	54	4	54	2	35	8	61.6	2.8
Ireland	60	1	65	0	56	1	48	3	42	5	42	5	52.2	2.5
Israel	66	1	60	3	48	5	50	4	50	4	50	4	54.0	3.5
Italy	72	0	81	0	66	1	67	1	51	3	47	4	64.0	1.5
Jamaica	80	0	58	1	33	7	25	9	25	9	25	9	41.0	5.8
Japan	75	0	70	1	65	2	65	2	50	5	50	5	62.5	2.5
Kenya	65	1	65	0	50	3	50	3	32	7	30	8	48.7	3.7
Malawi	45	4	50	3	50	3	35	7	38	5	38	5	42.7	4.5
Malaysia	60	2	45	6	45	6	32	7	29	8	28	8	39.8	6.2
Malta	65	0	65	0	65	0	35	7	35	7	35	7	50.0	3.5
Mauritius	50	3	35	7	35	7	30	8	25	9	25	9	33.3	7.2
Mexico	55	4	55	4	40	7	35	7	40	7	35	7	43.3	6.0
Morocco	64	2	87	0	87	0	46	3	44	4	44	4	62.0	2.2
Netherlands	72	0	72	0	60	3	60	2	52	3	52	2	61.3	1.7
New Zealand	62	2	66	0	33	7	33	7	39	5	39	5	45.3	4.3
Nigeria	70	0	55	3	55	2	35	7	25	9	25	9	44.2	5.0
Norway	75	0	64	1	51	3	42	5	48	5	48	5	54.6	3.2
Pakistan	55	2	60	1	50	3	45	4	35	7	35	7	46.7	4.0

Panama	56	3	56	3	56	3	30	9	31	8	31	8	43.4	5.7
Paraguay			30	8	30	8	0	10	0	10	0	10	12.0	9.2
Peru	65	2	65	0	45	4	30	8	20	10	30	8	42.5	5.3
Philippines	70	1	60	1	35	7	35	7	32	7	32	7	44.0	5.0
Portugal	84	0	69	0	40	5	40	5	40	6	40	6	52.2	3.7
Senegal			65	1	48	4	64	0	50	3	50	3	55.4	2.2
Singapore	55	4	40	8	33	9	30	9	28	9	22	10	34.7	8.2
South Africa	60	2	50	4	45	5	43	4	45	4	40	5	47.2	4.0
South Korea	89	0	65	2	64	2	48	5	44	5	40	6	58.3	3.3
Spain	66	1	66	1	56	3	56	2	48	4	40	5	55.3	2.7
Sweden	87	0	80	0	65	0	50	3	55	2	56	3	65.4	1.3
Switzerland	37	7	40	7	38	8	37	8	36	9	36	9	37.3	8.0
Taiwan	60	3	60	3	50	5	40	7	40	7	40	7	48.3	5.3
Tanzania			95	0	50	3	30	8	31	7	31	7	47.4	5.0
Thailand	60	3	65	2	55	4	37	7	37	7	37	6	48.5	4.8
Trinidad & Tobago			50	4	35	7	38	5	35	7	30	8	37.6	6.2
Turkey	75	0	63	2	50	4	55	4	45	6	40	6	54.7	3.7
Uganda			70	0	50	3	30	8	30	8	30	8	42.0	5.4
United Kingdom	83	0	60	2	40	5	40	5	40	6	40	6	50.5	4.0
United States	73	0	55	4	38	7	43	7	43	7	40	8	48.7	5.5
Venezuela	45	7	45	7	45	7	34	7	35	8	34	7	39.7	7.2
Zambia	70	0	80	0	75	0	35	7	30	8	30	8	53.3	3.8
Zimbabwe	45	5	63	0	60	1	45	4	53	2	46	3	52.0	2.5
Average	*61.3*	*2.2*	*59.2*	*2.4*	*48.5*	*4.2*	*40.8*	*5.6*	*38.6*	*6.1*	*37.1*	*6.2*	*47.3*	*4.5*
Median	*60*	*2*	*60*	*2*	*50*	*4*	*40*	*6*	*39*	*7*	*35*	*7*	*48*	*4*
Number of countries	*68*	*68*	*77*	*77*	*77*	*77*	*77*	*77*	*77*	*77*	*77*	*77*	*77*	*77*

Source: James Gwartney and Robert Lawson, *Economic Freedom of the World, 2004 Annual Report* (Vancouver, BC: Fraser Institute, 2004).

tries maintained top marginal rates at high levels during the 1980s and most of the 1990s. For example, Austria, Denmark, France, Finland, Germany, Italy, Japan, and the Netherlands made only modest rate reductions while maintaining top marginal rates of 50 percent or more throughout the 1980–1995 period. In contrast, other countries made substantial reductions in their top marginal rates during this period. Table 4 provides a list of the countries that reduced their top marginal rates by 25 percentage points or more between 1985 and 1995. With the exceptions of Iran, Morocco, and Sweden, all of these countries had top marginal rates of 40 percent or less in 1995. This list of major tax cutters is highly diverse. It includes countries from all regions of the world. It includes low-income

TABLE 4. *Countries That Cut Top Marginal Tax Rates between 1985 and 1995*

Countries reducing top marginal tax rates by 25 percentage points or more between 1985 and 1995	Top rate in 1985	Top rate in 1995	Change in top rate from 1985 to 1995
Tanzania	95	30	−65
Dominican Republic	73	25	−48
Zambia	80	35	−45
Morocco	87	46	−41
Uganda	70	30	−40
Iran	90	54	−36
Bangladesh	60	25	−35
Peru	65	30	−35
Ecuador	58	25	−33
Jamaica	58	25	−33
New Zealand	66	33	−33
Argentina	62	30	−32
Malta	65	35	−30
Paraguay	30	0	−30
Sweden	80	50	−30
Portugal	69	40	−29
Thailand	65	37	−28
Panama	56	30	−26
Botswana	60	35	−25
Brazil	60	35	−25
Costa Rica	50	25	−25
Ghana	60	35	−25
Philippines	60	35	−25

Source: Authors' calculations. See table 3.

developing countries such as Tanzania, Zambia, and Bangladesh, as well as high-income industrial countries like New Zealand and Sweden. In some cases, the economies of the tax cutters had high growth rates prior to 1985. Botswana and Thailand provide examples. In other cases, like Peru, Ecuador, and Ghana, the top rates were slashed against a backdrop of dismal economic performance.

If marginal tax rates impact growth, countries that reduce their marginal rates should grow more rapidly than those that do not. Table 5 uses regression analysis to investigate the linkage between changes in top marginal rates and economic growth for all of the seventy-seven countries with a personal income tax. The dependent variable is the growth

TABLE 5. *The Impact of Changes in Top Marginal Tax Rates on Economic Growth*

	Dependent variable: GDP per-capita growth rate, 1990–2002 (t-statistics in parentheses)			
Independent variable	(1)	(2)	(3)	(4)
Intercept	1.432	1.429	−0.350	0.407
GDP per-capita growth rate, 1980–1990	0.537 (7.02)*	0.478 (7.05)*	0.523 (7.07)*	0.474 (7.25)*
GDP per capita, 1990 (purchasing power parity, US $1,000)	0.008 (0.29)	−0.010 (0.42)	0.014 (0.55)	−0.002 (0.08)
Top marginal tax rate, 1985	−0.024 (1.47)	−0.012 (0.80)		
Top marginal tax rate (EFW rating), 1985			0.133 (1.63)	0.067 (0.93)
Change in top marginal tax rate from 1985 to 1990	−0.049 (2.33)*	−0.025 (1.31)		
Change in top marginal tax rate from 1990 to 1995	−0.048 (2.46)*	−0.027 (1.54)		
Change in top marginal tax rate (EFW rating) from 1985 to 1990			0.241 (2.53)*	0.144 (1.68)*
Change in top marginal tax rate (EFW rating) from 1990 to 1995			0.304 (3.35)*	0.215 (2.64)*
Adjusted R-squared	40.1	38.7	43.7	42.4
Number of observations	77	76†	77	76†

*Indicates statistical significance at least at the 90 percent level.
†Democratic Republic of Congo omitted from analysis.

rate of real per-capita GDP during 1990–2002. Growth of real per-capita GDP during the 1980s, per-capita GDP at the beginning of the period, and the initial top marginal tax rate (or the EFW marginal tax rating equivalent) are included in the model as control variables.

The inclusion of the variable for growth during the 1980s is particularly important. It should capture many of the key institutional and cultural factors that influence cross-country differences in long-term growth. To put this another way, factors like political stability, an evenhanded legal system, a well-educated and highly skilled labor force, and sound monetary, financial, and trade institutions that resulted in strong growth during the 1980s are also likely to exert a positive impact on growth during the 1990s. Correspondingly, institutional and cultural factors that resulted in weak growth during the 1980s will also tend to retard growth during the 1990s.[7] The findings are supportive of this view. The coefficient for the growth rate during the 1980s was positive and significant in a statistical sense (t-ratios near 7.0 in all of the regression equations).[8]

In this section, we are most interested in the variables that reflect changes in marginal tax rates. In regressions 1 and 2 in table 5, these marginal tax rate changes are measured by the percentage point change during 1985–1990 and 1990–1995. In regressions 3 and 4, the change in marginal rates is measured by the change in the EFW marginal tax rating during the same two periods. Because the EFW measure considers both the marginal tax rate and the income level at which the rate applies, it is a more refined measure than the rate change alone. The higher ratings are indicative of lower marginal tax rates (and initial application of high marginal rates at higher income levels), so the rating variables will have positive signs if lower top marginal rates enhance growth.

In regression 1, both the change in the top marginal rate during 1985–1990 and the change during 1990–1995 were negative and significant.

[7] Other researchers have used similar techniques in an effort to hold other things constant. For example, when analyzing the impact of changes in the top state income tax rates on income growth, Holcombe and Lacombe compared the growth of per-capita income in counties on state borders with income growth in adjacent counties across the state border. This border-matching technique made it possible for them to hold constant many factors such as climate, culture, and proximity to markets that might also influence the growth of income. Their findings indicate that over the thirty-year period from 1960 to 1990, states that raised their top income tax rates more than their neighbors had slower income growth and, on average, a 3.4 percent reduction in per-capita income. See Randall G. Holcombe and Donald J. Lacombe, "The Effect of State Income Taxation on Per Capita Income Growth," *Public Finance Review* 32, no. 3 (May 2004): 292–312.

[8] A t-ratio is a statistic that allows one to estimate the probability that a statistical result has simply occurred by chance. A "high" t-statistic indicates a low probability (p-value) that a given result is by chance, and, in such a case, the result is said to be "statistically significant." How high the t-statistic has to be is somewhat subjective, but t-ratios with corresponding p-values under 10 percent are generally considered statistically significant. A t-ratio of 7.0 (given the sample size in the model) would correspond with a p-value of essentially zero—meaning we are virtually certain that the result is not the product of chance alone.

Regression 1 implies that, holding the other variables of the model constant, a 10 percentage point reduction in the top marginal rate is associated with approximately a 0.5 percentage point increase in long-term growth. The R-squared implies that the model represented by regression 1 accounts for 40 percent of the variation in the growth rate of GDP among the seventy-seven countries during 1990–2002.

However, an outlier observation for the Democratic Republic of the Congo exerted a strong influence on the regression.[9] Therefore, this country was dropped from regression 2. Indeed, this makes a difference. As regression 2 shows, the coefficient for the change in the marginal tax variables is reduced and is no longer statistically significant at usual levels of acceptance.

Regressions 3 and 4 are identical to 1 and 2 except that the EFW marginal tax rating is substituted for the top marginal rates in the case of both the change variables and the initial (1985) top marginal tax rate. In regression 3, a one-unit increase in the rating between 1985 and 1990 enhances growth during the 1990s by 0.241 percentage points. A one-unit increase in the rating between 1990 and 1995 is associated with a 0.304 percentage point increase in growth during 1990–2002. The substitution of the EFW marginal tax rating, which takes both marginal tax rates and the income threshold at which they begin to apply into account, increases the explanatory power of the model. Nonetheless, Congo continues to exert disproportional influence. In order to avoid misleading results from this source, the model is re-run with the omission of Congo. These results are presented in regression 4. In this regression, both of the changes in the marginal tax ratings (from 1985 to 1990, and from 1990 to 1995) remain statistically significant. A one-point change in the EFW rating reflects a 5 percentage point change in the top marginal tax rate, holding the income level at which the rate applies constant. Thus, the coefficients of 0.144 for the rating change during 1985–1990 and 0.215 for the change during 1990–1995 indicate that a 10 percentage point reduction in a country's top marginal rate increases the annual rate of long-term growth by around 0.3 or 0.4 percentage points. The model represented by regression 4 accounts for 42.4 percent of the variation in growth rates among the seventy-six countries (omitting Congo).[10]

Clearly, these estimates do not indicate that changes in marginal tax rates are a growth panacea. They do suggest, however, that changes in

[9] The average annual growth rate of per-capita GDP for the Democratic Republic of the Congo was *minus* 2.0 percent during the 1980s and *minus* 7.2 percent during 1990–2002. The latter figure was, by far, the worst growth record of any country in our study. Because Congo also maintained a high (60 percent) marginal tax rate throughout the period, it exerted a strong impact on the marginal tax rate coefficients of the regression.

[10] Neither the initial (1990) per-capita GDP nor the marginal tax rate prior to the change (1985) in marginal rates was significant in this model. To the extent that low per-capita GDP and high marginal tax rates influence growth, the effects would be present in the 1980s as well as the 1990s. Thus, the insignificance of these variables merely indicates that they did not influence growth in the 1990s, over and above their impact on growth during the 1980s.

marginal rates, particularly rates that are exceedingly high, influence the growth rate of an economy. Interestingly, these estimates are in line with the experience of the United Kingdom, the United States, and New Zealand, the three high-income industrial countries that have cut their top rates from the 60 to 70 percent range to 40 percent or less since 1980.[11] During the period following their major tax reductions, the per-capita GDP of each of these countries has grown at approximately a 2 percent annual rate. By way of comparison, the per-capita GDP growth rates of Japan, France, Germany, and other members of the European Union maintaining top marginal rates of 50 percent or more have been about 1.5 percent since 1990.

Of course, our results are subject to the usual limitations accompanying cross-country regression analysis, particularly bias emanating from an inability to control for other factors influencing growth. To the extent that countries reducing their marginal rates between 1985 and 1995 were more likely than the non–tax cutters to adopt other growth-enhancing reforms, the estimates presented here will overstate the impact of the changes in the top tax rates. However, there are also biases in the opposite direction. As we discussed above, real GDP (and its growth rate) will fail to register several of the negative side-effects accompanying high marginal tax rates. This is particularly true of those side-effects associated with price distortions and tax-avoidance activities. Because the estimates presented here use the growth figures for real GDP as a measure of the negative side-effects of high marginal rates, they will understate the negative impact of the high marginal rates.

IV. Marginal Tax Rates, Income Inequality, and Tax Payments

A. Theoretical considerations

Tax cuts are often more or less across-the-board because, from a political viewpoint, rates in the lower income brackets will have to be cut in order to make the cuts in the top brackets politically feasible. Thus, it is important to understand that across-the-board cuts in marginal tax rates will have different incentive effects up and down the income distribution.

[11] The United Kingdom and the United States are not included among the countries of table 4 because they had two major tax reductions since 1980 and one of them occurred prior to 1985. The United Kingdom reduced its top rate from 83 percent to 60 percent in 1980 and then sliced it to 40 percent in 1988. The top marginal rate in the United Kingdom has remained at 40 percent since 1988. The United States cut its top rate from 70 percent to 50 percent in 1981, and then reduced it to approximately 30 percent in 1987–1988. The top rate in the U.S. has been both increased and decreased modestly since 1988, but it has remained below 40 percent during all of this period. New Zealand's major tax change occurred during 1988–1989, when the top rate was cut from 66 percent to 33 percent, and the rate has remained below 40 percent since that time.

Suppose that a government with graduated income tax rates ranging from a low of 15 percent to a high of 75 percent reduced tax rates across the board by one-third. The top tax rate would then fall from 75 percent to 50 percent. After the tax cut, taxpayers in the highest tax bracket who earn an additional $100 would get to keep $50 rather than only $25, a 100 percent increase in their take-home wage at the margin. These taxpayers will have a strong incentive to earn more taxable income after the rate reduction, and the revenues collected from them will decline by substantially less than a third. In fact, given the huge increase in their incentive to earn, the revenues collected from taxpayers formerly confronting such high marginal rates may actually increase, an outcome suggested by the Laffer curve.

Meanwhile, the same one-third rate reduction will cut the bottom tax rate only from 15 percent to 10 percent. In this range, the tax cut means that an additional $100 in gross pay increases take-home pay by $90 instead of $85, only a 5.9 percent increase. Because cutting the 15 percent rate to 10 percent exerts only a small effect on the incentive to earn in the lower tax (and lower income) brackets, the incomes of persons in these marginal tax brackets will be largely unchanged. Thus, the taxable income base of persons in the lower tax brackets will not be altered much by the tax cut. Therefore, in contrast with the situation in high tax brackets, tax revenue will decline by almost the same percentage as tax rates in the lowest tax brackets.

The bottom line is that when all rates are cut by approximately the same percentage, the increase in the incentive to earn will be greatest in the upper tax (and income) brackets. There will be two major side-effects of this change in the incentive structure. First, income inequality will increase. Predictably, the incomes of those in the high tax brackets will expand by larger amounts than those in the lower tax brackets. Some of this increase in income will reflect a decline in tax-avoidance activities, and some of it will reflect the substitution of work for leisure. Both will show up as an increase in the observed income of persons in the upper tax and upper income brackets.

Second, a larger share of the income tax will be paid by high-income taxpayers. Because the tax cut will increase the incentive to earn more in high-income brackets than in low-income brackets, taxable income will expand more and the taxes paid will decline less in the upper income brackets. When the top marginal rates are extremely high, taxes collected from the high-income taxpayers may even increase after a tax cut. Even if this is not the case, however, a larger share of the income tax will still be collected from those with high incomes.

B. Marginal tax rates and the distribution of income: Empirical evidence

If our analysis is correct, even across-the-board rate reductions will lead to an increase in income inequality. If the rate reductions are greater in the high tax brackets than in the lower brackets, the expected increase in income inequality will be even greater. Thus, countries that reduce their highest rates by substantial amounts should experience increases in income inequality. Reliable data on the distribution of income are unavailable for many of the seventy-seven countries that comprise the central data base of this study. Furthermore, even when income distribution data are available, there are often serious problems with comparability across countries.[12] Therefore, we are unable to use regression analysis to undertake a detailed statistical analysis of this issue.

Comparable data are available for the United States both before and after the major personal income tax cuts that have occurred since 1960. Data are also available for other countries, including several that reduced their rates substantially during the 1985–1995 period. These data can be compared with data from countries that have persistently maintained high marginal tax rates. These comparisons will shed light on the relationship between high marginal tax rates and income inequality.

In the United States, the personal income tax is the largest single source of revenue for the federal government. The marginal rate structure of the income tax is progressive; taxpayers with larger incomes face higher marginal and average tax rates. However, the structure of the rates has changed substantially since 1960. In the early 1960s, there were twenty-four marginal tax brackets ranging from a low of 20 percent to a high of 91 percent. The Kennedy-Johnson tax cut was roughly an across-the-board proportional rate reduction. The 91 percent top rate was sliced to 70 percent, and the 20 percent rate was cut to 14 percent. In 1981, the first tax cut of the Reagan years reduced the top rate from 70 percent to 50 percent, and the lowest rate was cut from 14 percent to 10 percent. The second Reagan tax cut sliced the top marginal rate to approximately 30 percent beginning in 1988. The top rate was increased to 33 percent in 1991, and two years later it was increased again to 39.6 percent, but the tax reductions during the administration of George W. Bush rolled the top rate back to 35 percent. Thus, since the late 1980s, Americans with the highest incomes have paid sharply lower top marginal tax rates—rates in the 30 to 40 percent range, compared to top rates of 91 percent in the early 1960s and 70 percent prior to 1981.

What has happened to the distribution of income in the United States? Table 6 provides income distribution data for the U.S. since 1970 and distributional data after taxes (and after taxes and transfers) since 1980.

[12] Several factors reduce the comparability of income distribution data across countries and time periods. Sometimes the underlying figures are based on income, and in other cases they are based on consumption expenditures. Sometimes the income figures are for households, and in other cases they are for individuals. Sometimes the figures are derived from national samples, while in other instances they only reflect figures for urban (or rural) dwellers. Some data are after-tax and some are before-tax. Thus, extreme care must be exercised in this area.

TABLE 6. *The Distribution of Household Income in the United States, 1970–2001*

	Income share of the bottom quintile	Income share of the middle three quintiles	Income share of the top quintile	Income share of the top 5 percent
Before taxes				
1970	4.1	52.7	43.3	16.6
1980	4.3	52.1	43.7	15.8
1990	3.9	49.5	46.6	18.6
2001	3.5	46.3	50.1	22.4
After taxes*				
1980	4.9	54.6	40.6	14.1
1990	4.5	52.0	43.5	16.5
2001	4.4	50.7	44.9	18.2
After taxes & transfers*				
1980	5.6	54.0	40.3	n.a.
1990	5.2	51.5	43.3	n.a.
2001	4.7	48.7	46.5	n.a.

Sources: http://www.census.gov/hhes/income/histinc/h02.html; http://www.census.gov/hhes/income/histinc/rdi3.html; and http://www.census.gov/hhes/income/histinc/rdi7.html.
*Comparable data after taxes and after taxes and transfers were unavailable for 1970.

The distribution of income before taxes and transfer payments (e.g., welfare and Social Security payments) can be very different from the distribution after taxes and transfers. Since the system tends to tax more from higher-income households and give more through transfers to lower-income households, the distribution of income will be more equal after taxes and transfers than before. In 2001, the before-tax income share of the top quintile was approximately fourteen times that of the bottom quintile. After taxes, the ratio of the income share of the top quintile to the share of the bottom quintile was approximately ten to one.

Second, income inequality in the United States has increased, and most of that increase has taken place since 1980. Between 1970 and 1980, there was little change in the before-tax distribution of income. In fact, the income share of the bottom quintile rose slightly (from 4.1 percent in 1970 to 4.3 percent in 1980), while the share of the top 5 percent of earners declined (from 16.6 percent to 15.8 percent) during the decade. Since 1980, however, the situation has been dramatically different. The income share of the bottom quintile fell from 4.3 percent in 1980 to 3.5 percent in 2001.

Over the same period, the income share of the top quintile of earners rose from 43.7 percent to 50.1 percent, an increase of 6.4 percentage points. Furthermore, the increase in the income share of the top group was entirely the result of the higher incomes registered by the top 5 percent of earners. Between 1980 and 2001, the income share of the top 5 percent rose from 15.8 percent to 22.4 percent, an increase of 6.6 percentage points. This increase more than accounts for the larger income share of the top quintile.

The changes in the distribution of income after taxes (and after taxes and transfers) followed a similar path. In both cases, the income share of the bottom quintile declined during the 1980s and 1990s, and the share of the top quintile rose during both decades. Likewise, the growth of income among the top 5 percent of earners accounted for almost all of the increase in the after-tax income share of the top quintile.

The increase in income inequality in the U.S. may have other contributing causes. Other researchers have argued that increased trade openness and/or demographic changes, particularly the increase in the number of both single-parent and dual-earner households, have contributed to the increase in inequality.[13] However, both the timing and the structure of the increase in income inequality indicate that reductions in the highest marginal tax rates played an important role. The major increases in inequality began with the sharp reductions in the top marginal rates during the 1980s. Moreover, almost all of the large increases—those substantially above the average growth of income—were registered at the very top of the income distribution, precisely the place where the incentive effects of rate reductions are the strongest.

Table 7 presents data on the share of household income derived by the top and bottom quintiles in the 1980s and the 1990s–2000s. These figures are presented for (1) countries with persistently low (40 percent or less) top marginal tax rates during the 1990s and (2) countries with persistently high (50 percent or more) top rates during the 1980s and 1990s.[14] Many of the countries with low top marginal rates during the 1990s reduced their top rates substantially between 1985 and 1995. Therefore, to a large degree, the persistently low tax group is comprised of countries with substantially lower tax rates in the late 1990s than in the early 1980s.

Two things stand out with regard to the pattern of the data in table 7. First, the income inequality of the countries in the persistently low tax category is greater than for those in the persistently high tax group. In the late 1990s, the income share of the top quintile of earners was 43 percent

[13] For information on the linkage between trade openness and income inequality, see Gary Burtless, "International Trade and the Rise in Earnings Inequality," *Journal of Economic Literature* 33, no. 2 (June 1995): 800–816; and the symposium on "Income Inequality and Trade," *Journal of Economic Perspectives* 9, no. 3 (Summer 1995).

[14] All countries in these two categories for which comparable household income distribution data could be obtained are included here.

TABLE 7. *Top Marginal Tax Rates and the Distribution of Income: Persistently Low versus Persistently High Top Marginal Tax Rates during the 1990s*

	Top marginal tax rate, 1980	Top marginal tax rate, 1995	Income share of the bottom quintile, 1980s	Income share of the top quintile, 1980s	Year	Income share of the bottom quintile, 1990s–2000s	Income share of the top quintile, 1990s–2000s	Year	Is income inequality increasing or decreasing?*
Low tax countries during the 1990s									
Bangladesh	60	40	7.2	43.4	1983	9.0	44.5	2000	No change
Costa Rica	50	25	4.5	51.8	1983	4.2	51.5	2000	No change
Guatemala	40	25	2.7	62.1	1987	2.6	64.1	2000	Increasing
Hong Kong	15	20	6.2	46.5	1980	5.3	50.7	1996	Increasing
Indonesia	50	30	7.3	42.3	1980	8.4	43.3	2002	No change
New Zealand	62	33	6.0	40.6	1980	6.4	43.8	1997	Increasing
Philippines	70	35	5.2	52.1	1985	5.4	52.3	2000	No change
Singapore	55	30	6.5	46.6	1980	5.0	49.0	1998	Increasing
United Kingdom	83	40	5.5	41.4	1986	6.1	44.0	1999	Increasing
High tax countries during the 1990s									
Austria	62	50	6.6	38.6	1981	8.1	38.5	1997	No change
Belgium	76	61	8.6	34.7	1985	8.3	37.3	1996	Increasing
Denmark	66	64	6.7	37.2	1981	8.3	35.8	1997	Decreasing
Finland	68	57	6.8	36.9	1987	9.6	36.7	2000	Decreasing
France	60	51	6.6	42.0	1984	7.2	40.2	1995	Decreasing
Germany	65	57	6.8	37.4	1981	8.5	36.9	2000	Decreasing
Japan	75	65	6.3	39.6	1980	10.6	35.7	1993	Decreasing
Netherlands	72	60	6.1	39.8	1983	7.3	40.1	1994	No change
Sweden	87	50	9.0	35.3	1981	9.1	36.6	2000	No change

Sources: 1980s income distribution data are from Deininger and Squire Data Set, A New Data Set Measuring Income Inequality, http://www.worldbank.org/research/growth/dddeisqu.htm; 1990s income distribution data are from the World Bank, *World Development Indicators 2004* (Washington, DC: World Bank, 2004).
*The "No change" label indicates that the average difference between the two periods for the top and bottom quintiles was less than 1 percentage point.
Note: The income distribution data were unavailable for some countries.

or more in all of the countries in the low top marginal rate group. In contrast, the income share of the top quintile was between 35 percent and 41 percent for all of the countries in the high tax group.

Second, the general trend appears to be toward more income inequality in the low-tax countries but less inequality in countries with high top marginal rates. Income inequality rose in five of the nine low-tax countries, while the other four experienced no significant change. In contrast, five of the nine high-tax countries registered a reduction in income inequality during the period, and there was no discernible change in three others. An increase in income inequality was observed in only one (Belgium) of the countries in the high-tax group.

From our perspective, the figures for New Zealand and the United Kingdom are particularly interesting. Among the high-income industrial countries, these two countries (along with the United States) made the largest tax cuts during the 1980s. New Zealand reduced its top rate from 66 percent to 33 percent during 1987–1989. In the United Kingdom, the top marginal rate was reduced from 83 percent to 60 percent in 1980 and to 40 percent in 1988, and the lower rate has been maintained ever since. As table 7 shows, the income share derived by the highest quintile of earners increased in both countries. In New Zealand, the income share of the top quintile rose from 40.6 percent in the early 1980s to 43.8 percent in the late 1990s. In the United Kingdom, the share of the top quintile jumped from 41.4 percent in the 1980s to 44 percent in the late 1990s. Like the figures for the U.S., the income distribution data for New Zealand and the United Kingdom indicate that substantial reductions in the highest marginal rates will lead to rapid income growth in the upper income brackets and an increase in the observed income inequality.

We should make one final point about the empirical linkage between lower top tax rates and income inequality: Comparisons of the periods before and after rate reductions will tend to overstate the change in economic inequality. To some extent, the empirical data reflect the fact that the rate reductions increase the visibility of the income of the highest earners. High tax rates encourage tax-avoidance activities that tend to conceal income, broadly defined to include leisure, pleasurable activities, and ability to purchase many goods at a low personal cost. For example, when tax rates are high, those confronting the high rates take more of their "income" in the form of low-cost luxury offices and automobiles, business-related vacations in exotic places, pleasurable hobby business activities, interest on tax-free municipal bonds, and similar activities that conceal their true income. As lower rates make these activities less profitable, those with high incomes shift away from them. As they do so, their money income increases and their overall income becomes more visible. In turn, this makes it look like their overall income has increased by a larger amount than is really the case.

C. Changes in marginal tax rates and the taxes paid by those with high incomes

As we previously discussed, an analysis of the incentive structure associated with tax cuts indicates that a roughly proportional reduction in tax rates will increase both income levels and the share of taxes collected from high-income taxpayers. Because the income base will be more responsive in the upper income brackets, the share of taxes collected from those with high incomes may increase even if their rates are reduced more than proportionally.

Table 8 provides data related to this proposition for the United States. The share of the personal income tax collected from those with high incomes is indicated for various periods from 1963, when the top federal rate was 91 percent, through 1994–2001, when the top federal rate was 39.6 percent. These data show that the share of the personal income tax paid by high-income Americans has increased substantially since 1963, and the increase has been particularly sharp since 1980. The top 1 percent of earners paid 33.4 percent of the personal income tax during 1994–2001, up from 19.1 percent in 1980 and 18.3 percent in 1963. The top 10 percent of earners paid 63.7 percent of the personal income tax during 1994–2001, compared to 49.3 percent in 1980 and 47 percent in 1963. At the same time, the share of the personal income tax paid by the bottom half of income earners has steadily fallen from 10.4 percent of the total in 1963 to 7 percent in 1980 and just 4.3 percent during 1994–2001. In addition to reducing the highest marginal tax rates, the tax reforms of the 1980s also

TABLE 8. *Marginal Tax Rates and Income Taxes Paid by Various Income Groups in the U.S., 1963–2001*

	Top marginal tax rate (federal)	Federal income tax receipts as a share of GDP	Share of federal income tax paid by			
			Bottom 50%	Top 10%	Top 5%	Top 1%
1963	91	7.71	10.4	47.0	35.6	18.3
1980	70	8.75	7.0	49.3	36.8	19.1
1981–1986	50	8.30	7.2	50.5	38.0	20.9
1987–1993	30–33	7.90	5.5	56.7	44.7	26.3
1994–2001	39.6	8.99	4.3	63.7	52.3	33.4

Sources: Internal Revenue Service (available online at the Tax Foundation's website: http://www.taxfoundation.org/prtopincometable.html); *Economic Report of the President, 2005* (Washington, DC: U.S. Government Printing Office, 2005), table B-80.

TABLE 9. *Marginal Tax Rates and Income Taxes Paid by Various Income Groups in New Zealand and the United Kingdom*

	Top marginal tax rate	Share of income tax paid by			
		Bottom 50%	Top 10%	Top 5%	Top 1%
New Zealand					
1981	62	12.4	38.0	25.1	9.5
1991	33	13.6	37.3	25.3	10.6
1998	39	12.2	41.3	29.0	12.8
United Kingdom					
1980	83	18.0	35.0	n.a.	11.0
1990	40	15.0	42.0	n.a.	15.0
1999	40	11.0	50.0	n.a.	20.0

Sources: New Zealand, Inland Revenue memo to New Zealand Business Roundtable; Adam Smith Institute.

increased both the standard deduction and personal exemption allowances by substantial amounts. This means that Americans are now able to earn more income before they face any tax liability. In 2001, for example, 30 percent of those filing an income tax return had no tax liability whatsoever.[15]

Table 9 presents the share of income taxes collected from high-income earners before and after major cuts in the top marginal rates for New Zealand and the United Kingdom, the two other high-income countries that have substantially reduced their top marginal rates. The pattern for both countries is similar to that of the United States. As the top marginal rate in both countries was reduced from more than 60 percent in the early 1980s to 40 percent or less during the 1990s, the share of income taxes collected from those with high incomes increased. In New Zealand, the top 5 percent of earners paid 29 percent of the personal income tax in 1998, compared to 25.1 percent in 1981. The top 1 percent paid 12.8 percent of the personal income tax in 1998, up from 9.5 percent in 1981. In the United Kingdom, the shift of the tax burden toward those with high incomes was even more dramatic. In 1999, the top 10 percent of earners paid 50 percent of the personal income tax in the United Kingdom, up

[15] Many tax filers actually received funds on net from the IRS as the result of the Earned Income Tax Credit, a program adopted in 1975 that provides a subsidy to the working poor. The tax share data of table 8 reflect only tax liability; they do not include income transfers resulting from tax credits. If these payments to taxpayers were taken into consideration, the net taxes paid by the bottom half of income recipients would have been less than 1 percent in 2002. Thus, the data of table 8 actually understate the reduction in the net share of taxes paid by the bottom half of income recipients during recent decades.

from 35 percent in 1980. Correspondingly, the share paid by the top 1 percent of income recipients jumped from 11 percent in 1980 to 20 percent in 1999. At the same time, the share of the income tax paid by the bottom half of the income distribution declined substantially from 18 percent in 1980 to 11 percent in 1999.

The figures for the United States, New Zealand, and the United Kingdom indicate that the income base in high tax brackets—those with marginal rates of 50 percent or more, for example—is highly responsive to rate reductions. As a result, exceedingly high marginal rates can be reduced with little or no loss of revenue. In fact, in extreme cases, more revenue may be collected at the lower rates. In turn, the rapid growth of observed incomes and tax revenues in the upper brackets makes rate reductions for other taxpayers possible. This is precisely what has happened in the United States and the United Kingdom, and to a lesser extent in New Zealand. As the share of the personal income tax paid by those in the upper tax brackets has risen, the share paid by the bottom half of taxpayers has fallen. Perhaps policymakers, at least in these three countries, have found a way to soak the rich: keep their marginal tax rates relatively modest, at 40 percent or less.

V. Conclusion

Our findings indicate that high marginal tax rates, particularly rates of 50 percent or more, exert an adverse impact on long-term economic growth. We estimate that a 10 percentage point reduction in a country's top marginal tax rate will enhance the country's long-term annual growth rate of real GDP by approximately three-tenths of a percentage point.

Economic theory indicates that the incentive effects of a proportional reduction in marginal tax rates will be greatest in the upper income brackets. Therefore, even an across-the-board rate cut will result in larger income increases among those with the highest incomes. Thus, reductions in high marginal tax rates will tend to increase observed income inequality. Our findings are supportive of this view. The income share of the highest group of earners tended to increase following major reductions in the highest marginal tax rates.

However, because of the stronger incentive effects accompanying rate cuts in the upper income and highest tax brackets, across-the-board tax reductions will tend to increase the share of taxes paid by those with the highest incomes and will tend to reduce the share paid by low- and middle-income earners. Even if the rate cuts are greater in the upper brackets, the share of taxes paid by the "rich" may increase. This is even more likely to occur if the rate cuts are also coupled with increases in the personal exemption and/or standard deduction (the income a taxpayer is permitted to earn without a tax liability). The experience of the United States is consistent with this view. Compared to the situation in 1980, when the top marginal tax bracket was 70 percent, the share of the personal income tax paid by those with high incomes has been substantially greater in the United States since 1987, even though the top federal income tax rate has been less than 40 percent throughout the latter period. The records of New Zealand and the United Kingdom, the other two high-income countries that dramatically reduced their highest marginal tax rates in the 1980s, are also supportive of this view. In both cases, the share of the personal income tax paid by those with the highest incomes increased following the lowering of the top rates.

In brief, our findings indicate that high marginal tax rates—rates of 50 percent and above, for example—retard economic growth. Lowering these rates will increase income inequality, but it will also tend to shift the payment of personal income taxes away from low- and middle-income households toward those with the highest incomes.

Economics, Florida State University
Economics, Capital University

TAXES, GROWTH, EQUITY, AND WELFARE

By Richard Vedder

I. Introduction

Few subjects in modern economics have received more attention, both from professional economists and from policymakers, than the issue of economic growth as it relates to "equity." Is a more prosperous society a more just or even happier society? Does the pursuit of increased output come at the cost of a loss of welfare because of adverse distributional effects of output expansion? How does one even measure inequality? Should it be measured in terms of income distribution in a given year, wealth distribution at a given point in time, the present value of lifetime income distributions, or the distribution of consumption expenditures (either currently or over a lifetime)? Should one use pre- or post-tax measures of income or wealth? And so on. The questions are endless, and the answers are inconclusive, at least in the minds of some.

This essay touches on some of these eternal questions in the context of tax policy, although it does not even attempt to offer more than partial answers to them. The basic arguments advanced in this essay are threefold. First, high taxes very often have adverse effects on the growth in incomes. If higher incomes are desirable, *ceteris paribus,* then low taxes are most often preferred to higher ones, unless one makes what I would regard as probably implausible assumptions about positive external welfare effects of tax-financed governmental expenditures, or the income distributional effects of higher incomes. Second, some crude but useful indicators of economic welfare suggest that the inverse correlation between tax burdens and economic welfare (or happiness) exists. Low-tax areas have, on average, a better quality of life. Third, even if one takes the view that economic growth resulting from tax reductions leads to some forms of potentially welfare-reducing income inequality as conventionally measured, a broader perspective on equality measurement likely would lead one to a different conclusion, namely that the growth-equity trade-off is more illusionary than real.

II. Taxes and Economic Growth

Taxes impact human behavior. Should I take an overtime job paying $15 per hour? If I am taxed 80 percent of the additional income, my after-tax compensation of $3 an hour may well be too low to make it worthwhile for me to sacrifice leisure time for working. I am happier watching football games on television. In contrast, if the marginal tax rate is 20 percent, and I can keep $12 per hour, I am more likely to prefer working—the opportunity cost of watching football is perhaps too high. Likewise, businesses facing taxes on capital investments might make similar decisions—if marginal tax rates on profits are high, the expected after-tax return may be too low to justify the risk of making the investment, thus increasing the probability that an alternative use of the funds would be more desirable. Thus, taxes can have an adverse impact on the magnitude of labor and capital resources used in making goods. Moreover, such taxes can lower investment and capital formation over the long run, having further long-run consequences on output and income. For example, if income from savings is highly taxed, the reduced supply of savings may lead to higher interest rates, leading to lower investment. Conceivably, technological progress could be impeded as well, as investments in innovation and research and development become excessively risky relative to the after-tax expected rate of return.

However, there are other theoretical reasons to believe that new or increased taxes could conceivably have positive effects on output. Individuals facing higher taxes may feel the need to work more hours to match previous levels of disposable income—the "income effect" of taxes induces more work. Also, tax revenues are spent, and if spent in a way that enhances output, it is possible that the resource-reducing disincentive effects of taxes may be offset by positive effects of government spending and the income effect. Therefore, it is not obvious a priori if taxes will have positive, negative, or neutral effects on the growth in income and wealth.

What does the empirical evidence show? Obviously, such factors as the type of taxes imposed, the uses of funds, and the time horizon studied (short-run versus long-run effects) will have an impact on the tax-growth relationship. Moreover, on a variety of grounds one might expect that the impact of new taxes will depend in part on the magnitude of taxes and the overall size of government. A society with a small government and modest taxes might benefit from higher taxes to fund needed expenditures, such as protection of property rights by improving the effectiveness of the police and justice system. A society with a large government (and already relatively high tax burdens) might find that the gains in economic growth from added taxes are far more than offset by the adverse disincentive effects of the new taxes. With these caveats in mind, a large majority of the studies seen by this author show that new taxes have adverse effects on economic indicators such as income, output, employment, migration, business investment, and plant location.

The overwhelming evidence that taxes impact behavior, often adversely, is demonstrated by a little research done for this essay. I downloaded five working papers dealing with taxes issued in the past year from the website of America's most prestigious economic research organization, the National Bureau of Economic Research. Below are excerpts from the summaries of each study, in reverse chronological order:

> This evidence is consistent with the notion that wealthy elderly people change their real (or reported) state of residence to avoid high state taxes. . . .[1]

> The individual income tax burden on dividends was lowered sharply in 2003 from a maximum rate of 35% to 15%. . . . The surge in regular dividend payments after the 2003 reform is unprecedented in recent years.[2]

> Regressions on rich-country samples in the mid 1990s indicate that a unit standard deviation tax rate difference of 12.8 percentage points leads to 122 fewer market work hours per adult per year, a drop of 4.9 percentage points in the employment-population ratio, and a rise in the shadow economy equal to 3.8 percent of GDP.[3]

> This paper presents new evidence on how corporate payout policy responds to the differential between the tax burden on dividend income and that on accruing capital gains. . . . Time series estimates . . . imply that the recent tax reform could ultimately increase dividends by almost twenty percent.[4]

> Americans now work 50 percent more than do Germans, French, and Italians. This was not the case in the early 1970s. . . . I examine the effect of the marginal tax rate on labor income. . . . [T]his marginal tax rate accounts for the predominance of the differences at points in time and the large change in relative labor supply over time.[5]

[1] Jon Bakija and Joel Slemrod, "Do the Rich Flee from High Taxes? Evidence from Federal Estate Tax Returns," Cambridge, MA: National Bureau of Economic Research (hereafter NBER) Working Paper w10645, July 2004.

[2] Raj Chetty and Emmanuel Saez, "Do Dividend Payments Respond to Taxes? Preliminary Evidence from the 2003 Dividend Tax Cut," Cambridge, MA: NBER Working Paper w10572, June 2004.

[3] Steven J. Davis and Magnus Henrekson, "Tax Effects on Work Activity, Industry Mix, and Shadow Economy Size: Evidence from Rich-Country Comparisons," Cambridge, MA: NBER Working Paper w10509, May 2004.

[4] James Poterba, "Taxation and Corporate Payout Policy," Cambridge, MA: NBER Working Paper w10321, February 2004.

[5] Edward Prescott, "Why Do Americans Work So Much More Than Europeans?" Cambridge, MA: NBER Working Paper w10316, February 2004.

Two of the studies (the third and last one cited above) show that high taxes have significant negative effects on the supply of labor, thereby lowering output. Two of the studies (the second and fourth) show that lowering taxes on dividends powerfully increases the amount of dividends, while the remaining study suggests that the elderly rich migrate to low-tax states, lowering tax revenues in high-tax states in the process. Without exception, these studies are consistent with the view that taxes significantly impact human behavior, often in ways that lower income and labor and capital inputs (and thereby output).

Literally scores of other studies reach the same general conclusion. Some of the studies look at different geographic areas (nations or American states) at one moment in time; others look at the same area over different periods in time; still others use questionnaires or other means to assess behavioral impacts. Similarly, alternative economic indicators are used: the growth in income, output, employment, new business start-ups, etc. Some studies find modest-sized relationships between taxes and the economic indicator examined, while others find stronger relationships. Most of them find, however, that taxes on balance have at least some adverse impact on the growth in incomes, output, jobs, business investment, human migration, etc.

A full review of the literature is beyond the scope of this essay, but some examples will strengthen the points made above. In the third quarter of the twentieth century, say around 1960, the prevailing view was that "taxes do not matter" much in economic decision making. Speaking of the business location literature, the distinguished public finance professor John Due said in 1961 that studies "suggest very strongly that the tax effects cannot be of major importance."[6] Within two decades, however, the evidence was strongly supporting a different conclusion: taxes matter. In the interim, tax levels had risen appreciably, particularly at the state and local levels in the United States, and econometric techniques and computer advances had led to more and better research. Contrary to Due's 1961 pronouncement, a number of studies concluded that high taxes retarded business location in a given area.[7] A series of papers using American data appearing at roughly the same time similarly showed that

[6] John F. Due, "Studies of State-Local Tax Influences on the Location of Industry," *National Tax Journal* 14 (November 1961): 163–73.

[7] Ronald Grieson, William Hamovitch, and Richard Morgenstern, "The Effects of Business Taxation on Industry," *Journal of Urban Economics*, April 1977; Deborah S. Ecker and Richard F. Syron, "Personal Taxes and Interstate Competition for High Technology Industries," *New England Economic Review*, September/October 1979, 25–32; Thomas R. Plaut and Joseph E. Pluta, "Business Climate, Taxes and Expenditures, and State Industrial Growth in the United States," *Southern Economic Journal* 50, no. 1 (July 1983): 99–119; and Robert Premus, "Location of High Technology Firms and Economic Development," Staff Study, Joint Economic Committee of Congress (Washington, DC: Government Printing Office, 1983).

high taxes more generally retarded growth in incomes and output.[8] Other studies of that era and beyond reached similar conclusions using international data.[9]

Nor have the studies been confined to analysis of income or output growth. Just as Edward Prescott and others have noted that taxes reduce labor effort of those working, other researchers have studied the impact of taxes on the number of people holding jobs or, conversely, the number who are unemployed, most often finding that increased taxation has adverse employment effects.[10] A classic study observed that high property taxation had an adverse impact on property values.[11] Other studies have gone beyond location decisions of larger American businesses to argue that taxation has an adverse impact on small business start-ups or foreign investment in the United States.[12] Finally, a large number of studies have shown that taxes have an impact on migration decisions and,

[8] Thomas Romans and Ganti Subrahmanyam, "State and Local Taxes, Transfers, and Regional Income Growth," *Southern Economic Journal* 46, no. 2 (October 1979): 435–44; L. Jay Helms, "The Effect of State and Local Taxes on Economic Growth: A Time Series–Cross Section Approach," *Review of Economics and Statistics* 67, no. 4 (November 1985): 574–82; Bruce L. Benson and Ronald N. Johnson, "The Lagged Impact of State and Local Taxes on Economic Activity and Political Behavior," *Economic Inquiry* 24, no. 3 (July 1986): 389–401; Victor A. Canto and Robert Webb, "The Effect of State Fiscal Policy on State Relative Economic Performance," *Southern Economic Journal* 54, no. 1 (July 1987): 186–202; and Alaeddin Mofidi and Joe A. Stone, "Do State and Local Taxes Affect Economic Growth?" *Review of Economics and Statistics* 72, no. 4 (November 1990): 686–91.

[9] Five representative examples: Keith Marsden, "Links Between Taxes and Economic Growth: Some Empirical Evidence," Washington, DC: World Bank Staff Working Papers no. 604, 1983; Reinhard B. Koester and Roger C. Kormendi, "Taxation, Aggregate Activity, and Economic Growth: Cross-Country Evidence on Some Supply-Side Hypotheses," *Economic Inquiry* 27, no. 3 (July 1989): 367–80; Alan Reynolds, "Some International Comparisons of Supply-Side Policy," *Cato Journal* 6, no. 2 (Fall 1985): 545–55; Bernhard Heitger, "Convergence, 'The Tax State,' and Economic Dynamics," *Weltwirtschaftliches Archiv* 129, no. 2 (1993): 254–74; and Gian Maria Milesi-Ferretti and Nouriel Roubini, "Growth Effects of Income and Consumption Taxes," *Journal of Money, Credit, and Banking* 30, no. 4 (November 1998): 721–44.

[10] Six examples: Michael Wasylenko and Therese J. McGuire, "Jobs and Taxes: The Effects of Business Climates on States' Employment Growth Rates," *National Tax Journal* 38, no. 4 (December 1985): 497–511; Andrew Newell and James Symons, "Macroeconomic Consequences of Taxations in the '80s," Discussion Paper 121 (London: London School of Economics, Centre for Economic Performance), February 1993; Ernest Goss, Phillips Preston, and Joseph M. Phillips, "State Employment Growth: The Impact of Taxes and Economic Development Agency Spending," *Growth and Change* 25, no. 3 (Summer 1994): 320–33; Douglas R. Dalenberg and Mark D. Partridge, "The Effects of Taxes, Expenditures, and Public Infrastructure on Metropolitan Area Employment," *Journal of Regional Science* 35, no. 4 (November 1995): 617–40; Guido Tabellini and Francesco Daveri, "Unemployment, Growth, and Taxation in Industrial Countries," London: Centre for Economic Policy Research, Discussion Paper 1681, August 1997; and Stephen T. Mark, Therese J. McGuire, and Leslie E. Papke, "The Influence of Taxes on Employment and Population Growth: Evidence from the Washington, D.C. Metropolitan Area," *National Tax Journal* 53, no. 1 (March 2000): 105–23. For Prescott's work, see note 5 above.

[11] Helen F. Ladd and Katharine L. Bradbury, "City Taxes and Property Tax Bases," *National Tax Journal* 41, no. 4 (December 1988): 503–23.

[12] Robert Carroll et al., "Personal Income Taxes and the Growth of Small Firms," Cambridge, MA: NBER Working Paper w7980, October 2000; and James R. Hines, Jr., "Altered States: Taxes and the Location of Foreign Direct Investment in America," *American Economic Review* 86, no. 5 (December 1996): 1076–94.

TABLE 1. *Taxes and economic growth, United States and five European countries*

	Taxes as % of GDP		% Change	Annual GDP growth rate	
Nation	1970	2003	1970–2003	1950–1973	1973–2001
United States	30.1%	31.0%	0.9%	3.93%	2.94%
France	35.6	45.3	9.7	5.05	2.20
Germany	32.8	45.1	12.3	5.68	1.75
Italy	27.9	45.8	17.9	5.64	2.30
Sweden	40.7	59.3	18.6	3.73	1.83
United Kingdom	37.5	39.9	2.4	2.93	2.08

Source: Statistical Abstract of the United States: 1984, 870; *Statistical Abstract of the United States: 2004–2005*, 857; Angus Maddison, *The World Economy: Historical Statistics* (Paris: OECD, 2003), 260. Taxes are for all levels of government (national, provincial, local) and include social insurance taxes, although they do not include the impact of unfunded regulatory mandates.

therefore, population growth; high-tax areas grow slower than lower-tax ones.[13]

This huge body of evidence, only a small part of which is cited here, is confirmed by less rigorous, more casual observation. Western Europe, which in the 1950s and 1960s grew far faster than the United States, has grown far slower in recent years, as table 1 indicates.[14] While the tax burden showed little change in the U.S., the burden rose sharply in most European countries. In the 1973–2000 period, growth rates were far higher in the U.S. than in its European counterparts, in marked contrast to the earlier period. This relationship, I think, is not coincidental. Low-tax Ireland is the "Celtic Tiger" that leads Western Europe in growth, with real per-capita GDP rising 6.03 percent annually from 1990 to 2001, more than triple the average of 1.72 percent for twenty-

[13] A few representative samples from different time periods: Richard J. Cebula, "Local Government Policies and Migration: An Analysis for SMSA's in the United States, 1965–1970," *Public Choice* 19 (Fall 1974): 185–93; Lynn E. Browne, "The Shifting Pattern of Interregional Migration," *New England Economic Review*, November–December 1979, 17–32; William A. Niskanen, "The Case for a New Fiscal Constitution," *Journal of Economic Perspectives* 6, no. 2 (Spring 1992): 13–24; and Karen Smith Conway and Andrew J. Houtenville, "Elderly Migration and State Fiscal Policy: Evidence from the 1990 Census Migration Flows," *National Tax Journal* 54 no. 1 (March 2001): 103–23.

[14] It is true that the 1950s European growth rates were at least partially enhanced by the "catch up" effect of recovering from World War II related damage, although that factor clearly was not so important in the equally high-growth 1960s, long after the war's end and long after output had exceeded prewar levels.

nine European nations.[15] At the same time, very-high-tax Sweden has such low growth rates that its per-capita income now is actually below that of most of its Western European industrial peer nations, whereas in 1972 it had easily the highest per-capita income of the European members of the Organization for Economic Cooperation and Development (OECD), exceeding the average of that group of industrialized countries by 83 percent.[16] Russia's economic growth has spurted in the years since it inaugurated a low (13 percent) flat-rate income tax in mid-2000 (effective in 2001).[17] Within the United States, those nine states without general state income taxes have had a massive net in-migration (4,169,268 from 1990 to 2004) of native-born Americans from the forty-one states with such taxes.[18] Low-tax states like New Hampshire have generally had higher rates of growth of income and in-migration of people than higher-tax nearby states such as New York, Vermont, and Maine. In 1970, Ohio had the fourth lowest state and local tax burden in the United States according to the Tax Foundation; by 2004, it had the fourth highest burden, raising its overall tax burden by well over 25 percent when the typical state changed its burden very little. It is probably not a coincidence that in the same period, the Buckeye State went from having a per-capita income level that exceeded the national average to one that was more than 5 percent below that average.[19]

Before moving on, it is worthwhile to briefly ponder *why* the strong negative relationship between taxes and growth exists. The disincentive effects of taxation on savings, investment, innovation, and work effort have already been mentioned. But in the most fundamental sense, taxation takes resources from the relatively productive (in most modern societies with market economies and a strong rule of law) private sector, and diverts those resources to the public sector, which is less productive, since

[15] Angus Maddison, *The World Economy: Historical Statistics* (Paris: OECD, 2003), 69, and author's calculations.

[16] U.S. Bureau of the Census, *Statistical Abstract of the United States: 1973* (Washington, DC: Government Printing Office, 1973), 812.

[17] In the 1995–2000 period, Russia's economic growth was actually negative according to official statistics, while it has averaged about 5 percent a year since 2001. To be sure, the numbers are somewhat suspect because of a sizable underground economy in the years when tax rates were high, and because of transitional difficulties after the collapse of the Soviet Union in the early 1990s, including the Russian financial crisis of 1998.

[18] The data are from the U.S. Bureau of the Census, available at http://www.census.gov. The numbers are the sum of estimates for 1990 to 1999 and 2000 to 2004, and exclude the period from July 1, 1999, to April 1, 2000. The non-income-tax states are Alaska, Florida, Nevada, New Hampshire, South Dakota, Tennessee, Texas, Washington, and Wyoming. The exclusion of data from July 1999–April 2000 simply reflects the fact that between decennial censuses, the Census Bureau does annual population estimates (including migration) for states as of July 1, except in the year in which the Census was taken on April 1. Thus, the data for the short 1999–2000 period are unavailable.

[19] The Tax Foundation website, at www.taxfoundation.org, is a particularly good source of information on taxes in the United States. In addition to sluggish income growth, in large parts of the modern era (e.g., the early 1980s, in 2003–2005), Ohio's unemployment rate has exceeded the national average by significant amounts.

it is less competitive (more monopolistic) and does not face the accountability, the "bottom line," that markets impose. Private businesses strive for increased profits by becoming more efficient (lowering costs) and offering better products. The profit incentive is absent in most government enterprises.

III. Taxes and Human Welfare—Is There a Relationship?

It is one thing to present evidence that high and increased levels of taxation tend to reduce the levels of income, wealth, and employment, but quite another thing to demonstrate that high taxes lead to reduced levels of happiness or well-being. One fundamental problem is that utility (economist jargon for satisfaction or happiness) cannot be scientifically measured with any great precision—a major reason why, for example, economic historians still debate whether the Industrial Revolution that came to Great Britain was, in some ultimate sense, a success or a failure. Material gains do not necessarily equate with gains in happiness.

Economists say that "cardinal utility"—a precise quantitative measure of the satisfaction derived from an activity or good purchased—is not measurable, whereas "ordinal utility" (as determined by preferences for one activity or good relative to others) is. I can say with reference to new cars, "I prefer a Lexus to a Honda," but I cannot meaningfully say, "I believe I will be 42.17 percent more satisfied with a Lexus than a Honda."

There are two major arguments that can be used to suggest that the welfare of the general populace may be improved by large government financed by taxes even if the crowding-out of productive private-sector activity reduces levels of income and wealth. The first argument is that much of what government does has what economists call "positive externalities"—spillover benefits that accrue not only to the user of government-provided services, but to society as a whole. For example, education spending, it is argued, leads to higher literacy, which in turn leads to better communications, lowering the costs of transactions and making the market economy more efficient in allocating resources. Also, a well-educated electorate is more likely to pick leaders who are wise and moral, as opposed to corrupt charlatans. These positive spillover effects are not present, we are told, in most goods and services sold in the private sector.

The second argument states that the material well-being of individuals is related not only to the absolute amount of income or wealth that people have, but to the distribution of that income or wealth. As Karl Marx once said, "A house may be large or small; as long as the surrounding houses are equally small, it satisfies all social demands for a dwelling. But if a palace rises beside the little house, the little house shrinks into a hut."[20]

[20] Karl Marx, "Wage-Labor and Capital," in *Selected Works*, vol. 1 (New York: International Publishers, 1933).

Therefore, it is at least plausible that a society with average household income of $45,000 where the overwhelming majority (say, 85 percent) of households have between $25,000 and $75,000 in income will have a higher level of aggregate happiness, and an absolutely larger number of happier people, than a society with average household income of $50,000, but where there are a large proportion of households (say, 30 percent) with less than, say, $25,000 in income and another good-sized group (say, 15 percent) with more than $75,000. It is argued that income is subject to diminishing marginal utility, meaning that adding $1,000 in income to households who already have $200,000 in income will increase their happiness far less than adding the same $1,000 in income to households with $20,000 in income. Since both taxation and tax-financed government spending can be used to reduce inequalities in disposable (after-tax) income, taxation (particularly progressive taxation that is directed disproportionately to upper-income persons) can serve to increase the well-being of a large majority of the population, causing only modest losses in well-being to a relatively small minority. This is in keeping with the utilitarian ideal, attributable to Jeremy Bentham, of "the greatest good for the greatest number." [21]

Looking at the first argument, it is extremely hard to measure "positive externalities," a somewhat imprecisely defined concept that ultimately depends on evaluating the utility derived from governmental activity. One might argue equally that governmental activities sometimes have negative spillover effects or externalities. The government constructs a sewage plant that emits an odor. The residents in the area surrounding the plant see their utility decline—as well as the value of their houses. It is not unambiguously clear a priori whether governmental activities in the aggregate have positive or negative spillover effects. Moreover, private expenditures can have positive spillover effects as well—my neighbor puts up a gorgeous Christmas holiday display in his front yard, which I enormously enjoy. His spending provides utility to me, although I cannot precisely measure it given the inability to measure cardinal utility. In contrast, some private activity has negative externalities—an entrepreneur opens a bar near my house that brings a lot of noise and alcohol-induced reckless driving to my neighborhood. My utility declines. All in all, it is hard to say whether governmental or private activities have more positive or negative spillover effects impacting on human welfare.

Yet there is one form of human behavior that is measurable that does relate quite directly to the issue of positive and negative externalities—human migration. When a person moves from A to B, he or she is revealing a preference for B—in effect saying, "I think life will be better in coming years in B than if I were living in A." Implicitly, assuming people

[21] For a good discussion of utilitarian philosophy as it relates to this discussion and more specifically to Jeremy Bentham, see Joseph A. Schumpeter, *History of Economic Analysis* (New York: Oxford University Press, 1954), esp. 128–34.

in general wish to maximize their satisfaction or utility in life, the mover says, "I believe I will derive more utility living in B than living in A." Migration is an exercise in revealing one's ordinal utility rankings.

If area B has more taxes and governmental services than area A, but similar income levels, job opportunities, climate, etc., it may well be that the move to the high-tax area B reflects the fact that the governmental services provided there have external benefits not reflected in the dollar value of the services provided. If positive externalities result from governmental activity, this should be reflected in in-migration, as people move to acquire the benefits associated with the governmental services. If governmental activity produces net positive externalities, one would expect a positive relationship between the size of government (measured by tax burden or governmental expenditures) and the in-migration of people.

This is a testable proposition. Indeed, as mentioned above, a number of studies have looked at the relationship between government size and in-migration, and have found a negative or nonexistent relationship, inconsistent with the notion that tax-financed governmental activity produces large positive external benefits. I confirmed that directly by using regression analysis to explain variations in net domestic migration among the fifty American states and the District of Columbia over the period from 1990 to 2004. I regressed the tax burden of each state in the middle of that period (as measured by total state and local taxes as a percentage of personal income) against the net number of in-migrants. Doing so produced a statistically significant (at the 5 percent level) *negative* relationship—persons tended to move *away* from the high-tax states. Adding some other possible factors into the analysis for control purposes (e.g., average income levels and the number of days the sun typically shines), the relationship remains negative. This finding certainly is inconsistent with the notion that large positive externalities of government spending add significantly to the quality of life.[22]

For readers less acquainted with multivariate statistical techniques, I made a simple calculation. I took the ten states that in the middle of the period examined had the highest tax burdens. I found that those states had a net *out*-migration of 2,976,513 persons from 1990 to 2004. I then compared that with the ten states with the lowest tax burden. They had a net *in*-migration of 4,199,194.[23] There was a massive migration away

[22] For a more extended discussion, see my *Taxation and Migration: Do Tax Decisions of State and Local Government Officials Impact on the Movement of People?* (Cedarburg, WI: Taxpayers Network, March 2003). The Census data in question are not classified by age. Other data suggest that while it is true that the elderly migrate in moderately large numbers, an even larger group quantitatively is young adults—relatively new workers to the labor force.

[23] Data were provided by the U.S. Bureau of the Census (and available via www.census.gov). Data on state and local tax burdens in 1997 (from the Census of Governments of that year) were divided by state personal income (provided by Bureau of Economic Analysis via www.bea.doc.gov) to obtain the average tax burden. The year 1997 was the mid-year in the period.

from high-tax states—into low-tax ones. This is highly inconsistent with the idea that high-tax states have higher external benefits because of generous governmental services.

I turn now to the second argument discussed above. This argument suggests that economic growth fostered by low levels of taxation might not be welfare-enhancing because the unequal distribution of income or wealth affects well-being. Studies based on average data ignore income distribution, and widening income inequality might lower utility as much as (or more than) rising general income levels raise it. The validity of this scenario, however, is questionable for a variety of reasons.[24]

To begin with, the thesis that increasing economic equality associated with bigger government has positive welfare effects cannot be evaluated if we cannot agree on the appropriate measures of economic inequality. It is my contention that the measure most often used is inappropriate, and that alternative measures often show a dramatically different picture as to the amount and trends in inequality.

At least three different economic indicators are commonly used in evaluating inequality: personal income, wealth, and consumption expenditures. Of these, income is the most used indicator, consumption the least. Yet it is my contention that consumption is the best of the three indicators for measuring the welfare implications of the inequality of economic conditions in any given time period. People do not derive utility from the income they earn as much as from the income they spend. Income taken from individuals involuntarily in the form of taxes or voluntarily in the form of savings does not provide direct material satisfaction to those individuals, at least in the period in which the individual is taxed or saves. To be sure, savers are, in effect, bribed to forgo consumption by the prospects of receiving future interest, dividend, and capital-gains income. Yet the ultimate goal of economic activity is consumption, not the act of earning the income itself, and that is why people have to be induced (through interest and dividend payments) to save rather than consume.

Data on consumption spending is less readily available than income data, but the Bureau of Labor Statistics of the U.S. Department of Labor has a much respected Consumer Expenditure Survey that provides relatively good consumption data. Table 2 shows consumption data for 2002 classified by income quintiles, along with Census Bureau data on household income similarly classified.[25]

[24] The classic work questioning the policy of using government fiscal policy to bring about changes in the distribution of income and wealth is Walter J. Blum and Harry Kalven, Jr., *The Uneasy Case for Progressive Taxation* (Chicago: University of Chicago Press, 1953).

[25] U.S. Department of Labor, Bureau of Labor Statistics, Report 974, *Consumer Expenditures in 2002* (Washington, DC: Government Printing Office, February 2004), table 1; U.S. Census Bureau, *Historical Income Tables—Households*, available at http://www.census.gov/hhes/income/histinc/h02ar.html (accessed February 22, 2005).

TABLE 2. *Distribution of income and consumption spending in the U.S., 2002*

Income quintile*	Income	Consumption spending
Bottom 20% (poorest)	3.5%	9.0%
Second 20% (below average)	8.8	12.8
Third 20% (middle quintile)	14.8	17.3
Fourth 20% (above average)	23.3	23.7
Top 20% (richest)	49.8	37.2

*Income is measured for household units; consumption spending is for consumer units, which are similar conceptually to households.
Source: U.S. Bureau of the Census, U.S. Bureau of Labor Statistics.

The data show that consumption spending is far more compressed (equal) than income. The richest 20 percent have four times the share of total consumption compared to the poorest 20 percent, while the richest 20 percent of households have more than fourteen times as much income. While the poorest Americans have only 3.5 percent the nation's income, they are responsible for 9 percent of its consumption, a share two and a half times as large as their share of income. The rich save or pay taxes equal to large portions of their income, while the poor actually dissave significantly, spending far more than they earn in income.

The major reason why the distribution of consumption spending is only roughly half as unequal as the distribution of income is that consumption spending is heavily influenced by expected *lifetime* income, not just income receipts in a particular twelve-month period. Americans have extraordinary income mobility, moving up and down the economic ladder frequently and sometimes abruptly. A "poor" person one year may be a financially average American two years later, and in the following decade might be rich. The "poor" that the government might try to subsidize this year may be the "rich" that they "soak" through high taxes next year.

The data demonstrating high income mobility are striking. Treasury Department data from 1992 showed that 86 percent of the poorest Americans in 1979 (those in the bottom 20 percent of the distribution) moved to a higher quintile in the income distribution in the next nine years.[26] An Urban Institute study suggests that more than one-quarter of Americans change income quintiles (up or down) from one year to the next, and a majority do so over intervals of a decade.[27] Other studies done at the

[26] See *Income Mobility and the U.S. Economy: Open Society or Caste System?* Joint Economic Committee of Congress, 102nd Congress, Second Session, January 1992.

[27] Daniel P. McMurrer and Isabel V. Sawhill, "How Much Do Americans Move Up and Down the Economic Ladder?" Urban Institute, *Opportunity in America,* no. 3, 1996.

Federal Reserve Bank of Dallas and the Economic Policy Institute reach similar conclusions.[28]

To the extent that incomes tend to equalize over time, a case can be made for public tax and spending policies that are relatively neutral toward the distribution of income, since single-year income differences are of little long-term meaning in terms of life income equality. While no one claims that incomes perfectly equalize over time, lifetime income differentials are sharply smaller than the single-year differentials most often cited.

This brings us to another problem with the arguments that tax-financed government expenditures might be on balance utility-enhancing. Suppose that, despite the argument made above, it were concluded that promoting income equality is utility-enhancing on balance. Such conclusions could not be made with any confidence based on empirical evidence, particularly given the extreme difficulty of measuring utility. But even if one were to accept the notion that income inequality is an obstacle in maximizing the community's welfare (or utility), what assurances are there that tax-financed government spending would reduce that inequality? As the economist Gordon Tullock pointed out more than two decades ago, large amounts of government spending are essentially middle-class or even upper-class entitlements—subsidies for pro football stadiums, National Public Radio, and even farmers come to mind, not to mention corporate welfare such as the Export-Import Bank.[29] It is even arguable that high public assistance grants to lower-income Americans beginning in the 1960s and 1970s actually had such adverse effects on behavior (by lowering work effort and leading to the disintegration of two-parent families) that they actually increased poverty rather than reduced it, worsening the income distribution.[30] The cutback in welfare benefits after federal welfare reform in the mid-1990s led to dramatically lower welfare rolls and falling rates of poverty. The poverty rate, for example, fell from 13.8 percent in 1995 (the year before the welfare reform) to 11.3 percent in 2000.[31] During the same period, federal current expenditures fell from

[28] W. Michael Cox and Richard Alm, "By Our Own Bootstraps: Economic Opportunity and the Dynamics of Income Distribution," Federal Reserve Bank of Dallas, 1995 Annual Report, pp. 2-23; Lawrence Mishel, Jared Bernstein, and John Schmitt, *The State of Working America* (Ithaca, NY: Cornell University Press, 2000). See also Cox and Alm's book *Myths of Rich and Poor: Why We're Better Off Than We Think* (New York: Basic Books, 1999), esp. chap. 4.

[29] Gordon Tullock, *Economics of Income Distribution* (Boston: Kluwer-Nijhoff, 1983).

[30] For example, in 1983, after federal expenditures per capita on the poor had expanded nearly fourfold in real terms since the Great Society era, the poverty rate was higher than in 1966, before the War on Poverty had gotten far off the ground. Lowell Gallaway and I have argued that the federal government got on the wrong side of what we termed the "poverty-welfare curve." See our short monograph *Poverty, Income Distribution, the Family, and Public Policy*, Joint Economic Committee of Congress (Washington, DC: Government Printing Office, 1986).

[31] For details on poverty, see U.S. Bureau of the Census, Current Population Reports, P-60-226, *Income, Poverty, and Health Insurance in the United States: 2003* (Washington, DC: Government Printing Office, 2004).

21.29 to 18.60 percent of gross domestic product.[32] Falling poverty was associated with *declining* government (in a relative sense). From 2000 to 2003, there was a marked increase in relative government spending—and the poverty rate *rose*—to 12.5 percent. While the 2001 recession was a contributing factor, it would be hard to argue that increased government spending reduced poverty.

The notion that government spending might increase poverty (and increase income inequality) is hardly new: in 1848, Frédéric Bastiat opined that the state "produces more poverty than it cures."[33] Lowell Gallaway, David Sollars, and I have presented strong empirical evidence that suggests that tax-financed income transfers from government do reduce inequality when administered in moderation, but actually increase it when payments reach the high levels common in the modern welfare state.[34] Thus, the assumption that expansive government leads to greater income equality through poverty reduction is, at the very least, highly questionable.

As a general proposition, does economic growth (whether stimulated by lower taxes or other means) generally lead to greater or lesser amounts of income inequality? The most famous answer to that question comes from the painstaking work of economist Simon Kuznets (who netted a Nobel Prize for his efforts). Kuznets suggested, based on examining empirical evidence, that economic growth among poor nations may generate greater inequality, but that, as nations get wealthier, growth is associated with *lesser* inequality.[35] While the existence of such a "Kuznets curve" has been debated, there is a substantial body of evidence that supports Kuznet's contention.[36] In the context of developed nations like the United States or the nations of Western Europe, this suggests that fiscal policies promoting economic growth are, on average, likely to promote greater income equality. The income distribution argument against lower taxes is further weakened.

In short, arguments used to justify tax-financed expansions of government on the grounds that they promote the general welfare and human

[32] Author's calculations from the U.S. Council of Economic Advisers, *Economic Report of the President: 2003* (Washington, DC: Government Printing Office, 2003), from tables on pp. 373 and 276. Including state and local governments in the analysis does not change the conclusion, although the decline in the relative size of government is smaller (from 30.99 percent to 30.04 percent).

[33] Frédéric Bastiat, *Selected Essays on Political Economy* (Irvington-on-Hudson, NY: Foundation for Economic Education, 1964).

[34] Richard Vedder, Lowell Gallaway, and David Sollars, "The Tullock-Bastiat Hypothesis: The Inequality-Transfer Curve and the Natural Distribution of Income," *Public Choice* 56 (1988): 285–94.

[35] Simon Kuznets, "Economic Growth and Income Inequality," *American Economic Review* 45 (March 1955): 1–28.

[36] A representative recent study, using Italian time series data, is Gianni Toniolo, Nicola Rossi, and Giovanni Vecchi, "Is the Kuznets Curve Still Alive? Evidence from Italy's Household Budgets, 1961–1991," CEPR Working Paper No. 2140, May 1999, available at http://papers.ssrn.com/so13/papers.cfm?abstrract_id=175468 (accessed February 22, 2005). This paper is particularly appealing in that it uses consumption data.

happiness appear to me to be largely statements of faith not justified by the realities of the modern world. To the extent that empirical evidence speaks to this issue at all, it suggests that Americans prefer to live in relatively low tax areas where economic prosperity is enhanced by the relatively less fettered operation of market processes.

IV. Markets and the Elimination of Spatial Income Inequality

As the foregoing discussion suggests, it is an unproven hypothesis that reductions in income inequality are associated with advances in human satisfaction, and, even if it were proven, governments have a dubious track record in promoting equality. Yet, given the difficulties of measuring utility, it is still an unsettled question whether happiness is promoted by reducing the gap between the rich and the poor. The fact that people tend to migrate over time from poor to rich areas (for example, far more persons migrate from India, China, or Mexico to the United States than in the opposite direction) suggests that the acquisition of income is perceived to be utility-enhancing. If low-income countries have income gains relative to higher-income ones, they should witness some utility gains similar to what happens with migration from low- to high-income areas. Because of this, a case can be made, at least on a global level, for reducing income inequality (by having higher economic growth in lower-income countries relative to more affluent ones). The really huge disparities in income are not found *within* nations like the United States, but *between* rich and poor countries.

Table 3 documents these large international income disparities. Taking the average income levels in seventy-six countries for which data were available for 2002, I have treated each country as if it were an individual.

TABLE 3. *Income distribution: U.S. individuals versus seventy-six different countries, 2002**

Income quintile	Intercountry differentials	Interpersonal differentials, U.S.
Poorest 20 percent	1.9%	3.5%
Second lowest 20 percent	5.0	8.8
Middle 20 percent	12.5	14.8
Second highest 20 percent	23.2	23.3
Richest 20 percent	57.4	49.8

*Percentage of total income; intercountry differentials ignore interpersonal income differences within countries and weight each country equally.

Source: 2004–2005 *Statistical Abstract of the United States*, Table 1336, U.S. Bureau of the Census; author's calculations.

I have then compared the quintile shares of the total income of these seventy-six individuals (actually, countries) with the shares for individuals living in the United States in the same year. The data show that the richest 20 percent of countries have thirty times the proportion of total income as the poorest ones do, more than double the differential between the rich and poor for individuals within the U.S. The rich nations produce a larger proportion of total world income (so measured) than rich individuals do of total U.S. income. International inequality is greater than interpersonal inequality within the United States. Moreover, for a variety of technical reasons, the statistics in table 3 probably understate international inequality. Purchasing-power-parity income data are used instead of data based on exchange rates, which would show even greater international inequality, for example. Many nations are excluded, a majority of which are poor (e.g., Haiti). Since many poor countries are populous (e.g., India), a weighted (by population) table would probably show even more inequality than is indicated here.

It is arguable that the world would be a better place if these wide disparities were reduced. In a world with a strong rule of law and property rights, no significant barriers to moving people or resources, and only minimal governmental interferences and involvement in the economy, economists would predict that international differences in average income levels would be drastically reduced. In such a world, capital would migrate from high- to low-wage countries to minimize labor costs, while labor would migrate from low- to high-wage areas to increase worker earnings. The two moves would serve to equalize differences in the amount of capital available per worker, and thereby also help to equalize incomes. This basic framework was most explicitly developed in a model by Robert Solow and was an important factor in his receiving the Nobel Prize in Economic Science.[37] The convergence hypothesis has been strongly supported in important empirical work using both U.S. state and international data by Robert Barro and Xavier Sala-i-Martin.[38] Dozens of empirical studies in general confirm the existence of convergence, although often with some qualifications (e.g., during periods of financial crisis or wars, convergence may be interrupted).[39] Yet other scholars, using dif-

[37] Robert M. Solow, "A Contribution to the Theory of Economic Growth," *Quarterly Journal of Economics* 70 (February 1956): 65–94.

[38] Robert J. Barro and Xavier Sala-i-Martin, "Convergence," *Journal of Political Economy* 100, no. 2 (April 1992): 223–51.

[39] A few representative samples from the 2002–2004 period: Gasper A. Garofalo and Steven Yamarik, "Regional Convergence: Evidence from a New State-by-State Capital Stock Series," *Review of Economics and Statistics* 84, no. 2 (May 2002): 316–23; Leo Michelis and Simon Neaime, "Income Convergence in the Asia-Pacific Region," *Journal of Economic Integration* 19, no. 3 (September 2004): 470–98; David Cook, "World War II and Convergence," *Review of Economics and Statistics* 84, no. 1 (February 2002): 131–38; Frank S. T. Hsiao and Mei-Chu W. Hsiao, "Catching Up and Convergence: Long-Run Growth in East Asia," *Review of Development Economics* 8, no. 2 (May 2004): 223–36; S. Nahar and B. Inder, "Testing Convergence in Economic Growth for OECD Countries," *Applied Economics* 34, no. 16 (Novem-

TABLE 4. *Per-capita income in seven American states, as a percentage of per-capita income in New York, 1929–2003*

State	1929	1950	1970	1985	2003
California	85.5%	98.0%	98.7%	100.5%	92.0%
Colorado	55.3	79.4	83.1	91.5	95.1
Georgia	30.0	55.2	69.3	77.8	80.6
Illinois	82.4	97.4	93.8	92.8	91.5
New Hampshire	58.8	70.6	79.7	93.7	95.6
Tennessee	33.2	53.1	65.0	72.9	78.7
Texas	41.2	72.0	74.5	84.6	80.1

Source: U.S. Department of Commerce, Bureaus of Economic Analysis, Census.

ferent data sets (different countries or regions, alternative time periods) or methodologies, find no evidence of convergence, or, at best, mixed evidence.[40]

The reasons for this somewhat mixed evidence are explained by tables 4 and 5. In table 4, personal income per capita for seven states scattered around the U.S. is expressed as a percentage of the level prevailing in New York, the most populous and one of the most prosperous states at the beginning of the period examined. In every single state, a majority of the percentage income differential with New York was erased from 1929 to 2003—strong evidence of income convergence. In a majority of the states, income converged on the New York figure at every date included in the chart. Southern and border states like Georgia and Tennessee had less than one-third the per-capita income level of New York in 1929, but more than three-fourths that level by 2003. In Georgia, for example, 72.3 percent of the differential with New York was eliminated. To be sure, convergence was not always continuous or complete, but it was still substantial and real. Note that in California and Illinois income levels stopped converging on New York (at almost New York's level) around 1950 and actually have diverged slightly since. Convergence, then, does not appear to be complete, but the sharp narrowing of regional income differentials is still one of the most important dimensions of twentieth-century American economic history.

ber 2002): 2011–22; and Eric Neumayer, "Beyond Income: Convergence in Living Standards, Big Time," *Structural Change and Economic Dynamics* 14, no. 3 (September 2003): 275–96.

[40] Three recent examples: Richard Kozul-Wright and Robert Rowthorn, "Globalization and the Myth of Economic Convergence," *Economic Appliquée* 55, no. 2 (June 2002): 141–78; Stephen M. Miller and Mukti P. Upadhyay, "Total Factor Productivity and the Convergence Hypothesis," *Journal of Macroeconomics* 24, no. 2 (June 2002): 267–86; and Javier Andrés, José E. Boscá, and Rafael Doménech, "Convergence in the OECD: Transitional Dynamics or Narrowing Steady-State Differences?" *Economic Inquiry* 42, no. 1 (January 2004): 141–49.

TABLE 5. *Per-capita income in seven nations as a percentage of per-capita income in the U.S., 1913–2001*

Nation	1913	1950	1973	2001
China	10.4%	4.6%	5.0%	12.6%
Germany	68.8	40.6	71.7	66.8
Great Britain	92.8	72.6	72.1	72.0
India	12.7	6.5	5.1	7.0
Italy	48.4	36.8	63.7	68.1
Japan	26.2	20.1	68.5	74.0
Mexico	32.7	24.7	29.0	25.4

Source: Angus Maddison, *The World Economy: Historical Statistics* (Paris: OECD, 2003), 262; author's calculations.

The international data, however, are far more mixed. Only three of the seven nations shown in table 5 show any convergence with the U.S. over the very long run (1913 to 2001), with two of them (Japan and Italy) showing the classic convergence similar to that observed by states in the U.S., and one, China, showing very limited convergence. Three nations (Great Britain, India, and Mexico) actually diverged significantly from the U.S. over time, while the seventh nation, Germany, showed little change (modest divergence). In short, table 5 is a mixed bag of results not very strongly supporting the convergence hypothesis.

Yet an examination of tables 4 and 5 suggests a reason for these diverging patterns. In the U.S., there is a relatively uniform rule of law, protection of property rights, a regulatory regime that is moderate by world standards, and taxation that is low by the standards of modern welfare states. In that environment, the forces of markets work to greatly reduce geographically-related income inequality over time. In nations where those characteristics (e.g., the rule of law, low taxation, minimal regulation, etc.) have been absent (e.g., Mexico, India, or until the past generation, China) divergence occurs, as it does when wars (a form of massive government spending) absorb a large portion of national resources (see, e.g., the German, British, and Japanese divergence in the 1913–1950 period in table 5). Labor resources are not free to leave and capital resources have no desire to migrate into authoritarian societies where there are few if any private property rights. Some recent empirical work confirms that increased government taxes and spending have adverse effects on economic growth in general (in keeping with the discussion in Section II of this essay) and on convergence in particular.[41]

[41] On taxes and convergence, see Benjamin Russo, "Taxes, the Speed of Convergence, and Implications for Welfare Effects of Fiscal Policy," *Southern Economic Journal* 69, no. 2 (October 2002): 444–56; see also Michelis and Neaime, "Income Convergence in the Asia-Pacific Region."

Using American state data, I looked at the role of state and local tax burdens in income convergence over the period from 1970 to 2003, years for which good tax data are available.[42] I identified fifteen states that could be viewed as convergence success stories. Each of these states had below-average per-capita incomes in 1970, and by 2003 had closed the gap with the average by at least 30 percent, or raised its income as a percent of the national average by at least 10 percentage points (e.g., from 63 to 73 percent).[43] I then identified ten states that diverged from the average, starting with below-average per-capita incomes but falling even further below that average from 1970 to 2003.[44] A majority of the successful convergence states lowered the tax burden from 1970 to 2003. For the group as a whole, the tax burden fell on average by $2.80 for each $1,000 in income earned. By contrast, in the less successful, diverging states, a majority (60 percent) raised their tax burden, increasing it on average for the group by $1.50 for each $1,000 in personal income. While I would certainly not want to claim that "taxes alone matter," tax-reducing states were more likely to have a successful story than tax-raising ones.

Income equalization between areas is a by-product of convergence. High-tax welfare states and authoritarian societies that reject market solutions to problems have been slow to converge on the most affluent societies like the United States, where the discipline of the market plays a dominant resource-allocation role—witness the end to convergence in Britain and Germany after episodes of large growth in government (in the 1930s and 1940s in Britain, after 1973 in Germany). Not only are market solutions more conducive to the growth of incomes and prosperity, they are also more powerful and successful in equalizing economic opportunities across time and space. It may seem ironical to some readers that greater income equality can be achieved with less government, less taxation, and less redistribution—but that is what the evidence suggests. Well-intended government policies often have behavioral effects that lead to unintended consequences.

V. Conclusion

Humans have a finite time on earth, and most want to use it productively, which in some ultimate sense means having a fulfilling, happy

[42] The tax data are from the Tax Foundation website, http://www.taxfoundation.org/statelocal70.html, and also http://www.taxfoundation.org/statelocal03.html; the income per capita data are from the website of the Bureau of Economic Analysis, U.S. Department of Commerce, at http://www.bea.doc.gov/bea/regional/spi/drill.cfm.

[43] The states were Alabama, Colorado, Georgia, Maine, Mississippi, Nebraska, New Hampshire, North Carolina, North Dakota, South Carolina, South Dakota, Tennessee, Vermont, Virginia, and Wyoming.

[44] The states were Arizona, Florida, Idaho, Indiana, Iowa, Missouri, Montana, Oklahoma, Oregon, and Utah.

existence. Two visions for achieving this goal exist—a market vision where the "invisible hand" allocates resources and provides rich rewards for those exercising hard work and innovation, and a welfare state approach where collective action by government is used to provide security and to equalize opportunities, funded by high taxation. The low-tax, smaller-government model simply works better in delivering the goods—lower taxes (or lower government spending, for that matter) are associated with higher growth in incomes.

Which model works better in dividing up the goods? It is not altogether clear that it really matters from the standpoint of maximizing human welfare, given the difficulty of demonstrating that income equality is in some sense utility-enhancing. Even if it does matter, however, the evidence that bigger government brings about greater opportunities for the disadvantaged or eliminates poverty is very weak indeed. The fact that people migrate into low-tax, smaller-government areas is a powerful hint that people perceive themselves to be happier in a low-tax environment where individual responsibility takes primacy over group rights and entitlements. Moreover, in a very important sense, the market is a very powerful and effective institution in equalizing incomes as well. The poor in China are declining in numbers and in levels of destitution not because of the success of a benevolent socialist experience or welfare state, but because of the rejection of that approach by pragmatic "communists" who are far more embracing of markets than many Western political leaders. Market-induced globalization has brought job and investment opportunities to relatively poor Chinese, reducing their relatively inferior economic status. A low tax and spend society where markets and individuals, not collective organizations, make decisions appears better for promoting material prosperity, a better way of life, and reduced poverty and destitution on our planet.

Economics, Ohio University

THE CONSEQUENCES OF TAXATION

By Joel Slemrod

I. Introduction and Motivation

Tax system design has consequences for prosperity and economic growth. These consequences matter for policy evaluation even if one is not a consequentialist—that is, even if one does not accept the view that the normative properties of alternative policies depend *only* on their consequences. Although these consequences are central to the mainstream economics notion of an "optimal" tax system, in many noneconomic treatments of what is appropriate taxation these consequences are nonexistent or appear as an afterthought.

The consequences of taxation depend crucially on the behavioral response of individuals and businesses to the tax system. Loosely speaking, the more the tax system induces individuals and businesses to alter their behavior, the greater is the social cost of raising revenue. While, traditionally, economists have focused on the behavioral response of labor supply, saving, and investment—sometimes called "real" responses—in recent years the public finance community has recognized that *all* the behavioral responses to taxation, including avoidance and evasion, are symptoms of inefficiency. According to this view, it is the responsiveness, or elasticity, of taxable income that determines the social cost of collecting revenue. The social cost, in turn, sets the trade-off between the fairness of the tax distribution and the efficiency consequences of taxation—the trade-off that frames the modern economics discussion of the appropriate level of tax progressivity. In this essay, I address how the new view of the efficiency consequences of taxes, and the view's emphasis on the technology of tax collection, affects how one thinks about the appropriate level and distribution of the tax burden.

II. Taxation, Prosperity, and Progressivity

Economists' attempts to address the appropriate distribution of the tax burden can be divided into two eras. Until the early 1970s, the discussion was dominated by the search for the proper principles to guide progressivity, with the leading contenders being the benefit principle and the ability-to-pay principle, the latter often leading to arguments over what tax system equalizes individuals' levels of "sacrifice." Under benefit principles, taxes were conceived as a quid pro quo for what government provided, and this approach explicitly ruled out purposeful redistribution by the government as a whole. Ability-to-pay theories argued from the premise that the tax system should extract the minimum amount of sacrifice from the population and the plausible but unprovable assertion that a dollar of tax payment causes less sacrifice for higher-income families. These theories could certainly justify a substantial amount of progressivity, but the difficulty of comparing sacrifice across individuals and the lack of a compelling argument about exactly how, if at all, sacrifice should vary across individuals made quantitative policy pronouncements—pronouncements about exactly how much progressivity is appropriate—impossible.

The modern era began in 1971 with the publication of James Mirrlees's seminal article on optimal tax progressivity.[1] In this article, he posed the problem as maximizing a social welfare function that depends on individual utilities, weighted so that marginal social utility declines with income in a way to be specified by the analyst. The approach is thus consequentialist, in that policies are evaluated based only on their effect on individuals' well-being (utility). It is more general than simple utilitarianism, in that social welfare may depend not only on the sum of utilities, but may give more weight to some utilities (the lower ones) than to others; the more concave is the social welfare function, the more favorably evaluated are policies that sacrifice the simple sum of utilities for a more equal distribution of utilities. In this framework, high marginal tax rates effect more redistribution, but provide higher disincentive to work and earn income, so that individuals work less than the amount at which the marginal social product just equals the opportunity cost of the leisure forgone. For example, someone who believes policies should maximize a very concave social welfare function may be inclined to institute a new, high tax bracket for millionaires, but in this framework he must consider that the revenue thereby raised (which could be used to reduce taxes or provide transfers to low-income people) will also induce the millionaires to withdraw from the labor force, hire accountants to reduce taxable income, and pursue a host of other behaviors that would, in the absence of the new tax rate, be unattractive to the millionaires and are, from a social point of view, wasteful.

Thus, according to the modern view, the optimal extent of progressivity reflects a trade-off between equity and efficiency. What limits progressivity is the economic cost of progressive taxation, which arises from the disincentive it provides to all the activities that people would otherwise engage in to increase their income, and the incentive it provides to all the activities that people would otherwise not engage in to reduce their tax liability. This is sometimes called a moral hazard.

[1] James Mirrlees, "An Exploration in the Theory of Optimum Income Taxation," *Review of Economic Studies* 38, no. 2 (1971): 175–208.

Noneconomist commentators have recognized, but not stressed, the efficiency costs of progressive taxation. The philosopher Thomas Nagel worries that redistribution will undermine the incentives for the talented to produce wealth.[2] The legal scholar Richard Epstein, who is otherwise dismissive of the optimal progressivity approach,[3] allows that a progressive tax system, by causing economic damage, makes us weaker in dealing with foreign affairs, "since it could lead to reductions in defense spending in settings where God favors big battalions."[4] Epstein's argument for a flat, nongraduated tax-rate schedule seems to rest on the idea that administrative difficulties and arbitrariness win the day: "[T]he simplicity of a pro rata rule seems evident in its relative immunity from political machinations" and therefore "in general the added complexity does not seem to be worth the candle."[5] Determining whether the additional redistribution made possible by a graduated tax system is "worth the candle" is indeed the objective of the empirical public finance program, which seeks to come up with quantitative estimates of the efficiency cost of increasing progressivity. In this context, one may note that Shlomo Yitzhaki, Joram Mayshar, Michael Lundholm, and I have calculated that the increase in social welfare (the presumed objective of policy) from having two tax brackets rather than one is small, absolutely and relative to the gain in social welfare from having a flat-rate tax compared to a lump-sum tax.[6] Note, though, that this finding does not apply directly to Epstein's analysis, since Epstein favors a flat tax with *no* demogrant.[7]

The moral hazard that gives rise to inefficiency is not an inevitable cost of progressive taxation. Rather, it arises because of a *technical difficulty* of tax administration—the difficulty of measuring the unalterable aspects of individuals that lead to differential income-earning potential—call it their "abilities." If abilities could be measured, then tax liability could be based on this measured ability. Because, by assumption, ability is not alterable, this tax causes no moral hazard and no efficiency cost. Of course, certain parental decisions do affect children's ability, and over generations an ability tax will distort these decisions, so an ability tax would not be

[2] Thomas Nagel, *Equality and Partiality* (Oxford: Oxford University Press, 1991).

[3] "These models assume that interpersonal comparisons of utility can be made between strangers, that charitable activities do not matter much in the overall picture, that variations in administrative costs are small under all relevant systems, that the aggregation of wealth for investment purposes does not depend on the choice of taxation regimes, and that public-choice problems do not create serious impediments to sound government policy." Richard A. Epstein, "Can Anyone Beat the Flat Tax?" in Ellen Frankel Paul, Fred D. Miller, Jr., and Jeffrey Paul, eds., *Should Differences in Income and Wealth Matter?* (Cambridge: Cambridge University Press, 2002), 163.

[4] Ibid., 165.

[5] Ibid., 157.

[6] Joel Slemrod, Shlomo Yitzhaki, Joram Mayshar, and Michael Lundholm, "The Optimal Two-Bracket Linear Income Tax," *Journal of Public Economics* 53, no. 2 (February 1994): 269–90.

[7] A "demogrant" is a fixed payment to all households, a payment that is invariant to income but might depend on marital status.

completely nondistortionary, but it would be less distortionary than an income tax that also distorts decisions made during one's own life.

If ability cannot be measured, then implementing a progressive tax requires basing tax liability on something that is correlated with ability. One such correlate is income. By basing tax liability on income, the tax burden is positively correlated with ability or potential income but, as an unavoidable by-product, inefficiency arises because income can be affected by individual decisions.[8]

Thus, the cost of taxation—and therefore optimal progressivity—depends on the technical feasibility of tax systems that can minimize the distorting effects of taxation.

Given that we are limited to distorting (i.e., inefficiency-causing) taxes, what is the source of the efficiency cost of taxation? In the Mirrlees framework, it is how substitutable people consider goods and leisure to be. If goods and leisure are viewed to be good substitutes, then any income or consumption tax that reduces the real wage—the terms at which an hour of leisure can be converted into goods—will cause a relatively large reduction in labor supply, and a relatively high efficiency cost per dollar of tax revenue raised. The attempt to tax income—or its fruits, consumption—will cause people to forgo market (taxable) work for leisure. If, alternatively, people do not view leisure and goods to be good substitutes, a tax that reduces the real wage will not induce people to work much less, and the efficiency cost per dollar of revenue raised will be relatively low.

Optimal progressivity thus depends on a particular characteristic of people's tastes. At first blush, it may seem odd that something so profound—how redistributional the tax-and-transfer system should be—should depend on something so prosaic. Moreover, this prosaic aspect is usually considered by economists to be immutable. Outside of economics and even within some corners of economics, whether tastes are immutable is of course controversial. Very recently, however, the emphasis on

[8] Some ingenuity has gone into thinking about how to design a tax system in which tax liability is correlated with potential income but in which the cost from moral hazard is minimized or eliminated. One suggestion is to base tax liability on wage *rates* rather than wage *income*. At first blush, this seems promising, because unlike income one's wage rate does not depend on how much labor one supplies to the market. A key problem, however, is that a person's wage rate certainly depends not only on his or her ability but also on the amount of effort the employer expects the employee to provide. When the effort per hour of work varies across jobs, the choice of job itself becomes a decision that will be influenced (i.e., distorted) by a wage rate tax. Another idea is tagging, in which the tax liability depends not only on income but also on relatively (and preferably completely) unalterable characteristics of the individual that are correlated with income. For example, imagine that income was highly correlated with one's caste, and that one's caste was unalterable. By granting lump-sum subsidies to the lower castes and levying lump-sum taxes on the higher castes, a given amount of redistribution can be achieved with lower marginal tax rates on income. This system of differential lump-sum taxes was apparently in use in the Middle Ages, when there were differential levies on serfs, vassals, and lords, and the chance of moving from one class to another was negligible.

tastes as the source of inefficiency has given way to a broader view that I will discuss next.

III. The Postmodern Approach: The Elasticity of Taxable Income

The notion of a behavioral elasticity occupies a central place in the economic analysis of taxation.[9] Undergraduate textbooks teach that the incidence of a tax depends on the relative elasticity of supply and demand, and that the excess burden of a tax per dollar raised is proportional to the sum of the compensated elasticities of demand and supply. Graduate textbooks teach that the optimal pattern of commodity taxes depends on the matrix of compensated cross-elasticities of demand, and that the optimal progressivity of the income tax depends (inversely) on the compensated elasticity of labor supply. Revenue estimators doing "dynamic" analysis need to take into account how the tax base contracts or expands as the tax rate changes. Because of their central importance, an enormous amount of effort has gone into coming up with quantitative estimates of behavioral elasticities. As a result, the economics literature is chock-full of estimates of the elasticity of behavior X with respect to its tax rate, with one or the other elasticity being important for the question at hand.

Until recently, the central behavioral response parameter was the labor supply elasticity. In a static model where people value only two commodities—leisure and a composite consumption good—the real wage in terms of the consumption good is the only relative price at issue. This real wage is equal to the amount of goods that can be consumed per hour of leisure forgone (or, equivalently, per hour of labor supplied). At the margin, substitution possibilities, and therefore the excess burden of taxation, can be captured by a compensated labor supply elasticity, the percentage change in desired hours for a 1 percent change in the after-tax real wage rate, holding income or utility constant.

With some exceptions, the profession has settled on a value for this elasticity close to zero (i.e., no response at all of aggregate labor supply to the after-tax wage rate) for prime-age males, although for married women the responsiveness of labor force participation appears to be significant. Overall, though, the compensated elasticity of labor appears to be fairly small. In models with only a labor-leisure choice, this implies that the efficiency cost of income taxation is bound to be low, as well.

Although evidence of a substantial labor supply elasticity has been hard to find, evidence that taxpayers respond to tax system changes more generally has decidedly not been hard to find. Because, income effects aside, *all* responses to taxation are symptoms of inefficiency (because they

[9] This section draws on Joel Slemrod, "Methodological Issues in Measuring and Interpreting Taxable Income Elasticities," *National Tax Journal* 51, no. 4 (1998): 773–88.

would not have been undertaken absent taxation), these findings raise the possibility that the efficiency cost of taxation is, after all, high and researchers have just been looking for evidence in the wrong place. Because all of these responses are reflected in changes in the tax base, or "taxable income" in the parlance of the U.S. income tax system, the key parameter becomes the *elasticity of taxable income*. It is usually expressed as the percentage change in taxable income in response to a percentage change in the net-of-tax rate, or one minus the marginal tax rate (the fraction of income one keeps after taxes, at the margin).

If the modern era of the economics of taxation began with Mirrlees, the beginning of the postmodern era may be marked in the early 1990s, when both the theory and the empirical analysis of taxation began to focus on the elasticity of taxable income. Lawrence Lindsey was one of the first to point out that the 1981 top rate cut in the Economic Recovery Tax Act of 1981 from 70 percent to 50 percent coincided with a very large increase in the share of income reported to the IRS by the top 1 percent of the income distribution.[10] He argued that the tax cut was a principal cause of this increase, as it reduced the penalty for receiving (or, to be precise, reporting) taxable income, and he estimated the elasticity of taxable income with respect to the net-of-tax share to be between 1.6 and 1.8.[11]

Economists Daniel Feenberg and James Poterba used tax return data to calculate a time series of inequality measures that focuses on high-income households. Using interpolations of aggregated tax return data, they calculated the share of adjusted gross income (AGI) and several components of AGI that were received by the top 0.5 percent of households arranged by income. After being approximately flat at about 6 percent from 1970 to 1981, in 1982 the value began to increase continuously, reaching 7.7 percent in 1985. It then jumped sharply in 1986 to 9.2 percent. Feenberg and Poterba argued that this pattern is consistent with a behavioral response to the reductions beginning in 1981 in the tax rate on high-income families.[12]

Probably the most influential contribution to this literature was provided by Martin Feldstein, who investigated the high-income response to

[10] Lawrence B. Lindsey, "Individual Taxpayer Response to Tax Cuts: 1982–1984," *Journal of Public Economics* 33, no. 2 (1987): 173–206.

[11] An elasticity of taxable income of 1.6 means that an increase in (one minus) the marginal tax rate of 1 percent would cause taxable income to go up by 1.6 percent. For example, consider a taxpayer who reports a taxable income of $100,000 and who has a marginal tax rate of 0.3 (30 percent). A cut in the marginal tax rate to 0.25 would increase one minus the marginal tax rate from 0.7 (1 - 0.3) to 0.75 (1 - 0.25), or by 7.1 percent. If the elasticity of taxable income is 1.6, reported taxable income will rise by 1.6 times 7.1 percent, or 11.4 percent, increasing it from $100,000 to $111,400. If the average tax rate is equal to the marginal tax rate, then tax revenue falls from $30,000 (0.3 times $100,000) to $27,850 (0.25 times $111,400), or 7.2 percent; with no behavorial response, tax revenue would have fallen by 16.7 percent (from $30,000 to $25,000).

[12] Daniel Feenberg and James M. Poterba, "Income Inequality and the Incomes of Very High-Income Taxpayers: Evidence from Tax Returns," in James M. Poterba, ed., *Tax Policy and the Economy*, vol. 7 (Cambridge, MA: MIT Press, 1993), 145–77.

the Tax Reform Act of 1986 using tax return panel data that follows the same set of taxpayers from 1979 to 1988. He concluded that the 1985–1988 percentage increase in various measures of income (particularly taxable income excluding capital gains) was much higher, compared with the rest of the population, for those high-income groups whose marginal tax rate was reduced the most. Based on this finding, he estimated that the elasticity of taxable income with respect to the net-of-tax rate is very high, between 1 and 3 in alternative specifications. To put this into perspective, if the elasticity is greater than $(1 - t)/t$, where t is the tax rate, then increasing the tax rate will shrink the tax base so much that revenue will actually decline.[13] Given a top tax rate of 0.35, the upper-end range of Feldstein's estimate thus suggests the possibility that tax rate increases would actually *decrease* revenue collected. If this is true, tax increases may benefit no one—certainly not the people who are subject to the higher tax rates, and perhaps not other people who might otherwise gain from the revenue collected from those to whom the higher tax rate was applied.[14]

Unfortunately, Feldstein's data set contained only a very small number of high-income observations; for example, the top income class on which Feldstein focuses most of his attention (non-elderly couples in the 49 to 50 percent tax brackets in 1985) contains only fifty-seven observations. Because of the wide variation among this group in their financial situation and in income changes over time, generalizing from such a small sample is problematic.

Gerald Auten and Robert Carroll made use of a much larger longitudinal data set, consisting of 14,102 tax returns for the same set of taxpayers for 1985 and 1989. Rather than rely on group means, as Feldstein did, they employed a multivariate regression approach, regressing the change in adjusted gross income between 1985 and 1989 against the change in marginal tax rate and a set of demographic variables. The regression approach allowed them to control for occupation as a proxy for demand-side, non-tax factors that affected the change in compensation over this period. They concluded that changes in tax rates appear to be an important determinant of the income growth of the late 1980s, but their central estimate of the net-of-tax price elasticity of 0.6 was much lower than Feldstein found, and far short of the Laffer-curve tipping point.[15]

[13] The idea that increasing tax rates could reduce revenue is usually associated with the economist Arthur B. Laffer, who in the mid-1970s raised the possibility of an inverse relationship between tax rates and government revenue. His arguments apparently were very influential in the thinking of soon-to-be President Ronald Reagan and his economic advisers. Laffer defends his argument in Arthur B. Laffer, "Government Extractions and Revenue Deficiencies," *Cato Journal* 1, no. 1 (1981): 1–21.

[14] Martin Feldstein, "The Effect of Marginal Tax Rates on Taxable Income," *Journal of Political Economy* 103, no. 3 (1995): 551–72.

[15] Gerald Auten and Robert Carroll, "The Effect of Income Taxes on Household Behavior," *Review of Economics and Statistics* 81, no. 4 (1999): 681–93. On Laffer, see note 13 above.

All of the studies discussed so far focused entirely on the effect of tax reforms that lowered marginal tax rates. This is a problem if there are non-tax-related trends occurring simultaneously, a problem that could be ameliorated by the study of tax increases. Policymakers provided such an opportunity in 1990 and 1993. Carroll used a panel of taxpayers spanning the tax increases of the 1990 and 1993 tax reform acts to consider to what extent taxpayers change their reported incomes in response to changes in tax rates. The tax rate response was identified by comparing the changes in reported income of higher-income taxpayers to those of moderate-income taxpayers in the face of the change in the relative taxation of these two groups, controlling for many non-tax factors such as the taxpayer's age, occupation, and industry. Carroll concluded that the taxable income price elasticity is approximately 0.4, smaller than the earlier studies of the tax reductions in the 1980s, but nevertheless a response that is positive and significantly different from zero.[16]

Finally, Jonathan Gruber and Emmanuel Saez examined a long longitudinal data base of tax returns that spans a series of tax reforms in the 1980s. They found that the overall average elasticity of taxable income is approximately 0.4, that the elasticity of real income is much lower, and that the elasticity of tax-deductible preferences is the source of most of the overall elasticity. Strikingly, they found that the overall elasticity is primarily due to a more elastic response of taxable income for taxpayers who have incomes above $100,000 per year, who have an elasticity of 0.57, while for those with incomes below $100,000 per year the elasticity is less than one-third as large. The differential elasticity result suggests two things about optimal progressivity. One is that the optimal rate structure should feature a large demogrant that is rapidly taken away as income rises for low-income taxpayers (because the high implicit marginal tax rates this implies do not engender large efficiency costs), and lower marginal tax rates at higher income levels (because this group does respond significantly). Second, it highlights the importance of choosing enforcement and base-broadening measures that set the *optimal* elasticity for high-income individuals.[17]

There are staggering policy implications to whether the taxable income elasticity is 0.4, 3, something in between, or even something outside this range. Using an elasticity of 1.04, the lowest from his paper, Feldstein calculated the deadweight loss to be 30 percent of the revenue raised by the U.S. personal income tax; he estimated that a marginal increase in revenue achieved by a proportional raise in all personal tax rates would generate a deadweight loss of two dollars per incremental dollar of rev-

[16] Robert Carroll, "Do Taxpayers Really Respond to Changes in Tax Rates? Evidence from the 1993 Act," Working Paper No. 79 (Washington, DC: Office of Tax Analysis, U.S. Department of the Treasury, 1998).

[17] Jonathan Gruber and Emmanuel Saez, "The Elasticity of Taxable Income: Evidence and Implications," *Journal of Public Economics* 84, no. 1 (2002): 1–32.

enue raised; and he argued that repealing the 1993 increase in the top rate would reduce deadweight loss by $23 billion while *raising* more than $2 billion.[18]

If, however, the taxable income elasticity is 0.4, as Carroll as well as Gruber and Saez argue, rather than 1.04, then the deadweight loss is about 40 percent of what Feldstein calculated, the ratio of incremental deadweight loss to revenue raised is only about 20 percent as high, and repealing the 1993 top tax rate increase would certainly have reduced rather than raised revenue.[19]

IV. Policy Implications

In the standard model, where the focus is on the extent to which taxes cause people to substitute toward untaxed leisure, the behavioral elasticity depends entirely on people's preferences, in particular the degree of substitutability between the leisure and the goods that market work can provide. It is well understood that the elasticity of substitution need not be the same for all people, or even for the same person at different levels of income or at different consumption baskets; however, for analytical convenience it is often assumed that there is a single, indeed constant, elasticity for everyone.

As I have already discussed, the efficiency cost resulting from a tax increase also arises from such things as increases in tax evasion, in the use of tax shelters, in business reorganizations, and so on. What characterizes all of these responses is that the extent of response is itself subject to government control. For example, the evasion elasticity will depend on the enforcement system in place, the tax shelter response will depend on the extent of passive loss limitations and accelerated depreciation, and the extent of business reorganization will depend on how tightly drawn are the rules that govern under what conditions a corporation qualifies as a Subchapter S corporation.[20] The response of taxable capital gains realizations to the capital gains tax rate depends on the tax treatment of gains that remain unrealized at death.[21]

What this means is that the characterization of an optimal tax system must include not only the tax rate structure but myriad other policy instruments that subsume, but are not limited by, the definition of taxable

[18] See Feldstein, "The Effect of Marginal Tax Rates on Taxable Income."

[19] See Carroll, "Do Taxpayers Really Respond to Changes in Tax Rates?"; and Gruber and Saez, "The Elasticity of Taxable Income."

[20] Income of a Subchapter S corporation is directly attributed to the owners of the buskins, and is subject to individual income tax, in a manner similar to the way partnership income is taxed.

[21] If, as under current law, unrealized gains at death escape tax, and heirs owe tax as if they bought the assets at the price at the time of inheritance, there is an especially large incentive to bequeath assets with appreciated gains.

income. *The elasticity of taxable income will depend on the setting of these other instruments.* It is not an immutable function of preferences.

The notion that the taxable income elasticity is itself a policy choice has an important implication. If the taxable income elasticity is not set optimally, there is no presumption that the extent of tax progressivity that is optimal, given the current value of the other instruments, is also the global optimum. To be concrete, if the taxable income elasticity is "set" too high, so that the marginal cost of raising revenue is higher than it need be, then the optimal progressivity will appear lower than if the other instruments are set optimally; in general, optimal progressivity can be properly assessed only simultaneously with the instruments the government uses to control avoidance and evasion. Elsewhere I have constructed an example in which, taking as given the existing (but higher-than-optimal) taxable income elasticity, it is appropriate to reduce progressivity, but an even better outcome is to make the tax rate schedule *more* progressive while simultaneously undertaking tax system reforms (such as cracking down on tax shelters) that lower the taxable income elasticity.[22] Using the metaphor of Arthur Okun, the "leakage" in the revenue system that limits redistribution can (and should) be "fixed," albeit at some cost.[23]

Wojciech Kopczuk and I take this line of reasoning to its logical conclusion by arguing that choice of those policy instruments that affect the elasticity of taxable income should be made *optimally*. We investigate an example in which the taxable income elasticity is controlled via the broadness of the tax base: in choosing the broadness of the tax base, one is choosing the elasticity of taxable income (i.e., the broader the base, the lower the elasticity) and thus choosing the marginal efficiency cost of increasing progressivity. The optimal base broadness, and therefore the optimal progressivity of the tax system, depends on the administrative cost of expanding the tax base.[24]

The Slemrod-Kopczuk argument suggests that, looking across countries, countries with less administrative capacity would have higher elasticities of taxable income and thus would optimally keep the level and progressivity of taxes below that of other countries. Once one realizes that low-income countries generally have less administrative capacity, this can explain one of the most striking empirical regularities related to taxation: across countries, the higher the level of taxation, the more affluent the country. This is an embarrassing fact for those who maintain that high, and highly progressive, taxes are seriously detrimental to a country's

[22] Joel Slemrod, "Fixing the Leak in Okun's Bucket: Optimal Tax Progressivity When Avoidance Can Be Controlled," *Journal of Public Economics* 55, no. 1 (1994): 41–51.

[23] Arthur M. Okun, *Equality and Efficiency: The Big Tradeoff* (Washington, DC: The Brookings Institution Press, 1975), 91–95.

[24] Joel Slemrod and Wojciech Kopczuk, "The Optimal Elasticity of Taxable Income," *Journal of Public Economics* 84, no. 1 (2002): 91–112.

prosperity. But the positive association between real income per capita and tax level does not necessarily establish a positive causal relationship running from taxes to prosperity. Indeed, it could also mean that citizens of high-income countries prefer more government, more even as a fraction of their income. Separating out the effect that taxes have on GDP per capita from the effect that GDP per capita has on the demand for what government does is extremely difficult. The Slemrod-Kopczuk argument adds yet another possible causal explanation for the empirical correlation. Low-income countries generally do not have the administrative ability to dampen the elasticity of taxable income, and therefore find it in their interest to restrain both the size of government and the progressivity of the tax system with which that size is financed. This provides another explanation for a positive association between tax levels and progressivity on the one hand, and a country's level of prosperity on the other. Neither causes the other, but variations in the administrative capacity to raise taxes affect both.

V. The Consequences of Taxation in an Open Economy

Another class of consequences of taxation arises in a world of multiple taxing jurisdictions that have economies that are open to cross-border movements of people and capital, both financial and physical. In this setting, one consequence of certain kinds of taxation is that it causes people and capital to flee the country.

To keep the problem manageable, first imagine a stylized setting in which only physical capital, but not people, is mobile across countries. Further assume that capital is perfectly mobile in the long run, meaning that it will always end up where the return it can earn (after taxes) is the highest. In this setting, Roger Gordon has shown that it is never optimal for a small, open economy to levy source-based capital income taxes (i.e., taxes on income deriving from capital located within its borders).[25] The reason is straightforward. Because capital is mobile, the small country can do nothing to reduce the after-tax return earned by its resident (or any) capital owners—because they can move elsewhere, they need not accept a lower after-tax return than is available in the rest of the world. The burden of the tax will ultimately be borne by immobile workers. Given that inescapable fact, it is better to directly tax workers by levying taxes on labor income. Why? In either case, workers bear the burden, but if the small, open economy tries to tax the income from domestically located capital, it drives some capital offshore, which, by lowering the productivity of the domestic labor force, lowers the equilibrium real wage rate. Thus, either levying a labor income tax or levying a tax on the income of

[25] Roger H. Gordon, "Taxation of Investment and Savings in a World Economy," *American Economic Review* 76, no. 5 (1986): 1086–1102.

domestically located capital will ultimately make workers worse off (this is inevitable in a small economy open to capital movements); but the negative economic consequence of capital flight will be avoided by taxing workers directly.

This result is critically dependent on the technology of tax administration, because it applies to a source-based tax only. If a country is restricted to taxing only income earned within its borders, doing so creates a disincentive to earn income domestically. If a country can tax on a residence basis (where the base is the worldwide income of its residents), then the tax does not cause capital flight. (It might cause individuals to change residence, but that is a different question.) Taxing on a residence basis is administratively difficult, however, especially without extensive information sharing and even tax system harmonization among countries.

The importance of smallness and openness for optimal tax policy raises some intriguing questions. Consider the following experiment. Take a country and determine the optimal progressivity of its tax system. Now split the country into two, for noneconomic (say, ethnic) reasons, and allow a high degree of capital, but not labor, mobility between the two countries. Is it right that now the optimal tax system changes, and in particular lowers, the appropriate degree of progressivity and renders any attempt to tax capital income a dominated strategy? It is interesting to note that this result depends on an implicit assumption that taxpayers act as free-riders and that their indifference about the uses to which their tax payments are applied extends to being indifferent about which country receives their tax payments. If, instead, there is "home bias" in tax payments, the stark implications of the stylized model may not apply. It is reasonable to suspect that home bias is less relevant to "stateless" multinational corporations, unless governments do not have anonymous tax policies, but instead relate government expenditure policies (such as good roads leading to the company's factories) to taxes received. By so doing, governments can provide an incentive for multinational companies to remit taxes to them when the companies would otherwise be indifferent.

Some argue, often based on an analogy to the benefits of competition among firms, that competition among governments leads to optimal outcomes. Certainly the ability of individuals to choose among jurisdictions as they choose among products can be beneficial when people have diverse tastes about the value of public goods, and it can provide pressure to reduce bureaucratic inefficiency, inter alia. There is, though, a problem with this kind of reasoning by analogy to private markets that has been pointed out by, among others, Hans-Werner Sinn. Sinn argues in his "selection principle" that governments undertake precisely those activities that people value but private markets fail to provide. He emphasizes that competition between governments undermines the ability of governments to overcome the failure of markets to provide insurance for certain life and career risks and to provide infrastructure that is productive but, because of the free-rider problem, will not be adequately provided in the absence of government.[26] The ability of people to move across jurisdictions after the life and career risks have been resolved, so that the fortunate can avoid paying the "premium" due in the social insurance scheme, undermines its viability.

VI. Endowment versus Tastes

A large body of work, mostly written by noneconomists, stresses that the normative implications of inequality depend on whether the inequality arises from differences in endowments or from differences in tastes. For example, the philosopher Ronald Dworkin has argued that distributive justice requires compensating individuals for aspects of their situations for which they are not responsible, but only for those aspects.[27] Inequality that arises from choices individuals make—which presumably arise because of differences in tastes—is not a concern. Dworkin wants to treat differently *ambitions* and *endowments*.

Another line of argument emphasizes the role of luck. The philosopher Daniel Shapiro, citing Dworkin, characterizes egalitarianism as follows: "Inequalities or advantages resulting from choice are just. On the other hand, when luck rather than choice rules, fairness dictates that the unlucky be compensated for their disadvantages."[28] The connection between the two lines of argument is that from an individual's point of view, one's endowment is a matter of luck. As Shapiro puts it: "Egalitarians believe that genetic or native endowments are unchosen, and thus that inequalities in income and wealth resulting from such differences are unchosen."[29] Of course, to the extent that people's productivity and opportunities depend on the educational decisions made for them by their parents (for example, were they read to as toddlers, were they allowed to go to the best college they were admitted to?), the ability that a person brings to his or her adulthood depends on a set of choices that might be influenced by the tax system.

The distinction among endowment, tastes, and luck does not arise in the Mirrlees framework, in which differences in endowment are the *only* source of inequality, there is no uncertainty, and everyone shares the same

[26] Hans-Werner Sinn, *The New Systems Competition* (Malden, MA: Blackwell Publishing, 2003), 5.

[27] Ronald Dworkin, "What Is Equality? Part 1: Equality of Welfare," *Philosophy and Public Affairs* 10, no. 3 (1981): 185–246; Ronald Dworkin, "What Is Equality? Part 2: Equality of Resources," *Philosophy and Public Affairs* 10, no. 4 (1981): 283–345.

[28] Daniel Shapiro, "Egalitarianism and Welfare-State Redistribution," in Paul, Miller, and Paul, eds., *Should Differences in Income and Wealth Matter?*, 7.

[29] Ibid., 11.

preferences. Nonetheless, both uncertainty and taste heterogeneity can be introduced into the standard model to yield insights.

Variations in tastes for goods versus leisure at given levels of well-being could increase or decrease the inequality of income (as opposed to utility), depending on the correlation between ability and tastes. If high-ability people were more likely to be goods-lovers rather than leisure-lovers, that would tend to exacerbate income inequality. Whether it would also exacerbate utility inequality is impossible to say, because, with non-uniform preferences, interpersonal utility comparisons are difficult, if not impossible. The economist Agnar Sandmo has investigated optimal linear income taxation (also known as a negative income tax, when there is a grant made to everyone and a single rate levied on income received) when diversity of tastes (with respect to leisure versus goods) is the *only* source of inequality, as opposed to the situation in the standard optimal progressivity approach, where tastes are homogenous and ability is the only source of inequality. Sandmo first investigates the characteristics of an optimal regime of differential lump-sum taxes, in which tax liabilities could be tailored to individuals (i.e., differential) and also not dependent on any action of the individual (i.e., lump-sum). He concludes that, in the absence of further information about preferences, we cannot say whether such a tax system should be progressive or regressive. It depends on whether those with a high taste for work have a higher capacity for enjoyment, which Sandmo considers to be a value judgment. In the optimal linear (i.e., single-rate) income tax (where the tax is not lump-sum but instead based on income, and therefore is distortionary, and is tailored to individuals only because income varies), the same intuition applies, although in this case the amount of redistribution is limited by the distortionary effect of the marginal tax rate. In conclusion, there may exist a utilitarian case for redistribution even when individuals face exactly the same budget constraints so that there is perfect equality of opportunity. The case is a tenuous one, though, that depends on the unknowable correlation across individuals between their tastes for goods and leisure (on the one hand) and their ability to "produce" well-being from a given endowment (on the other). Without knowing this correlation, the amount and even the direction of optimal redistribution is ambiguous.[30]

Wojciech Kopczuk updates the Sandmo analysis by stressing heterogeneity in the propensity to undertake avoidance opportunities. He stresses that the standard optimal progressivity results need to be modified in the presence of tax avoidance because it affects the relationship between the taxable income and the social marginal utility of income. With avoidance, a low income may indicate a low skill level, as in the standard Mirrlees problem, or a high degree of avoidance (or some combination of the two).

[30] Agnar Sandmo, "Optimal Redistribution When Tastes Differ," *FinanzArchiv* 50, no. 2 (1993): 149–63.

Thus, a person with low taxable income may either be truly poor or else be able and willing to avoid a lot; only the former is a reason to transfer income. These differences reduce the correlation between income and ability, and therefore render a redistributive income tax less effective. The ultimate effect on optimal progressivity depends, however, on the relative welfare of avoiders. If, for example, tax avoidance reflects economic hardship, then avoiders are the ones who are worse off and tax progressivity should be higher than otherwise.[31]

Some theorists—for example, Hal Varian as well as Jonathan Eaton and Harvey Rosen—introduce luck into the standard optimal progressivity problem. They recognize that taxes provide valuable insurance for undiversifiable risks, and this provides a justification for more progressivity than otherwise. Moreover, mitigating the income inequality due to luck has less deleterious efficiency costs because the inequalities do not arise from a choice. In sum, while there may be a moral reason to differentiate inequalities due to hard work from inequalities due to luck, there is also a practical reason to do so, because the efficiency cost of offsetting the former is larger than for the latter. This is no coincidence. Effort is a choice, and a consequence of taxing away some of the fruits of that choice is that people will tend to choose less of it than otherwise.[32]

VII. Conclusion

The consequences of taxation matter for the optimal design of the tax system. Those consequences depend on behavioral responses to taxation, as summarized by the elasticity of taxable income. Although this elasticity depends on characteristics of utility functions—the elasticity of substitution between goods and leisure—it also depends on the avoidance technology, and on the response of government to avoidance behavior. It depends on the size of states, and the amount of tax coordination and harmonization. To some degree, the elasticity of response can be affected by government policies, and the government need not accept it passively, but rather should put in place policies that optimally determine it.

Business Economics and Public Policy, Stephen M. Ross School of Business, University of Michigan

[31] Wojciech Kopczuk, "Redistribution When Avoidance Behavior is Heterogeneous," *Journal of Public Economics* 81, no. 1 (2001): 51–71.

[32] Hal Varian, "Redistributive Taxation as Social Insurance," *Journal of Public Economics* 14, no. 1 (1980): 49–68; and Jonathan Eaton and Harvey Rosen, "Optimal Redistributive Taxation and Uncertainty," *Quarterly Journal of Economics* 95, no. 2 (1980): 357–64.

JUSTICE: A CONSERVATIVE VIEW

By John Kekes

I. Two Questions

Suppose you had the power to impose on a society one of two patterns. In the first, good and bad things are distributed randomly across the population. In the second, there are exactly the same good and bad things, but good people have the good things and bad people the bad ones. Let us call the first pattern "random," and the second "ordered." My first question is: Which pattern would you impose?[1] I have asked this question of many people, and I have yet to meet one who would not impose the ordered pattern. This leads to my second question: Why is the ordered pattern preferred?

Sophisticated people will quibble. They will say that my first question is not well formed because it ignores complexities. They may say, for instance, that human beings could not have only good or bad things in their lives because good and bad things are unavoidably mixed. Success is good but it often depends on painful effort, which is bad. Courage is good but it can be shown only in the face of danger, which is bad. Deep love of someone is good but it gives a hostage to fortune, which is bad. All this is true and pedantic. Understand the first question as asking about the preferred distribution of the most favorable good-to-bad ratio.

Another quibble is that my first question assumes that there is agreement about what things are good or bad, but there is no such agreement. If you impose on a society an ordered pattern, you in fact impose your preferences on other people, and a decent person would not do that. Suppose, then, that you are forced to choose because if you do not, you will be sentenced to live in a society that conforms to the pattern you would not choose. Moreover, it is nonsense to say that there is no agreement about good and bad things. There certainly are disagreements, but there is also much agreement. Everybody agrees that in normal circumstances it is better to satisfy one's basic physiological needs than to frustrate them; better to be respected than humiliated; better to feel secure than terrified; better to have an interesting than a soul-destroying job;

[1] This question was suggested to me by W. D. Ross, *The Right and the Good* (Oxford: Clarendon Press, 1946/1930), 138: "If we compare two imaginary states of the universe, alike in total amounts of virtue and vice and pleasure and pain present in the two, but in one of which the virtuous were all happy and the vicious miserable, while in the other the virtuous were miserable and the vicious happy, very few people would hesitate to say that the first was a much better state of the universe than the second."

better to like than loathe oneself; and so on and on. Understand the first question, therefore, as being about the preferred pattern of distribution of those good and bad things about which there is agreement in a particular society. If you are tempted to invent extraordinary cases in which normal preferences do not hold, resist it because such cases are irrelevant. The first question is about the pattern preferred in normal circumstances, not in a lifeboat, or in the Garden of Eden, or on your deathbed. And remember also that your choice of pattern is for a society in which you will not live, so self-interest is not involved in your choice.

Yet another quibble might be to object to asking hypothetical questions. It might be said that such questions postulate unusual situations and the reasonable answer to them is that one does not know what one would do in unusual situations. I have a great deal of sympathy for this. Nevertheless, I persevere in asking the first question because I fail to see why conservatives, such as myself, should not be entitled to it when liberals endlessly discuss hypothetical questions about the original position, the veil of ignorance, ideal speech communities, the prisoner's dilemma, the consent of totally reasonable people, deserted islands with miraculously available resources awaiting distribution, compulsory insurance schemes, and the economic man, not to mention the state of nature or the social contract.

I submit, then, that the first question is legitimate and that virtually everyone would answer it by preferring the ordered to the random society, and thus the second question naturally arises of what is behind this general preference. I can now confess that the first question does not interest me very much. I asked it merely to permit me to ask the second question. And I want not merely to ask but also to answer it: A society with the ordered pattern (from now on "ordered society") is preferable because people in it get what they deserve and do not get what they do not deserve. The trouble with the society in which the random pattern holds (from now on "random society") is that people in it have no reason to believe that their actions will lead to their goals. Hard work, intelligent choice, and self-discipline, for instance, have exactly the same chance of success as sloth, stupidity, and self-indulgence. The conservative view I aim to defend is that the ordered society is just because its arrangements increase the likelihood that good actions will be successful and bad actions will not. To climb even further out on a limb, I also claim that reasonable people are, in fact, committed to the conservative view, if only they would take the trouble to think through what they believe.

II. Why Should People Get What They Deserve?

Consider a simple sequence leading to an action. I am hungry, want to eat, decide to go home for lunch, and I walk there. Implicit in the sequence is that I have a set of beliefs (my house is nearby, there is food in the fridge, there are no obstacles in the way, and so on) and I have the required capacities (I can walk, rely on my memory, estimate distance, and the like). The sequence that precedes action, then, has the following elements: motive, belief, capacity, goal, and decision. Each may be defective: motives may be irrational, beliefs false, capacities inadequate, goals unattainable, and decisions wrongheaded. Suppose, however, that they are not defective and I perform the action to which the conjunction of these elements leads. I expect, then, that my action will be successful, that it will achieve its goal. In simple sequences of this sort, normal people in normal circumstances have normally good reason to suppose that the elements are free of defect and no reason to doubt it. Their expectation that their actions will be successful is generally reasonable. The well-being of individuals requires that such reasonable expectations be generally met.

It would be comforting if simple sequences were adequate for the business of living, but they are not. Complexities unavoidably arise because it is often difficult to tell whether an element is defective. Motives conflict and we constantly have to make choices about which of them we should act on. We routinely have to evaluate the reliability of our beliefs on the basis of imperfect knowledge and insufficient evidence. Our capacities are always limited, and we have to estimate whether they are adequate for the achievement of difficult goals. We usually have several incompatible goals, and we must decide about their respective importance. But what seems important at one time may become less so at another. The world changes, we change, and we have to make guesses about how these changes might affect our goals. The choices we make depend on understanding our circumstances and what we want, all things considered, out of life, and both are unclear at the time we have to choose, and it is even more unclear how they might be in the future. Coping with complexities requires, therefore, in addition to getting the facts right, also judging the significance of such facts as we have available. Good judgment about such matters is difficult.

Suppose I act on the basis of a complex sequence and my judgment is good. Might I, then, reasonably expect that my action will be successful? No, because even if I act as reasonably as anyone in my position could, I may nevertheless fail because others justifiably prevent me from succeeding. Most of the time my success depends on the cooperation of others, and they may have more important concerns; or they may also want what I want and may be better at getting it; or what I want may run counter to their interests or to the interests of an institution, cause, or collectivity they wish to protect. More is needed, therefore, before I can reasonably expect to get what I want, and the same, of course, is true of everyone else. We all have to take into account that we live together in a society and depend on the cooperation of others. The terms of cooperation, therefore, have to be set. In the vast majority of complex sequences, we can get what we want only on the terms our society sets. These terms, of course, may be more or less adequate to the purpose of maintaining the optimum conditions in which as many of us as possible can go about getting what we want.

Can people in general reasonably expect that their actions will be successful if they are based on good judgment and conform to the terms set by their society? The answer is still no, for two reasons. One is that the prevailing terms of cooperation may be defective. I shall shortly say more about this, but let us assume for the moment that the terms are adequate because they set optimal conditions. The other reason why the expectation of success may be premature is that not even adequate terms of cooperation can eliminate competition. People may fail to achieve their goals, although they have good judgment and conform to the terms, because they lose out in a competition with others whose judgment is also good and who also conform to the terms. Only one person can win the race, get the job, be the first to make the discovery, and only a few can make the best-seller list, get elected, add to the canon, or make a lasting contribution to science. For each of those who succeed, there are many who try and fail.[2] Not all goals are competitive, of course; having a good marriage, enjoying nature, developing a historical perspective, and listening to music are not. But many are, and because of them people may have good judgment, conform to the terms, and still fail to achieve their goals.

Putting all this together, the following requirements of successful action emerge: having good judgment; conforming to adequate terms of cooperation set by one's society; and, if goals are competitive, prevailing in the competition. The expectation of success is reasonable if these requirements are met. This finally allows me to make clear the point of the preceding discussion. What I mean by saying that people should have what they deserve is that they should succeed if their expectation of success is reasonable. And what I mean by saying that people should not have what they do not deserve is that they should not succeed if their expectation of success is unreasonable. The "should" and the "should not" above express requirements of practical reason.

Practical reason is the use of reason for making human life better. One way of doing that is to make it more likely that good people have good, rather than bad, things in life and that bad people have bad, rather than good, things in life. This is what happens in an ordered society. The reason for making a society ordered is to increase the likelihood that good judgment, conformity to adequate terms of cooperation, and prevailing in competition will lead to better lives. These are means derived from the

[2] "It is not the most beautiful and the strongest that are crowned but those who compete." Aristotle, *Nicomachean Ethics*, 1099a3–4, trans. W. D. Ross, revised by J. O. Urmson, in *The Complete Works of Aristotle*, ed. Jonathan Barnes (Princeton, NJ: Princeton University Press, 1984).

history of human trials and errors for the betterment of the human condition. The conservative view I am defending is that justice prevails if these requirements of practical reason are met. This is at once the aim and the justification of justice.

People living together in a society should, therefore, do what they jointly can to make justice prevail, but what joint efforts can achieve is limited. Individuals alone can make their own judgments good, and they alone can make themselves succeed in a competition if the prevailing terms are adequate. What can be done by joint efforts, however, is to make adequate terms prevail, which is our next topic.

III. Terms of Cooperation

There are countless terms of cooperation, and it would be futile and tedious to try to list all of them. I shall proceed instead by calling attention to three general types that a society can hardly do without, and then go on to consider what these terms imply. There are, of course, others. These terms are conventional. They embody the habits, customs, practices, and the more or less clearly formulated rules that have emerged in the course of a particular society's history. The terms change, but usually slowly. There goes with them a continuum of evaluations that range between the extremes of good and bad, and allow many intermediate judgments in between. The resulting evaluations praise or condemn whatever appropriately falls in the domain of a general type of term. They imply responsibilities that people are praised for discharging or condemned for violating, or from which, under specifiable conditions, they are exempted or excused. They imply also the reasonable expectations of others that these responsibilities will be met. And they serve as the basis on which good and bad things are distributed in a particular society. In short, the terms of cooperation are conventions regulating what people should or should not have or do in particular areas of life.

One of these terms concerns relationships. Lovers, competitors, friends, colleagues, parents and children, teachers and students, judges and defendants, physicians and patients, merchants and customers are connected by conventional ties. These ties create responsibilities and expectations about how people related in these ways should treat one another. The first four of these relationships are symmetrical. Lovers, competitors, friends, and colleagues typically have the same reciprocal responsibilities and expectations. The next five relationships are asymmetrical because one party has authority over the other, or provides a service the other needs, or sells something the other wants to buy.

A second term of cooperation has to do with agreements, such as contracts, promises, loans, memberships in organizations, employment, political or legal representation of others, or holding a license to drive a car, sell a product, or build a house. Some of these agreements are formal. The responsibilities and expectations are governed by written rules and are legally binding. Others are informal. What is owed or expected rests on a tacit understanding of the parties. The force behind such informal agreements is a shared sense of trust and mutual good will.

A third term is connected with actions that affect the security of others. A society cannot endure unless it protects the security of those living in it, but different societies have different conventions about how far the protection of security should go, what violations are permissible, excusable, or prohibited, how people outside of the society should be treated, what counts as cruelty, negligence, accidental injury, and, of course, how security should be understood. Take, for instance, homicide. All societies must have conventions about it; but conventions regarding when homicide is murder and when it is excusable or justifiable vary greatly, as do conventions regarding abortion, suicide, revenge, euthanasia, capital punishment, infanticide, and the like.

Part of the importance of these terms of cooperation, and of many others I have not discussed, is that they establish what people in a particular society deserve. They deserve to have what the terms of their relationships, agreements, and actions establish, and they do not deserve to have what would violate those terms. Thus, the terms of cooperation provide reasons for the responsibilities and the expectations that people living together in a society have. Children deserve a decent upbringing from their parents because that is part of how parenthood is understood by us. Incompetent physicians deserve to lose their licenses because a physician is assumed by us to be able to treat illness well. Murderers deserve to be punished because that is how we go about protecting security. These terms are not merely conventions that happen to hold in our society. Our well-being requires that children be brought up well, that illness be treated, and that life be protected. It is conventional how we do these necessary things, but it is not conventional that a human society must do them in one way or another. If they were not done in a society, the well-being of those living in it would be badly served and the society would disintegrate. When we say, therefore, that people deserve this or that, what we are saying is that this is our particular way of doing what is necessary for our well-being.[3]

Claims about what people do or do not deserve may be mistaken of course. I shall consider two ways in which this may happen. One is that the prevailing terms of cooperation are misapplied; the other is that they

[3] In formulating this view, I drew on the rapidly growing body of work on what it means to say that something is or is not deserved. See, e.g., Joel Feinberg, "Justice and Personal Desert," in *Nomos VI: Justice*, ed. Carl J. Friedrich and John W. Chapman (New York: Atherton, 1963); William Galston, *Justice and the Human Good* (Chicago: University of Chicago Press, 1980); John Kekes, *Against Liberalism* (Ithaca, NY: Cornell University Press, 1997), chap. 6; David Miller, *Social Justice* (Oxford: Clarendon Press, 1976); Michael J. Sandel, *Liberalism and the Limits of Justice* (Cambridge: Cambridge University Press, 1982); and George Sher, *Desert* (Princeton, NJ: Princeton University Press, 1987).

are faulty. I discuss misapplication now and faulty terms in the next section. Any term may be misapplied because those who apply it get the relevant facts wrong. If a person is mistaken for a murderer, he does not deserve to be punished. If a student passes a course by cheating, he does not deserve credit for it. If a pretended friend is an enemy, he does not deserve my loyalty. Even if the facts are as assumed, the terms may be misapplied by getting wrong the proportion of what is deserved. A novel may deserve good reviews, but not the National Book Award. A thief may deserve a term of imprisonment, but not to have his arm cut off. A physician may deserve payment for services rendered, but not the deed to my house. Mistakes of fact and proportion lead to people's getting good or bad things they do not deserve at all or to their getting more or less than they actually deserve.

A less obviously detectable mistake is to be wrong about the goodness or badness of particular relationships, agreements, or actions. Because what is taken to be good or bad is in fact not, people are rewarded or punished when they do not deserve it. Those who suppose that telling a lie is always wrong, that contracts between employers and employees are always exploitative, or that suicide is murder are wrong because they suppose that what may be morally excusable is always bad. Similarly mistaken are the suppositions that frugality is a sign of virtue, that flogging children is good for their character, and that belief in God makes people virtuous.

Terms of cooperation are associated with a wide array of relationships, agreements, or actions which are judged by a society to be good or bad. These terms are not invalidated if some few of the judgments conventionally made within them turn out to be mistaken about what is good or bad. The mistakes call for the correction of some conventional beliefs and practices, but they leave the large remaining part of that term intact. It may happen, of course, that not merely a few but most applications of the term are mistaken. Then the term must be regarded as faulty in its entirety, and it should be abandoned. This is just what happened, or should have happened, to magic, astrology, and human sacrifice.

Another kind of mistake, much closer to home, is to suppose that there is no special reason needed for the distribution of good and bad things. One way of making this mistake is to suppose that everyone is equally deserving of the good things in life and that the bad things are burdens that we all have to bear equally. To appreciate the force of this familiar but nevertheless mistaken claim, it should be remembered that the distribution of good and bad things we are discussing includes only those about which there is agreement in a society. Opinion is divided on whether owning a cat is good or bad. But there can be no reasonable disagreement about it being good to satisfy one's basic physiological needs. The mistaken claim, then, is that everyone in a society is equally deserving of those good things that everyone there regards as good and everyone is obliged to carry a fair share of the generally agreed upon onerous burdens. If asked why good and bad things are equally deserved, the usual answer is that everyone has the same basic moral worth, or that everyone is entitled to the same basic respect, or that everyone has the same basic freedom and welfare rights.[4]

This is one of the passionately held shibboleths of our egalitarian age. It comes packaged in a self-righteous, moralistic rhetoric that maligns doubt as indecent.[5] But those whose critical faculties are not numbed by the ceaseless repetition of these catchphrases will recognize their absurdity. They will ask how apparently reasonable and well-educated people trained to think analytically and critically could believe that terrorists and hostages, felons and their victims, friends and enemies of one's society, evildoers and decent, law-abiding citizens have the same basic moral worth, are entitled to the same basic respect, should enjoy the same basic freedom and welfare rights, and deserve to have the same good and bad things.

The familiar indignant reply is that they believe no such things. What they believe is that there is a presumption in favor of everyone being equally deserving. The presumption can be defeated, and it is defeated in the case of terrorists, felons, and other malefactors. But this presumption flies in the face of facts whose denial is absurd. Human beings differ in their characters, circumstances, talents and weaknesses, capacities and incapacities, and virtues and vices; in their moral standing, political views, religious convictions, aesthetic preferences, and personal projects; in how reasonable or unreasonable they are, how well or badly they develop their native endowments, how much they benefit or harm their society, and how hardworking or disciplined they were in the past and are likely

[4] I am, of course, referring to egalitarian theories of justice. This is not the place for a detailed criticism of them. I offer such criticism in *The Illusions of Egalitarianism* (Ithaca, NY: Cornell University Press, 2003).

[5] For instance, "All humans have an equal basic moral status. They possess the same fundamental rights, and the comparable interests of each person should count the same in calculations that determine social policy. . . . These platitudes are virtually universally affirmed. A white supremacist or an admirer of Adolf Hitler who denies them is rightly regarded as beyond the pale of civilized dialogue." Richard Arneson, "What, If Anything, Renders All Humans Morally Equal?" in *Singer and His Critics*, ed. Dale Jamieson (Oxford: Blackwell, 1999), 103. "We cannot reject the egalitarian principle outright, because it is . . . immoral that [the government] should show more concern for the lives of some than of others." Ronald Dworkin, *Sovereign Virtue* (Cambridge, MA: Harvard University Press, 2000), 1. "[A] distribution of wealth that dooms some citizens to a less fulfilling life than others, no matter what choices they make, is unacceptable, and the neglect of equality in contemporary politics is therefore shameful." Ronald Dworkin, "Equality—An Exchange," *Times Literary Supplement* (December 1, 2000), 16. "Some theories, like Nazism, deny that each person matters equally. But such theories do not merit serious consideration." Will Kymlicka, *Liberalism, Community, and Culture* (Oxford: Clarendon Press, 1989), 40. "Any political theory that aspires to moral decency must try to devise and justify a form of institutional life which answers to the real strength of impersonal values" and "impersonal values" commit one to "egalitarian impartiality." Thomas Nagel, *Mortal Questions* (Cambridge: Cambridge University Press, 1979). All critics of egalitarianism then fail in moral decency. Just imagine the wave of indignation that would descend on someone who would dare to say such things about defenders of egalitarianism.

to be in the future; and they differ also in the relationships they have, the agreements they have made, and the effects of their actions on the security of others. In view of these and other differences, surely the reasonable presumption is that there is an overwhelming likelihood that different people will deserve different things.

The implausibility of the egalitarian presumption is compounded if it is asked who should distribute what people deserve. Should parents regard their own and other people's children as equally deserving of the benefits they can bestow on them? Should married couples treat each other and strangers as equally deserving? If, by way of avoiding such absurdities, it is said that the egalitarian presumption is meant to guide the government, not individuals, then no less damaging absurdities follow. A government betrays its most elementary responsibility if it proceeds on the presumption that citizens and foreigners, law-abiding and criminal citizens, defenders and subverters of the society are equally deserving. The questions grow in number and urgency when it is asked, as it must be, what reasons might be good enough to count against the egalitarian presumption. If differences in morality, reasonability, law-abidingness, and citizenship count, then virtually nothing remains of the presumption since the great and undeniable differences among people in these respects constantly defeat the presumption. And if these differences are said not to count, then what would justify the government in ignoring them in the distribution of good and bad things at its disposal?

The conservative view is that the time has come to consign this egalitarian shibboleth to the dust heap of history, where it will join other passionately held follies of other ages, such as the divine rights of kings, classless society, possession by the devil, planned economy, damnation outside the church, and an idyllic prehistoric society from which civilization has caused us to fall farther and farther. What should take the place of this absurd belief about what people deserve is the recognition that different people deserve different things and any claim that people deserve this or that must be backed by reasons. I have been arguing in this section that the reasons must be derived from the terms of cooperation that prevail in a society. The reasons are good if they are free of mistakes in fact, proportion, the identification of good and bad things, and in missing the central importance of individual differences. It must be recognized, however, that even if good reasons of this kind are given in support of claims about what individuals deserve, the claims may still fail because the terms of cooperation that prevail in a society and from which these reasons are derived may be faulty.

IV. The Justification of Terms of Cooperation

An often heard objection to conservatism is that it is committed to the mindless perpetuation of the conventions that happen to prevail in a particular society. There may have been conservatives who actually held this commitment, but, if they did, they should not have. What conservatives should be committed to is the perpetuation of conventions that have endured for a considerable length of time, measured in decades or more rather than months, because people have voluntarily adhered to them—and have been right to do so because the conventions have made their lives better.[6] I shall say that conventions that meet these criteria (endurance, voluntary adherence, and contribution to well-being) have stood the test of time.

Terms of cooperation are conventions, and their justification depends on whether they have stood the test of time. There are deplorable, coercive, unfair, exploitative, ignorant, and stupid conventions, and they fail the test of time. Since the conservative view is that justice consists in people having what they deserve and not having what they do not deserve, and since terms of cooperation that fail the test of time fail to distribute good and bad things according to what people deserve, conservatives are committed to abandoning or reforming unjust terms of cooperation and to perpetuating just ones if, and only if, they have stood the test of time.

One crucial task conservatives have in justifying terms of cooperation, therefore, is to provide reasons for thinking that adherence to them contributes to human well-being. These reasons emerge from reflection on life in a good society, by which I understand a society that protects the conditions in which people can make good lives for themselves. Or, to put it in another way, if individual lives go badly in a good society, it is not because of adverse social conditions but because of personal failure or misfortune. Good societies are cohesive and enduring partly because their members largely agree about what they owe one another, what sorts of lives are good or bad, and what are many of the good and bad things that tend to make lives good or bad. Their agreement rests on shared values, and the prevailing conventions embody them. These values have endured and members of the society express in their terms what they want, and the conventions govern permissible and impermissible ways of trying to get it. Individuals make sense of their lives partly in the conventional framework of their society.

One of the benefits a good society provides is order. A good society makes it possible for its members to have reasonable expectations about each other's conduct. These expectations rest on the justified assumption that fellow members are most of the time guided by the same conventions. Thus, they know what counts as kind or cruel, routine or exceptional, appropriate or inappropriate in countless different contexts, such as marriage, child-raising, employment, competition, joking, electioneering, quarrelling, and so on. This knowledge comes from a shared moral

[6] For a full defense of conservatism, see John Kekes, *A Case for Conservatism* (Ithaca, NY: Cornell University Press, 1998).

education, which is the usually informal initiation into the prevailing conventions. As a result, members of the society can count on each other because there is a social bond between them. They recognize each other as having the same allegiances. Their individual identity is partly defined by their shared conventions, including the shared terms of cooperation.

If you doubt that this picture fits American society, consider this random list of our shared conventions to assuage your doubt. Parents are responsible for their children; breaking a promise requires excuse; politicians speaking in their public capacity should not lie; winners must not gloat over losers; people ought not brag about their talents; a life of idleness is wrong; following one's conscience is right; eating people is wrong; one must not torture animals; parents should not have sexual intercourse with their children; disagreements should not be settled by violence; people ought to be allowed to express unpopular views; it is wrong to spread malicious lies about rivals; permission must be asked before borrowing anything; handicapped people should not be ridiculed; white lies are permissible; we should not publicly rejoice in our enemy's misfortune; deliberate cruelty is wrong; one should be loyal to friends; confidential information should not be made public; courage, honesty, and fairness are good, and their opposites are bad.

This list is not exhaustive or representative. The items on it are more or less randomly selected, and many of them are uncodified. They are often held unconsciously, and conformity to them is usually habitual. People often go against these conventions, but when they do they can normally be shown, in a cool moment, the wrongness of their actions. Habitual violators of these conventions are regarded as immoral or abnormal.

No society is perfect, of course. None can dispense with the need for improvement, and that is true of American society as well. The prevailing conventions should always be open to change, and are always likely to be changing in one respect or another. Nonetheless, there must also be continuity, because the reasons for change depend on criticizing some prevailing convention in terms of other prevailing conventions, which are thought to be deeper or more important. Our society is presently in moral turmoil about abortion and euthanasia. A significant feature of these controversies is that both sides try to justify their position by appealing to conventions they can assume to be generally shared, even by their opponents. Supporters of abortion and euthanasia appeal to freedom rights; opponents appeal to the importance of protecting life.

At this point, the objection is likely to be made that the conservative attempt to provide reasons for terms of cooperation is circular, question-begging, and hence a failure. According to the conservative view, it may be objected, justice consists in people having what they deserve and not having what they do not deserve; what is or is not deserved is said to depend on the prevailing terms of cooperation; and these terms are explained by the conventions governing relationships, agreements, and actions that affect the security of others. But how could it be decided, on this view, whether the terms of cooperation are themselves just? On what grounds could the prevailing terms be criticized if they are conventional but unjust? This objection, however, is misplaced; the answer to it is obvious, and follows from what has already been said.

Terms of cooperation could be criticized on the grounds that they rest on some mistake of fact, proportion, identification of good and bad things, or the recognition of relevant individual differences, and that the mistake prevents people from having what they deserve or not having what they do not deserve. Master-slave relationships are prejudice-ridden because they wrongly suppose that slaves are inferior to masters. Marriage contracts in which the husband acquires control over the wife's property are unfair because they falsely deny the wife's capacity to make reasonable decisions. The punishment of theft by cutting off an arm is deplorable because of its disproportionality. Depriving people of the fruits of their work in order to benefit those who do not work although they could is wrong because it ignores the difference in what they deserve. In all these cases, the terms governing the distribution of benefits are unjust because they lead to people having more or less than what they deserve. The bases for these criticisms are the mistakes on which the terms of cooperation appealed to rest.

It must be acknowledged, of course, that there may be serious disagreements about whether or not a particular term of cooperation is mistake-free. These disagreements, however, concern the question of what is deserved. They arise because, and only because, the parties to them accept the conservative view that justice depends on people getting what they deserve and not getting what they do not deserve. The existence of such disagreements thus strengthens, rather than weakens, the conservative view.

The conservative view, therefore, should not be understood as advocating that what people deserve depends merely on the prevailing terms of cooperation. The conservative view is that what people deserve depends on those prevailing terms that are free of mistakes in fact, proportion, identification, and the recognition of individual differences. That it is reasonable to maintain terms of cooperation that are mistake-free and have passed the test of time—those that endure, are voluntarily adhered to, and contribute to the well-being of members of a society—may be the conservative view, but it is also the view that reasonable people are likely to share.

V. Is the Conservative View Practical?

It has been said by more than one critic that the distribution of good and bad things on the basis of what people deserve is impractical.[7] One reason critics give is that in contemporary Western societies there is no agreement about what a good life is. There are many conceptions of a good life; what people are thought to deserve depends at least partly on which conception is accepted; consequently, there is bound to be much disagreement about what people deserve. The problem is exacerbated by the fact that what people deserve partly depends on their beliefs and efforts, and these are not open to observation. It is unrealistic to suppose that political decisions about the distribution of good and bad things could take such subjective factors into account.

This objection rests on two assumptions that have led to misunderstanding the conservative view: one is that what people deserve depends on their personal qualities; the other is that the distribution of deserved good and bad things is the responsibility of the government. Both assumptions are mistaken, but neither is totally mistaken. Personal qualities may provide reasons for saying that people do or do not deserve something, but they are merely one possible kind of reason among many. The government does have responsibility for distributing some deserved good and bad things, but there are many others distributed by civic institutions that function independently of the government.

The reasons I have given for the distribution of what people deserve were derived from terms of cooperation governing relationships, agreements, and actions affecting security. Personal qualities—virtues and vices, for instance—may be reasonably added to the three I have considered. But even if it were true that there are great practical difficulties in ascertaining what personal qualities people have, this is not true of their relationships, agreements, and actions. The latter are open to public observation, and there is no greater practical difficulty in identifying them than there is in identifying countless other features people have.

It adds to the implausibility of this objection that it is often possible to identify personal qualities, even though they have a subjective dimension. What, according to this objection, runs into insuperable practical difficulty is routinely done by families, teachers, coaches, selection committees, employers, and countless other people who are charged with making judgments about the personal qualities of some people. These judgments, of course, can be good or bad. If they are good, the alleged practical difficulties have been overcome. If they are bad, it need not be because practical difficulties stand in the way.

This last rejoinder, however, will be regarded as irrelevant because of the second mistaken assumption on which the objection rests. If the distribution of deserved good and bad things were the responsibility of the government, then the success of individuals in identifying personal qual-

[7] "The idea of rewarding desert is impracticable." John Rawls, *A Theory of Justice* (Cambridge, MA: Harvard University Press, 1971), 312. See also Friedrich A. Hayek, *The Constitution of Liberty* (Chicago: University of Chicago Press, 1960), chap. 6.

ities would be irrelevant. The question then is whether governments, not individuals, can succeed in formulating policies about the distribution of good and bad things on the basis of personal qualities. The answer to this question is twofold. First, as we have seen, the distribution of deserved good and bad things is not based exclusively on personal qualities; it is also based on the relationships, agreements, and actions of the recipients. Second, the distribution of deserved good and bad things is not the exclusive prerogative of the government; the institutions of a civil society have a very large role in it.

These institutions are families, schools, universities, corporations, athletic competitions, small businesses, orchestras, museums, quiz shows, honor societies, foundations, committees that award prizes, parole boards, neighborhood groups, arbitration panels, and many other more or less formal associations of people that stand between the private concerns of individuals and the political responsibilities of the government. They distribute money, honors, status, prestige; they distinguish between excellence, mediocrity, and deficiency; they set standards and evaluate performance by them; they assign rewards and mete out punishments; they have ways of rectifying violations of their procedures and standards; and they continually face and resolve disputes among their members about these matters. The institutions of a civil society, therefore, routinely identify personal qualities relevant to their concerns, and, of course, they do the same with the relevant relationships, agreements, and actions of their members.

Even if it were true, therefore, that practical difficulties prevent the government from knowing what the deserved distribution of good and bad things is, the same would not be true of the institutions of a civil society. But, of course, the government can also do what these institutions do. The government has no great practical difficulty in identifying some requirements of relationships, such as marriage, parenthood, or citizenship; of agreements, such as taking out a mortgage, enlisting in the army, buying a car, or being a patient in a hospital; and of actions affecting the security of others, such as driving a car, having a fight, or owning a gun. All these cases may constitute reasons for the distribution of good and bad things. There is, therefore, no good reason to suppose, as this objection does, that distribution based on what people deserve is vitiated by great practical difficulties.

An entirely different kind of objection to the practicality of the conservative view is that it is unrealistically optimistic. It supposes that if terms of cooperation are free of mistakes and have stood the test of time, then justice will prevail because there will be no obstacles left to people's having what they deserve and not having what they do not deserve. This supposition is false, it will be objected, because it ignores human wickedness that often leads people to act unjustly, the scarcity of resources that may make it impossible for people to have what they deserve, and the contingency of life that may result in undeserved misfortune.

There is a great deal to this objection. Wickedness, scarcity, and contingency undoubtedly stand in the way of justice, and this has an important effect on how the conservative view should be understood. This view is not the description of any existing society. It is a description of what a society would be like if it were just. It is perfectly compatible with this description to acknowledge that wickedness, scarcity, and contingency are likely to be permanent obstacles to a society's actually being just. This, however, does not make the conservative view impractical. On the contrary, it provides a special impetus for trying to make one's own society as just as possible in the face of these obstacles. In order to come closer to this highly desirable goal, it must be recognized that justice has two aspects.

One is the distribution of good and bad things, which is what I have been discussing up to now. The other is the rectification of injustice that is bound to occur in distribution as a result of wickedness, scarcity, and contingency. The standard to which just distribution and rectification should aim to conform is that the good and bad things in life should be proportional to the goodness or badness of their recipients.

The fact remains, however, that this standard is unattainable because the human condition stands in the way. Scarcity limits just distribution through the insufficiency of available resources. No matter how strong is the commitment to just distribution, if there is not enough money, food, medicine, prison space, police protection, or hospital care available, people cannot have what they deserve. Rectification is concerned with correcting unjust distribution. Its purpose is to make good and bad things proportional to what is deserved.

Disproportionality, however, is often an insurmountable obstacle to rectification. Some forms of injustice cannot be rectified. Nothing could compensate people who sacrificed their lives for a noble cause, who were blinded or disfigured in an accident for which they were not responsible, or who were forced to spend the best years of their lives in concentration camps on trumped-up charges. Nor is there a proportional punishment for mass murderers, torturers, or fanatics who destroy great works of art. Nothing could redress such imbalances because no punishment could be commensurate with what is deserved by these evildoers. Disproportionality, therefore, unavoidably limits efforts at rectification.

Wickedness seems to be another obstacle to justice. The same familiar vices recur throughout recorded human history. Cruelty, greed, destructiveness, selfishness, malevolence, envy, fanaticism, and racial, religious, and ethnic prejudice have motivated people in very different times, places, and circumstances. There is no reason to suppose that in this respect the future will be different from the past. No doubt, the forms in which these and other vices are and will be expressed are bound to change, but they will be expressed and they will inflict much injustice on innocent victims. There are, of course, also virtues, but they coexist with the vices in any given society and often in the same person. If vices are part of human nature, as virtues are, then they cannot be eliminated from the human repertoire. The best we can do is to limit their scope.

But even if, *per impossibile*, scarcity and wickedness could be overcome in some way, the contingency of life will remain and it will be responsible for much misfortune befalling undeserving victims. Lightning will strike, buildings will collapse, volcanoes will erupt, earthquakes will occur, cancer will strike, metal fatigue will make bridges collapse, viruses will mutate and invade the human immune system, cars, ships, and airplanes will crash, and so on and on.

As a result, the conservative view should not be understood as having the unattainable aim of making society just, but as having the much more modest aim of making society as little unjust as scarcity, wickedness, and contingency allow. The aim is to decrease imperfection, not to achieve perfection. That is a realistic aim that cannot be convicted of undue optimism.

VI. Implications

The conservative view of justice has implications for many actual or possible policies of the government. I will now venture a few remarks about its implications for taxation and prosperity, but I do so hesitantly because I can claim no expertise in policymaking. To begin with taxation, I take it that everyone agrees that tax laws need justification. Let us ask what such justification or criticism may be of tax laws affecting individuals. (I ignore businesses and other organizations.) Levying taxes on the legitimate income of individuals means that individuals must give up a portion of what they deserve to have. This requires justification, and the government bears the burden of providing it. Part of the justification is the tacit agreement that the government provides services that people need and want, even if they do not use them personally, and they must pay for them.

The government provides one kind of service that all reasonable citizens benefit from. In a large society, such as that of the United States, individual well-being requires the protection of security, the maintenance of infrastructure and a legal system, the negotiation of treaties, and so forth. Since everybody benefits from such services, everybody should pay for them. Taxation for this purpose seems to me justified. The government also provides services that people may reasonably choose not to use because they are willing to do without the benefits, or because they prefer the services of private firms. Social Security, unemployment insurance, Medicare, various publications, licenses, TV channels, and so on, according to the conservative view, should be paid for by taxing only those who choose to use them in the present or the future. A third kind of service the government provides is help for those who are in need because of poverty, illness, misfortune, or some other reason. From the mere fact that people are in need it does not follow that they deserve to be helped or that other people deserve to be deprived of a portion of their legitimate income in order to help them. The needy deserve help only if the creation of their need is not their fault and if others have an obligation to provide the help at considerable cost to themselves and over and above their other obligations. Egalitarians favoring existing welfare policies ignore the question of fault and take for granted that there is an obligation to help without explaining its basis.[8] According to the conservative view, taxation for this purpose is unjust because it deprives people of what they deserve to have in order to give it to others without inquiring whether they deserve it. This implication of the conservative view will outrage many people. It might mitigate their outrage to realize that the implication is not that people have no obligation to help others, but only that the obligation, if there is one, has not been derived from justice. Whether it

[8] "Non-utilitarian moralities with robust substantive equality ideals cannot be made coherent." Arneson, "What, If Anything, Renders All Humans Morally Equal?" 126. "The justification of the claim of fundamental equality has been held to be impossible because it is a rock-bottom ethical premise and so cannot be derived from anything else." Brian Barry, "Equality," *Encyclopedia of Ethics*, ed. Lawrence C. Becker and Charlotte B. Becker (New York: Garland, 1992), 324. "Equality is one of the oldest and deepest elements in liberal thought and it is neither more nor less 'natural' or 'rational' than any other constituent in them [*sic*]. Like all human ends it cannot be defended or justified, for it is itself which justifies other acts." Isaiah Berlin, "Equality," *Concepts and Categories*, ed. Henry Hardy (London: Hogarth, 1978), 102. Equality "is not grounded on anything more ultimate than itself, and it is not demonstrably justifiable. It can be argued further against skeptics that a world with equal human rights is a *more just* world . . . a less *dangerous* world . . . and one with a *more elevated and civilized* tone. If none of this convinces the skeptic, we should turn our back on him and examine more important problems." Joel Feinberg, *Social Philosophy* (Englewood Cliffs, NJ: Prentice-Hall, 1973), 94 (emphasis in original). "Every plausible political theory has the same ultimate source, which is equality. . . . A theory is egalitarian . . . if it accepts that the interests of each member of the community matter, and matter equally. . . . [I]f a theory claimed that some people were not entitled to equal consideration from the government, if it claimed that certain kinds of people just do not matter as much as others, then most people in the modern world would reject that theory immediately." Will Kymlicka, *Contemporary Political Philosophy* (Oxford: Clarendon Press, 1990), 4–5. Another author says that he will explore a "type of argument that I think is likely to succeed. It would provide a moral basis for the kind of liberal egalitarianism that seems to me plausible. I do not have such an argument." This does not stop him, however, from claiming that "moral equality, [the] attempt to give equal weight, in essential respects, to each persons' point of view . . . might even be described as the mark of an enlightened ethic." Nagel, *Mortal Questions*, 108 and 112. Years later he says: "My claim is that the problem of designing institutions that do justice to the equal importance of all persons, without unacceptable demands on individuals, has not been solved," but he nevertheless "present[s] a case for wishing to extend the reach of equality beyond what is customary in modern welfare states." Nagel, *Equality and Partiality*, 5. "Essential equality is . . . equality of consideration. . . . [O]f course none of this is literally an argument. I have not set out the premises from which this conclusion follows." Rawls, *A Theory of Justice*, 507, 509. Another author offers "a coherent, systematic, non-ad hoc method for accommodating, explaining, and ultimately guiding our egalitarian judgments. . . . [A]lthough I think most of the arguments that have been offered against equality can be refuted, let me emphasize that this book is neither a defense, nor an attack on, the ideal of equality. I do not address the question of whether one *should* care about inequality." Larry Temkin, *Inequality* (Oxford: Oxford University Press, 1993), 5–6.

can be derived from justice or from something else, such as benevolence, pity, prudence, or decency, I leave as an open question that those who favor the policy have the burden of answering.

I need now to say something about prosperity. Prosperity is clearly a good thing, but it is overrated. Individual well-being does not depend on living in a prosperous society, and it depends on many social and individual goods that are not economic (so that prosperity cannot provide them). What individual well-being requires is to have sufficient resources for living in a particular way, not the amplitude of resources that prosperity implies. The individual goods needed for well-being vary from life to life and from society to society, but there are some social goods that are necessary regardless of how well-being is understood. Without security, freedom, justice, order, health, division of labor, cooperation, and so forth, well-being is impossible. It is, therefore, a bad mistake to suppose that the well-being of individuals in a society can be measured by the prevailing prosperity. The prosperous life of Al Capone and the prosperous society of Nazi Germany were bad, and lives and societies can be good even if only merely adequate resources are available.[9]

A further implication of the conservative view concerns social change. All societies are always changing because the conditions to which people have to respond change. A society cannot endure unless it adjusts itself to new circumstances. Having some control over change requires asking and answering the questions of what makes change desirable and to what should the change lead. The conservative answer is that it is desirable to change if the prevailing conventions are not mistake-free or no longer pass the test of time. And the change should be to a revised form of the same convention that does not have the shortcomings of its predecessor. The reason for change, then, is to remedy the specific shortcomings of a specific convention. The conservative view is that change should be incremental, piecemeal, specific, and as little as is sufficient to remedy the shortcoming that prompts it.

Part of the significance of this conservative attitude toward social change emerges by noticing what it does not involve. It does not involve change according to a theory, an overall design, a general plan, the approximation of a distant goal; it does not involve wholesale changes, or abandoning conventions that have no discernible shortcomings, or change simply to try something new. The conservative view is that unless there is a shortcoming, there is no reason to change, and when there is no reason to change, there is reason not to change. The justification of this view is simply to point out that because the prevailing conventions are mistake-free, pass the test of time, are tried and true, command the allegiance of people, and set terms for agreements, relationships, and actions affecting

[9] See Harry Frankfurt, "Equality as a Moral Ideal," in his *The Importance of What We Care About* (Cambridge: Cambridge University Press, 1988).

the security of others, they have advantages that theories, overall designs, distant goals, and new possibilities lack. It is never reasonable to abandon satisfactory actualities in the present for the sake of uncertain possibilities in the future.

It may happen, of course, that the bulk of the conventions prevailing in a society are seriously defective. In that case, conservatives of course would not be in favor of maintaining them. Societies may be rotten through and through, as we know well from history, and then they should go under. To admit this is damaging only for a view that favors maintaining conventions simply because they have endured. This, however, is not the conservative view. The conservative view is to favor only those conventions that are reasonably regarded as mistake-free and passing the test of time.

Yet another implication of the conservative view is that the content of justice is likely to differ from society to society, or indeed, with the passage of time, within one and the same society. A society aiming to be just is committed to its members' having what they deserve and not having what they do not deserve. But what is and is not deserved depends on the prevailing conventional terms of cooperation. Different societies are likely to have different conventions about relationships, agreements, and actions affecting the security of others, and the conventions are likely to change with time in all societies. Commitment to justice, therefore, is not commitment to rules or principles that can be set a priori or with finality. It is commitment to treating people as they deserve to be treated, while recognizing that what they deserve depends on variable and changing conventions that are mistake-free and pass the test of time. It is necessary for justice that there be such conventions, but it is not necessary that these conventions should have the same content in all societies.

The last implication of the conservative view I shall mention here is that justice is essentially inegalitarian. Justice has to do with the distribution of what people deserve, and what they deserve is different because they have different relationships and agreements, and because their actions affect the security of others differently. To be sure, conservatives could agree that justice requires treating equals equally and unequals unequally. The crucial question, however, is about the respect in which people are supposed to be equal or unequal.[10] If that respect is what they deserve, then it will happen only rarely and exceptionally that they deserve to be treated equally. The conservative view of justice is thus incompatible with all egalitarian views of justice. Moreover, if the conservative view is right in stressing the essential connection between justice and what people deserve, then egalitarian views, ignoring that essential connection, cannot

[10] "All men think justice to be a sort of equality. . . . But there still remains a question: equality or inequality of what?" Aristotle, *Politics*, 1282b16–22, trans. B. Jowett, in Barnes, ed., *The Complete Works of Aristotle*.

even qualify as views of justice. Since the most widely accepted current views of justice are egalitarian, the prevailing consensus about justice is basically mistaken.

Egalitarian views advocate the redistribution of economic resources in order to decrease the difference between the rich and the poor. They thus advocate taking resources from people who have more and giving them to those who have less without asking whether the first deserve what they have and whether the second deserve to get what egalitarians want to give them. Proceeding this way may conceivably be justified, but its justification cannot be that justice requires it. If egalitarians had the courage of their convictions, they would simply provide such justification as they can instead of misappropriating justice and hanging it as a label on the unjust policy they advocate.

VII. Conclusion

I hope it will not be thought that in presenting the conservative view I have offered a theory of justice. I do not think that we need such a theory.[11] What we need is to remind ourselves of what we already know: justice is when people have what they deserve and do not have what they do not deserve. And that we do know this is shown, for instance, by the fact that virtually everyone prefers the ordered society to the random one. We prefer it because it is just, whereas the random society is unjust. That this is a reason for our preference is obscured from us by the pervasive egalitarian rhetoric. What I have been doing is "assembling reminders for a particular purpose."[12] Reminders can be what they are only if people already know what they are reminded of. And they do know what I have been saying about justice: everybody knows that our imperfect world would be better if the good and bad things of life were proportional to the goodness or badness of their recipients. Justice aims to make the world less imperfect. Working for that aim does not call for revolution or radical social change, and certainly not for a theory of justice. It calls for small, everyday efforts, political or personal, to correct injustice.[13] We can do that because we all know in our society what injustice is in a very large number of cases. That in some cases we are not sure, or that people in

[11] By a theory of justice I mean a structured argument that begins with well-established premises and deduces from them the conclusion of what justice must be if the premises are true. The most notable attempt to provide such a theory is John Rawls's. The attempt does not succeed. See my *The Illusions of Egalitarianism* (Ithaca, NY: Cornell University Press, 2003), esp. chap. 4.

[12] "The work of the philosopher consists in assembling reminders for a particular purpose." Ludwig Wittgenstein, *Philosophical Investigations*, no. 127, trans. Elizabeth Anscombe (Oxford: Blackwell, 1958).

[13] "He who would do good to another, must do it in Minute Particulars / General Good is the plea of the scoundrel hypocrite & flatterer." William Blake, "Jerusalem," chapter 3, plate 55, II. 60–61.

Timbuktu, Tehran, or Tianjin might disagree, affects what we know as little as the occasional optical illusion affects the reliability of what we see. This is behind the claim I made at the beginning that reasonable people already hold what I have called the conservative view of justice. If they would only think through their own beliefs, they would realize this. The reminders I have assembled in this essay have the particular purpose of aiding that realization.

Philosophy, State University of New York

NON-ABSOLUTE RIGHTS AND LIBERTARIAN TAXATION*

By Eric Mack

I. Introduction: Libertarian Theory and Taxation

Libertarian political theory is renowned—or notorious—for its ascription to individuals of robust moral rights that morally preclude others from killing, assaulting, maiming, enslaving, or otherwise extracting benefits from those individuals. It is renowned—or notorious—for holding that among the robust moral rights that persons have or would have under morally legitimate regimes are property rights, that is, entitlements to extrapersonal objects. Moreover, libertarian theory is renowned—or notorious—for holding that, insofar as individuals have legitimate property rights to their holdings, coercively depriving them of any of those holdings impermissibly violates their rights. Insofar as individuals acquire (and retain) genuine property rights, all taxation is theft. I am myself a friend of this sort of rights-oriented libertarian theory. Moreover, I confess to a fondness for the dictum that all taxation is theft. Nevertheless, in this essay I am interested in exploring whether there is room within rights-oriented libertarian theory for some taxation that is not theft.

More specifically, I want to examine one particular challenge to the taxation-is-theft dictum. This is what I will call the "non-absolutism challenge." This challenge arises within rights-oriented libertarian theorizing and, therefore, has to be taken seriously by rights-oriented theorists. I believe that the non-absolutism challenge is modestly successful in the sense that, starting with the challenge, one can by way of a long chain of speculative reasoning get to a vindication of taxation that would fund something like a minimal safety-net for individuals who would faultlessly find themselves in dire straits without that net. The success of the non-absolutism challenge is modest precisely because (i) the line of reasoning from some initial claims about the non-absoluteness of rights to the vindication of taxation is much longer and more speculative than one might initially think and (ii) the taxation that is vindicated if that speculation is sound is much more modest than many (other than myself) would hope for. In this essay, however, my purpose is to explore what is plausibly involved in the claim that rights are non-absolute and in the

* I thank Ellen Paul, the other contributors to this volume, and Mary Sirridge for their helpful comments.

inference from this non-absolutism to a vindication of taxation, rather than to trumpet any conclusion about justified taxation.

Before proceeding to the non-absolutism challenge, it is important to note and set aside other challenges to the taxation-is-theft dictum that are also internal to rights-oriented libertarian theory. To begin with, there are the "consent challenges." According to these challenges: (1) taxation of legitimate property would be theft if consent to that taxation has not been given; but (2) that consent has been given; and therefore (3) that taxation is not really theft. Different consent challenges invoke different accounts of who gave what consent to whom and how (and how directly or indirectly). However, all such challenges from consent fail because the necessary consent does not obtain. Of course, by their uncoerced consent, individuals can and often do make it permissible for another agent to take portions of what, absent that consent, was their inviolable property. But there has never been and there is unlikely ever to be a pattern of uncoerced consent on the part of individuals that would make permissible the sort of configuration of governmental takings that we normally think of as taxation.[1]

Consent challenges to the taxation-is-theft dictum accept the crucial premise that legitimate property rights are absolute and, hence, that permissible intrusions upon legitimate property do require freely given consent.[2] Nonconsent challenges to the dictum must reject this premise. They must hold that sometimes it is permissible to intrude upon an individual's legitimate property even if he has not waived (or forfeited) his rights with respect to that property. In this sense, all nonconsent challenges to the taxation-is-theft dictum assert the non-absoluteness of property rights. They assert that there are conditions under which it is permissible to infringe upon certain rights.[3] Such nonconsent challenges proceed by proposing a refinement in our understanding of robust property rights. The refinement is intended to introduce just enough of a loophole to make room for some special sort of taxation. Different possible refinements of libertarian rights may be proposed with different underlying justifications and leading to different vindications of different sorts or ranges of taxation.

[1] Rights-oriented libertarians will be theoretically opposed to any appeal to a hypothetical consent that is supposed to render permissible the violation (through taxation) of otherwise inviolable rights and to any hypothetical-consent account of why, to begin with, rights are not inviolable.

[2] Or they require the voluntary performance of impermissible actions through which those rights are forfeited.

[3] For ease of expression, I will use "trespass" or "intrude" to cover both rights-infringing entry and rights-infringing taking of property. One "infringes" a right when the right exists and one acts in a way that would "violate" that right if one did not have a dispensation. (One neither infringes nor violates a right if the right is no longer there to be infringed or violated. If F gives E permission to punch F in the nose, E neither violates nor infringes F's right against E not to be hit in the nose—because the permission eliminates the right.)

The most common and modest refinement involves the idea that persons' rights to their just holdings do not exclude those takings of their holdings that are necessary to finance the production of public goods—especially public goods that protect persons' rights, e.g., the public good of national defense.[4] Given this refinement, taxation that is necessary for the financing of a public good would not be a violation of rights.[5] This taxation—which would provide each taxed individual with compensation in the form of enjoyment of the financed public good—would not be theft.[6] Rights-oriented advocates of this refinement will have to argue that the refinement is not merely a device to bring libertarian thought into line with the conventional view that, of course, taxation for public goods must be justified. They need to point to a basis for the refinement within the libertarian theory of rights, and they need to argue that this refinement has limited, theoretically containable, implications. It cannot be a noose disguised as a loophole. For example, the defender of the refinement might argue that the only sort of benefit that will count as satisfactory compensation for such an infringement upon a property holder's right is an enhancement of the protection of his rights that is more extensive than the present infringement of his rights. Thus, the refinement would not even open the door to coercive funding of public goods—such as mosquito control—that do not take the form of rights protection.[7]

In this essay, however, I explore a refinement of rights and an associated challenge to the taxation-is-theft dictum that is *more* dangerous to rights-oriented libertarian theory. For it is a refinement and challenge that opens the door to dispossessing persons of rightfully held property for the sake of supplying something like a minimal safety-net

[4] The crucial characteristic of a public good is that, if it is produced, it is not feasible to prevent individuals from enjoying it. National defense is always the prime example. Because of this characteristic, individuals may be significantly less motivated to purchase this good voluntarily than they would be motivated to purchase an equally valuable private good. As a consequence, the public good may not be funded or may be markedly underfunded unless individuals who gain from its production are required to fund it. For one general discussion, see Gerald F. Gaus, *Social Philosophy* (Armonk, NY: Sharpe, 1999), chap. 10. The view that it is permissible to force beneficiaries to fund public goods need not, of course, be cast in terms of a refinement of rights that creates this permissibility. For tentative accounts that do follow the refinement of property rights line, see Eric Mack, "The Ethics of Taxation: Rights versus Public Goods?" in D. Lee, ed., *Taxation and the Deficit Economy* (San Francisco: Pacific Research Institute, 1986), 487–514; and Eric Mack, "Self-Ownership, Taxation, and Democracy: A Philosophical-Constitutional Perspective," in D. Racheter and R. Wagner, eds., *Politics, Taxation, and the Rule of Law* (Dordrecht: Kluwer Academic Publishers, 2002), 9–32.

[5] If taxation is not really necessary because mechanisms can evolve or be devised to overcome the difficulty of marketing this protection of rights to those who will benefit from it, then the takings will not be justified. They will be theft.

[6] The modesty of the refinement is manifest in the fact that the taxation that it permits is not redistributive.

[7] For explorations of this refinement, see Mack, "The Ethics of Taxation," and Mack, "Self-Ownership, Taxation, and Democracy."

for others.[8] I specifically designate this refinement and challenge as non-absolutist because it begins with a basic, commonplace intuition about the permissibility of infringing upon legitimate property rights in order to escape dire (and undeserved) injury. For instance, hiker A does not have to bear freezing to death in the unpredicted blizzard in order to avoid entering B's well-insulated wilderness cabin without B's permission. Similarly, faultlessly impoverished C is not morally required to starve to death in order to avoid consuming without D's permission the freshly baked pie cooling on the sill of D's open window. The commonplace idea is that when an agent faultlessly finds himself in a situation in which the cost to him of abiding by another's admitted right is enormous and the cost to the right-holder of having the right infringed is very small, a reasonable normative theory will not insist that the agent must bear that enormous cost.[9] The implication of this intuition is that rights are not absolute—in precisely the sense that sometimes their infringement is permissible. Moreover, if the grounding of rights itself appeals to the reasonableness of individuals' declining to bear costs for the sake of others, then it will be very difficult for the advocate of rights to deny that this intuition has traction. However, the embrace of such an intuition threatens to unravel rights; it threatens to spawn an almost unending series of justified infringements of rights and even threatens systematic substitution of calculations about comparative costs for invocations of restrictive rights. What is needed, then, from the friend of robust rights is an account of the limits on the costs that individuals must bear to accord others their rights. The limits themselves must be strictly drawn for the recognition of the limits not to unravel rights.

Rights-oriented libertarian theorists tend to try to push consideration of the non-absoluteness of rights to the periphery of their doctrines. Robert Nozick confines to a footnote his remark that "[t]he question of whether these side constraints [i.e., basic protective rights] are absolute, or whether they may be violated in order to avoid catastrophic moral horror, and if the latter, what the resulting structure might look like, is one I hope largely to avoid."[10] This remark exiles non-absoluteness to the far outer reaches of our moral experience. Nozick's banishment of non-absoluteness to those distant reaches is reminiscent of the strategy of the nonacademic

[8] I briefly discuss the distance between acknowledging a type of non-absoluteness in rights and validating taxation to support welfare in my essay "Libertarianism Untamed," *Journal of Social Philosophy* 23, no. 3 (Winter 1991): 64–72. For a related discussion, see Douglas Rasmussen and James Sterba, *The Catholic Bishops and the Economy: A Debate* (New Brunswick, NJ: Transaction Books, 1987).

[9] Perhaps the number of individuals who are *faultlessly* in dire straits is small enough so that, given the various interests others have in eliminating those dire straits, voluntarily funded assistance to those individuals will be feasible and, for this reason, the case for the coercive funding of a safety-net fails. I would like this to be true.

[10] Robert Nozick, *Anarchy, State, and Utopia* (New York: Basic Books, 1974), 30 n.

rights-oriented theorist Ayn Rand—from whom Nozick was usually eager to distance himself. According to Rand, in *emergency* situations an individual is at least morally at liberty to treat others in ways that ordinarily would be violations of their rights. This treatment is permissible because rights do not obtain within emergency situations. However, according to Rand, the fact that rights do not obtain in the context of emergencies in no way unsettles or complicates our understanding of rights in normal situations. Emergencies are metaphysical anomalies; they are so discontinuous with metaphysically normal social circumstances that our best judgments about how persons may act in emergencies should not carry over at all to the principles that govern our conduct within normal social states.[11] One motivation for my essay is the conviction that much more is needed than is provided by Nozick or Rand to mark off the cases in which a person in dire straits may permissibly do to another what would ordinarily be an impermissible violation of rights.

I have said that the line of argument from the non-absoluteness of rights to the vindication of taxation to fund something like a safety-net for faultlessly desperate people is longer and more speculative than one might think. The key reason for this is that to affirm that an individual like the freezing hiker A is *at liberty* to intrude upon the property of cabin-owner B is merely to affirm that A is not under his normal obligation to abide by B's property right. A's not having this obligation does not imply that B has an obligation to A to provide the needed shelter; A's not having the obligation to stay out of the cabin does not even imply that B is obligated to permit A to trespass.[12] Thus, the sort of non-absoluteness of an owner's right that we are envisioning here is, at most, the beginning of a line of argument for the taxation of property owners to fund a safety-net to prevent people from falling into dire straits. Further points along that line of argument will involve (i) the reasons that owners have to avoid situations in which their property rights are subject to permissible infringement, (ii) the reasons owners have to get out of such situations by preventing other members of their society from falling into dire straits, (iii) the reasons for believing that a safety-net that would prevent that fall will be a public good that will only be financed if the owners are required to pay for it, and (iv) the final normative premise that, if individuals have reason to want some public good to be funded but it will not be funded unless they are required to pay for it, then it is permissible to require them to pay for it. Notice that the final point along this line is the modest—but

[11] Ayn Rand, "The Ethics of Emergencies," in Rand, *The Virtue of Selfishness* (New York: Signet, 1961), 43–49.

[12] To assert the non-absoluteness of a right that B holds against A is *not* to assert that A possesses a right against B that conflicts with and may override the right held by B. Failing to distinguish between non-absoluteness of rights and conflicts among rights is a weakness in Tara Smith's interesting essay, "Rights Conflicts: The Undoing of Rights," *Journal of Social Philosophy* 26, no. 2 (Fall 1995): 139–56.

not incontestable—claim that the property rights of individuals do not exclude their being taxed to cover the costs of the public goods they will thereby enjoy. Thus, the whole argument from the non-absoluteness of rights to the permissibility of taxation to fund a safety-net can be no stronger than this public-goods premise; and because of other necessary points in this long line, this whole argument can easily be weaker. Friends of the taxation-is-theft dictum may take heart when they see how long and speculative this argument from non-absoluteness to taxation is.

The plan for the remainder of this essay is as follows: In Section II, I sketch the opening phases of arguments for rights. In particular, I emphasize the origination of rights in the proposition that it is not reasonable for individuals to opt for or accept personal losses in order to provide gains for others. It is because this emphasis on the "separateness of persons" is so essential to the case for rights that rights theorists must be receptive to the claim that a reasonable theory of rights will not require the freezing hiker to sit and freeze. In Section III, I look at cases in which one's intuitive judgment is that an individual in very difficult circumstances may infringe upon another's legitimate property rights if that will ameliorate those circumstances. I maintain that in such very difficult circumstances, rights infringement is permissible even if the individual in dire straits will not be able to compensate the owner for the infringement. This is the eye of the needle through which libertarian taxation for a safety-net needs to pass if there is a route from the non-absoluteness of rights to that taxation. In the remainder of Section III, I consider examples in which an individual is (faultlessly) in very dire straits but can escape a great loss by way of a pretty minor infringement of another's rights. If dire straits ever make trespasses permissible, if they ever reveal rights to be non-absolute, they do so in these cases.

How dire must individual A's circumstances be in order for him not to be bound to abide by B's various rights (which may differ in their degree of importance)? In Section IV, I examine—albeit only in a very rudimentary way—how difficult an individual's circumstances have to be for it to be permissible for him to infringe upon another's rights. This examination gives us some idea of how frequently property owners are faced with situations in which other individuals—especially other individuals who cannot compensate the owners for infringements—are morally at liberty to infringe upon their rights. In Section V, I examine how the institution of a safety-net might be defended as a public good for property owners because of the way it allows them to escape from the dangerous and morally difficult condition that obtains when others are morally at liberty to infringe upon the owners' rights. A key feature of my overall argument is that there are several different ways in which a person in dire straits may have a dispensation from his normal obligation to respect another's property rights, and the permissible response by the property owner to that person's permissible trespass will depend on what mode of dispensation (if any) the trespasser has. Therefore, the owner will be able to avoid overreaction and underreaction only if she can determine what mode of dispensation (if any) the trespasser has. It is because this determination is likely to be difficult and costly in itself that owners have an interest in the institution of a safety-net that prevents persons from falling into dispensation-generating straits. In Section VI, I sum things up.

II. Rights and Axiological Separateness

I have said that the non-absolutism refinement of our understanding of rights is grounded in the best arguments for libertarian rights and, for that reason, must be credible to advocates of such rights. A full defense of this claim would lay out those best arguments and point to the ground that the non-absolutism refinement has in them. Clearly, however, the laying out of those arguments cannot be attempted in one section of one essay. In this section, then, I will do something very much less than laying out those best arguments. I will say something about the underlying purpose or function of a system of robust rights, and I will say something more about the "separateness of persons" that friends of rights need to invoke to drive competing systems of enforceable interpersonal rules from the field.

Defenses of rights almost always begin with a recognition or defense of the reasonableness of individuals' pursuing their own good. Each person has a prospective well-being, and the attainment of that well-being stands as that person's ultimate end. Each person has a life of his own, and the first postulate of practical rationality is that an agent rationally aims at ensuring that his own life goes as well as possible. Rights come in as devices for the protection of each individual in the pursuit of his own ends from being trampled by other people in the pursuit of theirs. Rights do this by drawing boundaries between what one individual may deploy as he chooses in pursuit of his ends and what another individual may deploy as she chooses in pursuit of her ends. Rights preclude trampling. They thereby encourage the discovery by individuals of more and more non-trampling ways to achieve their respective goods—including ways of cooperation and ways of cooperatively reshaping those boundaries in order to facilitate yet further gains. Rights facilitate cooperation among individuals without requiring them to serve any common substantive goal—such as the goal of greatest social utility or greatest social equality. That is why friends of such substantive social goals cannot in the final analysis be friends of rights, and that is why friends of rights must reject systems of enforceable rules that are grounded upon some enshrined substantive social end. The rejection of all such doctrines of the social good is not in itself a positive argument on behalf of the system of rights, but it is a necessary negative part of the overall argument. If the basis for rejecting such doctrines of the social good gives rise to the non-absolutism refinement of rights, the friend of rights must give credence to that refinement.

Utilitarianism is, of course, the standard version of a conception of the overall social good that is advanced as the basis for a system of enforceable interpersonal rules. Utilitarianism calls upon individuals to incur costs within their own lives if doing so will more extensively diminish costs within others' lives or more extensively enhance benefits within others' lives. Indeed, it also seems to call upon individuals to impose costs on other persons if doing so will more extensively diminish costs within the lives of third parties or more extensively enhance benefits within the lives of third parties. The most prominent critique of utilitarianism in recent decades is the one offered by John Rawls in *A Theory of Justice*.[13] That critique is that utilitarianism is guilty of not taking seriously the separateness of persons. Utilitarianism ignores the separateness of persons by recommending that individuals ignore *who* is bearing costs and *who* is obtaining benefits. Indeed, Rawls depicts the utilitarian as ignoring the empirical separateness of persons to the point of conflating individuals into moments within an all-encompassing social being. In *Anarchy, State, and Utopia*, when Robert Nozick repeats Rawls's charge of not taking seriously the separateness of persons,[14] he too depicts the utilitarian and other theorists who are guilty of not taking seriously the separateness of persons as believing in a social entity that experiences both the costs that one individual is supposed to bear and the benefits for another individual that are supposed to justify those costs. However, this representation of the utilitarian provides too easy and, therefore, to fleeting a victory for Rawls and Nozick. The utilitarian can obviously disavow any empirical conflation of individuals; he can credibly insist that he does not believe in a social entity that experiences both the recommended costs and the compensating benefits.

What this shows is that the real critique of utilitarianism cannot consist in pointing to the empirical separateness of persons. Rather, it consists in pointing to what I shall call "axiological separateness."[15] This is the claim that, for each individual, the gains that make it rational for an individual to opt for certain losses within her life must be gains within her life. The enhancements to life and well-being that make it sensible for an individual to accept certain impairments to her life and well-being must be enhancements to her life and well-being. The profit generated by a costly action will render that action rational only if the profit is recorded in the same personal ledger of profits and losses as is the cost. To invoke this axiological separateness is to hold that each individual has her own system of ends and that, for each individual, the promotion of her own

[13] John Rawls, *A Theory of Justice* (Cambridge, MA: Harvard University Press, 1971), sections 5 and 6.

[14] Nozick, *Anarchy, State, and Utopia*, 30–31.

[15] Axiology is, of course, the science of values.

system of ends is the value-oriented measure of the rationality of her actions and choices.[16] Persons' separate systems of ends do not jointly form a comprehensive system of ends—a collective or overall social good—the optimal realization of which serves to direct each individual's choices and actions. As Nozick puts it when his critique comes closest to invoking axiological separateness,

> Using one of these people for the benefit of others, uses him and benefits the others. Nothing more.... To use a person in this way does not sufficiently respect and take account of the fact that he is a separate person, that his is the only life he has. He does not get some overbalancing good from his sacrifice, and no one is entitled to force this upon him....[17]

Unlike Rawls, Nozick realizes that the separateness of persons has much broader negative implications than the undermining of utilitarianism. It also undermines nonaggregative (i.e., distribution-sensitive) conceptions of an overall social good. Such distribution-sensitive conceptions rank alternative available social outcomes on the basis of how extensively they would realize some favored profile or pattern of goods among members of the society in question. For instance, one might think—as Rawls himself does—that alternative available social outcomes are to be ranked in accordance with how well served the least-advantaged members of society are. The better an outcome serves the least advantaged (i.e., the more that is allotted to them within it), the more highly ranked it is.

This distribution-sensitive conception of the overall social good, like any distribution-sensitive conception for which advocates can be found, will sometimes call upon individual A to opt for or accept a loss for herself so as to make possible a *smaller* gain for B; for circumstances can easily obtain in which such a loss for A will yield a social outcome that more extensively realizes the favored profile or pattern of goods.[18] This is obvious in the case of the conception of the overall social good that ranks social states by the size of the smallest allotment of goods that obtains within the available social states. Suppose that in the status quo distribution of goods, individual A possesses a substantial allotment of the units of whatever good we are focusing upon and B possesses a very small allotment, and a loss to A of a large number of the units of that good will marginally increase the number of units possessed by B. If this is the case, then that much smaller gain to B will be thought to justify A's opting

[16] I am not saying that the only measure of reasonableness in action is the value-oriented measure of how well one's ends are satisfied. Another measure of reasonableness is how fully one complies with sound constraining interpersonal norms, e.g., others' rights.

[17] Nozick, *Anarchy, State, and Utopia*, 32.

[18] If the favored profile is strictly egalitarian, then losses to A that do not generate *any* gains for B may still count as yielding a better overall social state.

for or accepting his much larger loss. (Even the *utility* loss to A may be greater than the *utility* gain to B.) Thus, if Rawls is correct that the separateness of persons undermines the utilitarian claim that an individual ought to opt for or accept a loss to himself if that loss will engender a larger gain (even a much larger gain) for another individual, it seems that Nozick must be right to think that the separateness of persons all the more undermines all distribution-sensitive conceptions of the overall social good. For, again, each of these conceptions will assert that it is sometimes rational for individual A to opt for or accept a loss to himself for the sake of a smaller gain for individual B.

In this section, then, I have maintained that the first phase of any defense of a system of rights as the basis for enforceable interpersonal norms requires the rejection of all candidates for the role of authoritative social good, and that an essential move in the rejection of these candidates is the invocation of axiological separateness. I have pointed out that to invoke axiological separateness is to validate each individual's questioning of demands that he bear costs for the benefit of others. This validation certainly does not mean that it is never reasonable for individuals to bear costs in order to remain respectful of others' rights. If there is a case for rights as general protective norms that enable each individual to pursue his own valued ends in his own way, then it must be reasonable for individuals to be required to bear some costs—perhaps very considerable costs—so as to comply with those rights. Nevertheless, a doctrine which so focuses on the separateness of individuals' systems of ends, and on the rationality of individuals' seeking the realization of their own ends, cannot comfortably insist that it is all-things-considered reasonable for individuals to bear enormous costs even in order to abide by other persons' relatively minor rights. Because of his appeal to axiological separateness, the friend of robust rights has to give credence to the intuition that an individual need not accept great loss (for example, loss of his life) in order to abide strictly by others' rights.

It should be noted that axiological separateness is not axiological atomism. To accept axiological separateness is not to believe that our valued ends are isolated and unconnected. For all or almost all of us, what gets recorded in others' respective ledgers of gains and losses affects—and not just instrumentally—what gets recorded in one's own ledger. Among the things that all or almost all of us value are things going well for other individuals. More specifically, all or almost all of us value very highly things going well for a limited number of other individuals, value somewhat things going well for a greater number of others, and value slightly (down to barely perceptibly) things going well for most individuals at large. Moreover, all or almost all of us disvalue to various degrees things going well for various other individuals. (We differ from one another in what aspects of things going well or going badly in others' lives we value or disvalue.) Often, then, a gain to another will have some—possibly barely perceptible, possibly highly salient—value to the individual whose loss makes that gain possible. This factor will reappear in this essay when we note that many owners of property may be willing to bear the costs of minor trespasses by individuals who are escaping serious dangers; the owners may be willing to bear these costs precisely because they value others' escaping such dangers.

III. Dire Straits and the Permissible Infringement of Rights

Let us begin with the most standard sort of case that intuitively supports the non-absoluteness of rights, the Freezing Hiker case. Here are the stipulated facts of the case:

> While on a well-planned wilderness trek and through no fault of his own, Hiker finds himself in fatally freezing weather. The full use of his carefully selected gear will not keep him alive given the unpredicted plunge in temperature. Fortunately, Hiker stumbles across Owner's wilderness cabin and through the window he can see nice cords of wood by the fireplace and life-saving blankets. But the cabin is locked and Owner is not around. Worse yet, there is a sign near the front door that reads, "Private Property! Keep Off No Matter What Your Sob Story." Hiker, however, will escape death only if he breaks the lock, burns some of Owner's wood, and makes use of her blankets.

The most basic intuition here is that no plausible moral theory says that Freezing Hiker must accept his freezing to death. Even more clearly, no moral theory that builds upon the separate value of each person's life and well-being can hold that Freezing Hiker is morally bound to grin and bear it. Since plausible rights theory itself builds upon the axiological separateness of persons, it especially must give credence to this basic intuition.

Having given this credence, however, the rights theorist will have a great need for an account of *the limits on the limits* to individuals' being required to grin and bear it. Here is another case—Sore Hiker—that conveys the intuitive need the friend of rights—including property rights—has for such limits on the limits:

> While on a well-planned wilderness trek and through no fault of his own, Sore Hiker finds himself one long day from his exit point but very sore and tired and a bit chilled. The ground is rocky and his sleeping pad has sprung a leak. He faces a sleepless and somewhat chilly night and a difficult and physically uncomfortable hike on his final day. Fortunately, Sore Hiker stumbles across Owner's wilderness cabin and through the window he can see nice cords of wood by the fireplace and comforting and chill-averting blankets. But there is that sign that reads, "Private Property! Keep Off No Matter What

> Your Sob Story." Sore Hiker, however, will escape that fairly miserable night and a good portion of the next day's misery only if he breaks the lock, burns the wood, and so on.

The loss that Sore Hiker would escape is much less drastic (and permanent) than the loss faced by Freezing Hiker. If we take Owner's rights at all seriously, we will judge that Sore Hiker is required not to enter the cabin even though the cost to himself that he would avert by doing so is distinctly greater than the cost he would impose on Owner. The rights-oriented libertarian theorist needs to provide an account that explains why Freezing Hiker is not morally required to grin and bear it while Sore Hiker is. Then that theorist has to address whether his account—or whatever fragments of an account he can come up with—is a refinement within rights theory that opens the door to more systematic permissible takings of private property—in particular, takings to finance a social safety-net. I offer the rudiments of such an account in the next section of this essay.

However, within this section I am concerned to point out that a given faultless and seriously endangered hiker—like Freezing Hiker—may possess one of a number of different dispensations from his normal obligation to respect Owner's property rights. Which dispensation a given hiker possesses will depend upon further particular features of his case. Consider these four distinct—and successively more modest—dispensations that a seriously endangered hiker might be thought to possess. (The four dispensations represent different—and successively more modest—interpretations of the judgment that the endangered hiker is not morally required just to grin and bear it.)[19]

(a) The seriously endangered hiker has a claim-right to break the lock, burn the wood, and so on—that is, he is at liberty to break the lock, burn the wood, and so on, and Owner is obligated to facilitate the hiker's entry (for example, by using some form of telecommunication to reveal the location of the hidden door key).

(b) The seriously endangered hiker has a claim-right to break the lock, burn the wood, and so on if and only if he compensates Owner (either immediately or over time). But Owner is under no obligation to facilitate the hiker's entry. (She need not reveal the key's location.)

(c) The seriously endangered hiker is at liberty to break the lock, burn the wood, and so on; thus, correlatively, Owner has no claim-rights against the hiker's performing these actions. But

[19] It looks like there is room for a whole *theory* of dispensations. I suspect that there is a good deal in the common law of (intentional) torts that would be instructive to such a theory.

Owner is under no obligation to allow the hiker to act in this way; Owner is at liberty to prevent the hiker's actions—albeit not by the use of harmful force against him.

(d) The seriously endangered hiker is at liberty to break the lock, burn the wood, and so on; thus, correlatively, Owner has no claim-rights against the hiker's performing these actions. But Owner is under no obligation to allow the hiker to act in this way; Owner is at liberty to prevent the hiker's actions—even by the use of harmful force.

I will maintain that no hiker's serious endangerment confers dispensation (a) upon him.[20] However, some seriously endangered hikers enjoy dispensation (b), while others enjoy dispensation (c) and yet others enjoy dispensation (d). Dispensation (a) is really not a dispensation but, rather, a straightforward right to assistance—a right that is triggered by the hiker's need and that eliminates without a trace Owner's relevant property rights. I will argue that, if we take at all seriously Owner's rights, the most robust dispensation that it is reasonable to ascribe to a seriously endangered hiker is dispensation (b).

Let us begin by considering the case of a freezing hiker who is capable of compensating Owner for the property damage he causes in escaping from the blizzard. He is Freezing Capable Hiker (FCH). This feature of being able and willing to provide compensation makes FCH a stronger candidate for exemption from the requirement that he not trespass on Owner's property than similarly endangered hikers who are not able (or willing) to provide compensation. Thus, if even FCH possesses only dispensation (b), no seriously endangered hikers will—in virtue of their endangerment—possess dispensation (a). After making the case for FCH's possession of dispensation (b) rather than dispensation (a), I will turn to the dispensations possessed by faultless seriously endangered hikers from whom compensation cannot be expected.

If FCH possesses dispensation (a), he has an unqualified claim-right to break the lock, burn the wood, and so on. As a consequence, FCH may not be prevented from performing these actions *and* he may not be prevented from imposing the cost of his escape from death on Owner. If FCH has this unqualified right, he can do two distinguishable things to Owner that would (normally) be precluded by Owner's property rights. The first is that FCH may deprive Owner of her discretionary control over how the lock, the wood, and so on will be used. Rather than the deployment of these resources being determined by Owner's choice, it will be determined by FCH's choice. The second is that FCH may impose the costs of

[20] Indeed, if persons in dire straits did possess dispensation (a), the route from property rights being non-absolute in the face of individuals in dire straits to the vindication of taxation to undo those dire straits would be much shorter than I have claimed.

his escape from death on Owner. FCH does not have to bear the costs of his escape from death either by way of paying Owner in advance for Owner's permission to break the lock, and so on, or by way of compensating Owner afterward for his trespass. If FCH possesses dispensation (a), he is not rightly subject to punishment—which would serve at least metaphorically to nullify the deprivation of choice imposed on Owner—*and* he is not even rightly required to pay compensation to Owner—which would serve to nullify the imposition of costs upon the right-holder. One reason for rejecting the ascription of dispensation (a) to FCH is that, if FCH has this dispensation, then his actions (breaking the lock and so on) cannot be said to *infringe* upon any rights of Owner. If FCH has this dispensation, then we should no more say that FCH's actions infringe Owner's rights than we should say that just punishment infringes the rights of the criminal subject to that punishment. If we think that FCH's actions are infringements upon Owner's rights—albeit permissible infringements—we have to reject the ascription to FCH of dispensation (a).

We have further reason to reject this ascription. It is one thing for FCH not to be morally required to sit and freeze; it is another thing for morality to require that Owner bear the costs of FCH's escape from freezing.[21] FCH faces—through no fault of his own—that most severe of losses. He can escape this loss by imposing a minor, albeit rights-infringing, loss on the cabin owner. Suppose he proceeds to impose that cost on the cabin owner. He breaks the lock on the cabin door, burns some of the owner's wood in her fireplace, uses some of her blankets, and (when this becomes known to the owner) disrupts her valued sense of the security of her possessions. Given that these costs have been incurred, the question is this: Who should end up bearing them—the hiker who chooses to incur these costs and who benefits from their being incurred, or the cabin owner who does not choose to incur these costs and who does not benefit from their being incurred? The much greater plausibility of the view that the hiker should bear these costs—even if he is entirely faultless in being in his precarious position—strongly supports the ascription to FCH of dispensation (b); FCH is not required to sit and freeze, but he must compensate Owner for his life-saving trespasses.[22] FCH has a qualified claim-right not to be prevented from engaging in those life-saving actions[23]—a claim-right that is qualified by FCH's being required to pay compensation to Owner. FCH is subject to legitimate punishment if he

[21] I am not saying that, under dispensation (a), Owner would be required through her own actions to take on these costs; but under (a) she would be required to bear them if FCH imposes them on her.

[22] This essentially is the argument for why, no matter how reasonable the intentional tort-feasor is in, e.g., choosing to damage another's dock in order to avoid greater damage to his ship, he ought to be required to bear the costs of his reasonable action.

[23] However, as Ellen Paul has prompted me to point out, FCH does not have any claim-right to Owner's facilitating his trespass by, e.g., revealing where the door key is hidden.

fails to provide such compensation. The owner has an undiminished right to that compensation—that is, if it is not paid, she can demand restitution for the harm of (still) not getting the compensation that is owed to her, and she can demand punishment for the wrong of her being deprived of her discretionary control over the payment of the original owed compensation.[24]

Mode of dispensation (b) nicely fits the judgment that in special circumstances like those involved in the Freezing Hiker case, an endangered agent does not *wrong* an Owner by infringing upon her rights—until and unless compensation is not paid. Dispensation (b) is a nice solution to the Freezing Hiker case because it involves a pretty neat splitting of the difference. By allowing that the endangered hiker may not be precluded from engaging in his life-saving actions and that he may not be punished for them, we accommodate the judgment that the hiker is not morally required to grin and bear it. By insisting that the hiker is required to compensate Owner, we also accord to Owner a good deal of what her undiminished right would provide—in particular, her not having to bear the cost of FCH's loss-avoiding actions. Unfortunately, this nice solution depends upon the endangered hiker's being able and willing to compensate Owner. Things get tougher and more interesting as we move to situations in which our severely endangered hiker is not able and willing to compensate Owner for the costs imposed on her by the hiker's escape from danger. (And there is no one else prepared to pay compensation on behalf of this hiker.)

As for this endangered hiker who is incapable of paying compensation, let us call him Freezing Incapable Hiker (FIH). And let us presume that FIH is as faultless with respect to his incapacity to compensate Owner as he is with respect to his being caught in the deep freeze. If we have in mind the possibility of moving from some non-absolutist refinement of rights to justified taxation, it is especially appropriate that we focus on the case of FIH and the dispensation for which FIH qualifies. After all, the prime candidates for protection by a safety-net funded by taxation are individuals who (faultlessly) are in dire straits and who (faultlessly) are not capable of compensating those on whom the cost of the safety-net would fall.[25] We should note, however, that FIHs may be rarer than they first appear to be. Whenever the costs to the right-holder are minor, there is almost certainly something (permissible) that anyone who imposes those minor costs will be able to do to enable him to compensate the right-holder. As soon as he gets back to civilization, almost any hiker can

[24] Note that I have *not* said that an agent may impose a forced exchange *whenever* the loss to the agent that the agent averts is great enough for it to pay for that agent to compensate the victim of the forced exchange. The permissibility of infringement with compensation has only been asserted with respect to FCH.

[25] Again I note the possibility that the numbers of such people may be small enough that no coercion is necessary to raise funds and generate institutions to assist them.

sell his remaining hiking gear or some of his nicely thickened blood. It will be hard to find freezing *responsibly equipped* hikers who are incapable of paying compensation. In addition, there is always the possibility that third parties—for example, the Committee for the Aid of Freezing Hikers—will provide compensation on behalf of the trespasser. Nevertheless, we want to confront the case of FIH precisely because the situation of FIH corresponds to the situation of the most plausible candidates for protection by a social safety-net.

Here we need to ask and answer two related questions. Does FIH have as much moral latitude to break the lock, burn the wood, and so on as FCH? Is the fact that FIH is not capable of compensating Owner (and not capable of triggering anyone else's payment of that compensation) irrelevant? I think the answer to both these questions has to be "no." The sort of moral latitude that FCH has to break the lock and so on depends on the prospect of Owner's being compensated. FCH's capacity to compensate Owner makes it possible for FCH to escape his dire situation by (merely) depriving Owner of discretionary control over her lock, wood, and so on—without his having also to impose any (other) cost upon Owner. What we normally think of as the costs of FCH's escape from the deep freeze can be borne by FCH. It is this prospect of Owner's not having the cost of FCH's escape from his dire situation imposed upon her that makes it unreasonable under the circumstances for Owner to prevent or defend against FCH's intrusion. In effect, FCH's prospective payment of compensation to Owner buys FCH some of the moral latitude he possesses. It makes him eligible for dispensation (b). Unfortunately, FIH cannot escape his dire situation without both depriving Owner of her discretionary control over her property *and* imposing the costs of his escape on Owner. In the case of FIH, there is no prospect of compensation to Owner to purchase moral latitude for the endangered hiker. It is, of course, true that FIH avoids great loss to himself if he trespasses upon Owner's property and that the cost of the trespass to Owner will be markedly less than the cost to FIH of forgoing the trespass. In light of axiological separateness, however, this in itself cannot be a good reason for ascribing to FIH a dispensation that requires Owner to allow FIH to impose that lesser cost on her. What one should expect is that the latitude that FIH has with respect to depriving Owner of her discretionary choice and imposing the cost of his escape on her will be less than the latitude that FCH has with respect to (merely) depriving Owner of her discretionary choice. This is to say that we should expect FIH to possess a more modest dispensation than FCH.

This line of reasoning would lose credibility if it were to drive us to the conclusion that FIH is morally required to sit and freeze, but we are not driven to this conclusion. Rather, we are driven to dispensation (c). FIH is not required to grin and bear it. He is entirely at liberty to break the lock, burn the wood, and so on—that is, he is under no obligation to refrain from doing these things. If he does these things, he is no more subject to just punishment than FCH is—under dispensation (b)—if FCH breaks and burns *and* pays compensation to Owner. FIH's need to do these things if he is to stay alive frees him from his obligation not to trespass upon Owner's cabin. No theory of rights grounded in the separate importance of each person's life and well-being can reasonably hold that Owner's rights can, in these circumstances, reach in and bind FIH to eschew the modest trespasses that are necessary for FIH to avert death. But the fact that FIH's infringement of Owner's rights will impose the cost of his escape from death on her leaves Owner with the moral liberty to block this imposition of cost. Owner's liberty rests on her having no obligation to submit to any (uncompensated) cost-imposition at the hands of FIH, whereas FIH's liberty rests on the unreasonableness of any interpretation of Owner's rights that requires FIH to sit and freeze.

In anticipation of the arrival of FIH, Owner is at liberty to install a lock on her cabin door. From the comfort of her primary residence, she may press the button that causes steel shutters to descend around her cabin when the remote sensors she has left there report the arrival of FIH. I do *not* think, however, that in order to prevent FIH's breaking her lock, burning the wood, and so on, Owner may from the comfort of her primary residence press the button that fires the shotgun mounted on the cabin porch that tracks anyone attempting to break into her cabin. Unfortunately, I do not have a confident account of this judgment. Perhaps what underlines it is a doctrine of proportionality in just defense—a doctrine which states that, for any infliction by A of an injury on B that is not just, there is an upper limit on the harm that B may inflict on A to prevent that injury. Perhaps what underlies my judgment is a principle of moral caution. If Owner in the comfort of her primary residence is mistaken about the hiker approaching her cabin door—if the hiker is not actually planning to break in or if the hiker is prepared to compensate for any damage he does—then Owner's pushing the button that fires that shotgun is objectively a form of homicide—even if it would be a legitimate defense of her property if Owner were not mistaken. In pressing the button, then, Owner takes a huge moral risk to block a likely minor loss. Our judgment that the absentee Owner may not push the button that fires that shotgun may be based on the idea that the loss through trespass in this case is not great enough to justify that moral risk.

If, as I surmise, Owner may not use harmful force against FIH, we can distinguish between the cases of FCH and FIH as follows: FCH possesses dispensation (b). He is at liberty to break the lock and so on, and Owner may not thwart FCH's breaking in (e.g., by bringing down those steel shutters). However, FCH must compensate Owner and may be punished for not compensating her. In contrast, FIH falls under dispensation (c). He is at liberty to break the lock and so on, and he need not do what, by hypothesis, he cannot do (namely, compensate Owner for the costs imposed on her). However, Owner may thwart FIH's breaking in (e.g., by bringing down the shutters), even though Owner cannot thwart FIH's breaking in by the use of harmful force against FIH.

I have been giving FIH the benefit of *my* philosophical doubt about whether Owner may resist FIH's relatively minor trespass by way of harmful force. That philosophical doubt diminishes as there is an increase in the damage that an endangered hiker in dire straits has to impose in order to escape those straits. I am not thinking here of cases in which Owner is on the scene and the endangered hiker must do damage to her in order to escape freezing to death.[26] I think it is uncontroversial that, if Owner must use harmful force against the hiker to protect her person against being injured by the hiker, she is at liberty to do so. Rather, I am thinking here of cases in which the endangered hiker has to impose markedly greater damage on Owner's property than is the case with FCH and FIH. Suppose, for example, that once inside the cabin the hiker will have to warm himself by burning Owner's valuable collection of antique furniture, and suppose further that this hiker is incapable of compensating Owner for this damage.[27] Here we have Freezing Incapable Highly-Damaging Hiker (FIHDH). I take it to be controversial, but plausible, that there is some amount of damage to Owner's property such that, if a faultlessly freezing hiker has to cause that amount of damage (or more) to escape from freezing, he still is at liberty to do so—the hiker still does not have to grin and bear it—*but* Owner (perhaps through that remotely controlled shotgun) is at liberty to thwart that property damage *by harmful force*. Let us presume that the value (to Owner) of the antique furniture collection is high enough so that, in contrast to the case of FIH, Owner is at liberty to use harmful force against FIHDH. If we have a case with these features, we have a case in which the endangered hiker possesses dispensation (d). So we have (at least) three different sorts of cases involving faultlessly severely endangered hikers—exemplified respectively by FCH, FIH, and FIHDH—who possess, in turn, dispensations (b), (c), and (d). When we refocus our attention from the truncated world of cabin owners and hikers back onto society at large, we see that owners (and their families, employees, and customers) may encounter individuals who enjoy (or may appear to enjoy) any one of these three dispensations.

I have emphasized Owner's moral liberty to thwart the trespasses that, in virtue of their dire straits, FIH and FIHDH are at liberty to perform. I should add, therefore, that to take note of the permissibility of these

[26] For instance, suppose that Owner is also caught in the blizzard. She has enough clothing to protect her from harm, including a scarf that she has wrapped around her left hand. Hiker can save himself from freezing to death only by wresting that scarf from Owner and (barely) protecting himself with it. But the consequence of this will be severe frostbite in several of the fingers on Owner's left hand. It is uncontroversial, I say, that Owner is at liberty to use harmful force against the hiker to prevent his wresting the scarf away.

[27] If this endangered hiker can be expected to make compensation to Owner, it seems that he possesses dispensation (b).

thwarting actions is not to hold that Owner *should* engage in them. The costs or dangers involved in thwarting trespasses by FIH or FIHDH may make those thwarting actions imprudent. Moreover, when the direct cost in property damage to Owner is relatively low—as it is when the prospective intruder is FIH—a morally decent Owner will value the survival of the faultlessly endangered hiker over avoidance of that property damage. (Recall the complicating factor mentioned in Section II—the value that people place upon others' well-being.) Of course, if Owner is faced with FIHDH, she has a markedly greater stake in exercising her moral liberty to thwart the trespass.

We should also note that the situation is more epistemically complicated when Owner is on site—as *we* owners are on site in our real social circumstances. If she is on site, Owner has to wonder what else an (apparently) endangered hiker will trespass upon if he is admitted to the cabin or succeeds at breaking in. If she throws a nice high-tech sleeping bag and high-tech snacks out to the freezing hiker and yet he still pleads to be let in or still is fiddling with her lock, she has to worry about what he intends to fiddle with if he gains entry. Owner has full and uncompromised rights not to suffer any loss that an endangered hiker does not have to impose in order to escape his dire straits. She may thwart the imposition of such a loss both by means other than harmful force (i.e., by means of the steel shutters) and by means of harmful force (i.e., by means of the shotgun). If Owner is on site, she may have reasonable or at least understandable concerns about the endangered hiker's overstepping his dispensation and, thus, she may have a reasonable or at least understandable basis for resisting the hiker's actions in ways that are not objectively permissible if the hiker is in fact acting within his dispensation.

If the endangered hiker is FIH, that is, if he enjoys dispensation (c), then that hiker and the on-site Owner exist in something like a Hobbesian micro-state of nature. FIH is at liberty to break into the cabin (albeit not by way of using harmful force on Owner); and Owner is at liberty to thwart FIH's entry (albeit not by way of using harmful force on FIH). Unlike the case of FCH, there is no way to split the difference so that in some significant sense neither party has to lose. When at least one party has to lose, and neither is at fault, a reasonable moral doctrine does not declare that either party is bound to submit to the loss. The micro-state of nature that exists between FIH and on-site Owner is not a fully Hobbesian micro-state of nature because neither party is at liberty to thwart the other party's exercise of his or her liberties by the use of harmful force—that is, by attacks upon the other person. Nevertheless, these situations obviously have great potential for escalating into Hobbesian micro-wars of each against each. If the endangered hiker is FIHDH, that is, if he enjoys dispensation (d), then the hiker and on-site Owner exist in a fully Hobbesian micro-state of nature. Each may permissibly use harmful force on the other, and this normative state will almost inevitably escalate into a micro-war of each against each. This tendency for escalation when Owner is on site may be exacerbated by one further factor. If an individual who is not herself endangered wanders by as an endangered hiker is ineffectively attempting to break into Owner's cabin, the wanderer is at liberty to act as the hiker's agent; she may exercise the hiker's liberty to break the lock, burn the wood, and so on.[28] The presence of such willing agents—especially agents whom cabin owners may suspect are on course to overstep whatever dispensation the endangered hiker possesses—will add fuel to the wilderness's micro-Hobbesian fires.[29]

The point of mentioning these exacerbating factors is that they are factors that will come into play as we move from the truncated world of isolated endangered wilderness hikers, (mostly) absentee owners of wilderness cabins, and few (if any) aspiring nonendangered samaritans to the world of everyday society. I have offered here a (rudimentary) account of the diverse dispensations from the normal obligation to abide by others' property rights that individuals in dire straits may possess. We need to see what the implications of this account are for everyday society—or, more specifically, for a society like ours except for its being more systematically respectful of individual property rights. In such a social order, there will be lots of on-site owners or on-site agents of owners and lots of samaritans who may be prepared to act on behalf of individuals whose straits are dire enough to confer on them dispensation (b), (c), or (d). What we most need to know, then, is how widespread within such a society will be the possession (or apparent possession) of one or another of these dispensations. More specifically, we need to have some idea of how dire the loss that an individual (faultlessly) faces must be in order for it to be true that he is at liberty to infringe upon the rights of another. If it turns out that the costs of an individual's compliance with another's rights *readily* provides him with a dispensation from the obligation to respect property rights, then the prediction of the rights absolutist—that any departure from absolutism will lead to the unraveling of rights—will turn out to be correct. As I have already noted, then, the friend of rights who wants nevertheless to recognize that sometimes individuals in dire

[28] I would uphold two restrictions on one party's acting as the agent of another. The first is that, if there is some third party who is already supposed to be the agent of both the cabin owner and the endangered hiker, that third party cannot permissibly act on behalf of the hiker and against the cabin owner—absent something like the permission of the cabin owner. This means that we cannot go from the permissibility of some third party's acting on behalf of the endangered hiker to the permissibility of the *government's* acting on his behalf. The second restriction is that the costs that will be borne by each of a number of individuals—e.g., the various burdens of discomfort that will be borne by twenty chilled hikers—if no third party acts on their behalf do not aggregate into one much bigger burden, the group's collective burden, that provides the group or its agent with a dispensation.

[29] Other wilderness wanderers may leap to the defense of Owner's property and may be seen by endangered hikers and their agents as overstepping what may permissibly be done in resisting the present trespass.

straits are not obligated to grin and bear it must explain why only quite dire straits exempt individuals from that obligation.

IV. Limits on Permissible Infringement

Section III's crude sketch of moral dispensations yields this rough picture: If an individual will suffer a great enough loss unless there is a transfer of property from its legitimate owner to that individual, then that individual has a dispensation from his normal obligation to abide by the owner's property rights. Which dispensation that individual will have will depend upon (i) whether or not the individual can compensate the owner for the transfer of property and (ii) how much of a transfer of property is needed to prevent the prospective loss. If the endangered individual can compensate the owner, then the individual enjoys dispensation (b). If the transfer of property needed to escape the dire straits is more than modest, the individual enjoys dispensation (d). Otherwise, he enjoys dispensation (c). Thus, the crucial question we must ask in order to get some idea of how frequently owners in an everyday property-respecting society will encounter individuals who possess (or may appear to possess) some dispensation is this: How severe a loss must an individual face before some dispensation is triggered?

We have already taken note of some intuitions relevant to this question, namely, that a wilderness hiker facing death possesses such a dispensation, but a wilderness hiker facing soreness does not. Since we are abstracting from questions about whether the parties facing losses are capable or not of compensating for the trespasses they would have to perform to escape their losses, and about whether those necessary trespasses would be modest or not, let us simply designate the hiker who faces freezing to death as "F" and the hiker who faces soreness as "S." If we tell S that his trespass is not permissible, S will demand some explanation of why his case is so different from F's case. We can and should say that, *if* his case is significantly different, then a due regard for the rights of Owner requires that S eschew the break-in. But this still leaves us with the burden of saying why it is different.

What would be especially nice would be to show that, whereas it is advantageous to hikers that the danger of freezing to death triggers a dispensation from the obligation not to break into wilderness cabins, it is disadvantageous to hikers to so expand this exemption that the danger of soreness also triggers a dispensation. More generally, what would be especially nice would be to show that, whereas it is advantageous to individuals in everyday society that the prospect of death triggers a dispensation from the obligation not to trespass, it is disadvantageous to individuals in everyday society that the prospect of middle-ish discomfort also triggers a dispensation. All this would be nice because it would rebut a claim that the individual who demands a more permissive dispensation might make—the claim that a moral code that lacks this more permissible dispensation is not sufficiently solicitous of his interests. It would be still nicer to be able to say something about where the cut-off point is at which any further expansion of exemptions becomes disadvantageous. Friends of robust rights will want that cut-off point to be in the region of significant permanent injury, so that only individuals who have to trespass to avoid such injury or worse have a moral liberty to do so. If an argument from the non-absoluteness of rights to a tax-funded safety-net goes through, these will be the individuals saved by the net. But how could it even be shown that it is disadvantageous to S for there to be an exemption from obligatory respect for property rights that extends to individuals like S who face the prospect of soreness? Surely it is advantageous—not disadvantageous—to S that the prospect of his soreness triggers a dispensation. It is crucial to see why this apparently plausible proposition is false.

The first step in seeing this is to note that, if a given level of prospective loss triggers a dispensation for *any* hiker (e.g., for S), then that level of prospective loss triggers a dispensation for *every* hiker facing that level of prospective loss. We can hold that hiker F is at liberty to trespass in order to save himself from death only if we hold that every hiker is at liberty to trespass to avert his death. We can hold that hiker S is at liberty to trespass to save himself from a period of discomfort only if we hold that every hiker facing that increment of discomfort has this liberty. The second step is to note that there can be considerable blowback from others' having a liberty that, if not for the blowback, it would be advantageous for one to have. It is precisely on point here to cite that maximal state of moral liberty—the Hobbesian state of nature. First, picture individuals occupying an uncomplicated Lockean state of nature, where each individual possesses claim-rights to his life, limbs, freedom, and peacefully acquired holdings. None of these individuals has any moral liberty to trespass upon any other's life, limbs, freedom, or peacefully acquired holdings. Now imagine that one of these individuals—call him "Tom"—receives a dispensation from all his Lockean obligations not to trespass upon others' lives, limbs, freedoms, and property. At least at first blush, it seems that Tom's freedom from the bonds of Locke's "law of nature" would be highly advantageous to Tom. Let us suppose that it would be advantageous to Tom in and of itself—that is, before we take account of the *implications* of Tom's having this liberty and the *consequences* of those implications.[30] However, if Tom enjoys such unlimited Hobbesian liberty,

[30] At second blush, even this singular moral liberty is not advantageous to this individual—at least if others are aware of his being unbound. For he is now more dangerous to be around. Moreover, since he is at liberty not to keep his contracts, people will be very reluctant to enter into contractual relationships with him.

so too must everyone else.[31] And as we all know, that universalized enjoyment is not very enjoyable. The consequence for Tom of the implication that all must have unlimited Hobbesian liberties is that Tom will be fully engaged in a war of all against all.

Tom's life in a world of Hobbesian liberties will not be enjoyable because of the blowback to Tom from others' equally unlimited Hobbesian liberties. The most readily envisioned part of this blowback is the cost to Tom of others' being under no obligations at all to constrain their conduct *toward him*. For each of them, it is as much open season on Tom as for Tom it is open season on all of them. However, a less readily envisioned part of this blowback is crucial for an account of the limits on permissible infringement. This is the portion that derives from each of those other individuals' being unconstrained in his or her actions *toward each of those other individuals*. A great deal of the brutishness, nastiness, poverty, and shortness of life that will befall Tom in a Hobbesian state of nature will be the negative externality of the war of all these others against all these others. We can get a sense of the magnitude of this negative externality, that is, of this portion of the blowback, by imagining that Tom has Lockean rights against everyone else—so that everyone else is quite constrained in what they may do directly to him—but each of these others enjoys Hobbesian liberty with respect to each other. In other words, we imagine Tom as an island of Lockean rights in a sea of Hobbesian liberties.

That is going to be a pretty small, pretty poor, and pretty short island. It will, essentially, be only as good an island as Tom can create for himself without any trade or joint cooperative endeavors with anyone else. This is the case because others will, of course, have very little to trade and very few developed skills to bring to any cooperative endeavor with Tom. Moreover, since none of them will have rights to any of the goods they might offer to Tom in trade, Tom's Lockean right to anything he obtains in trade will be highly questionable. Thus, others' strict compliance with Tom's Lockean rights will not require them not to seize these goods. And, of course, even if some other individuals have some goods to trade with Tom or some developed skills to bring to cooperative endeavors with Tom, these other individuals will have little incentive to trade or cooperate with Tom. By hypothesis, they will have no Lockean rights against anyone else to the fruits of those trades or endeavors.

Here is one more exercise in imagination to convey the magnitude of the negative externality for a given individual of the dilution of *others'* rights vis-à-vis one another. Imagine, again, that Tom has Lockean rights against everyone else. Suppose, however, that each of the remaining people has what we might call Benthamite liberties against each other. Each

[31] Tom's unique unbounding *could* arise from a Lockean state of nature if everyone else were to waive all their Lockean rights against Tom. For Locke, that is the incredibly implausible story that would have to be told to vindicate a Hobbesian sovereign.

of these individuals is at liberty to infringe on the rights of any other of these persons whenever the cost that the infringer escapes through the trespass exceeds the cost that the infringer inflicts. It seems clear that, under such a regime, life would go much less well for everyone—including Tom—than it would if rights were not subject to so extensive a dilution. It would not be as bad for Tom as it would be if others were to have Benthamite liberties toward him, but it would still be very bad—because the enormous positive externalities for Tom of living in a well-ordered market society would largely disappear. Life would go markedly worse for Tom than it would if the only dilution of people's Lockean rights were to consist in people's being at liberty to infringe those rights when—as in the case of the freezing hiker—an agent's infringements were necessary for that agent to escape an extremely bad outcome.

It is probably obvious why I have emphasized the indirect portion of the blowback that originates with others' having the same liberty to infringe upon rights as our protagonist Tom has. For this is the portion of the blowback that hits our protagonist—as a negative externality or as a loss of a positive externality—even if others are not going to be exercising *against him* the liberty to infringe rights that he may be exercising against them. It is only this indirect portion of the blowback that is relevant if we think of the wilderness as something like a closed system in which there are hikers (who are not also owners) and owners (who are not also hikers). The hikers do not have to consider the cost to them of the owners' exercising *against them* the same liberty to trespass upon cabins that the hikers have or may be thought to have. Although the owners would also have the same moral dispensation that the hikers have, they would rarely have occasion to exercise it. Similarly, individuals who are in dire straits in *our* non-wilderness society, and to whom some dispensation regarding trespass might similarly be ascribed, do not face the prospect of direct blowback by way of non-indigent individuals exercising a comparable liberty to trespass *against them*. Though the non-indigent would have the same moral dispensation that the (faultless) indigents would have, the former would rarely (if ever) have occasion to exercise that dispensation. Thus, if there is a case to be made against a hiker who cannot compensate having a liberty of a certain extent to trespass on Owner's property, it has to be made in terms of the cost to that hiker of the indirect blowback of everyone's having that liberty to trespass. That is to say, it has to be made in terms of the indirect cost to that hiker if everyone were to have a liberty of that degree and, hence, if people were to act as they would if everyone were to have that exemption. If the cost to a hiker that would flow from everyone's having an increased dispensation to trespass would exceed the local gain to the hiker of having that increased dispensation, then the hiker would be better off without that increase in his (and hence in everyone's) dispensation. Thus, even from his own perspective, he cannot hold that a moral code that denies this increased dispensation is unreasonable. A moral code that denies this increased dispensation—while perhaps allowing a lesser exemption—is, on the whole, better for him than one that incorporates this increased dispensation. Similarly, if there is a case against the everyday indigent individual's having a liberty of a certain extent to trespass upon us, it has to be made (at least very largely)[32] in terms of the cost to that indigent individual of the indirect blowback of everyone's having that liberty of trespass.

We have, in effect, already envisioned the case against the indigent individual's having an unlimited Hobbesian liberty to trespass and the case against the indigent individual's having even the somewhat limited Benthamite liberty to trespass. But to see more clearly why such cases can be made and what liberties to trespass may survive, it is useful to go back to hikers F and S (Freezing Hiker and Sore Hiker) and to see why the indirect blowback on hikers increases as the level of loss to a hiker that triggers a dispensation from the obligation not to trespass is lowered. My hypothesis is that the cost to potentially endangered or discomforted hikers of the blowback from all hikers' having a dispensation will exceed the advantage to hikers of having that dispensation when the level of loss that triggers the dispensation is lower than serious lasting injury. The analogue hypothesis for everyday society is that the cost to potentially loss-suffering individuals of the blowback from all individuals' having a dispensation will exceed the advantage to those individuals of having that dispensation when the level of loss that triggers the dispensation is lower than serious lasting injury.

Here is the reasoning behind these hypotheses, cast in terms of wilderness hikers and the blowback cost to them of increasing permissive dispensations. Freezing hikers who need to break locks and so on in order to escape death are much rarer than sore hikers who need to break locks and so on in order to alleviate their discomfort. If hikers have only the liberty to break and burn in order to escape death, owners will face a much lower probability of this sort of trespass upon their cabins than they will face if hikers have the liberty to trespass in order to escape (considerable) discomfort. Besides there being *now* lots more sore hikers than freezing hikers, think of how many more sore hikers there will be when word gets around that they are morally at liberty to trespass to ameliorate their prospective discomfort. (In contrast, a liberty to trespass to save oneself from freezing to death—a liberty which one will be in a position to exercise only if one stumbles upon a suitable cabin—is not likely to increase the number of freezing hikers.) For these reasons alone, owners will have much less incentive to install strong locks, camouflage their cabins, or relocate them to warmer climes if hikers have only the narrow liberty of trespass rather than the broader liberty.

[32] I say "very largely," and not "entirely," because the indigent individual may well not remain indigent; thus, he may well become subject to the permissible trespasses being considered.

Moreover, many a cabin owner won't really mind a (faultlessly) freezing hiker saving himself through breaking her lock and burning her wood. Indeed, many such owners may positively value this happening. In contrast, many owners will really mind (faultlessly) sore hikers mitigating their discomfort through breaking the owners' locks and burning their wood. Owners may very well spend less to make their cabins less vulnerable to trespass by freezing hikers than it would be rational for them to do as pure *Homines economici* (economic men), and may very well spend more to make their cabins less vulnerable to trespass by sore hikers than it would be rational for them to do as pure *Homines economici*. The upshot is that there will be considerably fewer cabins available for breaking into if individuals are also at liberty to engage in break-ins in order to mitigate their discomfort than there will be if individuals are only at liberty to engage in break-ins in order to escape death. Since hikers (rationally) care very much more about escaping death than about mitigating their discomfort, they (rationally) have to prefer that the more permissive exemption not be added to a moral code that already contains the less permissive exemption. They cannot say that a morality that allows the lesser exemption but denies the greater exemption is insufficiently solicitous of their interests.

So it looks like an interesting and nonarbitrary line can be drawn between a dispensation that is triggered by a hiker's prospective death and one that is triggered by his prospective discomfort. But where between death and discomfort does the line fall? As I have said, my hypothesis is that it is nearer to death. Suppose hikers were also to have the liberty to trespass whenever this is necessary for them to escape deforming frostbite or permanent (or even long-term) loss of health. This would increase the percentage of hikers at liberty to intrude upon the cabins of owners, but it would not increase by much the total number of hikers having this exemption. This is because the addition of a liberty to trespass on a cabin—if one can find one—to escape from disfigurement or long-term loss of health is not going to recruit many more people into the ranks of wilderness hikers. Moreover, many (absentee) cabin owners will not mind being subject to trespass by individuals who (faultlessly) must engage in it in order to avoid frostbite disfigurement or long-term loss of health.[33] Thus, extending the liberty to trespass (to this extent) will not much diminish the likelihood of an endangered hiker's finding a cabin that he can break into. It will diminish the likelihood somewhat, but this seems to be offset by the value to hikers of not being morally required to grin and bear disfiguring frostbite or long-term loss of health.

However, as we extend the dispensation much beyond this point, we get a dispensation the consequences of which are less favorable to hikers

[33] The exception here would be the rare case of a hiker who must do more than minor damage to escape his dire straits and who, therefore, operates under dispensation (d).

than a less extensive dispensation; for we get both a substantial increase in the percentage of hikers who will be at liberty to trespass and, I think, a marked increase in the hiking population. For just this reason, then, owners will be moved to improve their locks, camouflage their cabins, build in warmer climes, and so on. Moreover, owners are likely increasingly to mind trespasses by hikers as the degree of the danger that hikers escape through trespass diminishes. Owners are likely to be more strongly moved to decrease the opportunities for trespass than they would be as pure *Homines economici*. Thus, as the liberty to trespass is extended much beyond the liberty to trespass to escape loss of life, limb, or health, the supply of cabins susceptible to trespass drops, and it seems as though the drop in supply accelerates as soon as owners' distaste for being trespassed upon becomes more salient than their sympathy for not-very-endangered hikers. (This point will vary from owner to owner.) At least beyond the liberty to trespass to escape loss of life, limb, or health, increases in liberty to trespass blow back toward those to whom the liberty is ascribed in the form of an accelerating drop in the supply of cabins susceptible to trespass. This drop in the supply of cabins susceptible to trespass is not offset by the more extensive liberty that can be exercised by the hiker if he (nevertheless) finds a cabin susceptible to trespass, for the loss escaped by the hiker whose escape is allowed only by the more extensive exemption is not a major loss.

In the truncated world of hikers and owners, the blowback toward hikers of a permissive dispensation from the obligation not to trespass on cabins comes entirely from the incentives the dispensation provides to owners (especially in light of a prospective increase in the number of hikers) to better barricade or camouflage their cabins or not to build in the freezing wilderness. But the permissive dispensation does not negatively affect the level of productive economic activity in the non-wilderness segment of society and, thus, does not negatively affect how much wealth there is to build cabins or keep them in useable condition. Suppose, however, that a dispensation more permissive than the life, limb, and health dispensation were part of the moral code for society at large. Property in general would then be substantially more likely to be subject to permissible trespass than if the code included only the life, limb, and health dispensation. Recall that as the dispensation becomes more permissive—as the cost to the "endangered" individual that engenders a liberty to trespass drops—the number of individuals who enjoy that dispensation rises at a greater rate. Statically, this is because more people within the current population come under the umbrella of the expanding dispensation. Dynamically, this is because as more of an umbrella is provided, more people will go out in the rain. As the dispensation becomes more permissive, then, one gets a substantial decrease in the security of property. It is not that some property is taken away and that is that. Rather, it is that all property (in practice, no doubt, some types of property more than other types) is subject to a substantial but not very calculable risk of permissible trespass.

Each owner is directly somewhat less well off, just as each wilderness cabin owner is directly somewhat less well off if the dispensation for hikers becomes more permissive. But owner O_1 will also be less well off because prospective trading partner O_2 is less secure in her capacity to determine by her choice what will be done with her holdings; for this will make O_2 a less attractive trading partner for O_1 (and vice versa). Beyond this, O_1 will be less well off in virtue of O_3 and O_4 being less eligible trading partners to one another; for, except when O_1 is a direct competitor of either O_3 or O_4, the more nifty mutually beneficial interactions there are between O_3 and O_4, the more attractive as trading partners they will become for O_1 (and vice versa). And so on. *All* are likely to be worse off because of the general undermining of mutually beneficial bilateral interactions between owners *and* between owners and *nonowners* (of extrapersonal holdings). As we noted with respect to a Benthamite liberty of trespass, as dispensations become more permissive, this increasingly deprives people—including nonowners—of the positive externalities of life within a smoothly functioning market order. As a general (society-wide) dispensation becomes more permissive, that which is available to be trespassed upon by people who are in dire straits (and who would be at liberty to trespass under a less permissive dispensation) diminishes. Moreover, there will be more people in dire straits because of the undermining of economically productive interaction.

Rights protect individuals in their capacity to determine by their own choice how they will act—including how they will deploy the resources that they have acquired for the sake of carrying out their respective valued plans. Right-holders benefit, of course, from their possession of (respected) rights, but others benefit as well. I have concentrated here on the benefit to others—other property owners and other nonowners—derived from the productive economic actions and interactions that secure enjoyment of rights engenders. However, we should not forget a harder to quantify general benefit that rights and respect for them provide. Rights provide resolutions of disputes about how particular resources will be employed—resolutions that do not hopelessly appeal to claims about which employment of those resources would most advance some specious social good. The nice resolution is that the party who has rights over a particular resource gets to determine by her choice what is done with the resource. We need only determine who has jurisdiction over the resource whose use is in dispute to know which deployment of it—the deployment favored by the owner—is to be allowed and protected.[34] The more extensive dispensations are, the more this nice mechanism for resolving

[34] Obviously, those who favor a different use of the resource have an opportunity to put their money where their mouths are.

social disputes is disrupted and the more the local internal benefits and the general external benefits of this mechanism will be lost. The point, then, of this and the two preceding paragraphs is that there is more reason not to extend a liberty to trespass (beyond something like the life, limb, and health dispensation) if we are thinking in terms of a general, society-wide dispensation than if we are thinking in terms of a dispensation only for wilderness hikers.

In the next section, I turn to the taxation implications of these rudimentary thoughts about the types of dispensations that individuals in dire straits have and how dire the straits have to be in order for them to obtain. Before doing so, however, I want to try to deal explicitly with a natural objection to the form of argument I have been offering. Suppose Sore Hiker responds as follows to the argument that it is not reasonable for morality to include an exemption permissive enough to allow him to trespass:

> My concern is with my specific situation here and now. I have stumbled upon a cabin susceptible to trespass. It will be costly to me in terms of soreness and discomfort not to trespass. I understand the argument that the cabin is the rightful property of Owner and, for *that* reason, I must bear the cost of complying with that right. But once you allow that the costliness of compliance may exempt someone from compliance, I want to know why the costliness of my compliance *here and now* does not exempt me. I do not see the relevance of all this talk about how Abstract Hiker is better served by a moral system that does not include a liberty to trespass in circumstances like those I am in here and now. (Isn't this the sort of talk about abstract individuals beyond veils of ignorance to which libertarian theorists usually object?) Of course, I am not saying that I am the only hiker with the liberty to trespass in order to escape discomfort. I am quite willing here and now to say that all hikers have this degree of dispensation—though, of course, I recognize that, insofar as this liberty obtains and actual and potential owners respond to it, lots less hikers in *their* here and now will stumble upon cabins to break into—even to escape from death.

Here is my answer to Sore Hiker's objection:

> A crucial feature of dispensations from the requirement not to infringe upon rights is their tendency to generate blowback—their tendency to generate negative externalities or to undermine positive externalities. For this reason the relevant assessment of a proposed further dispensation must be prospective and dynamic. That is, besides considering what individuals who receive this further exemption would gain if the inclusion of it within a refined doctrine of rights would not

> generate any blowback, we must consider what individuals receiving the dispensation would lose as a consequence of everyone's having the proposed further exemption. Sore Hiker's static assessment—*after* he knows that whatever blowback there has been has passed him by—is not the appropriate sort of assessment for proposed refinements that tend toward blowback. The appropriate assessment must (also) be dynamic—and this necessarily means prospective and probabilistic.

Moreover, the static assessments of some less-lucky hikers will conflict with lucky Sore Hiker's static assessment. These unlucky hikers, including most strikingly some of those in danger of death, disfigurement, or long-term ill health, will, when making their assessment *from their here and now,* rationally bemoan the inclusion of this liberty to trespass to avoid discomfort. For, in their cases, the nonavailability of cabins susceptible to life-, limb-, or health-saving trespasses will be due to the inclusion of that dispensation. Thus, if we sanction static assessments like Sore Hiker's, every proposed dispensation will be both reasonable and unreasonable.[35] Only the dynamic analysis will enable us to avoid such conflicting assessments.

V. Out of the Trespass Frying Pan and into the Taxation Fire

An important difference between the everyday social world and the truncated world of the winter wilderness is that in the former there is a significant prospect of interactions between owners (of apple pies, recreational vehicles, homes and businesses) and individuals who possess or appear to possess some dispensation from the obligation to respect the owners' property. Owners or their agents will face the big problem of differentiating among the trespassers they may encounter—the problem of determining whether any given approaching trespasser has any dispensation and (more difficult yet) determining what specific mode of dispensation (if any) this approaching trespasser has. Yet the permissibility of the response of owners or their agents depends upon what dispensation, if any, the trespasser has. If an owner fails to identify correctly whether an approaching trespasser has a dispensation, or fails to identify correctly what mode of dispensation that approaching trespasser has, that owner will either overreact or underreact to the pending trespass. She may overreact by either forcibly or nonforcibly thwarting a trespass when

[35] The language of "static" versus "dynamic" assessment almost certainly comes to my mind because of its use in David Schmidtz's essay "Taking Responsibility," in David Schmidtz and Robert Goodin, *Social Welfare and Individual Responsibility* (Cambridge: Cambridge University Press, 1998).

it is not permissible for her to do so—because the trespasser possesses dispensation (b). Or she may overreact by resisting the trespass with harmful force when only nonforcible resistance is permissible—because the trespasser possesses dispensation (c). She may underreact if she desists from any resistance in the false belief that the trespasser has dispensation (b) or if she desists from forcible resistance in the false belief that the trespasser has dispensation (c). It is bad to overreact because this wrongs the trespasser in dire straits; it is bad to underreact because the owner thereby forgoes the permissible protection of her property.

The prospect of overreaction and apparent overreaction on the part of owners and their agents to approaching trespassers, and the prospect of overreaction or apparent overreaction on the part of trespassers to the actions of owners and their agents, is precisely the prospect of escalation of actual and apparent partial and full Hobbesian micro-states of nature into micro-wars of each against each. Indeed, the numbers of individuals who will have some dispensation or who may take themselves to have some dispensation, combined with the prospect of actual or apparent overreaction against these individuals, combined with the prospect of individuals who possess or take themselves to possess one or another dispensation themselves reacting or overreacting to the reactions against their anticipated trespasses, adds up to the prospect of pervasive micro and not-so-micro wars of each against each. Moreover, while diverse owners may have friends or employees who are willing to join them in a bit of Hobbesian smack-down (even at the cost of opening themselves up to permissible counter-force), there may also be champions of the folks in dire or apparently dire straits who are eager to mix it up with the owners and their capitalist lackeys. The prospect of third parties acting as agents for owners and other third parties acting as agents for trespassers adds further fuel to the Hobbesian fires. Recall also that, insofar as actual partial or full Hobbesian micro-states of nature exist between a given owner and a given indigent individual, neither party can expect the official *neutral* rights-protecting agencies of his or her society to intervene on his or her behalf.

Lastly, even if all and only actual possessors of dispensations had highly visible badges of their status and owners were prepared to surrender whatever would enable those in dire straits to escape the loss of life, limb, or health, the resulting world of unpredictable permissible intrusions and acquiescence to those intrusions would be unsettling to the owners—above and beyond the economic costs they would incur. "Good evening, sir," says the certified local (faultless) indigent individual, after one answers the knock on one's front door. "This evening, in the exercise of my dispensation, I have chosen to have dinner with your family in your lovely dining room." Or: "Good afternoon, madam. Today I have chosen to exercise my dispensation by reaching into your car and removing the emergency cash you keep in the car's ash tray."

Or: "Good morning, Motel 6 owner. I presume you've been keeping that light on for me."

Thus, if rights are non-absolute to something like the extent I have suggested, and non-absolute in something like the range of different ways I have suggested, then the social world is going to be at least somewhat dangerous, morally risky, and irritatingly messy both for owners and for nonowners—including nonowners who are not in dire straits. Those in dire straits are, by definition, not in a position to eliminate the "underlying causes" of this danger, moral riskiness, and messiness—namely, those dire straits and the dispensations that they engender. But those against whom those dispensations would operate can eliminate those underlying causes.[36] Without going beyond the broadest generalities, what would do the trick is some system for certifying that individuals are faultlessly (or faultlessly enough) in sufficiently dire straits (e.g., in danger of loss of life, limb, or health), coupled with a system of provision of a minimal income (perhaps in the form of vouchers for shelter, food, and basic medical care) that would undo that direness. Our early contrast between the freezing hiker who is capable of compensating the cabin owner, and the freezing hiker who is not, suggests one slightly more specific feature of the proposed system. The recipients who are capable of compensating for the aid that gets them out of dire straits would be required, in exchange for assistance, to exercise the skills that make them capable of compensation. That is, they would be recipients of workfare rather than welfare. Aside from helping out those in dire straits, such a system would absolutize property rights, that is, it would remove the conditions that trigger dispensations from the obligation to respect those rights. Thus, it would benefit owners (and nonowners) by generating the positive externalities of a regime of well-defined, certain, and secure rights.

An obvious complicating factor here is that it may not be feasible to restrict the benefits of this absolutization to those who voluntarily fund the system of aid that engenders it. As the familiar story goes, the publicness of these benefits may so remove the incentive for individuals to pay for the system that the system will not get funded voluntarily (or will be significantly underfunded). Whether that story would be plausible depends on lots of things that we do not know—for example, how much the system would cost, what the total gain from the system would be to potential contributors, and what clever techniques could be devised to exclude noncontributors from free-riding on the system.[37] Nevertheless, let us add to our premises the *assumption* that this story is plausible. Then, to reach the conclusion that the beneficiaries of this system (other than

[36] Of course, there will always be the kinds of dire straits into which someone—e.g., one of our wilderness hikers—may stumble.

[37] The administrators of a system that is less well-funded than it would be if all contributed to it may discover that they can only afford to give those in dire straits free rides by bus to the homes of the noncontributors.

those removed from dire straits) may be required to fund it, we need one more, but only one more, premise. That is the narrow normative premise that I mentioned in the discussion of the public-goods refinement of our understanding of property rights (in Section I). According to this normative premise, individuals may be required to contribute to the funding of a public good if it really is not feasible to fund it voluntarily *and* if the good that each receives in return is the greater realization of his or her rights. Given all the other premises, this final narrow principle is enough because a system that removes the dire straits that engender dispensations from the obligations to abide by rights absolutizes those rights.[38] Such is the argument from the non-absoluteness of rights to the justification within a rights-oriented libertarian theory for taxation to fund a social safety-net.

VI. Conclusion

In this essay, I have argued that the non-absoluteness of rights has to be taken seriously. It has to be taken more seriously than it is when friends of rights acknowledge certain cases in which acts that would normally violate rights are permissible, but then confine those cases to the far outer limits of our moral experience. I have also argued that friends of rights and friends of taxation are both correct to think that, if one takes the non-absoluteness of rights seriously, one is on the road to some vindication of taxation—indeed, taxation to relieve the dire straits in which some people may faultlessly find themselves. I have also argued, however, that friends of rights and friends of taxation are both wrong to think that, if one takes the non-absoluteness of rights seriously, one is on a short road to taxation. The road is long and convoluted and full of potholes that will be welcomed by enemies of taxation and bemoaned by friends of taxation. It is long and convoluted and full of potholes because the non-absoluteness of rights involves different modes of dispensation, none of which implies obligations on the part of legitimate owners to assist those in dire straits and most of which allow legitimate owners to thwart (albeit sometimes not by way of harmful force) the permissible infringements upon their rights. The length, convolutions, and potholes show how much exploration has to be done to understand the non-absoluteness of rights and the true significance of their non-absoluteness.

Philosophy, Tulane University

[38] That is, it absolutizes them except with respect to the right-holders' being subject to taxation to support such public goods.

TAXATION, THE PRIVATE LAW, AND DISTRIBUTIVE JUSTICE*

By Kevin A. Kordana and David H. Tabachnick

I. Introduction

Taxation is traditionally conceived of as the sector of the public law through which governments raise revenue needed for their justifiable distributive aims. The rules of tax law, in this view, control the manner in which governments raise revenue, while rules of transfer guide government spending. Distributive aims are understood to be met largely through selecting and implementing, from among competing "tax and transfer" schemes, that scheme which best serves the demands of a conception of tax policy. The question of what constitutes justified distributive aims varies, of course, from political theory to political theory. Some theories maintain, for example, that governments may rightly use systems of tax and transfer (only) for the provision of public goods (i.e., nonrivalrous, nonexcludable goods) and the protection of basic rights. Other theories maintain that governments might justifiably engage in additional taxation for the provision of goods that are not, strictly speaking, public goods (e.g., hospitals, schools, and the arts), as well as the provision of economic distributions to the poor or needy (e.g., food and housing subsidies).

Our aim in this essay, however, is *not* to directly weigh in on this debate (roughly) between libertarians and liberals over the proper aims of taxation. Instead, we intend to focus on somewhat more basic questions concerning "equity-oriented values"[1] and distributive justice, and their justificatory relationship to taxation and the private law. We are interested in the questions of what exactly constitutes the proper domain of taxation and what taxation's proper relationship is to the private law.[2] In partic-

* We are grateful to John G. Bennett, Harry Dolan, Edward McCaffery, and Ellen Frankel Paul for written comments on a previous draft and to Eric Mack, Fred Miller, Jeffrey Paul, A. John Simmons, and the other contributors to this volume for valuable discussions.

[1] We use the phrase "equity-oriented values" to mean values that serve as the basis for legal rules that are not justified solely by concerns of either (1) negative rights or (2) wealth-maximization. As we use the phrase, "equity-oriented values" include, for example, charity, beneficence, equality, and utility, and are not limited to matters of the moral value of *equality*, per se.

[2] We employ, for the purposes of this essay, the conventional distinction between public and private law: namely, on the one hand, areas of law in which the state is a party to legal actions (for example, taxation, criminal law, and constitutional law), and, on the other hand, areas of law where the state merely provides rules and judicial fora for the enforcement of legal action, but private parties conduct legal actions against one another (for example, tort

ular, can the rules of the private law, as a matter of principle, be justifiably leveraged in service of equity-oriented values and, if so, why? Taxation is traditionally conceived as an independent module limited to the rules of tax and transfer schemes. An interesting question arises, however, over whether the very values that serve as the normative underpinning of tax and transfer schemes, in particular a conception of *justice,* may also (as a matter of principle) serve as the normative basis for creating private-law rules that assist in meeting bona fide equity-oriented aims.

We maintain that the answers to our questions (unsurprisingly) turn to a large extent upon one's conception of political theory and—importantly—upon one's conception of private property. In addressing our questions, we distinguish between two important camps in contemporary political theory: on the one hand, those who hold deontic "pre-institutional" or (roughly) Lockean "natural right" conceptions of private property (for example, libertarians and Lockean liberals); and, on the other hand, those who hold maximizing "post-institutional" conceptions of property (for example, Rawlsians[3] and some utilitarians).

For deontic pre-institutional liberals, property claims derive their moral force from the commitment to a prepolitical or pre-institutional moral doctrine. In this view, the authority of a justified system of property law is derived from the moralized prepolitical account of natural rights in property. In contrast, political liberals who hold a maximizing post-institutional conception of property maintain that private property is a political institution constructed in service of distributive aims.

We argue that for such post-institutional theorists—for example, Rawlsians employing the difference principle (maximizing the position of the least well-off), or utilitarians employing the utility principle (maximizing general utility)—taxation cannot be *conceptually* independent of the private law. In post-institutional maximizing conceptions, the entirety of law must answer to the demands of the overarching distributive scheme. Our central claim with regard to post-institutional maximizing theorists is that there are no conceptually *independent* or distinct principles of taxation—

and contract). See, e.g., Jeffrie G. Murphy and Jules L. Coleman, *Philosophy of Law,* rev. ed. (Boulder, CO: Westview Press, 1990), 143–46.

[3] We consider Rawls's two principles of justice to be maximizing principles. They demand that the complete scheme of legal and political institutions adopted (in comparison with all other potential schemes) maximizes the position of the least well-off in terms of primary goods (subject to the liberty constraints generated by the maximizing component of the first principle and to the opportunity principle, taken in lexical priority). The principles of justice are properly viewed as not only consequentialist, but also maximizing, in this inter-schemic selection. This is correct even given the fact that the values embodied in the principles of justice are informed by deontic considerations (i.e., in the first principle, equal liberty, and, in the second, the egalitarian considerations embodied in the difference principle). It is correct even given the fact that people living within the selected scheme are not required to act so as to maximize anything (i.e., are not required directly to apply the maximands of the principles of justice). The principles of justice are thus consequentialist and maximizing in their application in the inter-schemic comparisons they make in selecting the complete scheme of legal and political institutions.

there is no philosophically interesting distinction between "taxation" and the "private law." For such theorists, we maintain that both taxation and the private law are matters of distribution.

In contrast, we argue that the situation is different for theorists who hold a deontic pre-institutional conception of property. Since such views do not conceive of justice as flowing directly from an overarching distributive scheme (or set of distributive principles) that defines a conception of justice, the private law does not answer to the demands of distributive justice. Thus, there *is* for such pre-institutional theorists *conceptual* space for a distinct body of private law—independent of distributive demands or aims. The private law for such pre-institutional theorists can claim a conceptual or normative independence from distributive aims. We argue, however, that this independence of the private law from distributive justice does not entail that, for at least some such pre-institutional views, the private law cannot reflect equity-oriented values. We maintain that while some such pre-institutional theorists may justifiably leverage the rules of the private law to reflect equity-oriented concerns, an interesting question arises as to whether or not meeting such concerns can properly be understood (for them) as a matter of *justice*.

In Section II, we discuss the maximizing post-institutional conception of taxation, property, and the private law. In Section III, we discuss the deontic pre-institutional conception of property and the role that taxation and equity-oriented values play in such pre-institutional schemes. Section IV provides a conclusion.

II. Taxation and the Private Law for Post-Institutional Maximizing Theorists

The traditional or conventional view of taxation holds that justified tax and transfer schemes must meet the demands of some independent conception of tax policy (e.g., the benefit principle[4] or the equal sacrifice principle[5]). In their philosophical treatment of tax policy, *The Myth of Ownership: Taxes and Justice,* Liam Murphy and Thomas Nagel argue against this conventional view, maintaining that tax policy is of only instrumental

[4] The benefit principle is the principle of tax policy according to which people should be taxed in proportion to the benefits they receive from the state. "Benefit" is typically understood as measured against the baseline of life in the absence of a state. See Liam Murphy and Thomas Nagel, *The Myth of Ownership: Taxes and Justice* (New York: Oxford University Press, 2002), 16.

[5] The equal sacrifice principle is the principle of tax policy according to which taxation should reduce the welfare of each taxpayer by the same amount, measured against a baseline of pretax market outcomes. Given the diminishing marginal utility of money, equal sacrifice does not entail equal or even proportional taxation in dollar terms. The equal sacrifice principle distinguishes taxpayers according to their income, creating post-tax incomes that equally reduce the welfare (given the diminishing marginal utility of money) of each taxpayer, as compared to a pretax baseline. Ibid., 24.

value to meeting the demands of the overarching requirements of distributive justice. Therefore, they argue, independent modules of tax policy analysis are morally irrelevant (indeed, incoherent). There are no questions of justice or fairness that are independent matters of tax policy.[6] While we have elsewhere argued that this claim is overbroad—that it is not true for all forms of political liberalism[7]—we have also commented that "Murphy and Nagel's argument is most powerful if one's conception of distributive justice is maximizing or teleological."[8]

Consider a conception of liberalism with a post-institutional view of property (i.e., property is viewed as merely conventional, rather than natural) and a maximizing theory of distribution (e.g., Rawlsianism or utilitarianism). Given that property is merely instrumental, and because the demands of distributive justice are maximizing, the tax system is required to satisfy (in conjunction with other institutions) the demands of the distributive principles. (Again, these principles might be Rawlsian or utilitarian, but their content is unimportant for present purposes. We will refer to them below as "the distributive principles" without specifying their content.) This implies that tax-specific notions of justice or fairness (e.g., perhaps those tied to the benefit principle, or to "fairness" in the tax base)[9] are irrelevant. To the extent that these notions conflict with a tax policy that violates their tenets but better satisfies the demands of the distributive justice aim, they will be ignored, and the tax policy violating their tenets will be implemented, in service of the overarching demands of distributive justice. This is what Murphy and Nagel mean when they argue that tax policy is merely instrumental to the aims of the distributive scheme.

Interestingly, in this view, tax policy, while merely instrumental, is immune to (new) charges of unfairness—even if, for example, it were to feature a striking absence of uniformity in the tax base.[10] This is because the conception of distributive justice *defines* fairness. The entire tax system is therefore suffused with "fairness"—it has been constructed in order

[6] Ibid., 98–99: "[C]hoice of tax base has only instrumental significance for economic justice.... [T]he issue of the tax base does not disappear, but it takes on a purely instrumental significance as far as justice is concerned: Different tax bases may be better or worse suited to the tax system's task of helping to secure just social outcomes."

[7] Kevin A. Kordana and David H. Tabachnick, "Tax and the Philosopher's Stone," *Virginia Law Review* 89, no. 3 (2003): 655–56.

[8] Ibid., 654.

[9] For example, it is sometimes argued that fairness requires a measure of equity in the tax base—i.e., in what is taxed (income, consumption, "sin," etc.).

[10] "Since justice in taxation is not a matter of a fair distribution of tax burdens measured against a pretax baseline, it cannot be important in itself what pretax characteristics of taxpayers determine tax shares." Murphy and Nagel, *The Myth of Ownership*, 98. "[Y]ou may still feel the force of the initial intuition: Isn't it *obviously* unfair to tax food more heavily than clothes . . . ?" Ibid., 108 (emphasis in original).

best to satisfy the demands of the distributive principles, which define justice or fairness.[11]

Importantly, however, this argument may be pressed even further. If tax policy is, for the post-institutional, maximizing theorist, understood as entirely instrumental to meeting the demands of distributive justice, then tax policy has lost any principled claim to play a unique role in distributive justice. For post-institutional maximizing theorists, *all* economic matters—not only the system of tax and transfer, but also matters of the private law (i.e., property, contract, tort, etc.)—are properly understood, conceptually and normatively, as distributive concerns.[12]

That is, for post-institutional maximizing theorists, there is no principled distinction between taxation and the sectors of what are traditionally understood to be matters of the private law. For such theorists, all economic matters, including matters of the private law, are to be constructed in service of the post-institutional distributive scheme. Therefore, theories that hold a post-institutional, maximizing conception of property lack the resources to draw a principled distinction between taxation and the pri-

[11] Kordana and Tabachnick, "Tax and the Philosopher's Stone," 664: "The reference to 'intrinsic fairness' and talk of 'instrumentality' diverts attention from the fact that, for Murphy and Nagel, the choice of tax base should be understood as *suffused* with fairness. It is this very fact that . . . makes arguments grounded in *new* fairness claims incoherent. In other words, we think that the best way to understand Murphy and Nagel's view is to imagine that the response to . . . fairness claims . . . is not the rather puzzling 'choices of the tax base are purely instrumental' but rather, 'fairness has been taken care of already'" (emphasis in original).

[12] To be clear, our discussion is limited to post-institutional theorists for whom the conception of private property is maximizing. This, however, is not exhaustive of all post-institutional views. There are nonmaximizing post-institutionalists; see, for example, Jean-Jacques Rousseau, *On the Social Contract*, in *The Basic Political Writings*, trans. Donald A. Cress (Indianapolis, IN: Hackett Publishing Co., 1987), bk. 1, chap. IX. One might object that Rawls is not a post-institutional maximizing theorist with regard to the private law, since the difference principle is the second of two lexicographically ordered principles and is itself constrained by conditions of fair equality of opportunity. This objection holds that considerations other than economic distribution are at stake. For instance, one might argue on the basis of Rawls's first principle that private law must be independent of economic distributive considerations (for Rawls, first-principle matters are distributive albeit not economic). Our response is this: for Rawls the construction of a property baseline is a second-principle (i.e., economic) matter, and since private-law constructions require a property baseline, contract and tort law must, therefore, also be second-principle matters. Rawls does allow that the first principle of justice constructs what he calls personal property, and we have argued elsewhere that (analogously) the first principle may require (at the most abstract level) that (at least) some contracting options be open. See Kevin A. Kordana and David H. Tabachnick, "Rawls and Contract Law," *George Washington Law Review* 73, no. 3 (2005): 609. Our point, however, is that the specific details of rights of ownership, transfer, and compensation for harm require a property baseline that is not available at the first-principle level; thus, the private law is, for Rawls, a second-principle matter constructed in service of maximizing the position of the least well-off. See John Rawls, *A Theory of Justice* (Cambridge, MA: Harvard University Press, 1971), 298. This point would seem to hold true for any post-institutional view of property constructed in service of maximizing distributive concerns. Since, in such a view, the details of the private law (e.g., transfer and compensation for harm) are constitutive of the property construction, independent (or pre-institutional) conceptions of private law are rendered incoherent.

vate law. For such theories there is no independent subject of taxation—there is simply government action that is instrumental to the distributive scheme and government action that is not. For post-institutional maximizing theorists, there is no public/private distinction in economic matters that patterns deontic pre-institutional commitments[13] and therefore no subject of tax law independent of all other areas of economic governance.

In this view, not just tax policy but all of a society's legal and political institutions[14] must be designed in instrumentalist fashion to the satisfaction of the demands of the distributive principles. Just as independent metrics of tax policy are rendered irrelevant by the demands of distributive justice, so too are independent metrics of justice in contract law (e.g., Charles Fried's contract-as-promise)[15] and bankruptcy (e.g., the principle of respecting prebankruptcy entitlements as much as possible).[16] Rules of contract and bankruptcy—as well as the rest of the private law—are constructed to serve, instrumentally, the demands of the distributive scheme. Such rules cannot coherently reflect commitments to other (independent) goals or values. Note as well that, due to the lack of commitment to other values, such bodies of law might not be constructed at all; that is, they would be constructed if and only if their existence were instrumental to meeting the demands of the distributive principles.

Thus, for the post-institutional maximizing theorist, distributive justice is not, at the level of principle or theory, tied to taxation and transfer.[17]

[13] For a contrasting view, see Arthur Ripstein, "The Division of Responsibility and the Law of Tort," *Fordham Law Review* 72, no. 5 (2004): 1814–15: "Tort law protects property as well as persons, however, so a Rawlsian account of its normative structure must take account of property, and explain how it can merit protection as a matter of justice. Justice requires that private law—tort, contract, property and unjust enrichment—have a certain kind of independence. . . . [P]articular transactions can be judged on their own terms, rather than being subordinated to distributive justice. The same point applies to property, and to the involuntary transactions governed by tort law" (footnote omitted).

[14] More precisely, this statement applies to the set of legal and political institutions subject to the domain of the distributive principles. It is possible that the maximand's domain might be limited. See Kordana and Tabachnick, "Rawls and Contract Law," 602 and n. 16.

[15] Charles Fried, *Contract as Promise: A Theory of Contractual Obligation* (Cambridge, MA: Harvard University Press, 1981), 17. Fried argues that what separates contractual liability from other forms of liability is the moral significance of a promise. Barring procedural defects, contracts are understood to be fair because they embody the "will" of the consenting (promising) parties. In Fried's view, the conception of justice in transaction (again, barring procedural defects) is *endogenous* to the "will" of the parties. External values (e.g., general welfare or economic efficiency) are not capable of imposing *contractual* duties or liability.

[16] Thomas H. Jackson, *The Logic and Limits of Bankruptcy Law* (Cambridge, MA: Harvard University Press, 1986), 27–33.

[17] Of course, the locus of equity-oriented moves might be concentrated, based on instrumental concerns, in a particular area of law. See, e.g., Louis Kaplow and Steven Shavell, "Why the Legal System Is Less Efficient Than the Income Tax in Redistributing Income," *Journal of Legal Studies* 23, no. 2 (1994): 667. Our point is that it is important to keep in mind that such a concentration does not arise as a matter of principle. It is the very lack of a principled distinction between tax and the private law that allows the evaluation of instrumentalist trade-offs to be made between the various bodies of law.

The entire scheme of political and legal institutions, including the private law, is subject to the demands of distributive justice. That complete scheme of political and legal institutions which best satisfies the distributive principles will be selected. Schemes of taxation and transfer are not the particular or exclusive domain of distributive justice.

To illustrate, take an example from the private law—bankruptcy—in conjunction with taxation, and consider how a post-institutional maximizing theorist would go about constructing a system of bankruptcy. There are various possibilities. First, and most simply, there might be no bankruptcy law. In other words, there need be nothing in the distributive principles that directly entails the existence of bankruptcy law. Second, to the extent that the scheme of political and legal institutions selected by the distributive principles were to have a fairly detailed system of private law in place, it seems likely that there would be some rules governing actions taken against insolvent persons and firms. For example, to the extent that a mandatory stay (of collection),[18] and/or a mandatory right to discharge of indebtedness in personal bankruptcy,[19] are welfare-enhancing, they might be required in order to (indirectly) satisfy the demands of the distributive principles. Thus, contracting options that might otherwise have been constructed as "open" or "free" (in the post-institutional sense) would be closed in order to make the stay and the right to discharge mandatory.

Thus, we can see that the post-institutional maximizing theorist cannot begin the inquiry into designing bankruptcy policy by appealing to an antecedently held (pre-institutional) conception of property or contract; nor can he begin within the framework of a traditional conception of bankruptcy law. Much of what jurists working within such a post-institutional scheme might come to deem "bankruptcy law" would arise through the opening and closing of contracting options, in service of the distributive principles. In other words, the distributive principles obliterate any notion of what bankruptcy law, or tax law, "should" look like (in pre-institutional terms). The distributive principles construct a complete scheme of political and legal institutions which, overall, best serves their demands. Lawyers operating within this scheme might label certain of its aspects "tax law" or "bankruptcy law" as a matter of their profession's division of labor, but there is no principled patterning of pre-institutional conceptions of property, contract, bankruptcy, or tax "fairness" in the post-institutional scheme. Instead, such bodies of law would have been selected for their usefulness in meeting the demands of the distributive principles.

The distributive principles might require that contracting options closed by traditional bankruptcy law (e.g., the mandatory stay) instead be constructed as open. In this case, the bankruptcy scheme might approximate

[18] Jackson, *The Logic and Limits of Bankruptcy Law,* 16–17.
[19] Ibid., 225.

something like that advocated by legal scholar Alan Schwartz, who advocates a more contractual approach to bankruptcy law, on grounds of its efficiency.[20] In contrast, if those contracting options were to be closed, it might look something like current law. In the latter case, the options might be closed for a variety of reasons—for example, those advocated by bankruptcy scholar Thomas Jackson or by the "traditional fairness camp."[21] But these last two illustrations are simply that—illustrations. The exact contours of bankruptcy policy (should it exist) need to respond to the demands of the distributive principles, not to pre-institutional values. The upshot is that taxation and transfer are not in any interesting philosophical sense distinct from other bodies of law: all are designed (in conjunction with one another) to best meet the demands of the distributive principles. For post-institutional maximizing theorists, all of law, not just "tax" law, is suffused with distributive aims and designed solely with those aims in mind.

To think otherwise, that is, to speak of whether a particular bankruptcy policy (or any other area of law) is more or less "fair" than another in isolation, would be to commit the fallacy of division. The modules of the private law, including bankruptcy policy, are not to be understood as fair or just in and of themselves; rather, each has a part in an overall scheme of distributive justice that is guaranteed to be fair.[22] The ultimate comparison is interschemic[23] (that is, between complete schemes, rather than between particular policies or subsets of distributive schemes).[24]

[20] Schwartz argues that the cost of capital is higher when lenders and borrowers face the application of mandatory bankruptcy terms in insolvency situations, rather than being able to select bankruptcy terms tailored to their particular situation. See Alan Schwartz, "Bankruptcy Contracting Reviewed," *Yale Law Journal* 109, no. 2 (1999): 344: "If there is a possibility that free contracting over bankruptcy systems would increase welfare, and if there otherwise is nothing wrong with free contracting, then free contracting should be permitted."

[21] Jackson argues that creditors face a "common pool" problem. That is, once a debtor is insolvent, creditors have an incentive to "race to the courthouse" to enforce their claims, which might result in the firm being dismembered piecemeal, even though creditors as a whole might be better off with a coordinated procedure (such as selling off the firm as a going concern). For Jackson, this justifies bankruptcy law's mandatory stay (of collection). Jackson, *The Logic and Limits of Bankruptcy Law*, 16–17.

The "traditional fairness camp" is concerned with job preservation, as being in the interest of workers and communities. Thus, its proponents tend to favor bankruptcy policies that will preserve a firm's operations as opposed to shutting them down.

[22] "[W]e cannot tell by looking only at the conduct of individuals and associations in the immediate (or local) circumstances whether, from a social point of view, agreements reached are just or fair. For this assessment depends importantly on the features of the basic structure, on whether it succeeds in maintaining background justice." John Rawls, "The Basic Structure as Subject," in Rawls, *Political Liberalism* (New York: Columbia University Press, 1996), 266–67.

[23] Thomas W. Pogge, *Realizing Rawls* (Ithaca, NY: Cornell University Press, 1989), 66–67.

[24] Of course, one could object that bankruptcy policies could be compared interschemically; that is, one policy could be compared to all other available policies. Our point here is that that independent judgment is only instrumentally relevant. The distributive principles must always adjudicate in favor of the overall or complete economic scheme that complies with the principles of justice.

Thus, for post-institutional theorists, arguments about property, contract, bankruptcy, and tax policy per se are moot. The post-institutional maximizing theorist needs to select bankruptcy policy as part of the overall scheme that best satisfies the distributive principles. While this is a complex endeavor, a simple example can help explain the spirit of the analysis, and highlight the essential unity between taxation and bankruptcy policy in such a scheme. Consider an economy with four agents: (1) a lender, (2) an owner/manager, (3) a worker, and (4) a disabled person. The nongovernmental economic transactions in this economy consist of the following: at t_0 the owner/manager borrows money from the lender, and the owner/manager uses this money to hire the worker and to invest in a research project. At t_1 the project has a 90 percent chance of succeeding, in which case the lender is repaid and the firm remains in business with the owner/manager having profited. Assume that, given such an outcome, the distributive principles would demand the taxation of the owner/manager's profits (and perhaps those of the lender) in order to make a transfer payment to improve the position of the disabled person (who otherwise has no income). Perhaps the worker would receive transfer payments as well. At any rate, bankruptcy policy would not be relevant at t_1 if the project succeeds (of course, at t_0 it might affect the interest rate charged by the lender, which in turn could affect the probability of the firm's solvency at t_1).

There is, however, a 10 percent chance that the research project will fail. In this event, assume that the firm is to be liquidated (perhaps because its liquidation value is greater than its going-concern value). There are two creditors of the firm: the lender and the worker. Post-dissolution, the worker will be jobless, so his economic position will fall to that of the disabled person. Consider two (of the many) possibilities for how the creditors are to share in the liquidation value of the firm: they could be treated equally (i.e., receive an equal percentage of their claim), or the worker could be preferred in some manner to the lender. If the worker is so preferred, he will have more assets going forward, and thus, presumably, will not require as many transfer payments as will the disabled person. If the worker is not so preferred, he will have fewer assets going forward, and presumably will require more transfer payments going forward than if he were preferred.

Our point is that, in essence, the post-institutional nature of the maximizing scheme has obliterated the principled distinction between bankruptcy policy and taxation, vis-à-vis the choice to be made in the preceding example. There is no principled reason for the post-institutional maximizing theorist to have an *ex ante* bankruptcy policy commitment either to treat the lender and the worker equally or to prefer the worker. Moreover, a worker preference operates as, in essence, a tax (here, on the lender). The post-institutional maximizing theorist would compare the consequence of imposing that sort of tax on the lender with the consequence of not doing so—that is, the worker falling all the way to the disabled person's position in society, which would likely require the imposition of some sort of other taxation (and transfer). Thus, taxation and the private law can be traded off against each other in meeting the demands of the distributive principles. In other words, a tax policy and a bankruptcy policy would ultimately be selected, but they would be those policies that best satisfy, in conjunction with the other areas of government action, the demands of the distributive principles—not those policies that satisfy any tax-specific or bankruptcy-specific goals. In this sense, the private law, for post-institutional theorists, is "tax."

The latter point, we think, has been insufficiently appreciated in the literature. For example, bankruptcy scholar Robert Rasmussen, apparently sensing a discrepancy between the bankruptcy policies advocated by the "traditional fairness camp" and what a prominent category of post-institutional maximizing theorists—Rawlsians—*ought* to think about bankruptcy law, has argued that a Rawlsian "would enact an economically-derived bankruptcy regime rather than current law."[25]

In his analysis, Rasmussen appears to recognize that, for a Rawlsian, bodies of law other than bankruptcy may be constructed in order to advance the position of the least well-off in the overall scheme of political and legal institutions. For example, Rasmussen seems to suggest that tort law would be a likely candidate as a subject of equity-oriented distribution. It is his conjecture that the tort regime could aim at reducing accidents in a manner maximally beneficial to the least well-off.[26] Rasmussen goes on to argue that even under the assumption that current bankruptcy law "saves some jobs in firms which experience financial distress that would be lost under an economic approach,"[27] a Rawlsian would reject that employment-preserving aspect of the current bankruptcy regime out of a concern that the increase in interest rates that results from such a policy causes more job losses throughout the economy than it saves in bankruptcy.[28]

For Rasmussen, the preference for lower interest rates over specific instances of job preservation is an instance of a law-and-economics or wealth-maximization analysis. Rasmussen assumes that the bankruptcy regime that maximizes the position of the least well-off is the regime that embodies minimal overall unemployment. Rasmussen maintains that the law-and-economics approach to the design of possible bankruptcy schemes is the normative framework that, interestingly, produces the scheme

[25] Robert K. Rasmussen, "An Essay on Optimal Bankruptcy Rules and Social Justice," *University of Illinois Law Review* 1994, no. 1 (1994): 40.

[26] "[T]hose in the original position would consider ... minimizing the number of accidents in the first instance." Ibid., 31. Note that Rasmussen is imprecise here. For Rawls, representatives in the original position merely select the two principles of justice, not the policies to be used to implement them.

[27] Ibid., 39.

[28] Ibid., 39–40.

that best serves Rawls's difference principle. The law-and-economics approach to the design of bankruptcy would, by selecting the bankruptcy policy that embodies the least unemployment, be most consistent with Rawlsianism.

We have two objections. First, while not impossible, it seems highly curious that two maximizing principles with different maximands (wealth on the one hand, and the position of the least well-off on the other) would yield extensionally equivalent outcomes. Second, it is unclear to us why Rasmussen attempts to construct bankruptcy with only economic efficiency in mind, while assuming that all the equity-oriented work of maximizing the position of the least well-off will come in *other* areas of law.[29] Surely, maximizing the position of the least well-off will require *some* policy differences as compared to a pure wealth-maximization system, given the different maximands. For example, if the argument of the previous paragraph concerning unemployment is that the Rawlsian would prefer low interest rates to particular instances of job preservation (in an effort to create more jobs in total), then the same analysis should be regenerated with regard to tort law. However, Rasmussen assumes that the Rawlsian would construct tort law to result in fewer accidents, not more jobs. In other words, for Rasmussen, the Rawlsian constructs tort law to protect tort victims and bankruptcy law to promote job-creation (via lower interest rates).

However, it is unclear why the Rawlsian does not instead construct bankruptcy law to better protect tort victims (e.g., via granting them priority as creditors)[30] and tort law to promote job-creation. It is possible, for example, that there would be more jobs if more torts went uncompensated (through a reduction in liability and/or damages).[31] Thus, if, as Rasmussen assumes with respect to bankruptcy, job-creation via lower interest rates is the path to maximizing the position of the least well-off, perhaps tort law could be relaxed in a manner that would create jobs—for

[29] Kaplow and Shavell have argued that given a commitment to utility maximization, all equity-oriented distributive moves are most efficiently made via tax and transfer. Kaplow and Shavell, "Why the Legal System Is Less Efficient Than the Income Tax in Redistributing Income." Note, however, that *Rawls* is not concerned merely with the distribution of constitutional liberties and economic benefits and burdens, but focuses rather on what he calls "the objective index of the primary goods" (i.e., those goods that reasonable people would want independent of whatever else they want). Prominent among these goods, for Rawls, is "the social bases of self-respect." Thus, even if Kaplow and Shavell are correct—given a commitment to utility (or wealth) maximization—their argument need not hold for Rawlsianism. Assuming that self-respect might be affected by, for example, one's amount of leisure time, then even if the subjective utility of the least well-off were higher with less leisure, the Rawlsian difference principle might select a scheme with more leisure (which might arise from closing some contracting options), if it provided a higher level of the objective index of the primary goods. Kordana and Tabachnick, "Rawls and Contract Law," 617–18.

[30] See, e.g., Lucian Arye Bebchuk and Jesse M. Fried, "The Uneasy Case for the Priority of Secured Claims in Bankruptcy," *Yale Law Journal* 105, no. 4 (1996): 904; and Lynn M. LoPucki, "The Unsecured Creditor's Bargain," *Virginia Law Review* 80, no. 8 (1994): 1908.

[31] Recall the popular Rust-Belt bumper sticker: "No Smoke, No Jobs."

example, jobs manufacturing luxury goods that are latently dangerous to the user.

Our claim is that taxation, in conjunction with the private law, is used to meet the demands of the distributive principles. There is no principled reason to think that distribution—in particular, the equity-oriented component of distribution—need be limited to taxation. To underscore our general thesis, there is no principled reason to think that equity-oriented distribution, for the post-institutional maximizing theorist, is done only in one module of the overall political and legal scheme. The overall scheme that best satisfies the distributive principles will likely include a number of equity-oriented distributive moves across the entire range of political and legal institutions.

III. Taxation and the Private Law for Deontic Pre-Institutional Theorists

There are (of course) a set of political theorists for whom private property is not simply a matter of institutional or political convention. Such theorists maintain that rights in private property are a pre-institutional or prepolitical matter.[32] Property rights, in this view, are taken (for various reasons) to be "natural" or among the set of basic or fundamental human rights, the existence of which does not depend upon any particular political institution. Indeed, in this view, the extent to which various political institutions respect and protect such pre-institutional rights in private property often serves (in part) as the benchmark for the moral evaluation of such political institutions.

This set of political thinkers is widely diverse—including egalitarians, moderate liberals, left-libertarians, and right-libertarians. Despite the theoretical space between these different theorists, they share the view that property arrangements are *moralized.* These thinkers hold that rights in property or property arrangements (for one reason or another) are derived from pre-institutional or prepolitical moral doctrine.

There is, of course, no general agreement among the various types of pre-institutional theorists over the strength of such pre-institutional rights in property. From the diversity of political views in this camp, however, it is clear that a pre-institutional conception of private property does not commit one to the view that rights in property are absolute. The dispute between pre- and post-institutional theorists, then, is not

[32] See, e.g., David Boaz, *Libertarianism: A Primer* (New York: Free Press, 1997); Loren Lomasky, *Persons, Rights, and the Moral Community* (New York: Oxford University Press, 1987), 120–21; Jan Narveson, *The Libertarian Idea* (Philadelphia, PA: Temple University Press, 1988); Robert Nozick, *Anarchy, State, and Utopia* (New York: Basic Books, 1974); A. John Simmons, *The Lockean Theory of Rights* (Princeton, NJ: Princeton University Press, 1992), 222; and Peter Vallentyne, Hillel Steiner, and Michael Otsuka, "Why Left-Libertarianism Is Not Incoherent, Indeterminate, or Irrelevant: A Reply to Fried," *Philosophy and Public Affairs* 33, no. 2 (2005): 201.

over the substantive *strength* (or weight) of rights in private property but is instead over the source, justification, and derivation of such rights or arrangements.

For deontic pre-institutional theorists, property holdings that flow from an entitlement theory that includes the correct principles of acquisition, transfer, or rectification are taken to be legitimate.[33] There are, however, different conceptions of these principles. In what follows, we distinguish four types of pre-institutional views, focusing chiefly upon their respective conceptions of the principles of acquisition and the role that conceptions of justice play in each. We distinguish between what we call the "libertarian view," the "negative deontic view," the "mixed deontic view," and the "non-justice-oriented mixed deontic view."

In the libertarian view, property acquisitions can only be justified via principles in which negative rights (or liberty interests) exclusively determine holdings. In this view, values other than absolute negative rights (e.g., duties of beneficence or charity) are not included among the correct principles of acquisition, nor do they play a role in the ultimate justification of holdings. Legitimacy, in this view, is understood in terms of negative liberty interests. Liberty, however, is often thought not to be exhaustive of moral value, so proponents of the libertarian entitlement theory must explain away the seeming moral force of moral values that are not oriented toward the promotion of negative liberty (e.g., utility or beneficence).

Robert Nozick's strategy, for example, is to argue that non-negative-liberty-oriented values are of little (or no) relevance to the ultimate justification of rights in property.[34] Non-negative-liberty-oriented values are not included in the correct principles of entitlement or legitimacy that define Nozick's conception of justice;[35] nor are they capable of serving as "trumps"[36] over legitimate holdings. Nozick concludes that property rights are "essentially" absolute. Because property rights are (nearly) absolute and liberty-preserving, taxation cannot be justified, either as a matter of justice or of other values.

[33] "The legitimate means of moving from one distribution to another are specified by the principle of justice in transfer. The legitimate first 'moves' are specified by the principle of justice in acquisition." Nozick, *Anarchy, State, and Utopia*, 151 (note omitted).

[34] "The general outlines of the theory of justice in holdings are that the holdings of a person are just if he is entitled to them by the principles of justice in acquisition and transfer, or by the principle of rectification of injustice. . . . If each person's holdings are just, then the total set (distribution) of holdings is just." Ibid., 153.

[35] Rawls, for example, characterizes Nozick's view as follows: "It is maintained that the principles of just acquisition and transfer preserve the justice of holdings throughout the whole sequence of historical transactions. . . . The only way injustice is thought to arise is from deliberate violations of these principles, or from error and ignorance of what they require and the like." Rawls, "The Basic Structure as Subject," 263–64.

[36] Ronald Dworkin, *Taking Rights Seriously* (Cambridge, MA: Harvard University Press, 1978), 184.

However, pre-institutional theorists holding a roughly Lockean view of property need not be drawn to Nozick's absolutist conclusion,[37] which turns on (1) the libertarian conception of entitlement and (2) the absolute nature of legitimate rights in property. A second type of pre-institutional theorist holds that property rights are a matter of pre-institutional entitlement, though non-absolute. This view can be divided into two sub-positions: (1) those holding a "negative deontic view" and (2) those holding a "mixed deontic view." In the negative deontic view, the conception of justice is identical to that of the libertarian view—the entitlement theory is definitive of justice. The negative deontic view, however, is not absolutist with regard to claims of justice or legitimacy—which are capable of being traded off against, for example, weighty claims of utility or charity. Thus, the view is not absolutist with regard to property rights.

The mixed deontic view, in contrast, is distinct in that it allows for non-negative-liberty-oriented values to be enshrined in the principles of entitlement. To put the point differently, the principles of entitlement, for the mixed deontic view, are conceived of as autonomy preserving (i.e., legitimacy preserving) and are definitive of justice or fairness. However, the conception of autonomy is inclusive of values other than negative freedom.[38] The principles of entitlement, as a result, differ from those in the libertarian and negative deontic views. In the mixed deontic view, justice is also conceived of as non-absolute—it can be traded off against weighty non-justice-oriented values (e.g., utility).

For both the negative deontic view and the mixed deontic view, the entitlement theory defines justice. The concept of justice, however, is understood as only one of several sectors of morality or one of the many dimensions of a complete normative evaluation of institutions.[39] While justice is (perhaps) the sector of morality most prominently or chiefly concerned with the evaluation of rights, duties, obligations, institutional

[37] "Suppose, for instance, that justice in acquisition (or transfer) allows my taking the product of another's labor when I am in dire and unavoidable need. . . . To believe Nozick, we must have good reason to believe that honest industry, inheritance, and free transfer are just grounds of property in a fashion sufficiently strong to exclude conflicting or limiting grounds of other sorts." Simmons, *The Lockean Theory of Rights*, 323–24.

[38] "Charity . . . requires that our basic needs be met, and that the property of others be correspondingly limited or overridden. . . . [O]nly what we need for preservation is in principle immune to the claims of need. . . . Rights to charity are necessary, for instance, so that need is not allowed to make us subject to others' wills, make us dependent on them, or make us their vassals. The same reasoning in Locke that justifies rights of property or justice, then, also justifies rights of charity." Ibid., 332 (footnotes omitted).

[39] This conception of justice, interestingly, is shared by John Rawls, though he is not a pre-institutional liberal. See John Rawls, "Justice as Fairness," in Samuel Freeman, ed., *John Rawls: Collected Papers* (Cambridge, MA: Harvard University Press, 1999), 48: "Justice is not to be confused with an all-inclusive vision of a good society; it is only one part of any such conception. It is important, for example, to distinguish that sense of equality which is an aspect of the concept of justice from that sense of equality which belongs to a more comprehensive social ideal. There may well be inequalities which one concedes are just, or at least not unjust, but which, nevertheless, one wishes, on other grounds, to do away with."

arrangements, and property, to say of an action or institution that it is *just* or *fair* is to have evaluated that action or institution only along *one* normative dimension. Thus, it does not follow (merely) from the fact that an action or institution is just, fair, or legitimate that it is all-things-considered justified or morally sound. When one acknowledges that an action or institution is just, there is still more, morally speaking, to say about the matter.

There is a final pre-institutional view, which we term the "non-justice-oriented mixed deontic view." This conception is identical to the mixed deontic view, except that the entitlement theory is *not* definitive of justice. In this view, claims that arise from the entitlement theory are taken to be legitimate, but not definitive of justice. For those holding the non-justice-oriented mixed deontic view, justice is understood neither as a single sector of morality, nor as a single dimension along which institutions may be evaluated. Instead, justice is understood more loosely, as all-things-considered right action, or this view does not admit of a conception of justice. Justice is conceived of in a much broader fashion—or, indeed, it disappears entirely—compared to the other three views.

Now, consider the possible justification of taxation for these differing pre-institutional views. In the libertarian view, the conception of liberty enshrined in the entitlement theory rules out the possibility of non-negative-freedom-oriented values serving as the basis of just holdings, and the view is also absolutist about the conception of justice. Thus, for the libertarian conception of entitlement, there essentially can be no justification for taxation.

Return to the negative deontic view. Here, the justification of taxation must be understood as other than a matter of justice or distributive justice. Lockean political philosopher A. John Simmons, while not himself holding what we have called the negative deontic view, has drawn an instructive distinction between *legitimacy* and *justification*.[40] Claims of legitimacy can (at times) be "trumped" for reasons of justification, that is, general utility or beneficence. This distinction is helpful in understanding the role of taxation for theorists who hold the negative deontic view.[41] For the negative deontic view, the private law is best understood as embodying an account of justice or fairness that conceives of justice (solely) in terms of the preservation of a negative-freedom-oriented conception of entitlement. Taxation (if it is to exist) must be understood not as a matter of *justice* but rather as a matter of *all-things-considered morally right action*.

[40] A. John Simmons, "Justification and Legitimacy," *Ethics* 109, no. 4 (1999): 739; A. John Simmons, *Moral Principles and Political Obligations* (Princeton, NJ: Princeton University Press, 1979), 195–201.

[41] While Simmons appears to hold what we have termed the "non-justice-oriented mixed deontic view," the distinction between justification and legitimacy makes good sense for the negative deontic and mixed deontic views as well.

The crucial point is that taxation, in the negative deontic view, cannot be required or justified by appeal to claims of justice or distributive justice. For pre-institutional theorists holding the negative deontic view, the entitlement theory of justice *defines* the conception of justice,[42] and, therefore, sets the baseline of *just* entitlements. Taxation, because it upsets or alters this *just* system of entitlement, cannot therefore be justified by appeal to a (new or distinct) conception of *justice.*[43] It does not follow from this, however, that values exogenous to the conception of justice are irrelevant, *simpliciter.* Taxation may be justified by appeal to values that are independent of justice (e.g., beneficence or utility). With regard to the latter point, this entails that beneficence or utility, for example, are values independent of justice, rather than themselves conceptions of justice in competition with the negative deontic view. The result is that, for theorists holding the negative deontic view, taxation can be implemented, but not as a matter of *justice.*

From the perspective of justice, for the negative deontic view, taxation can be regarded as an unfortunate upsetting of the requirements of justice, itself required by some non-justice-oriented moral value. This has implications for how taxation should be implemented—namely, that justice should be upset only as much as is necessary to satisfy the other, trumping value(s). This does not imply, however, that tax assessments need to be *proportional* as assessed against the baseline set by justice. While proportionality is a feature of an important tax policy that might seem intuitively applicable—the equal sacrifice principle—it is not *required.* This is for two reasons: First, the proportionality requirement embodied in the equal sacrifice principle can itself be understood as an independent conception of justice; however, justice has already been defined by the entitlement scheme, which is now being trumped by other values (i.e., weighty reasons of utility, if the taxation is raising funds for the funding of important public goods; or beneficence, if it is raising funds to be redistributed to the needy). Second, taxation is, in this view, being implemented to achieve specific outcomes. Its aim is to yield net *benefits* for at least some against the baseline of justice, so it seems unmotivated to require proportionality or equal sacrifice in the assignment of tax "burdens" even to those who will, on net, benefit.[44] Since the equal sacrifice principle is not required, this leaves open the possibility that some of the aims of the trumping values could be accomplished through changes to

[42] See Kordana and Tabachnick, "Rawls and Contract Law," 628: "For the will theorist, a contract that is otherwise legitimate . . . but that contains one-sided terms is, by definition, fair."

[43] See, e.g., Murphy and Coleman, *Philosophy of Law,* 163: "In [Fried's] view, because contract is based on and enforces promises, courts are not entitled to use a dispute that arises in contract either to promote an independent ideal of *justice* by refusing to enforce hard or bad deals, or to further the economic or other aims of society as a whole."

[44] Murphy and Nagel, *The Myth of Ownership,* 25.

the rules of the private law, rather than only through the imposition of a tax and transfer scheme.

Return now to the mixed deontic view. In this view, non-negative-liberty-oriented values, such as beneficence or charity, can play a role in correct principles of entitlement, thereby defining legitimacy in holdings.[45] This suggests that the rules of property themselves may embody equity-oriented distributive values (e.g., meeting claims of beneficence) as a matter of *justice*. What are conventionally viewed as rules of tax and transfer could be used to create entitlements. That is, the rules of tax and transfer could be viewed as one aspect of property rules, just as the taxation of particular transactions renders the rules of tax that apply to such transactions (at least conceptually) part of contract law.[46] It follows from this that, to the extent that "tax" is constructed in service of the principles of entitlement that define justice, those rules of tax are *just*, because the principles of entitlement define *just* entitlements. Also, for the mixed deontic view, *additional* rules of tax and transfer could be constructed, in the same manner as for the negative deontic view, by appeal to values exogenous to the conception of entitlement or justice (e.g., general utility). Such appeals to exogenous values function for the mixed deontic view as they do for the negative deontic view: they construct rules that are matters of all-things-considered right action, but not by appeal to *justice*.

Consider now the role of taxation in what we have called the non-justice-oriented mixed deontic view. Here, as with the mixed deontic view, non-negative-liberty-oriented values can be drawn upon in constructing correct principles of entitlement. To the extent that the correct principles of entitlement embody equity-oriented values, the legal rules constructed in service of them may therefore also embody such equity-oriented values. Thus, the entitlement principles, as is the case for the

[45] "The important point for Locke is that the needy can have a right to the property of others (or what was formerly their property—i.e., the fruits of their honest industry)." Simmons, *The Lockean Theory of Rights*, 329.

[46] See Anthony T. Kronman, "Contract Law and Distributive Justice," *Yale Law Journal* 89, no. 3 (1980): 503–4 (criticizing the view that tax law is somehow unobtrusive vis-à-vis individual transactions).

Thomas Scanlon has distinguished between legal rules or legal rights and underlying values, maintaining that legal rules and rights can take many forms, but must ultimately be designed to account for the correct balance of values or principles:

> Rights, understood as institutional constraints and prerogatives, can "clash." . . . What we need to do in such a case is to adjust our understanding of these [legal] rights so as to make them coherent. This adjustment is not best understood, I think, as a matter of "balancing" [legal] rights against one another. . . . It is true, however, that in deciding which readjustment of these [legal] rights to accept, we may need to "balance" certain values . . . against one another. . . . [V]alues are balanced, [legal] rights are adjusted, or redefined.

T. M. Scanlon, "Adjusting Rights and Balancing Values," *Fordham Law Review* 72, no. 5 (2004): 1478–79. Given this view, there is no reason of principle that would require that equity-oriented aims be met via any specific body of legal rules or doctrine.

mixed deontic view, may serve as the basis of either taxation or private law rules that contain equity-oriented aims. In this view, the entitlement principles generate legitimate holdings; however, the non–justice-oriented mixed deontic view is importantly distinct from the mixed deontic view in that the conception of legitimacy is not definitive of justice.

Since, in the non–justice-oriented mixed deontic view, (1) justice is conceived of as all-things-considered morally sound action, or falls out of the picture, and (2) legitimacy is not viewed as absolute, it follows that taxation (or equity-oriented distributive aims) can be justified by appeal *either* to the equity-oriented aspects of the entitlement principles *or* by appeal to other non–legitimacy-based values. Justice, in this view, is found in the full working-out of the balancing between legitimacy and justification, or else is not of primary moral concern. In any event, through the full working-out of the balancing of legitimacy and justification, a possible source of equity-oriented values in either the private law or taxation arises.

The non–justice-oriented mixed deontic view, like the mixed deontic view, is non-absolutist in both of the two respects that Nozick's view is absolutist: (1) the duty of beneficence or charity is conceived of as a component of the correct principles of entitlement, and (2) claims of legitimacy can be overridden for reasons of justification (e.g., general utility). However, for the non–justice-oriented mixed deontic view, ultimate claims of *justice* are derived from the balancing of claims of legitimacy and justification, or justice has fallen out of the picture altogether. The result is a non-absolutist view of pre-institutional rights in property, a view which, when taken in its totality, is understood as all-things-considered morally right action. In this view, however, no isolated or particular sector of morality is conceived of as *justice* that may serve as the basis of taxation; in the strict sense of the term, as discussed (for example) by Rawls and Nozick, justice falls out of the picture.

The following passage may be instructive in illustrating the role of justice in these theories. In discussing the legitimate nature of consensual institutions and their relationship to a "liberal egalitarian" conception of justice, Simmons writes:

> [T]he libertarian consent theorist will simply reject the liberal egalitarian theory of justice that is alleged to have [certain] implications, arguing that if one cannot point to clear wrongdoing in the process that creates the polity, one has no grounds for claiming that the resulting polity is unjust.[47]

Here, Simmons appears to be positing what we have called a libertarian conception of legitimacy, pointing out that this conception of legitimacy

[47] A. John Simmons, "Consent Theory for Libertarians," *Social Philosophy and Policy* 22, no. 1 (2005): 354.

or justice is inconsistent with a liberal egalitarian (e.g., Rawlsian) conception. Simmons continues:

> But suppose that one finds it difficult to follow the libertarian this far, committed as one might be to a more moderate, left-libertarian or liberal egalitarian conception of social justice. Even in that event, I think, there is nothing to prevent one from nonetheless accepting consent theory's standards for legitimacy.[48]

Simmons then writes:

> A liberal egalitarian theory of justice and a consent theory of political legitimacy can be consistently conjoined if one accepts the distinction between what I have called "justification" and "legitimacy"—which I take to be two kinds of favorable evaluations of political institutions within quite different dimensions of evaluation. General good qualities and virtues of a political society—such as benevolence or *justice*—are what is appealed to in *justifying* that society's existence, in showing why such a society is *a good thing*.[49]

The invited conclusion is that the consensual arrangement is *legitimate,* but ultimately not fully *justified.* Simmons, here, must be conceiving of "justice" as an areteic (or excellence-oriented) value for the purpose of evaluating the goodness or badness of institutions.[50] Our point is that, given our distinctions above, it is not possible to ground the claim that the consensual polity is *legitimate* but *unjustified* in a liberal egalitarian conception of justice qua rightness. In this case, there appear to be three possible conceptions of legitimacy at stake (given that absolutism is not at issue): what we have called the "negative deontic," "mixed deontic," and "non-justice-oriented mixed deontic" conceptions of legitimacy (or entitlement). It is true that, for each of these positions, claims of legitimacy

[48] Ibid.

[49] Ibid. (emphasis added on the word "justice"; footnote omitted).

[50] When Simmons, here, appeals to "justice" as a matter of justification, he is *not* conceiving of justice as a "function of [society's] specific interaction and [something that] consists (in part) in its having a particular set of rights over subjects," but rather as one of "the general good qualities and virtues of a political society" (ibid). This move renders Simmons's view consistent with our own. However, one must be clear that Simmons is appealing to "justice" as other than a sector of the concept of "right," as it is articulated in Rawls's schematic on page 109 of *A Theory of Justice.* It is true, of course, that Rawls does at times elsewhere write of "justice [as] the first virtue of social institutions" (ibid., 3), which would (contra the schematic) cast justice as an areteic (i.e., excellence-oriented) value.

Our point (consistent with Simmons's passage) is that once one sets out a conception of justice as a matter of "legitimacy," one cannot then appeal to a differing conception of justice qua rightness (as opposed to goodness) as a matter of "justification." However, why one would hold two differing conceptions of justice—one as rightness and the other as goodness—remains an open question.

may sometimes be "trumped" by claims of justification (e.g., general utility). However, if one is to take seriously the conception of justice of any one of the three entitlement theories, it is difficult to ground claims of *justification* in a (distinct) conception of *justice*. The trouble is that the negative deontic and mixed deontic conceptions of entitlement each *constitute* a conception of justice, while the non-justice-oriented mixed deontic conception of entitlement is (itself) a *component* of a conception of justice—one distinct from the liberal egalitarian's conception of justice, or a component of all-things-considered right action in which justice plays no role. The result is that if one accepts any of the three entitlement conceptions, one cannot then appeal to an independent conception of *justice* as a trumping value. Our point is this: Something other than claims of *justice* (qua rightness) is required to advance the claim that the arrangement is (in Simmons's sense of the term) *unjustified*.

It also seems important to distinguish between (1) moderate Lockeans or left-libertarians and (2) liberal egalitarians. The former are pre-institutional theorists, who may hold either the negative deontic, mixed deontic, or non-justice-oriented mixed deontic conceptions of entitlement. However, if by "liberal egalitarian conception of social justice" Simmons were invoking a post-institutional liberal view of justice qua rightness such as Rawlsianism,[51] then the claim that the arrangement is *legitimate* but ultimately not *justified* seems problematic. As we saw above in Section II, the Rawlsian conception of justice qua rightness requires that all bodies of law serve, instrumentally, the demands of the principles of justice. If that is true, it does not appear that the liberal egalitarian has the resources to adopt consent theory in any meaningful way; entitlements instead must be constructed in a fashion instrumental to the demands of the distributive principles.

Return now to the four types of pre-institutional views we distinguished above. One difference between the non-justice-oriented mixed deontic conception and the other three conceptions appears to reflect a disagreement over the *concept* of justice itself, rather than a disagreement over competing *conceptions* of justice. In the latter three conceptions, justice is conceived of as the sector of deontic morality that is chiefly (or in the first instance) responsible for the evaluation of institutions and the manner in which rights, duties, and holdings in property are assigned. In this view, the concept of justice is exclusive of other sectors of morality. For those who hold this position there is, of course, disagreement over the *correct* conception of justice. For Rawls (though he is not a pre-institutional liberal), justice is conceived of as the principles that flow from the original position; for Nozick, justice is conceived of as the entitlement theory. Both, however, despite their disagreement over the correct principles of

[51] On the previous and subsequent pages, Simmons follows "liberal egalitarian" with "(e.g., Rawlsian)." Simmons, "Consent Theory for Libertarians," 355.

justice, view justice as a distinct and important sector of morality. That is, they appear (roughly) to agree over the very *concept* of justice.

In contrast, one who conceives of justice (roughly) as all-things-considered morally right action, or believes that the concept of justice plays no primary role in all-things-considered morally right action (the view of the non–justice-oriented mixed deontic pre-institutional theorist), appears not simply to disagree over the conception of the correct principles of justice, but rather over the very concept of justice itself.

Consider, again, the question of taxation. As we saw above, in the mixed deontic and non–justice-oriented mixed deontic conceptions, correct principles of entitlement reflect a commitment to positive rights, such as beneficence (or charity). These equity-oriented values may serve as the basis of equity-oriented legal rules. For these two conceptions, equity-oriented legal rules can also be implemented as a matter of justification. The negative deontic conception can only implement such rules as a matter of justification, as opposed to legitimacy (or entitlement).

It is interesting to consider what form these equity-oriented rules might take. One could hold (1) that these rules should include what are traditionally thought of as property rules (or other areas of the private law), or (2) that all equity-oriented moves should be made as a matter of "tax and transfer." Consider the well-known claim made by the law-and-economics scholars Louis Kaplow and Steven Shavell: that income taxation is more efficient than other legal rules in accomplishing equity-oriented ends.[52] While the claim has attracted critics,[53] assume for the sake of argument that it is correct. The conclusion it invites is that even though either position (1) or position (2) is *morally* justifiable, the second is preferable in terms of economic efficiency and should be chosen (given that morality is not at issue), as long as economic efficiency is taken to be of (some) value.

We think, however, that there are reasons to doubt that the Kaplow and Shavell claim applies to pre-institutional theorists.[54] We maintain, there-

[52] Kaplow and Shavell, "Why the Legal System Is Less Efficient Than the Income Tax in Redistributing Income."

[53] See, e.g., Chris William Sanchirico, "Taxes versus Legal Rules as Instruments for Equity: A More Equitable View," *Journal of Legal Studies* 29, no. 2 (2000) (constructing a counterexample to the Kaplow/Shavell thesis); and Helmuth Cremer, Pierre Pestieau, and Jean-Charles Rochet, "Direct versus Indirect Taxation: The Design of the Tax Structure Revisited," *International Economic Review* 42, no. 3 (2001): 797 ("differential commodity taxes *do* have a role to play as instruments of optimal tax policy—an optimal (general) income tax will not suffice"). But see also Louis Kaplow and Steven Shavell, "Should Legal Rules Favor the Poor? Clarifying the Role of Legal Rules and the Income Tax in Redistributing Income," *Journal of Legal Studies* 29, no. 2 (2000): 821 (contesting the significance of Sanchirico's counterexample); and Louis Kaplow, "On the Undesirability of Commodity Taxation Even When Income Taxation Is Not Optimal," National Bureau of Economic Research Working Paper 10407 (Cambridge, MA: NBER, 2004).

[54] This is not to suggest that Kaplow and Shavell believe that their thesis does apply in this context. See Kaplow and Shavell, "Why the Legal System Is Less Efficient Than the Income Tax in Redistributing Income," 667 n. 2: "Our discussion concerns the overall distribution of income or wealth, not entitlement to payment based on desert."

fore, that for such theorists, the private law may justifiably embody equity-oriented values. Kaplow and Shavell contrast tax and transfer with other "legal rules."[55] They compare the efficiency of a tort rule to the efficiency of an income tax with equivalent distributive effect.[56]

Kaplow and Shavell appear to assume the existence of an underlying system of property ownership and free markets. Our issue, however, is the very question of the form that *property* rules should take; that is, we are interested in the question of whether the equity-oriented values that differing theorists hold are best met through tax and transfer, or through (in part) the rules of property law. Thus, it is not clear that Kaplow and Shavell's discussion, which compares tax and transfer to a tort rule (in isolation) and concludes that tax and transfer is superior in terms of economic efficiency, would (also) apply to the question of the underlying set of property rules. In other words, one interpretation of Kaplow and Shavell is that *given* a system of property law, tax and transfer can more efficiently achieve an equity-oriented end than can the rules of tort. The underlying system of property law, however, may (or may not), it seems, reflect equity-oriented aims. Their discussion does not appear to directly address this question.

We claim that for certain pre-institutional theorists the rules of the private law can answer to equity-oriented concerns. Consider this claim in the context of legal scholar Ernest Weinrib's view that the private law ought to maintain a form of conceptual independence from the realm of the political and from distributive aims.[57] Weinrib defends what he calls "legal formalism," maintaining that sectors of the private law ought to take the form of moral values derived from Kantian moral philosophy.[58] Weinrib distinguishes between what he calls the realm of the "juridical" and the realm of the "political." The elements of the juridical realm are the set of legal concepts drawn from moral theory, while the elements of the

[55] They write: "For purposes of this article, the term 'legal rules' refers to rules other than those that define the income tax and welfare system." Ibid., 667 n. 1.

[56] Ibid., 669–74.

[57] "The choice of distributive program is therefore political in its nature. . . . Distributive justice implies that a political authority must define and particularize the scope or criterion of any scheme of distribution. . . . The situation in corrective justice [i.e., the private law] is categorically different. Corrective justice involves no decision as to the selection of a collective purpose. When construing a transaction in accordance with corrective justice, the adjudicator does not choose one scheme of correction over another but rather specifies the meaning of corrective justice with respect to the transaction in question. The contrast with distributive justice is stark. . . . The rationality of corrective justice is entirely immanent." Ernest J. Weinrib, *The Idea of Private Law* (Cambridge, MA: Harvard University Press, 1995), 211–12.

[58] "[O]ne understands a legal relationship through its unifying structure, or 'form.' Applied to private law, the thesis of immanent intelligibility is a version of legal formalism. . . . [The private law's] normative force derives from Kant's concept of right as the governing idea for relationships between free beings. For Kant, freedom itself implies juridical obligation. On this view, the doctrines, concepts, and institutions of private law are normative inasmuch as they make a legal reality out of relations of corrective justice." Ibid., 18–19.

political realm are those bodies of law that are properly constructed by the political process. For Weinrib, property, contract, and tort law constitute the "juridical," while distributive justice constitutes (in part) the "political." The point is that, for Weinrib, property,[59] contract, and tort law are to be derived directly from Kantian moral theory and are therefore, he believes, conceptually and normatively distinct from distributive justice and the political process.

Weinrib holds what one might view as a negative-rights-oriented[60] pre-institutional view of property, combined with a political conception of distributive justice. This appears to lead Weinrib to hold the view that what we have called equity-oriented concerns are all a matter of the political process and, therefore, a matter of distributive justice—not private law.[61] Given our arguments, however, one need not accept Weinrib's conclusion.

First, it is important to note that, in Weinrib's view, if distributive justice (as a sector of the "political") were to construct within the body of positive law a minimum wage requirement, that law would *not* be a rule of "contract law" as Weinrib conceives of the term and, thus, would not constitute a part of the private law.[62] For Weinrib, the "private law" is understood to be (as a conceptual matter) only that body of law that is derived from pre-institutional moral notions, which need not be coextensive with the body of positive law more typically thought to constitute the private law (i.e., laws regulating accidents, exchange, and holdings). However, even in Weinrib's view, the latter body of positive law *can* include equity-oriented moves (constructed by the demands of distributive justice). Therefore, even for Weinrib, the body of positive law typically understood as private law (though not so conceived by Weinrib's narrower and monistic conception) admits of equity-oriented moves.

[59] "Even the idea of property takes its normative character from the abstractness of right rather than the promotion of welfare." Ibid., 131.

[60] "[O]ne person's need does not serve as the basis of obligating another to satisfy that need; accordingly, there is no liability for nonfeasance, that is, for not providing another with a needed benefit." Ibid., 97.

[61] Weinrib, in other words, appears to hold that the private law protects negative rights, and that welfare is relevant "only inasmuch as it is crystallized in the holding of a right." Ibid., 131. He writes: "Under Kantian right two kinds of rights . . . are relevant to private law. The first is the right to one's bodily integrity. . . . The second kind of right is to external objects of the will. Rights to external objects, including rights to property and to contractual performance, are not innate to the actor but are acquired through the execution of a juridically effective act. . . . Because external objects are categorically different from free will, they can be owned without contravening the freedom of others under the principle of right. And their being owned entails an obligation in nonowners to refrain from their use." Ibid., 128–29.

[62] For example, Weinrib allows that values drawn from the "political" rather than the juridical (i.e., what he understands as a conceptual matter to be "the private law") can inform the content of accident law. He writes: "Assume . . . that one wanted to *replace* or *supplement* tort law by introducing a distributive scheme of compensation for personal injuries . . ." (ibid., 210; emphasis added). The point for Weinrib is that such replacement or supplemental values are not properly understood as a matter of his (narrow) conception of tort law.

Second, even if we accept Weinrib's conception of the private law, it is important to note that, as a conceptual matter, arguments about equity-oriented moves in the private law could still arise from within the juridical realm. This is because, as we saw above, there exist plausible arguments for incorporating positive rights into correct principles of acquisition. In other words, equity-oriented values can be drawn directly from moral theory as much or as little as can the negative moral values that Weinrib takes to define the realm of the juridical. The point is this: a pre-institutional liberal can maintain the claim that the private law is normatively independent of *distributive* aims, while at the same time holding that the private law can also contain rules that serve equity-oriented values.

IV. Conclusion

For post-institutional theorists (for example, Rawlsians and utilitarians), there is no principled reason for limiting the domain of distributive justice to tax and transfer. For such theorists, not only tax policy, but also the rules of the private law, are constructed in service of distributive aims. If our argument is correct, such theorists should have no commitment to any particular normative conceptions of the private law that are *independent* of their overarching distributive principles. While this conclusion with regard to utilitarianism is widely acknowledged, it is less well understood in the context of Rawlsian political theory.

In pre-institutional theories, in contrast, the private law derives from correct principles of entitlement and reflects no overarching distributive aims. Thus, pre-institutional theorists are free to derive conceptions of the private law from sectors of morality independent of distributive justice. If our arguments are correct, this does *not* entail that the private law, for all pre-institutional theorists, is sanitized of equity-oriented values. However, it is true that pre-institutional libertarians, given their lack of commitment to equity-oriented aims in general, may justifiably conceive of the private law as free of such values. We have shown, nonetheless, that nonlibertarian pre-institutional theorists who hold principled commitments to equity-oriented values are free to invoke *either* tax and transfer *or* the rules of the private law to attain these values. Thus, for such theorists, the private law can embody equity-oriented aims, and there is no principled reason to believe that all equity-oriented aims need to be pursued through the system of tax and transfer. We conclude, then, that for post-institutional (maximizing) liberals there is no principled distinction between tax and the private law, and that for nonlibertarian pre-institutional liberals the private law can contain equity-oriented values—such values need not be understood as pertaining only to the rules of tax and transfer.

Law, University of Virginia
Philosophy, University of Virginia

THE UNEASY CASE FOR CAPITAL TAXATION*

By Edward J. McCaffery

I. Introduction

I write not to praise all tax-reductions but to bury one particular set of taxes. Over a decade ago I began writing on the subject of comprehensive tax reform, in a piece titled "The Uneasy Case for Wealth Transfer Taxes,"[1] echoing the classic work on tax-rate progression by the law professors Walter Blum and Harry Kalven.[2] While I have never viewed the case for progressivity in tax burdens as especially uneasy, I have now come to see that the case for *any* tax on capital (that is, any *direct* tax on capital, a qualification to be made clear below) is indeed uneasy. Simply put, my argument is that there is no compelling reason of fairness or justice to tax capital qua capital, that is, the mere possession of material resources in the hands of an individual or, even more strongly, in the hands of an entity such as a corporation. We can and should abolish capital gains and other capital taxes under the income tax, wealth and wealth transfer taxes such as the gift and estate tax, and, perhaps especially and paradigmatically, corporate income taxes. Since this is a claim that I suspect many (if not most) readers will find surprising, I shall limit my argument here to a moral case against direct capital taxation, a case grounded in considerations of fairness; suffice it to say that others, writing in an economics tradition, have raised considerable doubts as to the (possibly related) efficiency of these levies as well.[3]

* I thank the editors, my research assistants Alex Baskin and Nina Kang, and the other contributors to this volume for their helpful comments.

[1] Edward J. McCaffery, "The Uneasy Case for Wealth Transfer Taxes," *Yale Law Journal* 104, no. 2 (1994): 283–365 (hereafter cited as "The Uneasy Case"); this article advocates the abolishment of the gift and estate tax and the establishment of a progressive consumption-without-estate tax.

[2] Walter J. Blum and Harry Kalven, Jr., "The Uneasy Case for Progressive Taxation," *University of Chicago Law Review* 19, no. 3 (1952): 417–520 (later published as a book). Blum and Kalven found that most arguments for progressivity in tax burdens, such as those resting on the idea of the declining marginal utility of money income, are "uneasy" or unpersuasive; in the end, the case rests on little more than aesthetics and subjective value judgments.

[3] Arnold C. Harberger, "The Incidence of the Corporation Income Tax," *The Journal of Political Economy* 70, no. 3 (1962): 215–40; Martin Feldstein, "The Welfare Cost of Capital Income Taxation," *The Journal of Political Economy* 86, no. 2 (1978): S29–S51; Joseph E. Stiglitz, "Notes on Estate Taxes, Redistribution, and the Concept of Balanced Growth Path Incidence," *The Journal of Political Economy* 86, no. 2 (1978): S137–S150. The "fair tax," a proposal for a progressive national sales tax, would also entail the elimination of all direct taxes on

I should clarify, from the outset, that mine is not any of the three most familiar arguments against capital taxation.[4] It does not follow from the argument, owing to Thomas Hobbes, that capital represents a "common pool" of social resources that ought not to be taxed until individuals withdraw from it.[5] To the contrary, mine is not an argument about the aggregate capital stock; it does not depend on the idea of savings as a public good, or on any instrumental quest to get more social capital. Nor is mine an argument of "horizontal equity," of failing to treat likes alike or (equivalently) equals equally, such as the argument most famously sourced to John Stuart Mill. I do not claim that any "income" tax—any tax that includes both the initial receipt of wealth and the subsequent yield to capital in its base—is a "double tax" on wealth or resources that are not immediately consumed, penalizing savers over spenders, noble Ants over spendthrift Grasshoppers (taken to be *ex ante* equals by Mill and the traditional view of taxation).[6] To the contrary, I accept that, under some circumstances, savers ought to be taxed more, and other times less, than spenders; and, like other thoughtful commentators in the increasingly sophisticated tax-policy literature, I eschew a naive, formalist, horizontal equity approach to taxation.[7] Nor, finally, is my argument against capital taxation the simple, lay argument against "double" taxation, come what may. It is true that capital can often be triply or quadruply taxed: at the individual level, both when received and when invested, at the corporate or entity level, and again at the individual level when transferred. But many dollars are taxed multiple times in the flow of funds, and the number of times an element of value is taxed is simply less important than the rate at which it is taxed. A single high-rate tax can be more burdensome than a panoply of trivial-rate ones. My argument happens to be for a one-time tax on individuals, at the moment of spending or ultimate private preclusive use, but this is because I argue that this one time is the right time to make social judgments over the appropriate level of taxation, and not on account of any foundational constraint on the number of times individuals or elements of value can be taxed.

---

capital, including the gift and estate tax and corporate income taxes. See Laurence J. Kotlikoff, "The Case for the 'Fair Tax,'" *Wall Street Journal*, 7 March 2005; see also www.FairTax.org.

[4] See generally Barbara H. Fried, "Fairness and the Consumption Tax," *Stanford Law Review* 44, no. 5 (1992): 961–1017.

[5] Thomas Hobbes, *Leviathan* (1651; New York: Penguin Classics, 1985). Barbara Fried, in "Fairness and the Consumption Tax," argues against this Hobbesian position, calling it the "foundational argument." See also Liam Murphy and Thomas Nagel, *The Myth of Ownership: Taxes and Justice* (New York: Oxford University Press, 2002).

[6] John Stuart Mill, *Principles of Political Economy, Books IV and V* (1848; reprint, New York: Penguin Classics, 1985), chap. 2, pp. 162–69.

[7] See Louis Kaplow, "Horizontal Equity: Measures in Search of Principle," *National Tax Journal* 42, no. 2 (1989): 139–54; but see also Murphy and Nagel, *The Myth of Ownership*; and C. Eugene Steuerle, *Contemporary U.S. Tax Policy* (Washington, DC: Urban Institute Press, 2004).

Rather, my argument is about progressivity, the very thing that Blum and Kalven found "uneasy." The central, animating question is when judgments about progressivity in tax burdens should be made, which necessarily runs out to questions about how capital and its yield fit into a normatively attractive account of the fair distribution of tax burdens. I argue that, given that we are going to have a progressive tax system, in which the better-able-to-pay pay more, in percent terms, than the less-able-to-pay do—a proposition that I happen to accept as both factually accurate and normatively compelling, but, more to the point, one I simply assume to move forward the analysis of this essay—the next question for policymakers is when to levy such a tax. The goal of any comprehensive progressive tax is to effect a fair distribution of burdens among individuals; this calls for individuated judgment. "Genuinely progressive taxation is necessarily personal taxation," as the Nobel laureate William Vickrey began his classic 1947 treatise.[8] When should we decide how much individuals ought to share with the body politic or, perhaps better put, when should we decide what is private and what is public, what is a fair *distribution* of resources, in the first instance?[9] The key insight is that we ought to tax people when they finally use their wealth—that is, when they spend—and not when they save, give, or die: our ordinary and reflective moral intuitions ought to consistently run out to the *uses* of material resources, and not to their *sources*. Capital is presently unused, unconsumed, wealth. It can be put to different final uses at different times at the individual level. Society can reasonably make different judgments about the propriety of taxing different uses of capital. We can and should, that is, wait and make judgments about capital in the hands of individuals when their ultimate private preclusive uses of that capital become manifest.

These thoughts lead out naturally enough—with the aid of insights gleaned from tax-policy tradition—to a specific form of comprehensive individuated tax: namely, a progressive postpaid consumption tax, a progressive spending tax in short. These are terms that I shall make clearer in due course. The critical understanding is to see that such a tax *is* a tax on capital, at the individual level, when (but only when) capital is used to finance enhanced lifestyles or greater consumption of material resources—spending—and not when capital is used simply to move around in time, within or between generations, uneven labor-market earnings. This is a compelling moral endpoint for taxation. Once we get the major comprehensive tax system down right—from a strictly moral point of view—there is no longer any compelling reason for, and there are good reasons against, any of the traditional direct taxes on capital.

[8] William Vickrey, *Agenda for Progressive Taxation* (New York: The Ronald Press Company, 1947), 3.

[9] See Murphy and Nagel, *The Myth of Ownership*, 31–37, 90–93, and passim.

It is time to better explain and defend these claims. In Section II, I set out the traditional view of taxation and a new understanding, using two types of consumption tax plus the income tax. In Section III, I develop two norms about the propriety of taxing capital and its yield: the ordinary-savings norm and the yield-to-capital norm. In Section IV, I set out two positive uses of savings: to smooth out consumption profiles over time, and to shift them up or down. Then, in Section V, I present the case against direct taxation of capital, pointing out that a consistent progressive postpaid consumption tax, alone among alternative tax forms, implements the two norms set out in Section III. In Section VI, I address the counterargument that direct taxes on capital are needed to correct the inequities of power that capital accumulation generates, and in Section VII, I address the argument that taxes on capital are good because they are "hidden." I offer some concluding remarks in Section VIII.

II. Three Types of Tax

A. The traditional view

Much of tax policy in the United States and elsewhere has been consumed with debating the relative merits of an income tax versus a consumption tax.[10] This debate has been framed by the so-called Haig-Simons definition of "income," which holds, in essence, that income equals consumption plus savings (I = C + S).[11] This accounting identity—a mere tautology—tells us no more and no less than that all "sources" equal "uses" or, even more simply put, that all material resources (income) are either spent (consumption) or not (savings).[12] This is hardly profound, but great wisdom can be built on simple truths. The Haig-Simons definition of income has been enormously influential in tax policy. Perhaps most important, it has been used, through a simple rearrangement of terms, to show the essential difference between an income tax and a consumption tax. If income equals consumption plus savings, then consumption equals income minus savings. It appears as if the difference

[10] Noel B. Cunningham, "The Taxation of Capital Income and the Choice of Tax Base," *Tax Law Review* 52, no. 1 (1996): 17–44; Fried, "Fairness and the Consumption Tax"; David A. Weisbach and Joseph Bankman, "The Superiority of a Consumption Tax over an Income Tax" (draft on file with author); Murphy and Nagel, *The Myth of Ownership*; Joel Slemrod and Jon Bakija, *Taxing Ourselves: A Citizen's Guide to the Great Debate over Tax Reform*, 2d ed. (Cambridge, MA: The MIT Press, 2001). For a brief look at tax policy in Canada, see David Duff, "Tax Policy in a Libertarian World: A Critical Review," *Canadian Journal of Law and Jurisprudence* 18, no. 1 (2005): 23–45; and for a brief look at tax policy in the developing world, see Richard Bird and Eric Zolt, "Redistribution in Developing Countries," *UCLA Law Review* 52, no. 6 (2005): 1627–95.

[11] Henry C. Simons, *Personal Income Taxation: The Definition of Income as a Problem of Fiscal Policy* (Chicago: University of Chicago Press, 1938), 50.

[12] Edward J. McCaffery, *Fair Not Flat: How to Make the Tax System Better and Simpler* (Chicago: University of Chicago Press, 2002).

between an income tax and a consumption tax is that the former includes, and the latter does not include, capital or savings in its base.

In fact, however, there are three major choices of broad-based tax systems in ideal theory: the income tax, prepaid consumption taxes, and postpaid consumption taxes. We get to the three-view perspective when we see that the two broad types of consumption taxes are not created equal under progressive rates. First, however, let us understand the traditional view of matters, which equates the two forms of consumption tax.

An income tax, as we can see from the Haig-Simons definition, applies to all inflows into a household or taxpaying unit, whether from capital or labor (or, indeed, beneficence). This means, as Mill pointed out in his 1848 treatise *Principles of Political Economy,* that savings are "double taxed": in order to have principal to invest, one has to have paid tax on some prior receipt, but the yield to capital is taxed again. In Mill's words, this is to "tax the same portion of the contributor's means twice over"; if a taxpayer "has the interest, it is because he abstains from using the principal."[13]

Consumption taxes, in contrast, are *single* taxes on the flow of funds into and out of a household. This way of putting the matter allows us to comprehend the two basic forms of consumption tax, which are distinguished according to when the single tax is levied. In one model, the tax is imposed up-front and never again: a wage tax, or a so-called prepaid or yield-exempt consumption tax. Roth IRAs in the United States work on this model (pay tax now, never again).[14] The second form of consumption tax imposes its single tax on the back end, when resources flow out of households: this is a sales tax, a postpaid, cash-flow, or "qualified account model" consumption tax. Traditional IRAs in the United States work this way (no tax now, only later).

Under flat or constant tax rates, the two principal forms of a consumption tax are in fact largely equivalent, a result that can be proven in relatively simple algebraic terms.[15] This equivalence has led to a confusion in the traditional view of taxation, an over-quick equation of prepaid and postpaid consumption taxes. To see this equivalence and also to

[13] Mill, *Principles of Political Economy,* 165.

[14] There are two types of individual retirement accounts (IRAs), tax-favored savings accounts in the U.S. for individuals' retirement contributions: traditional IRAs and Roth IRAs. A traditional IRA is an account to which individuals can make tax-deductible contributions. Tax on earnings is deferred until withdrawal from the account at the age of at least fifty-nine and a half. Contributions to a Roth IRA, in contrast, are not tax-deductible, but withdrawals are not taxed. For more information on traditional IRAs, see the Internal Revenue Code ("IRC"), 26 U.S.C. section 408; for Roth IRAs, see IRC section 408A.

[15] Consider what happens to a principal sum, P, invested over time, for n periods, at a rate of return r. Untaxed, the sum grows at the rate of $(1 + r)$, which gets compounded by the n periods. A single tax, t, is taken away from the taxpayer at one time, leaving her with $(1 - t)$. Now, under the commutative principle of multiplication, which holds that $ab = ba$, it does not matter where, or, better, when, the $(1 - t)$ is levied. Assuming constant t and r—assumptions to be discussed in the text—the following identity holds: $\{(1 - t)P\}(1 + r)^n = \{P(1 + r)^n\}(1 - t)$.

consider further Mill's celebrated "double tax" argument against the income tax, a simple numeric example proves illustrative.

Suppose that Ant and Grasshopper each earn $200 in wages, the tax rate is 50 percent, and the interest rate on savings is 10 percent. Grasshopper, as is his way, spends all of his available money at once. Under any tax—income, prepaid consumption, or postpaid consumption—the government takes its 50 percent cut, or $100, and Grasshopper consumes the remaining $100. This demonstrates an important point: the choice of income versus consumption taxation has no direct impact on most taxpayers, for the simple reason that they do not save. (If I = C + S, and S = 0, then I = C.) But, of course, patterns of progressivity, saving, borrowing, and spending across the entire income and wealth scale matter to all citizens, even if not directly so.

Ant, in contrast, does save, and so the choice of tax does matter directly to her. Suppose that Ant saves her initial wage-earnings for two years, at the conclusion of which she consumes these initial wages plus any interest received on account of her saving them. How do the three different taxes treat her?

An income tax reduces Ant's $200 to $100 right away, which she puts in the bank. Ant earns 10 percent on her savings, or $10, in year 1, but the income tax hits this, too—Mill's double tax—taking away $5, leaving her with $105 at the end of year 1. In year 2, this $105 again earns 10 percent, or $10.50; again the income tax strikes, taking $5.25. This leaves Ant with $110.25 to consume at the end of year 2. If the 10 percent interest rate simply compensated Ant for inflation—if the cost of goods were rising at 10 percent per year—Ant would be losing real value, actual purchasing power, over time under the income tax: $110.25 at the end of two periods of 10 percent inflation is worth—has the same real purchasing power as—$91 at the start of the two periods.[16]

Consider next the two forms of consumption tax. First, the prepaid model: Ant is taxed on initial receipt under this system, reducing her $200 to $100. But she is not taxed again: recall that consumption taxes are single taxes, escaping Mill's double-tax label. The $100 grows by the full 10 percent interest rate, to $110, after year 1. In year 2, the $110 earns another 10 percent, or $11, to $121, and Ant is left to consume this much at the end of year 2. Unlike the case with the income tax, this end of year 2 consumption is worth the same as $100 at the start of year 1, under a 10 percent inflation or discount rate.

Under the postpaid consumption tax model, Ant pays no tax up-front and thus can save her entire $200. This grows by 10 percent, or $20, in year 1, to $220. The $220 grows by another 10 percent, or $22, to $242 in

[16] Since the future value (FV) of a present sum, P, invested over time at a rate of return r is $P(1 + r)^n$, the present value of any fixed future sum can be obtained by dividing such future sum by $(1 + r)^n$. Dividing Ant's $110.25 of year 2 dollars by $(1 + .10)^2$ or 1.21 yields approximately $91 in start of year 1 value.

year 2. When Ant goes to consume this, the government collects its 50 percent share, leaving Ant with $121 to consume. This is just as under the prepaid model. And it is more than the income tax. There is no smoke and mirrors here. There are only two critical assumptions needed to make out the equivalence of prepaid and postpaid consumption taxes: that the interest and tax rates have stayed constant in the two periods.[17]

The Ant-Grasshopper example, or something rather like it, stands at the center of the traditional view of tax. The income tax is a double tax on value that is not immediately consumed, which has led many conservatives to oppose it as an unfair burden on the noble Ant, but has led many liberals to support it as a necessary means of capturing some of the return to capital, the nearly exclusive domain of the wealthy. Both forms of consumption tax get put on the other side of a divide, as not reaching the yield to capital at all. It becomes a matter of either indifference or administrative convenience which of the two forms is chosen. In this traditional view, the debate over income taxation versus consumption taxation is an all-or-nothing one over whether to tax capital (all capital) at all. This traditional view of taxation is flawed.

B. *A new understanding*

The traditional view's equivalence of prepaid and postpaid consumption taxes does not hold under nonconstant or progressive rates. Once we assume at least some progression in the rate structure, the traditional understanding of consumption taxes is no longer accurate.

Progressive rates under most comprehensive tax systems work through a series of marginal rate brackets that form, in mathematical terms, a step-function. To have a simple and illustrative structure in mind, suppose that no tax is paid on the first $10,000, followed by a 15 percent marginal rate on the next $40,000, and a 30 percent rate on all value in excess of $50,000 (though further differentiation is, of course, possible). See table 1.

Such a system effects progression in average or effective tax rates. A taxpayer who has $100,000 subject to this tax, for example, will pay total taxes of $21,000 ($6,000, or 15 percent of $40,000, plus $15,000, or 30 percent of $50,000), for an average tax rate of 21 percent. This is a higher average tax rate than the one faced by someone who makes $50,000, who pays $6,000 (15 percent of $40,000), or 12 percent in average tax.

The two forms of consumption taxes differ in their effects under progressive rates. Now there are three—not two—alternatives for the tax

[17] For a fuller discussion, see Edward J. McCaffery, "A New Understanding of Tax," *Michigan Law Review* 103, no. 5 (2005): 825–26. It may seem as if the need for constant inflation is a third assumption, but inflation is built into the interest rate; in the running example, if inflation were running at 10 percent per year, then Ant would be breaking even with inflation, before tax, but losing real value after it. See note 15 and accompanying text.

TABLE 1. *Simple Marginal Tax Rate Schedule*

Income or consumption	Marginal tax rate
$0 to 10,000	0 percent
$10,000 to 50,000	15 percent
Over $50,000	30 percent

policymaker to choose. The differences depend on when the tax is imposed; this impacts choices of work, savings, education, and so on, and, most important, it determines how the tax redistributes material resources. The time-path of earnings and spending, inflows and outflows—and with them, the role of capital transactions—now matters critically to the total tax burden, given these progressive rates. Consider each tax in turn.

First, an income tax falls on all labor-market earnings and on the yield to savings, at the time they come into a household. Savers are hurt by the "double taxation" of savings, whatever their intended or actual use. Individuals, like the athletes, artists, and highly educated persons who see their earnings come in relatively short, concentrated bunches, are also hurt by the timing of the imposition of progressive rates.

Second, a prepaid consumption tax falls on labor-market earnings alone, again at the time they come into a household. Once more, people whose earnings profiles are uneven throughout their lifetimes are hurt by the timing of the imposition of the progressive rate structure. However—and here is the rub for most liberals and even moderates—those who live off the yield to capital are never taxed.

Third, a postpaid consumption tax does not come due at the time of initial inflows, but rather at the time of outflows, when money is spent in consumption. This means that a progressive postpaid consumption tax stands between an income tax, which double-taxes all savings, and a prepaid consumption tax, which ignores all savings. A consistently progressive postpaid consumption tax treats savings differently depending on their use, as I shall continue to explore in the following sections.

III. Two Norms of Capital

Before continuing with an exploration of how individuals in the normal course of their lives use capital and its yield, a matter that is critical to the new three-tax perspective on tax policy, let us pause and reflect on the norms of capital—that is, our ordinary moral intuitions about capital. Mill's claim that the income tax is a double tax on savings is descriptive, an analytic fact. It is true both within the income tax's own base, where savers are penalized vis-à-vis spenders, and relative to a hypothetical no-tax world, where the income tax destroys the equivalence, in present value terms, between savers and spenders, Ants and Grasshoppers. Yet neither of these facts exerts a strong pull on our moral intuitions; it is hard to get from Mill's *is* to any compelling *ought*. This tension featured prominently in an extended debate that began in the 1970s between the American law professors William Andrews and Alvin Warren, over income taxation versus consumption taxation. Andrews first pressed Mill's position, arguing that "the most sophisticated argument" for consumption taxation rested on preserving the pretax equality of spenders and savers.[18] This is an argument grounded in horizontal equity (comparing savers and spenders) and also one that takes an *ex ante* perspective (looking at the moment of decision to save or spend as the right time to make social judgments about fair taxation). Warren counterpunched by taking both an *ex post* (after the distribution of capital market returns) and a vertical equity perspective, arguing that those with greater "ability to pay" or (equivalently) more material resources ought to pay more than those with less: Ant has more material resources in the later, second period than Grasshopper does, so why shouldn't we tax Ant more?[19]

Arguments like Warren's had prevailed, decades before Warren actually made them, at the dawn of the creation of comprehensive individual taxation systems in the United States in the early years of the twentieth century, and elsewhere later in the century. Reformers actively desired an income tax because it included the yield to savings, and thus would impose an added burden on financiers and the like.[20] Those were, however, simpler times. Things changed as the income tax expanded both in scale, becoming a higher burden and more steeply sloped in its rate progression, and in scope, reaching the majority of earners in the U.S. and elsewhere.[21] Lawmakers began to have second thoughts about double-taxing the yield to savings, anywhere and everywhere. A near century of experience with a so-called income tax in the United States and in other countries in the developed world has by now shown a deep split over the

[18] William D. Andrews, "A Consumption-Type or Cash Flow Personal Income Tax," *Harvard Law Review* 87, no. 6 (1974): 1113–88.

[19] Alvin C. Warren, Jr., "Fairness and a Consumption-Type or Cash Flow Personal Income Tax," *Harvard Law Review* 88, no. 5 (1975): 931–46; see also Alvin C. Warren, Jr., "Would a Consumption Tax Be Fairer Than an Income Tax?" *Yale Law Journal* 89, no. 6 (1980): 1081–1124. See also Barbara Fried, "Ex ante/Ex post," *The Journal of Contemporary Legal Issues* 13, no. 1 (2003): 123–60.

[20] Consider, for example, the argument of Senator William E. Borah in the debates leading up to adoption of the Sixteenth Amendment in 1913, permitting the modern income tax in the United States. Referring to the founding fathers, Senator Borah claimed that "it was a republic they were building, where all men were to be equal and bear equally the burdens of government, and not an oligarchy, for that must a government be, which exempts property and wealth from all taxation." Quoted in Steven R. Weisman, *The Great Tax Wars* (New York: Simon and Schuster, 2002), 224. See also Steven A. Bank, "The Progressive Consumption Tax Revisited," *Michigan Law Review* 101, no. 6 (2003): 2238–60.

[21] Carolyn C. Jones, "Class Tax to Mass Tax: The Role of Propaganda in the Expansion of the Income Tax during World War II," *Buffalo Law Review* (Fall 1988/1989): 685–737.

normative propriety of taxing the yield to capital. More and more exceptions to the income tax's theoretical commitment to double-taxing savings have been piled on one another, whether by happenstance, inertia, deliberate policy, or mere mistake. Examples include tax-favored medical, educational, and retirement savings accounts, the nontaxation of "unrealized" appreciation, and the rather systematic exclusion of the financial gains from personal residences.[22] The result is that we now observe "hybrid" taxes, perched (typically, uneasily) between an income tax model, with its double tax, and a consumption tax, with its principled nontaxation of savings. The trouble is, the compromises to bring about this state of affairs have been effected without suitable normative or practical reflection, resulting in a tax system in which the well-endowed—the capitalist class—can live well and *consume* away, tax-free. We are neither favoring savings nor effecting a fair distribution of tax burdens across taxpayers; individuals who can live off the yield to capital quite simply need pay no tax.[23]

Consider a simple example, drawn from my earlier work on this subject.[24] Take the case of Artful Dodger, who happens to have the sum of one million dollars. It does not matter much for the illustration how Dodger got this wealth. If he earned it via wages, he would have paid income and payroll taxes on it; if he received it as a gift or as the proceeds of life insurance, for example, he would never have paid tax on it, and, depending on the circumstances of his benefactor, it is possible that no one ever paid tax on it.[25] The point is that Dodger need never pay tax again. He can invest his million dollars in non-income producing property, such as growth stocks; such property rises in value without producing taxable cash each year. Dodger can borrow, income tax free, to finance his lifestyle. When he dies, his heirs can sell their inherited property, tax free, and pay off Dodger's debts, continuing the pattern with any value that is left over. The details vary, but the basic point is that those who live off the fruits of financial capital need pay no federal taxes in the United States, at least, while those who live off human capital—those who get paid for their labor—are hit, and hit hard, by income and payroll taxes combined.

On reflection, the schisms in contemporary tax systems between income tax and consumption tax elements are not random. Looking back to the Andrews-Warren, income-versus-consumption debate, settled reflection reveals that ordinary moral intuitions reasonably reach different norma-

[22] For an extended discussion of these and other deviations from the U.S. income tax's theoretical commitment to taxing savings, see McCaffery, "A New Understanding of Tax," 885–907.

[23] See Edward J. McCaffery, "A Voluntary Tax? Revisited," *National Tax Association Papers and Proceedings* (2000): 268–74.

[24] See McCaffery, *Fair Not Flat*, 33–34.

[25] IRC section 101 exempts the proceeds of life insurance from income taxation; IRC section 102 exempts gifts.

tive judgments about different uses of savings. On the one hand, many citizens are indeed sympathetic to the noble Ant, especially when she is manifest as a middle-aged wage-earner, struggling to make ends meet while paying her taxes and setting aside some funds for her later retirement, or for medical or educational needs within her family. Why should we punish her, with a second tax, for her prudence? Thus, we observe tax-favored retirement, medical, and educational savings accounts. On the other hand, many citizens are also bothered by the specter of the socially privileged, such as a second- or third-generation rich child, like Artful Dodger, living well off the fruits of someone else's prior capital accumulation. Surely this "trust fund baby" should be taxed, at least as much as the hard-working Ant. Surely his income, in the form of rents, royalties, interest, dividends, and the like, should count in the tax base, at least as much as the product of noble Ant's blood, sweat, and tears.

These simple insights and intuitions cash out into two discrete norms about capital. Not all uses of savings are the same. One norm I call the "ordinary-savings norm": Capital transactions (borrowing, saving, investing) that are simply used to move around uneven labor-market earnings in time, allowing people to save for their retirement, or for periods of high spending needs/low earnings, such as times of education or medical urgency, should not be double-taxed or otherwise discouraged and burdened. The second norm I call the "yield-to-capital norm": Capital that enables a higher, better—more costly—lifestyle than the yield to labor, alone, should bear *some* burden, one at least commensurate with normal wage earnings.

Ordinary moral intuitions thus agree with both Andrews's horizontal equity position and Warren's vertical equity one, and this agreement is revealed through these two norms, the ordinary-savings norm and the yield-to-capital norm. Savers should not be penalized for saving, rather than consuming, in the ordinary course of their lives, so as to provide for rainy days or times of greater need or urgency. But the yield to capital is also an increment of value that should not be simply and completely ignored in the tax base. The trick is to design a tax system that implements both norms, simultaneously, without undue complexity. It turns out that, with the right understanding of taxation—*mirabile dictu*—this is surprisingly easy to do.

IV. Two Uses of Savings

With this new normative vocabulary in hand, we can now return to the discussion of the uses of material resources, focusing especially on the uses of capital. Consider in financial terms how most of us live out our lifetimes. As any parent knows full well, we spring forth into the world nearly fully formed as consumers: we cost money from the get-go. As any parent also knows, however, we do not earn anything for quite some time. When we do start earning, we have to earn more than we spend (let us hope!), to pay off the debts of our youth, including school loans, and to set aside funds for our retirement, so that we do not have to keep working all the days of our lives. Our lives look like one fairly steady consumption profile, from cradle to grave, financed by a lumpy period of labor-market earnings concentrated in midlife. If we lived as islands, unto ourselves, we would have to balance the books on our own account, borrowing in youth, first paying off our debts and later saving for retirement in our midlife, and spending down in old age. Financial intermediaries such as banks and insurance companies would help us to effect these results. In practice, many families work as more or less informal annuities markets, between generations. Thus, our parents pay for our youths, and we pay for our children's youths; we also stand ready to pay our parents back, should their needs exceed their resources in their old age.[26] And so on.

In this stylized depiction of a typical life, note two broad uses of savings. One is to *smooth out* consumption profiles, within lifetimes or across individuals—to translate uneven labor-market earnings into even consumption flows. We do this by borrowing in youth and saving for retirement (and/or other times of special need, such as health and education demands) in midlife. We can do this using third-party financial intermediaries, or within the family, as noted above: perhaps we pay for our children's youth, and they pay for the youths of their children, our grandchildren, in a recurring "overlapping generations" model.

A second use of savings is the analytic complement of smoothing: capital transactions can *shift* consumption profiles, up or down. An upward shift occurs when the fruits of our own or another's savings (via beneficence) allow us to live a "better" lifestyle than we could on the basis of our own labor-market earnings alone, smoothed out over time. Suppose that the noble Ant has gotten wondrously lucky on the $200 of wage-earnings that she has saved; some investment has yielded her millions of dollars. Ant can then, quite simply, enjoy a "better"—more costly—lifestyle than other ants or grasshoppers earning the same amount of labor-market wages. The progressive postpaid consumption tax would thus tax her, on her spending. A downward shift, in contrast, occurs when our Ant's beneficence or bad fortune means that she will live at a lower—less costly—lifestyle than she otherwise could, all measured against the baseline of her smoothed-out labor-market earnings profile alone.

The two norms considered in the prior section map up perfectly with these two uses of capital. Smoothing effects the ordinary-savings norm;

[26] See, e.g., Laurence J. Kotlikoff and Avia Spivak, "The Family as an Incomplete Annuities Market," *The Journal of Political Economy* 89, no. 2 (1981): 372–91; and Laurence J. Kotlikoff and Lawrence H. Summers, "The Role of Intergenerational Transfers in Aggregate Capital Accumulation," *The Journal of Political Economy* 89, no. 4 (1981): 706–32.

shifting effects the yield-to-capital one. Ordinary moral intuitions, reflected in nearly a century of experience with actual taxation systems, suggest that society ought not to burden smoothing transactions with a double tax, but that the yield to capital is an element of value that can properly be taxed when used to enable a "better," more expensive lifestyle. This is not envy. That is, it is not the concept that the rich should be penalized, or that those who earn wealth from capital should be brought down and laid low. It is, rather, the sensible thought that the yield to capital is an increment of value that deserves to be counted in one's resources available to pay tax, except when savings are used simply to move values around in time. Such movements in time are one thing; greater material enjoyment is another thing. It is all, in essence, about the fair timing of taxation.

Return now to the three basic tax systems: income, prepaid consumption, and postpaid consumption. Under progressive rates, these three basic tax systems affect different patterns of savings and spending differently. An income tax double-taxes all savings, come what may, and makes its judgments of progression on the basis of inflows, however uneven. A prepaid consumption or wage tax ignores all capital transactions, again whatever their use, and also makes its judgments of the fair degree of progression on the basis of inflows, burdening the uneven wage earner. But a consistent progressive postpaid consumption tax, wondrously enough, implements the ordinary-savings and yield-to-capital norms, simultaneously, seamlessly, and by design.

A simple example helps to make these points clearer. One taxpayer, Steady Earner, makes and consumes $50,000 a year for the relevant years of comparison, say beginning in her early twenties. A second taxpayer, Lumpy Earner, stays in school until he is thirty, and then makes $100,000 a year. But Lumpy Earner spends $50,000 a year, too, using prudent borrowing and saving to effect this result.[27] Finally, Trust Fund Baby lives off his parents' fortune, getting and spending $50,000 a year (which represents a 5 percent yield off a trust corpus of $1,000,000, small change for the rich today). How do the three taxes affect these three individuals, under the simple progressive rate structure posited above (in table 1)?

An ideal progressive income tax burdens all three taxpayers, but falls most heavily on Lumpy Earner, because of the timing of the imposition of the progressive rates. In the simple rate structure posited above, Lumpy Earner pays 21 percent of his earnings in income tax (as calculated from table 1), whereas Steady Earner and Trust Fund Baby each pay 12 percent.

A progressive prepaid consumption tax also burdens Lumpy Earner most heavily, at a 21 percent level, given the same rate structure. Such a tax continues to burden Steady Earner at the 12 percent level, but it

[27] My simple example ignores interest, which I discuss at greater length in McCaffery, "A New Understanding of Tax," 864, note 159 and accompanying text.

altogether ignores Trust Fund Baby—taxing him at 0 percent, and thereby accepting the tax, if any, on some prior generation of labor earnings as sufficient for his contribution to society.

A progressive postpaid consumption tax, in contrast, falls equally on all three taxpayers, at the 12 percent level. Note, moreover, that if any of the three taxpayers should get lucky in the capital markets—win the lottery, say, or simply get extra high returns from investments—then the progressive postpaid consumption tax stands ready to tax that good fortune when and as it is used to enhance, or elevate, that taxpayer's lifestyle.

In sum, whereas an ideal income tax double-taxes all savings, whatever their use, and a prepaid consumption tax ignores all savings, again whatever their use, a consistent progressive postpaid consumption tax splits the difference, in a principled way and by design. It allows taxpayers to lower their taxes by smoothing, but it falls on the yield to capital when such yield is used to enhance lifestyles. This reflects simple, commonsensical attitudes about life, income, and savings. These attitudes are reflected imperfectly under the status quo in the United States and other advanced Western democracies, with a nominal income tax rife with pro-savings provisions for retirement, health, and education.

V. The Case against (Direct) Capital Taxation

The better understanding of the analytics of taxation that we have now attained can lead to a dramatically simpler tax system that is, at the same time, far fairer, one that perfectly incorporates our ordinary moral intuitions about savings—namely, that savings for some purposes, which we can broadly call "smoothing," should not be burdened twice over, but that savings that enable a higher material lifestyle can and should be subject to tax: some positive tax burden commensurate with all other sources of material enjoyment or private preclusive use. The central insight is that a consistent progressive postpaid consumption tax is a tax on the yield to capital, under just the circumstances in which ordinary moral intuitions suggest taxing such yield, and no other. Such a tax can be implemented easily enough, taking advantage of the rearrangement of the Haig-Simons definition of income noted above: consumption equals income minus savings (C = I − S). This handy formula shows that a consistent postpaid consumption tax can be obtained by tallying up sources of income as under current law, and systematically subtracting savings (and adding in dissavings).[28]

The tax law would thereby, however surprisingly, look much like it does today, in the United States at least. There would be annual wage reporting from one's employers and annual income tax returns like the dreaded 1040 forms used in the U.S. Instead of the myriad of tax-favored

[28] See McCaffery, *Fair Not Flat*, 97–111.

accounts we observe today, however, there would be a single, unlimited savings account for every individual, which we can call, to make things clear, a "trust account." All contributions to these accounts would be deductible, and all withdrawals from them would be includable in taxable "consumed income." Debt that was used to consume, as dissavings, would likewise be taxable; repayments of principal, as positive savings, would be deductible. In such a fashion, the law would work out the logic of "income minus savings." Ordinary saving for retirement would lower the burden of taxation, by changing the time of taxation from one's high-earning, midlife years, to the smoother, lower levels of one's consumption. Saving for medical needs or other special circumstances, such as education, could also lower the burden of one's taxes, especially if the law imposed a lower (or no) taxation on these uses, parallel to the United States' current limited deduction for extraordinary medical expenses.[29] Lumpy Earner, for example, who makes $100,000 in wages but saves $50,000 for his retirement, would pay tax on $50,000 ($100,000 minus $50,000). Trust Fund Baby would pay tax on the $50,000 he withdrew from his trust account. Steady Earner, who neither borrows nor saves, would pay tax on her earnings, which equal her consumption, $50,000. Note that there is no need whatsoever to tally up particular items of expenditure; this is all quite general. To this base, a progressive rate structure can apply, like the structure illustrated by table 1.

The important point to see is that this progressive postpaid consumption tax would, in and of itself, make for an individuated tax on capital, when, but only when, capital is used to enhance lifestyles. No other tax on capital would therefore be needed—and, in part because any other tax on capital is *not* so individuated, and hence risks falling on ordinary savings as well as on the yield to capital, all "direct" taxes on capital should be eliminated.

Consider first the role of "second" taxes on the yield to capital under the basic individuated tax system, such as capital gains under the income tax. These are simply not needed under a consistent progressive postpaid consumption tax. On the one hand, if a taxpayer sells an asset and reinvests the proceeds, she has continued to save, and there is no reason to tax her. This can all be done inside her trust account. On the other hand, *any* mechanism to finance her lifestyle—wages, the ordinary yield to capital (interest, dividends, and the like), someone else's beneficence, the proceeds of sales of capital assets or, for that matter, borrowing against present assets or future earnings—is taxed, at the moment of private preclusive use, when withdrawn from the trust account. Whether or not to sell an asset can be left to the personal decisions of investors, for the sake of efficiency. How to tax the proceeds of investments can be left to the

[29] IRC section 213.

moment of consumption, when society can better judge what kind of lifestyle these investments enable.

Consider next the gift and estate tax. The current system in the United States at least aims to "backstop" the income tax, which tax is (in ideal theory) supposed to burden savings, by levying a hefty tax on those decedents who die with large estates or those persons making large *inter vivos* gifts. This tax is obviously desired as a matter of fairness. But its very existence encourages the rich to consume more, and die broke, whether they spend on themselves or on their heirs.[30] In contrast, a consistent progressive postpaid consumption tax never taxes savings directly. Assets saved in the trust accounts thus have a zero "basis" in technical tax terms, meaning that they have not yet been taxed, and thus all proceeds from their sale or disposition are subject to tax, if and when consumed.[31] The trust accounts can therefore be passed on to heirs during one's lifetime or at death, without the moment of transfer itself triggering tax. Of course, at a different time, *spending* by the heirs will generate tax, under a progressive rate structure, on withdrawal from the trust accounts. A consistent progressive postpaid consumption tax does not need, in principle, a separate gift and estate tax, because the very design of the tax entails an accessions or inheritance tax—Trust Fund Baby pays the progressive spending tax. Note, by the way, that intergenerational transfers, just as intragenerational ones, can effect smoothing or shifting: parents can help to equalize spending across generations, or they can self-sacrifice to allow their children to live better. In the latter, shifting case, the familial burden will increase under a consistent progressive spending tax; in the former, smoothing case, it will decrease. This pattern has normative appeal.

Finally, parallel—though indeed stronger—arguments can be made against a separate corporate income tax. The problems with this tax begin with its uncertain incidence: since corporations are not real people, they do not really pay taxes. They must pass these on. A corporate tax falls on workers and consumers, on capital generally, or on some combination thereof.[32] To the extent that it falls on ordinary workers and consumers, a corporate income tax's claims to fairness are fairly obviously questionable. But even to the extent that such a tax falls on capital, it cannot do so in any *individuated* way. Savers bear the burden of the corporate income tax whether they are rich or not, whether they are saving for lifetime needs or emergencies or to support a high-end lifestyle. Once again, under a consistent progressive postpaid consumption tax—which falls on

[30] See Stephan M. Pollan and Mark Levine, *Die Broke* (New York: Harper-Collins, 1997). For my own thoughts on estate or wealth transfer taxation, see McCaffery, "The Uneasy Case"; Edward J. McCaffery, "The Political Liberal Case against the Estate Tax," *Philosophy and Public Affairs* 23, no. 4 (1994): 281–312; and McCaffery, *Fair Not Flat*, 62–77.

[31] IRC section 1011 (basis); I define "basis" in McCaffery, *Fair Not Flat*, 161, as after-tax dollars.

[32] See generally the sources cited above in note 3.

the yield to capital as a source of personal consumption, making individuated judgments at that time—a direct tax on capital, such as a corporate income tax, is not needed.

The elimination of these other taxes follows from the principle of a consistent progressive postpaid consumption tax: to tax individuals as they spend, not as they work, save, give, or die. Such a tax will enhance simplicity, transparency, and efficiency while promoting fairness. Specifically in terms of capital, the tax would apply to the yield to capital, when (but only when) it is appropriate to do so. The rich would not be let off the social hook; their tax would come due when, as, and if they spent wealth on themselves. Progressivity could be maintained, even strengthened.

VI. Capital as Power

An argument that supports direct capital taxation, manifest in a recent rise in scholarly reflection over a separate freestanding wealth tax,[33] pivots on the idea that capital itself—the mere possession of material resources, unspent—is a phenomenon that bears taxing. I have long written that this argument, as an objection to a consistent progressive postpaid consumption tax, is confused.[34] To see why this is so requires us to take a deeper, better look at why the wider society might find it troubling that capital should rest in private hands. Two potential problems come to mind.

One possibility is that the capital today represents potential consumption, or spending tomorrow: capital qua potential use. But the consistent progressive postpaid consumption tax, best understood, exerts a present lien on capital for any future use. Such a tax redefines property rights, what it means to be "private" or "public." A taxpayer cannot use "her" capital without running through the gauntlet of the tax system; that tax system stands ready to exercise a greater toll on higher, less urgent private use. Thus, this argument rests on a confusion.

A second possibility is that capital today represents use, or power, *today*; there is the problem, as I have called it, of capital qua present use. This is a question of what one does with "his" capital. It is possible to save in a way that exercises power, or confers pleasure, as by buying up newspapers, sports franchises, or, for that matter, elected offices. The response to this problem tracks the response to the first. Once again, the tax system defines or redefines property rights, what it means to be "private" or "public." Problems with how capital is used are best met by regulation, as we have today in all advanced capitalist countries, for "private" endowments, pension plans, IRA accounts, and so on. Simply

[33] See generally the articles in *Tax Law Review* 53, no. 3 (2000): 263–498; and *Tax Law Review* 53, no. 4 (2000): 499–696.

[34] McCaffery, "The Uneasy Case"; McCaffery, "The Political Liberal Case."

forbidding taxpayers from using "their" trust-account money to affect political outcomes without first withdrawing the funds from the account and paying a tax will go a long way—farther than any mechanism we have in place in the U.S. today—toward curbing the power of capital qua capital. Therefore, this argument, too, is misplaced as a criticism of a consistent progressive postpaid consumption tax. In practice and in theory, such a tax creates a structure in which capital is, indeed, a common pool, and can be regulated as such—though it bears noting, again, that this is not the only or the best justification for the tax, Hobbes notwithstanding. It is, rather, a happy by-product of doing the right thing—getting the fair timing of taxation down right on an individual level.

VII. One Last Uneasy Argument

Another argument for direct capital taxation, pressed particularly vis-à-vis the corporate income tax, bears noting. It is that these taxes are desired precisely because they are "hidden." People do not notice the true incidence of the corporate tax, and this allows governments to have a higher revenue base than they otherwise might.

This may at first seem a weak argument to press in the name of fairness, resting as it does on trickery, and coming in the face of the near-certain regressive incidence of the tax. But recent research that I and others have conducted does indeed suggest that perhaps the best way to effect redistribution of material resources to the poor is to have large and relatively flat taxes, accompanied by progressive redistributive *expenditure* programs.[35] It is, after all, the net of tax and transfer programs that matters to any robust and compelling sense of distributive justice. So perhaps we want capital taxes, bad as these levies are, to get the money with which to effect social justice, on the spending side of the government's tax and spending scheme.

In the end, this might be a compelling practical political argument for corporate taxation, though not for gift and estate taxes or capital taxes more generally, and though it bears noting that corporate taxes have been declining as a source of revenue in all advanced states, and may not, in the end, be worth the candle. As philosophers and scholars, however, we should know this argument for what it is and label it as such. It bears noting that "hidden" taxes have real costs: the corporate income tax affects prices, distorts decisions, and effects no compelling distributive goal, once a suitably designed progressive spending tax is in place at the individual level. Thus, maintaining it, even to get funds for doing "good," is not without cost; in a perfect world, we could generate all the revenues

[35] See Jonathan Baron and Edward J. McCaffery, "Unmasking Redistribution (Or Its Absence)," in Edward J. McCaffery and Joel Slemrod, eds., *Behavioral Public Finance* (New York: Russell Sage Press, 2006); and Bird and Zolt, "Redistribution in Developing Countries."

we need for just social spending programs by just social taxation schemes. In public finance as in life, we can pay a dear price for our illusions.

VIII. Conclusion

Advocates for fairness in taxation have long supported an income tax, precisely because it gets at the yield to capital, and because, they think, consumption taxes do not. In fact, a better understanding of the analytics of taxation shows otherwise. Under progressive rates, the two canonical forms of consumption taxation, prepaid and postpaid, are not equivalent. An income tax is a double tax on all savings, come what may. A prepaid consumption or wage tax does indeed ignore the yield to capital, everywhere and anywhere. But a postpaid consumption tax splits the difference, by design. It falls on the yield to capital when (but only when) this yield is used to elevate lifestyles, not when it is used to smooth out in time, within or between generations, uneven labor-market earnings.

It turns out that this is the right thing to do. Not only can we derive that from first principles, and the ordinary-savings and yield-to-capital norms, but we can also observe it from a century of practice with a so-called income tax. Whatever one thinks of ideal taxation, we ought to note well the fact that we have never had, and almost certainly never will have, an ideal income tax in practice, or anything close to it, at all. The real debate in practical tax politics is and always has been over what form of consumption taxation to have. Here the stakes are large and dramatic for the fate of progressivity in taxation, and point toward a consistent progressive postpaid consumption tax.

The final insight is that, once we have gotten the comprehensive tax system down right, strictly from a fairness point of view—by adopting a consistent progressive postpaid consumption tax—we no longer need any direct taxes on capital. This is not because capital per se is good, or because of a naive horizontal equity approach to policy. Rather, it is because we are now taxing the yield to capital, in an individuated way, at the right time. We can and should repeal all capital taxes under the income tax, the separate gift and estate tax, and corporate taxes of all forms. This will add considerably to the simplicity, administrability, and efficiency of the tax system, but these are side effects. The principal and principled reason we should take this approach is that it is the fair thing to do.

Law and Political Science, University of Southern California

HOUSEHOLDS AND THE FISCAL SYSTEM*

By Daniel N. Shaviro

I. Introduction

One of the most vexed issues in the history of the federal income tax is how family or household status should affect tax liability. The relative treatment of different types of households, such as singles versus married individuals as well as those with and without children, has fluctuated significantly over time and between countries, reflecting not just varying political trends but the general lack of an underlying theoretical consensus concerning how to think about household issues.[1] The rise of feminist concerns in recent decades has strongly affected the tenor of the discussion, but without creating anything approaching theoretical closure.[2] In this essay, I suggest a general approach for thinking about household issues, grounded in advances over the last fifteen years in the broader normative tax policy literature. I then apply this general approach to a number of the main tax and transfer issues posed by households.

The discussion proceeds as follows. In Section II, I discuss the need for a normative framework and my use of utilitarianism to provide such a framework. In Section III, I discuss why households matter in setting the treatment of individuals by the fiscal system. In Section IV, I discuss the definition of a household. In Sections V and VI, I discuss the commonly cited but often irreconcilable principles of equal taxation of equal-income couples and marriage neutrality. In Section VII, I discuss the relative treatment of single individuals, one-earner couples, and two-earner couples. In Section VIII, I discuss the fiscal system's incentive effects on work

* I am grateful to Lily Batchelder and Louis Kaplow for comments on an earlier draft.

[1] Classic articles from the 1970s that note the long-standing lack of political stasis and theoretical consensus include Boris I. Bittker, "Federal Income Taxation and the Family," *Stanford Law Review* 27 (1975): 1389–1463; and Michael J. McIntyre and Oliver Oldman, "Taxation of the Family in a Comprehensive and Simplified Income Tax," *Harvard Law Review* 90 (1977): 1573–1630. Among the very numerous more recent treatments of the subject are Louis Kaplow, "Optimal Distribution and the Family," *Scandinavian Journal of Economics* 98, no. 1 (1996): 75–92; Edward J. McCaffery, *Taxing Women* (Chicago: University of Chicago Press, 1996); and Lawrence Zelenak, "Doing Something about Marriage Penalties: A Guide for the Perplexed," *Tax Law Review* 54 (2000): 1–76.

[2] See, e.g., Grace Ganz Blumberg, "Sexism in the Code: A Comparative Study of Working Wive and Mothers," *Buffalo Law Review* 21 (1980): 49–98; Marjorie E. Kornhauser, "Love, Money, and the IRS: Family, Income-Sharing, and the Joint Income Tax Return," *Hastings Law Journal* 45 (1993): 63–111; Nancy C. Staudt, "Taxing Housework," *Georgetown Law Journal* 84 (1996): 1571–1647; McCaffery, *Taxing Women*; and Anne L. Alstott, *No Exit: What Parents Owe Their Children and What Society Owes Parents* (Oxford: Oxford University Press, 2004).

decisions by secondary earners in a household. In Section IX, I discuss the distributional and incentive issues raised by the treatment of households with children. In Section X, I conclude by noting some possible practical implications of the prior analysis.

II. A Normative Framework

The main advance in the tax policy literature on which I draw in this essay is the shift to a more sophisticated normative stance. Rather than assigning canonical status to the Haig-Simons income concept, which defines income as the market value of the taxpayer's consumption and change in net worth during the tax year,[3] writers about tax policy increasingly recognize that one cannot coherently ground a normative position without venturing "into the territory of more abstract controversies of political and social philosophy."[4] Leading early studies argued that "the Haig-Simons formulation of the income concept can and should play a central role in the development of a normative model for the taxation of the family."[5] Or, finding that "nothing in the [Haig-Simons] concept . . . tells us anything about the extent to which tax rates should take account of marriage bonds or family responsibilities,"[6] they argued instead that there is simply an unresolvable conflict between "marriage neutrality," which requires that marriage and divorce have no effect on tax liability, and "couples neutrality,"[7] or equal taxation of equal-income couples.

More recent work has rejected the traditional doctrinal approach in favor of focusing on such central issues in household taxation as the tax system's discouraging married women from working and its favoring traditional one-earner families over those in which both spouses work.[8] However, it mostly has tended to emphasize particular issues, such as

[3] Henry Simons, *Personal Income Taxation* (Chicago: University of Chicago Press, 1938), 50. The adoption of an income tax in various Western European countries in the late nineteenth century, and in the United States in 1913, prompted extensive scholarly discussion of what "income" (typically assumed to be a desirable tax base on poorly specified grounds relating to the "ability to pay" concept) really meant. Simons championed the term's generalization to cover the market value of all consumption and changes in net worth, even in the absence of an observed market transaction such as a sale of appreciated property. The Haig-Simons income ideal held a dominant position in U.S. legal tax scholarship from at least the 1950s through the 1980s, although more recently it has increasingly been challenged by support for consumption taxation.

[4] Liam Murphy and Thomas Nagel, *The Myth of Ownership: Taxes and Justice* (Oxford: Oxford University Press, 2002), 6.

[5] McIntyre and Oldman, "Taxation of the Family," 1576.

[6] Boris I. Bittker, "A 'Comprehensive Tax Base' as a Goal of Income Tax Reform," *Harvard Law Review* 80 (1967): 974.

[7] Bittker, "Federal Income Taxation and the Family."

[8] See, e.g., McCaffery, *Taxing Women*. I have also examined these issues in earlier work. See Daniel N. Shaviro, *Making Sense of Social Security Reform* (Chicago: University of Chicago Press, 2000), 65–66 and 72–73; and Daniel N. Shaviro, *Who Should Pay for Medicare?* (Chicago: University of Chicago Press, 2004), 69–71, 128–30, and 134–35.

gender bias in the tax system or the treatment of children, in lieu of a full overview. An important exception, systematically applying a normative view like mine, is the work of Louis Kaplow, from which I have benefited in thinking about these issues.[9]

The need to specify an underlying, inevitably controversial normative stance undermines the possibility of achieving broad consensus, but at least it means that one's cards are on the table. My own preference, utilitarianism, has come nowhere near universal acceptance. Nor even has welfarism, or the broader set of positions holding that only individuals' well-being matters, whether or not toted up in utilitarian fashion.[10] Most people would agree, however, that well-being is important, whether or not it is exclusively so, and that utilitarians are generally right to prefer greater to lesser well-being even if one has qualms about some applications of their aggregation method. A utilitarian approach should be relevant, therefore, even to people who are not utilitarians.[11]

The basic idea I use in operationalizing utilitarianism is that we should think of the fiscal system, including the income tax, in terms of an expanded notion of "social insurance."[12] We can approach this concept by starting with private insurance. On the supply side, private insurance involves using the law of large numbers to reduce variance. For example, the rate of automobile accidents is relatively predictable, while who will have an accident is not, so drivers can reduce their individual variance by pooling their risks through the medium of an insurance company.

On the demand side, however, the role of the law of large numbers is incidental rather than fundamental. Indeed, even offsetting a bad financial outcome is merely a means, not the end. A rational consumer buys insurance, even though (assuming an actuarially fair bet with a compensated service provider) it reduces her expected financial return, because it increases her expected utility. The idea is to direct more dollars to states of the world where the consumer expects to value them more, by agreeing

[9] See Kaplow, "Optimal Distribution and the Family"; Kaplow, "Families, Tax Treatment of," in Joseph Cordes et al., *Encyclopedia of Taxation and Tax Policy* (Washington, DC: Urban Institute Press, 1999); and Louis Kaplow, "Taxation," in A. Mitchell Polinsky and Steven Shavell, eds., *Handbook of Law and Economics* (forthcoming).

[10] But see Louis Kaplow and Steven Shavell, *Fairness Versus Welfare* (Cambridge, MA: Harvard University Press, 2002), arguing for welfarism.

[11] The form of utilitarianism that I apply is hedonic rather than preference-based, and thus permits overriding people's observed preferences if we have sufficient grounds for believing that they are making mistakes from the standpoint of their own welfare. (Their preferences would, however, typically serve as powerful empirical evidence regarding what best serves their welfare.) In addition, I assume a utilitarian aim of maximizing total rather than average welfare. I concede that there are grave difficulties with the view that people's mental states can generally (even assuming full information) be given cardinal or even ordinal welfare rankings, reflecting the diversity of our psychological sensations and experiences.

[12] See Shaviro, *Making Sense of Social Security Reform*, 44–58, for a broader discussion of social insurance.

to accept fewer dollars in states of the world where she expects to value them less.

Due to the declining marginal utility of wealth, this often involves compensating losses. For example, I may value getting a million dollars from the insurance company much more in the state of the world where I owe an injured pedestrian one million dollars than in that where I have avoided collisions. But some bad outcomes are not worth betting against, because they would not increase the marginal value of a dollar. Thus, for example, parents typically do not insure against the death of a child, because, terrible though it would be, it would not add to the value of getting cash. Moreover, we sometimes "bet" against good outcomes rather than bad ones, by using insurance or similar contracts to direct dollars to states of the world where we are better off but expect to derive greater utility from a marginal dollar. One example is a life annuity, which insures you against the "risk" of living longer—a good outcome, but one that means you will need more money to meet your lifetime material needs. Similarly, medical insurance, when conditioned on available treatments, offers you a bigger payoff if expensive new treatments that could help you are newly developed—again, a good outcome, but one that makes money more valuable to you.

With rational consumers and complete, well-functioning markets, private insurance would advance utilitarian aims because, by definition, every arrangement that increased expected utility would arise in response to consumer demand. Indeed, even arrangements that were Kaldor-Hicks efficient rather than Pareto-efficient—that is, arrangements that made people on average better-off but with some losers—would arise if there were a stage where people could make insurance bargains behind a veil of ignorance regarding how their odds would change once they knew more about their circumstances. Thus, suppose that transferring ten dollars from A to B would increase B's utility more than it reduces A's. While A might not like this arrangement once she knew she was A, if there were a stage where she could decide whether to mandate the transfer before knowing whether she was more likely to end up as A or as B, then it would be no different from the case where she is buying insurance for her future self. Hence the insight of economist John Harsanyi, writing before John Rawls's more famous use of the behind-the-veil rubric,[13] that this rubric readily supports a utilitarian approach.[14]

[13] See John Rawls, *A Theory of Justice* (Cambridge, MA: The Belknap Press of Harvard University Press, 1971).

[14] John Harsanyi, "Cardinal Utility in Welfare Economics and in the Theory of Risk-Taking," *Journal of Political Economy* 61 (1953): 434. To be sure, positing a veil of ignorance is an extra step relative to simply valuing everyone's welfare equally in the world we actually observe, a step requiring justification and potentially raising such questions about its "thickness" as what degree of risk aversion people should be deemed to have if they do not know who they are. From a utilitarian standpoint, however, the veil of ignorance is merely a way of expressing morally required indifference between oneself and other people. Treating

Where market failure leaves private demand for insurance unsatisfied, including due to the lack of a behind-the-veil stage, there is a case for government intervention if the government can better address the failure. The two classic insurance problems that might lead to private market failure, but that government intervention could try to address, are moral hazard and adverse selection. Moral hazard arises when the insured reduces her effort to avoid or mitigate the circumstances that would give rise to a claim, because of how the insurance affects her incentives. An example would be driving less carefully due to one's car insurance coverage. Adverse selection involves using superior information about one's own risk profile to buy coverage disproportionately in situations where the odds are against the insurance provider. An example would be buying generous health insurance coverage based on your knowledge, which the insurance company does not share, that you have a condition calling for costly surgery.

In general, governments may have a hard time outperforming private firms with respect to moral hazard. Greater power to compel information disclosure, thus addressing the information asymmetry about the insured's decisions that underlies the problem, is the only extra tool governments have, and this tool may not always help very much. A government can, however, powerfully address adverse selection if exit from its zone of control is costly. By taxing residents to fund benefits, it can limit the effect of people's superior information about their own circumstances on enrollment outcomes.

Government insurance provision also has a major disadvantage. The weakness of competitive constraints on government actors creates incentive problems regarding the provision of welfare-enhancing insurance. Unlike businesses in a competitive market with informed consumers, governments do not have to make enrollees better off unless the governments themselves face either competitive pressures or control by informed voters (that is, exit or voice).

The most prominent instance where the case for social insurance is widely accepted pertains to lifetime income risk, or the risk that one's lifetime income will be low rather than high for reasons outside one's control.[15] People face such income risk due both to the "ability lottery" that affects their capacity to produce earnings through effort, and to "unpredictable circumstances beyond their control that may determine their success or failure after they have acted, such as by starting a particular business or acquiring a particular workplace specialization."[16]

oneself as equally likely to be A or B is a way of treating A's and B's welfare as equally important, rather than importing selfish bias if one knows that in fact one is A. See ibid., 453; and Shaviro, *Making Sense of Social Security Reform*, 52.

[15] As I discuss later with respect to having children, a social insurance rationale potentially applies even to risks within one's control, but this may greatly raise the stakes regarding moral hazard issues.

[16] See Shaviro, *Making Sense of Social Security Reform*, 51.

Income risk is addressed by means-based tax systems such as the income tax, which cause one's tax liability to rise with some measure of one's material well-being, and by means-based transfer systems such as, in the United States, Temporary Aid to Needy Families (TANF, the current official name for welfare), food stamps, and Medicaid. These various systems could all be described as engaging in vertical redistribution, or redistribution from the presumptively better-off to the presumptively worse-off, based, under a utilitarian social welfare function, on the assumption of declining marginal utility with respect to material resources.[17] A normative preference for greater equality as between the better-off and the worse-off, although not part of my normative framework in this essay, would provide additional motivation for vertical redistribution, potentially favoring it even in cases where it reduced total welfare. Such redistribution could involve either a nonutilitarian variant of welfarism or the assignment of moral weight to values apart from increasing welfare.

From a utilitarian standpoint, however, the assumption of declining marginal utility that supports vertical redistribution by no means exhausts the set of cases where a transfer of money from A to B would be expected to increase total welfare. There also are cases where we would expect B to gain more welfare than A loses from the transfer, based on information wholly apart from their relative levels of well-being.

Suppose, for example, the following: A and B have the same preferences; they are comparably threatened with imminent heart attacks, but only A's condition can be treated; this treatment is very expensive, and A cannot afford it; A would choose this treatment if given the money; and B, if given the same amount of money, would have nothing better to spend it on than eating out more and going on nice vacations during the period before the heart attack struck. On the surmise that A would benefit more from the money because her condition is treatable, we might prefer giving the money to her rather than to B, without regard to which of them is at a higher well-being level.[18] After all, if both of them were buying medical insurance coverage before they learned about their conditions, it is plausible that both would have selected coverage against incurring the treatable condition but not the untreatable condition.

Or suppose that C and D are both retired, and no longer physically capable of paid work, but that neither has entered retirement with significant savings. We might decide, in the fashion of Social Security, to give each of them a life annuity. If C had a greater life expectancy, this would amount to giving him a larger expected benefit than D. The motivation

[17] A transfer system such as Medicaid further reflects a view that medical needs are distributionally important independent of income.

[18] More precisely, this reason for giving the money to A would apply without regard to the parties' relative well-being levels. This is not to deny that one's overall distributional decision might reflect both this reason for giving money to A and information about the parties' relative well-being levels.

for favoring C would be that, even though living longer is presumably a good thing, it increases one's post-retirement needs.[19] Again, this motivation for favoring C would be independent of information about the two parties' relative well-being levels.

Where an assumption other than declining marginal utility supports the view that a dollar would do more to benefit people in circumstance 1 than in circumstance 2, the utilitarian case for redistributing wealth to the former group from the latter could be described as involving lateral redistribution, rather than vertical redistribution. We are not, to the extent of this redistribution, systematically engaged in transferring resources from the better-off to the worse-off. Rather, we are using other types of information to guide our distribution policy. We might even, on average, be favoring better-off individuals through this redistribution. For example, it is presumably better to be longer-lived and have a treatable rather than an untreatable condition, and both life expectancy and treatability might be positively correlated with an individual's earnings. While this would not have to imply reduced vertical redistribution, it would mean that some notional portion of our total redistributive effort was purely in response to what I call lateral differences, or those based on observed characteristics other than well-being level.[20]

With this framework in place, I turn to a number of the main issues posed by imposing tax and transfer rules on the individuals in different kinds of households. My aim is to provide a basic of survey of how a

[19] This example ignores the possibility of inducing people with higher life expectancies to work longer or save a larger proportion of their lifetime earnings for retirement. It also does not take account of moral hazard, which could take the form of under-saving given one's above-average life expectancy because one knows that the retirement system will make up the difference.

[20] Since part of my aim here is to offer an analysis that is relevant to people who have sympathy for increasing total well-being even if they are not utilitarians, it is worth noting two common criticisms of utilitarianism. The first relates to hypothetical "utility monsters who get enormously greater gains in utility from any sacrifice of others than these others lose. . . . [Utilitarianism] seems to require that we all be sacrificed in the monster's maw, in order to increase total utility." Robert Nozick, *Anarchy, State, and Utopia* (New York: Basic Books, 1974), 41. This objection will not arise here, as I will be emphasizing differences in people's preferences and circumstances that do not raise issues of differing intensity as to their overall sets of preferences. The second common criticism pertains to expensive tastes, or the concern, first raised by Kenneth Arrow, and developed most notably by Ronald Dworkin, that it is unfair to favor individuals by reason of their having freely chosen tastes that are unusually expensive to satisfy. See Kenneth J. Arrow, "Some Ordinalist-Utilitarian Notes on Rawls's Theory of Justice," *Journal of Philosophy* 70 (1973): 245; Ronald Dworkin, "What Is Equality? Part 2: Equality of Resources," *Philosophy and Public Affairs* 10, no. 3 (1981): 283. Anne Alstott, writing about households with children from the standpoint of liberal egalitarianism, treats this as an objection that needs to be met on nonutilitarian grounds that relate to parents' responsibility for their choices and to effects on children's development. Alstott, *No Exit*, 61–66. One should keep in mind, however, that the apparent underlying concerns about the social costs of accommodating expensive tastes and encouraging people to develop such tastes are relevant under utilitarianism. Thus, while concern about rewarding expensive tastes, depending on its underlying basis, might affect a nonutilitarian's degree of acceptance of the approach taken in this essay, it does not necessarily suggest reaching radically different conclusions.

utilitarian might think about these issues, all of which could be explored in another setting at much greater length.

III. Why Do Households Matter?

Under the U.S. federal income tax, the question of whether household status should matter, via the use of joint returns for married couples, is typically posed as one of what is the "appropriate taxable unit."[21] Ostensibly, we must decide whether people should be taxed as "isolated individuals, or as social beings,"[22] perhaps based on the question of whether Haig-Simons income is most truly earned, enjoyed, or controlled (as the case may be) at the individual or at the family level.

This formulation can lead to confusion. For one thing, the "taxable unit" is only of administrative interest. As an illustration, it commonly is recognized that joint returns, where the dollar amounts in each rate bracket are double those applying to single individuals' tax returns, are arithmetically equivalent to separate returns for married couples that are prepared under the assumption that each couple splits its total income fifty-fifty. Joint returns are merely one way of bringing household information to bear on tax and transfer outcomes, which can also be done through separate returns that make use of information about other household members.[23] It should be clear, moreover, that we can only tax individuals. Even if, as an administrative matter, we recognize as "taxpayers" certain legal entities such as corporations and family groups of one kind or another, this is merely a device for collecting money from the underlying owners or members. The issue of real interest, then, is whether we use household information in determining individuals' taxes and transfers. It should be clear that there are powerful reasons for wanting to use such information.

Two simple examples may help to dramatize the importance of household information to distribution policy. First, suppose that we offer net transfers to people with low earnings and assets, and consider only individual rather than household information in deciding who needs the transfers. If Mrs. Bill Gates did not work and did not own any of the Gates assets but lived the Gates lifestyle, would it make sense to think she needed a net transfer?

[21] Kornhauser, "Love, Money, and the IRS," 92.

[22] Bittker, "Federal Income Taxation and the Family," 1391.

[23] An example of using household information without joint filing is the federal income tax treatment of minor children, who must file their own returns if they have sufficient income, but may be claimed by their parents as dependents and also may be taxed on certain unearned income at the parents' marginal rate. A proposed example of using household information along with separate filing is McCaffery's proposal that spouses file separate returns but with a "more generous rate schedule, or greater deductions, for the lesser-earning spouse." McCaffery, *Taxing Women*, 277.

Second, suppose we observe two same-aged single individuals earning $20,000 a year, one of them with no children and the other with ten. Even if we just focused on these two individuals, without considering the needs of the ten children, would it really make sense to surmise that their material circumstances, like their earnings, are the same, and thus to figure that neither of them would value an extra dollar more than the other? If you started out with no children and suddenly found yourself with ten, doesn't it seem likely that this would increase the value that you placed on an extra dollar?

Put more generally, these examples illustrate two broad points. The first is that, in assessing an individual's well-being level and likely marginal utility of a dollar, we must evaluate the significance, not only of self-owned resources, but of those owned by other members of the individual's family or household. The second is that, in making this same assessment, we must consider not only the individual's own needs but also those of others in the same family or household. The reason we need to make these broader assessments is that resources actually flow between members of the household in ways that we would not ordinarily expect as between third parties. Thus, we may need to look at other household members' resources and wants in order to understand either the current circumstances of any household member or how those circumstances would change if an extra dollar were given to her or taken away. Moreover, since we cannot look at each household individually to determine how it actually operates, we may need to apply generalizing assumptions about various types of households' internal distribution behavior that we determine are more realistic, on average, than assuming that each household member is an island.

One further implication is that we cannot understand tax and transfer incidence, or who economically gains or loses from the government's extracting or providing a dollar, without looking inside the household. Suppose, for example, that we wanted to penalize sexist husbands while aiding their wives, or that we wanted to aid the children, as distinct from the parents, in a given set of households. Making the husband write a check while sending a check to the wife, or writing government checks that were made out to the children rather than the parents, would not necessarily accomplish the desired intrahousehold distributional aim. Maybe it would, but we would have to understand or observe the household's internal decision rules—how it allocates its various resources—in order to know.

IV. What Is a Household, and How Might It Be Officially Defined?

A. *Households in concept*

The reasons why households matter for tax and transfer purposes suggest how, as a basic conceptual matter (leaving aside, for now, practical implementation), they ought to be defined. Households are groups of people who, to a significant degree, pool their individually owned resources for allocation among group members based on some set of rules or norms that are not limited to respecting individual ownership.

Equal sharing of resources among household members without regard to who contributed them would be one example of a norm that a household might use, but is by no means exclusive.[24] Suppose instead that a given married couple's rules for pooling and allocating resources included the norms that (1) the man's consumption priorities are more important than the woman's and (2) the person who earns or owns a given dollar has extra say about it. We might be appalled by norm (1), and also by norm (2) if the woman was a homemaker whom it disadvantaged. In addition, we might note that, to the extent it follows norm (2), the household does less to change legal title-based resource allocations than it would under a norm of equal sharing. Nonetheless, the reasons for believing that households matter to tax and transfer policy would still apply. For example, we still might need household information to form a realistic appraisal either of the woman's material welfare level or of how it might change if we tried to give her a dollar.

For reasons that merge human biological nature with contemporary Western cultural nurture, household affiliations between individuals in contemporary Western societies are most commonly of two types. The first involves couples, defined as pairs of individuals who decide to form lasting personal relationships.[25] The second involves blood or adoptive relationships between family members, typically strongest between parents and children but capable of further extension, such as through grandparents or laterally among siblings. Other prototypes, such as religious communities or hippie communes, may comparably function as households, but are statistically a great deal less common.

I use the word "household" rather than "family," although neither is a perfect fit, because blood relationships do not always involve significant resource pooling and reallocations (which typically are quite limited, for example, between adult siblings), and because the question of whether a given couple should be called a "family" is a political hot-button issue for reasons that have nothing to do with how individuals share their resources.

[24] In some past literature, relevant pooling and allocation have been defined more narrowly. For example, Kornhauser, "Love, Money, and the IRS," 97, argues that viewing households as economic units requires "assum[ing] that the family is a monolithic, homogeneous group in which all members share the same tastes and resources, including income, equally. . . . True pooling presumes equality, if not in contributions to the pool, then at least in free access to the pool."

[25] Given the practice of polygamy at various times and places in world history, and indeed its apparent survival in portions of Utah (see Jon Krakauer, *Under the Banner of Heaven: A Story of Violent Faith* [New York: Doubleday, 2003]), a more universal definition would have to permit extension of this definition beyond the case of two individuals who form a couple.

The term "household" can also be misleading, however. In common usage, it typically includes roommates who physically live together but do not significantly pool their resources, while excluding spouses who have separate primary residences but engage in resource pooling.[26] That usage differs from mine in this essay.

While resource pooling and allocation are the main features of interest here, it is true that living in one residence versus two may be relevant to distributional policy. Economies of scale, which roommates may enjoy without any pooling beyond that of common living space, appliances, and various food items, are often mentioned as potentially increasing one's level of material well-being.[27] This factor therefore is typically invoked as suggesting that people enjoying economies of scale should pay higher taxes (or get lower transfers) than would otherwise be appropriate. Under utilitarianism, however, it also has the opposite implication, since people who enjoy economies of scale may be more efficient consumers, in the sense that they can get more total utility out of an extra dollar. As an illustration, if one were donating a TV set to be put in either of two apartments, one might choose to put it where several people could watch it, rather than just one. Which of these offsetting effects predominates in analyzing economies of scale is ambiguous without further information.[28]

B. Households in practice

In identifying couples, the federal income tax, Social Security, and Medicare rely purely on marriage, but welfare rules often cast their net more broadly for purposes of disqualifying potential recipients through asset or income limits and work requirements. One of the well-known demographic trends of recent decades is a decline in marriage as a predictor of couple status, both because heterosexual couples face less pressure to marry than in earlier times and because acknowledged same-sex couples are now freer to form but, in nearly all states and generally for federal legal purposes, no freer to marry. Marriage has therefore become an increasingly poor proxy for identifying couples who function as a household unit.

The case for trying to identify unmarried couples who should be viewed as members of the same household is therefore growing ever stronger. Helping to make it quite difficult, however, is the fact that, just as the federal income tax has marriage penalties in some situations and marriage bonuses in others, so the verification and enforcement problem with respect to unmarried couples could go in either direction. One might, in principle, need either to verify claims of couple status (as in the case

[26] See Kornhauser, "Love, Money, and the IRS," 67.
[27] See, e.g., Bittker, "Federal Income Taxation and the Family," 1422–25.
[28] See Kaplow, "Optimal Distribution and the Family," 80–81.

today where immigration authorities try to root out sham marriages between Americans and foreigners), or to assert it in cases where the involved individuals were not doing so.

As an example of the different ways these issues may play out, same-sex couples typically benefit under the federal income tax from not being identified as married if both individuals are working and their earnings are comparable. Likewise, same-sex couples may benefit under the welfare laws from not being amalgamated for purposes of income and asset tests and work requirements. In contrast, if only one member of the same-sex couple works, then they are denied the marriage bonus that the federal income tax, Social Security, and Medicare extend to one-earner couples.

If we find ourselves at some point living in more enlightened times, it is possible that some of these issues will be addressed, at least for same-sex couples that at present cannot marry, and at least where claiming couple status favors the claimants. In principle, however, tax and transfer recognition of a couple should not depend upon whether it helps or hurts the claimants. While assertion of couple status by the government may seem to raise the specter of IRS bed-checks to determine whether roommates are more than just roommates, the fiscal system could piggyback on other filings, such as filings to claim partner benefits from employers, in cases where the other benefits exceeded any tax or transfer penalties that might result from acknowledging couple status. (This would, however, affect incentives to claim and indeed to offer such benefits, making piggy-backing a trade-off rather than an unambiguously desirable approach.)

With regard to children, determining household status is more straightforward. Where there is possible uncertainty regarding a child's status as a dependent or regarding the identity of the main supporting parent, the available cues include the child's age, residence, custody, and who provides financial support. Such tests can likewise be used to determine whether other family members, such as siblings or aged parents, are dependents in one's household.[29]

The general social expectation in the United States of achieving financial independence when one reaches adulthood lessens the importance of tracing household connections between adults and their surviving parents. Nevertheless, the fact that there are economic links, whether through bequests from the older generation or support from the younger, helps make intergenerational tax and transfer incidence a challenging subject. For example, one's estimate of the transfer through Medicare to older generations would be a lot lower if one thought that seniors' adult children would otherwise have borne most of the seniors' medical expenses. The links between

[29] See Internal Revenue Code section 152, defining dependents for federal income tax purposes relating to the allowance of deductions for personal exemptions, for an example of a rule addressing children's and other relatives' household status.

adults and their surviving parents also create difficult issues under the Medicaid rule denying subsidized medical benefits to people with assets above a specified level, since generally only one's own assets are counted and the rule therefore encourages asset transfers to family members, such as one's children, as a means of establishing eligibility.[30]

V. Equal Taxation of Equal-Income Couples

Boris Bittker, the renowned Yale Law School professor and tax expert, first made the point that, with graduated marginal tax rates, one cannot have both (1) a marriage-neutral system, in which the combined tax on two individuals' income is not affected by whether they are married or not, and (2) a regime of equal taxes for equal-income married couples.[31] As an illustration, exaggerating actual rate graduation to make the point clear, suppose single individuals face a zero tax rate on their first $50,000 of income, along with a 50 percent rate on all income above that amount. The question still to be decided is how to tax married individuals. A and B are married, and each earns $50,000. C and D are married, and C earns $100,000 while D earns zero. Our options include the following:

(a) If we ignore marriage and have separate returns, then C pays $25,000 of tax while none of the others pays anything. Thus, we violate equal taxation of equal-income couples by failing to tax C and D the same as A and B.

(b) If we have separate returns and mandatory income-splitting, so that C and D are taxed as if they were unmarried individuals earning $50,000 each, then we have equal taxation of equal-income married couples, but we also have a marriage bonus for C and D rather than marriage neutrality. Marriage lowers their collective tax bill from $25,000 to zero.

(c) If we have joint returns, then we will have equal taxation of equal-income married couples, but we will also have marriage bonuses or penalties, depending on where we set the zero bracket relative to that for single individuals. If we set the zero bracket at $100,000 or double that for singles, the result is the same as in (b) above. If the zero bracket is any lower than $100,000, we have a marriage penalty for A and B, who now owe tax that they could avoid by being divorced, but we also have a marriage bonus for C and D so long as the zero bracket for married couples exceeds, by even a dollar, the zero bracket for singles.

Whether this inconsistency is a problem depends on what we think of Bittker's two objectives: marriage neutrality and equal taxation of equal-

[30] Intrafamily asset transfers for this purpose became sufficiently prominent that Congress in 1996 enacted a new law creating criminal penalties in cases where the transfers were designed to circumvent the Medicaid asset limit. See 42 U.S.C. sections 1396a and 1396p; and Helen Hershkoff and Stephen Loffredo, *The Rights of the Poor* (Carbondale, IL: Southern Illinois University Press, 1997), 184.

[31] Bittker, "Federal Income Taxation and the Family," 1395.

income married couples. Starting with the second objective,[32] its appeal rests on applying the principle that like cases should be treated alike. From a social insurance standpoint, redistributing between identical cases (in marginal utility terms) fails to direct marginal dollars to where they are valued more, and is likely to reduce total well-being given the generally declining marginal utility of a dollar. But are equal-income married couples relevantly alike? There are two types of objections to assuming that they are, the first devastating but applicable only in a subset of cases, and the second significant but hard to draw conclusions from.

The objection that is devastating where it applies can be illustrated through the preceding example. If C and D with one spouse working can earn as much as A and B with both working, then it seems pretty clear that C and D are better off economically, rather than in the same position as A and B. Suppose both households have young children. D is available to offer childcare during working hours that A and B must pay a lot of money to procure. Or to put it another way, suppose D, like A and B, could earn $50,000 if she (or he, to take the statistically less common case) so chose. We would recognize that C and D were better off than A and B if D took the job and her household therefore was taking in $150,000. But C and D evidently prefer the actual state of affairs, where D does not work, so even at $100,000 they apparently consider themselves better off still.

From a social insurance standpoint, we use an income tax and means-based transfers to address income risk by redistributing from high earners to low earners. However, people who voluntarily choose lower earnings because some nonpaid use of their time has greater value to them presumably think they are better off by reason of the choice. Moreover, the mere fact that one-earner couples are voluntarily earning less need not suggest that their marginal utility for a dollar is greater. Secondary earners within couples, especially though not uniquely when they have minor children in need of extensive care, are a group in which low earnings are unusually poorly correlated with ability to earn.

Thus, the notion that equal-earning couples are relevantly alike and should be taxed the same can be ruled out immediately if we are not comparing likes in terms of their levels of labor market involvement. Even where they are alike in this sense, however, the second objection that I mentioned above must be considered. Suppose we compare E and F, spouses who each earn $100,000, to G and H, where G earns $180,000 and H, despite working full time, earns only $20,000. Keeping in mind that we are interested in evaluating individuals in light of household information, rather than households as such, do we really have the posited equals here? Suppose that both households apply an internal distri-

[32] On the importance of this principle, compare ibid., 1438, describing proposals to abandon it as "nothing less than astonishing," with McCaffery, *Taxing Women*, 25: "Taxing equal-earning couples equally is terribly unfair, because in fact it leads to massive discrimination against women."

butional norm under which the earner of a given dollar has extra say about its use. Then it is plausible that, as indicated by the differences in individual earnings, G is better off than E or F, while H is worse off. Unfortunately, however, we cannot use this information to transfer resources away from G and toward H, nor can we even tell which of the two households should gain or lose overall, until we know more about how the G/H household determines its internal resource allocation.[33] The net result is that we might end up falling back on equal taxation of equal-income households with similar levels of labor market participation, based on uncertainty about which way the transfers should go, unless it turns out that we can use observable general information or inferences about intrahousehold allocation to do better.

VI. Marriage Neutrality

The other prong of the dilemma that Bittker considered central to taxation of the household was marriage neutrality, or the idea that the combined tax on two individuals' income should not be affected by whether they are married or not. Under a system that did a good job of identifying unmarried couples who pool and allocate their collective resources, this issue would be transformed into couples neutrality (or neutrality concerning whatever characteristics were now being used to assess couple status). The fact that, at present, the only neutrality practically at issue, at least in the income tax, is that concerning possession of a marriage certificate importantly affects what is at stake in the analysis.

Neutrality is an old but still potent idea in tax policy, reflecting the fact that, under specified conditions, it advances both efficiency and equity. When you are choosing between activities or assets X and Y and will internalize all of the consequences of your choice, tax and transfer neutrality as between the two choices keeps your personal incentives aligned with increasing total welfare. Likewise, under a utilitarian view of equity, if people who choose X are not relevantly different (i.e., in marginal utility of a dollar) from those who choose Y, favoring one group over the other is likely to reduce total welfare under the assumption of declining marginal utility.[34] Given these underlying assumptions, the utilitarian case for marriage neutrality depends on the view that the couple internalizes all of the effects of its marriage choice (and on the choice being sufficiently price-elastic for neutrality to matter) and on the view that marriage choices are not informative about the marginal utility of a dollar.

[33] See Kaplow, "Optimal Distribution and the Family," 78–80, for a similar view of the significance of unequal sharing within a household.

[34] As Bittker famously pointed out, marketplace responses to a non-neutral tax rule may eliminate the inequity problem, leaving only inefficiency. See Boris I. Bittker, "Equity, Efficiency, and Income Tax Theory: Do Misallocations Drive Out Inequities?" *San Diego Law Review* 16 (1979): 735–48.

Neither of these assumptions is necessarily correct. Even if we disregard most of the reasons why third parties, ranging from parents to friends to romantic rivals to pure busybodies, might care about the marital or relationship status of a given couple, there is the point that children's welfare may be affected. It is commonly agreed that divorce, on average, has bad effects on children, although in abusive households separation may benefit the children if a nonabusive spouse gets custody. Decisions to marry or form a couple may also have external effects through the fiscal system—for example, by easing burdens on other taxpayers where an earning spouse supports a non-earner, or increasing burdens if a worker who would have paid net taxes decides to quit working by reason of spousal support.

The effects of marriage (or forming a couple) on marginal utility are likewise ambiguous. For example, in the case of a high-earner married to a low-earner, if resources in the household are shared more equally than the split in earnings, we may be less inclined both to tax the high-earner and to support the low-earner than we would have been had they remained separate. Moreover, as I noted above, the economies of scale that may result from cohabitation are ambiguous, as they increase our estimate both of the cohabitants' welfare (relevant under the assumption of declining marginal utility) and of their efficiency as consumers.

These ambiguities may tend to push one back toward favoring marriage (and couple) neutrality, effects on children's welfare aside, if only in the weak sense of being unsure in which direction we should lean as a general matter. However, in a system with rampant marriage penalties and bonuses, which do not balance each other out because they occur in very different settings, the neutrality rubric may be too abstract and generalized to help very much. We can better come to grips with the issues by looking at the three main groups involved: one-earner couples (who get marriage bonuses), two-earner couples (who get marriage penalties), and single individuals. The issues of main interest here, which I address in the next two sections, are (1) how these different types of households ought to fare distributionally relative to each other, and (2) the incentive effects on women's labor supply decisions of strongly penalizing the decision to be a couple's second earner.[35]

VII. Single Individuals versus One-Earner Couples versus Two-Earner Couples

The mechanism by which the income tax yields a marriage bonus for one-earner couples and a marriage penalty for couples with two rela-

[35] A further important issue is the effect of taxation on decisions to marry, involving encouragement of forming a one-earner couple and discouragement of forming a two-earner couple.

tively equal earners is the use of joint returns on which various income-limited tax benefits, such as lower rate brackets, terminate at less than double the income levels used for single individuals. Thus, in terms of my earlier example with individuals A, B, C, and D, it as if the zero bracket of $50,000 for singles were adjusted only to $75,000 for marrieds. Accordingly, A and B, who earn $50,000 each, lose $12,500 per year as a result of being married, while C and D save $12,500 due to marriage if we assume that their labor supply decisions would have been the same in any event.

Adding a complication is the possibility that D would lose welfare benefits if unemployed and not married to C. However, for middle-class individuals with decent employment prospects, this assumption would often be unrealistic, and the income tax bonus from marrying therefore would not be eliminated by looking at a broader set of fiscal rules. In Social Security and Medicare, moreover, it is unambiguous that one-earner couples get a transfer from singles and two-earner couples. Both of these systems provide spousal benefits that nonworking spouses get to claim at retirement, but neither system makes the one-earner couples pay more for the extra retirement coverage. One-earner couples therefore get a two-for-one: two sets of retirement benefits for only one set of payroll taxes. A system that was designed to avoid this redistribution could still provide retirement benefits for nonworking spouses, who have at least as good a chance as anyone else of needing the support when they get to that stage, but it would require that the benefits be paid for. For example, workers might be required to make extra payroll tax contributions when they have nonworking spouses, so that the system would be more actuarially fair between different types of households.

To be sure, actuarial fairness is not an end in itself. Indeed, social insurance is meant to be actuarially unfair, in the sense of transferring expected resources to people who are expected to have greater needs at the time when their participation begins. (Examples include the income tax and means-tested transfers, which favor people with low as compared to high earning ability.) The transfer to one-earner couples may initially look like social insurance for income risk, since part of what triggers it is the nonworker's low earnings. However, this brings up again the point that low earnings are empirically much weaker evidence of bad circumstances, as opposed to rational optimizing amid good circumstances, in the secondary earner setting as compared with other settings. Moreover, while a two-person household has greater total needs than a one-person household, a nonworking spouse may still be an economic producer for the household's benefit, performing tasks that have value and that in some cases would require paying a third party if both spouses worked.

While earnings are therefore a bad measure of relative material well-being for one-earner couples as compared with two-earner couples, one should not too swiftly assume equivalent material well-being. Potential nonworking spouses are more likely to take that path when the earnings they would forgo are low rather than high. Moreover, even where nonworking spouses had good earnings prospects at the start, once they have been on the sidelines they may find that, as a prospective matter, their economic opportunities are limited. Thus, we should not exaggerate the point that one-earner households' relative economic resources are being underestimated if we rely on a measure of earnings. The point retains significant force, however, and might support increasing these households' relative fiscal burdens even without regard to the issue of effects on secondary earners' labor supply decisions (which I discuss next).

VIII. The Secondary Earner Problem

Perhaps the most important defect in existing fiscal rules for households is how they affect secondary earners' (mainly married women's) incentives to participate in the labor market. These incentive effects and their significance have been thoroughly and ably discussed elsewhere, such as by the economist Michael Boskin in the 1980s,[36] and more recently in Edward J. McCaffery's *Taxing Women*, but they are worth briefly reviewing here.

An initial point to keep in mind is that married women, who most often are their households' secondary earners in the sense of earning less and being less committed to market work, tend to be highly price-responsive in making work decisions. In other words, small changes in their net economic return from work can have large effects on what they decide to do.[37] From the standpoint of efficiency, it is a truism that the higher the compensated elasticity, the lower the tax rate should be.[38] Thus, there would be a strong efficiency case for taxing married women (or, to put it in more facially neutral but substantially overlapping terms, lower-earning spouses) at lower marginal rates than single individuals and higher-earning spouses.

Instead, we apply much higher marginal tax rates to secondary-earner married women than to nearly anyone else. The main causes are the following:

(a) While a joint return, on its face, applies a single income tax rate schedule to all of the couple's income, this may not be how the couple looks at it if the man is certain to work while the woman faces a genuine

[36] See Michael J. Boskin and Eytan Sheshanski, "Optimal Tax Treatment of the Family: Married Couples," *Journal of Public Economics* 20 (1983): 281–97; and Michael J. Boskin and Douglas J. Puffert, "Social Security and the American Family," in Lawrence H. Summers, ed., *Tax Policy and the Economy, Vol. 1* (Cambridge, MA: MIT Press, 1987).

[37] See McCaffery, *Taxing Women*, 179–82, and sources cited therein. This is especially true for couples with children, because nonmarket work in the home is such an important form of household economic production.

[38] See ibid., 170–75. "Compensated elasticity" refers to that which is measured holding income constant, so as to focus on substitution effects, or responses to incentives at the margin, as opposed to people's changing preferences as income changes.

choice. Under this circumstance, the woman may view her first dollar of earnings as facing the marginal tax rate into which the man's work was already expected to place the couple. Thus, the tax rate schedule she faces in making labor supply decisions may start at more than 30 percent, whereas for single individuals and primary earners in a couple it starts at zero and gradually proceeds through increasing rate brackets.

(b) Especially in the case where the couple has children, the woman's decision to work may result in the couple's incurring increased expenses, for items such as childcare, commuting, and work-related clothing, that generally are nondeductible for income tax purposes because they are viewed as consumption expenditures.[39] The result is that, if the wife goes to work, the couple's taxable income may increase far more than their pretax monetary gain from her going. As an illustration, suppose that her earnings would face a 35 percent rate, that she would earn $30,000 if she went to work, and that the household's extra nonrecoverable expenses would total $20,000 (not at all unreasonable if full-time childcare would be needed). After federal income tax, her decision to go to work would actually cost the household $500, or the excess of the income tax on her earnings over the pretax monetary gain.

(c) Social Security may add to the problem, due to its 12.4 percent tax rate (counting both the employer's and the employee's nominal shares) on earnings up to an annual ceiling. For primary earners and single individuals, this tax is somewhat offset by the fact that extra Social Security earnings may increase the retirement benefit for which one would qualify under present Social Security law. In effect, then, the wage tax is somewhat offset by a wage subsidy, in the form of retirement benefits that are based at the margin on earnings, although it is unclear to what extent workers take this into account when making labor supply decisions. If one is a secondary earner, however, there is no wage subsidy (in the form of increasing benefits) counteracting the wage tax until one reaches the point where one's expected own benefits exceed one's expected spousal benefits.

The end result, very high marginal tax rates affecting decisions by people who are highly tax-responsive, is a significant efficiency problem in a straightforward labor market sense, and also raises additional issues. The problem becomes a lot worse if one believes that reducing women's workforce participation has important adverse effects on our society as a whole that lie outside each worker's individual calculus in making labor supply decisions. Reduced workforce participation might, for example, entrench women's subordination, gender stereotyping, and gender bias in labor markets while reducing the availability of part-time work (by

[39] Internal Revenue Code section 21 provides a fairly limited childcare credit for two-earner married couples and heads of households with children, which I ignore in the text for ease of exposition.

reducing employers' capacity to benefit from restructuring their workplaces to accommodate it).[40] On the other side of the scale, there might be benefits to children from inducing a parent to remain home. Depending on the view one takes of these issues, they might turn out to be more important than the straightforward labor supply distortion that results from imposing high marginal rates on highly tax-responsive workers.

IX. Children and Distribution Policy

The topic of how the presence of children in a household should affect its taxes and transfers is, if anything, even more unsettled, albeit not as intensely controversial, as the various issues discussed above relating to adult couples. The issues are sufficiently complex to merit separate discussion, first of distributional considerations and then of possible incentive effects on having children, before evaluating the policies that we actually have.

A. The case for transfers to households with children (or more children)

Suppose initially that having children was entirely a random event, not reflecting any element of choice by those who became parents. I start with this assumption simply to isolate the static distributional effects before I turn to the incentive effects.

Under this scenario, people would likely want insurance against the risk of having children, whether they wanted the children or not, because having them would be economically costly in various respects. The case differs from that of affiliating with a nonworking adult partner in a new couple, because children cannot, for many years, be economic producers. Thus, unlike a nonworking spouse, they bring extra mouths to feed without also bringing extra pairs of hands that can be used productively, either in the labor market or in housework.

One further complication to the analysis is that children may be able to help support their parents after growing up. However, parents cannot borrow against their children's future earning capacity, except in the very limited sense that, if they are feeling very brave (and have not read *King Lear*), they might save less of their own resources for retirement based on this expectation. The proper way to account for children's earning capacity, therefore, is through consideration of the degree to which transfers to seniors should take account of their adult children's resources.

The case for the desirability (in marginal utility terms) of significant transfers to households with children (or with more children than other households) should therefore be clear enough if one puts oneself in the shoes of a prospective parent and asks how it would affect one's eco-

[40] See McCaffery, *Taxing Women*, 240–64; and Alstott, *No Exit*.

nomic wants. (Considered purely at the parental level, the case arguably is one of lateral redistribution, since a voluntary consumption choice to have children, even if costly, presumably is expected to make one better off.) Yet focusing just on parents undervalues the overall case for the transfer. From behind the veil of ignorance, you also might be the child, who also would likely prefer transfers to her household. From a utilitarian standpoint, it is not "double-counting" to value the child's welfare both directly and via the parent's altruistic preferences, since one is simply, as usual, counting the distinct preferences of each individual in the society.

Why, then, don't we observe private insurance markets offering coverage that pays off if you have children? To a small degree, we actually do observe this on a group basis, because employers frequently offer employees health insurance and other benefit packages that become more valuable as family size increases. Free public schools can also be seen in this light, if we think of neighboring jurisdictions as competing for residents in classic Tiebout fashion[41] by offering tax-benefit packages, and thus as akin to private firms. Broader efforts to offer coverage against the risk (even if desired) of having more rather than fewer children would presumably founder on adverse selection problems. Sign-ups would be expected to come disproportionately from people with private information about their own intentions concerning children.

Large-scale governments can solve this adverse selection problem by requiring all residents effectively to enroll in an implicit insurance program that uses highly child-adjusted taxes and benefits to provide the coverage. This, however, raises the question of moral hazard, which governments often cannot solve much better than private firms. Here moral hazard takes the form of having more children because of the coverage, thus increasing the payoff from households that are childless or have fewer children.

B. Possible incentive effects on having children

Suppose that we believe people would respond to the transfer policy described above by having significantly more children. While this is a necessary prerequisite to discerning an important moral hazard problem here, it is far from sufficient. The externalities of having a child are so great that it is difficult to see the parent's personal calculus of the costs and benefits as a good proxy for the social costs and benefits.

I start with two important externalities suggesting that, if anything, prospective parents' incentive to have a child is too weak, rather than too strong. Fiscally, from the standpoint of people in other households, if the

[41] See Charles M. Tiebout, "A Pure Theory of Local Expenditures," *Journal of Political Economy* 64 (1956): 416.

child is a net taxpayer during her life, her birth is likely to be a net revenue benefit over time, despite the transfers to her household early in her life. Thus, other households may benefit financially, on balance, from offering the implicit insurance coverage. Lifetime measures typically show that nearly everyone is a net taxpayer. Concededly, this could be misleading, because it involves ignoring the value of public goods that, even if highly invariant in the cost of provision to one extra person, may need to be gradually scaled up as population size increases. However, in the United States fiscal system and that of most other affluent countries, the financing structure of retirement programs such as Social Security and Medicare adds a positive revenue externality to population size. These programs were set up to provide large transfers to the initial cohorts of participants, financed by passing the burden forward to younger generations. This structure creates a general fiscal benefit to increasing population size. The benefit is divided between the members of different age cohorts based on how taxes and benefits are adjusted.

Second, and perhaps a bit more fundamentally, consider the benefit to the child of being born. Again, from a utilitarian standpoint this benefit should count independently of the parent's altruistic or other interest in having a child. The fact that this line of argument might lead us, on total welfare-based utilitarian grounds, quite far past the idea of merely treating households with children favorably in the fiscal system, is food for thought, but not a refutation of the argument as used in this more limited way.

Admittedly, this barely starts the process of examining the welfare consequences of increasing birthrates. Important negative externalities that come to mind are congestion and the potentially dire environmental effects of population increases. There may also be important effects of various kinds on wage and price levels. It seems clear, however, that the parent's cost versus benefit calculus in deciding whether to have a child falls very far short of capturing the social metric. So neutrality as to this decision has little appeal as a normative benchmark. A more pertinent question is whether we think the overall government policy should be pro-natalist or anti-natalist. If one concludes that it should be anti-natalist, then concededly there is a trade-off posed by favoring households with children to the degree suggested by the straight distributional or social insurance analysis, and the size of the transfer should be, at the least, reduced (depending on the elasticity of having children as well as the significance of the anti-natalist considerations).

Other than under that scenario, however, the case for significant transfers to households with children (or more children) remains strong, and might even be stronger than that suggested by the distributional analysis alone, if one is pro-natalist and believes that the behavioral response would be significant. It is therefore worth asking to what degree actual United States policies conform to the suggested approach.

C. Current policy toward households with children

If someone who was familiar with American political rhetoric but not with the actual details of the United States fiscal system were asked to guess whether we have the generous policy toward households with children that I suggest above, that person would very likely guess that we do. After all, concern for children is, if anything, an even more widespread sentiment than dislike for marriage penalties. While children's issues share some of the marriage penalty issue's culture-war overtones of crusading for traditional families, their appeal is arguably broader. For example, Democrats such as Hillary Clinton are no less eager than conservative Republicans to advocate pro-child policies, although the style of the policies they propose may differ.

Despite these reasons for expecting consistent pro-child policies, actual United States fiscal policy presents a mixed picture. At the bottom of the income distribution, households with children are indeed very strongly favored relative to those without children. Examples include the earned income tax credit for low-wage workers, which becomes much more generous as the number of children in a household increases from zero to two, and various welfare benefits, such as TANF, food stamps, and Medicaid, that aid children and/or households with children. In addition, public schools offer an important child benefit—free education—that, while not expressly income-linked (and probably tending to improve in quality as neighborhood income rises), is used less by higher-income people who can more easily afford private school.[42]

As income rises, however, the relative benefits for households with children tend to shrink or even disappear. In the federal income tax, for example, personal exemptions and child tax credits are allowed to taxpayers who otherwise would have positive income tax liability, but both benefits are reduced or phased out completely as adjusted gross income rises through the low six-figures range. Moreover, there is an ongoing trend toward increasing the relative tax burdens of households with children in the low six-figures range, through the rapidly rising applicability of the alternative minimum tax, which offers no adjustment for dependents.

This limitation of the policy favoring households with children to lower income levels is hard to rationalize. From a utilitarian standpoint, the distributional issues posed by poor households are clearly continuous with those posed by households above the poverty level. Take two households with the same economic resources and add children to the first but not the second, and the result will be that the first has fewer resources than the second relative to its needs. The children need not be facing the threat of inadequate food or shelter in order for this to be true. Thus, there

[42] See C. Eugene Steuerle, "Can the Progressivity of Tax Changes Be Measured in Isolation?" *Tax Notes* 100 (2003): 1187–88. As Steuerle notes, however, higher-income households get greater college education subsidies than lower-income households.

is a strong argument for favoring households with children at middle and upper income levels to a degree that is roughly comparable to that prevailing with respect to poor and near-poor households.

X. Conclusion

Although this essay aims to be conceptual and exploratory rather than being focused on concrete policy proposals, it may be worth describing the main types of policy changes that its analysis suggests would likely be desirable. These include the following:

(1) There should be greater consistency in the rules used by different parts of the fiscal system to identify couples, since the distributional issues posed by, say, TANF and income taxation are similar. Since marriage is an increasingly poor marker of couple status, other indicators of couple status should be used as well. These could include domestic partner-type statutes provided by the states, or piggybacking on claims of couple status with respect to employee benefits. Non-couples' incentive to make false claims of couple status where it was favorable would be an admitted problem, as would the issue of the government's asserting couple status where such status was denied by the individuals involved because it was unfavorable. Despite these problems, however, it is difficult to see marriage as retaining, in the twenty-first century, its adequacy as an exclusive marker of couple status.

(2) The United States fiscal system's present discouragement of work by secondary earners in couples, along with its distributional bias toward one-earner couples, should be mitigated. One means of doing this might be to require one-earner couples who are accruing spousal benefits in Social Security and Medicare to owe a minimum contribution for the lower earner, which might be collected through the income tax return to the extent it exceeded the payroll tax actually paid for the year with respect to the lower earner. Paid-for spousal benefits might even be defined as belonging, for future benefit computation purposes, to the spouse to whom they relate in the event of divorce, possibly offering the added advantage of increasing that individual's ability to leave the relationship without as much concern about facing future destitution.

The biases within the income tax in favor of one-earner couples and against work by secondary earners could also be addressed—for example, by reducing the tax burden on the earnings of the lower-earning spouse. One way to do this would be through an income tax exclusion for the first $X of this individual's earnings, similar to that which existed in the federal income tax from 1981 through 1986. In addition or alternatively, one could increase deductions or other tax benefits (such as credits) for the work-related expenses, such as childcare, of two-earner couples.

A further, frequently discussed possibility is eliminating joint returns. As I have noted, however, the official filing unit is mainly of administrative interest, rather than being as fundamental as is sometimes thought. Making use in some fashion of household information in tax and transfer filing seems unavoidable no matter how the filing is handled. And the aim of avoiding the first-dollar taxable rate effect on secondary earners that results under present law could be accomplished, with or without joint filing, through special rate schedules such as the 1981 to 1986–style secondary earner exclusion.

(3) Child benefits within the income tax probably should be increased and should not be subject to phase-out. In addition, if the alternative minimum tax is retained, it should be amended to allow child benefits. In principle, all this should be done on a revenue-neutral basis and without reducing overall progressivity, since the idea would be to change how we redistribute as opposed to addressing the separate question of how much should be redistributed. Obviously, the present budgetary environment, along with the political difficulty of imposing losses on anyone relative to prior law, makes this difficult, but it is an aspiration to keep in mind and one that, in principle, can raise just as much revenue as the existing system at a comparable efficiency cost (or, if at a greater efficiency cost, then in reasonable exchange for improving distribution policy).

Law, New York University

TAXATION, THE STATE, AND THE COMMUNITY

By Jeffrey Schoenblum

I. Introduction

This essay is concerned with taxation, the state, the community, and the approach of public finance to these topics. By "public finance" I mean the expert consideration of how revenue is and should be raised from private interests and then translated into public goods and/or direct redistribution by the state.[1] In what follows, I set out to make six principal points.

First, public finance has historically segregated the revenue-raising and revenue-spending functions of the state. An explanation for this failure to integrate lies in public finance's underlying assumptions about the state and the community it serves. While contemporary theories of public finance have developed abstract models of revenue-raising and its distributional effects, no serious accounts of the political process and its effects have been integrated into the models to any substantial degree.

Second, no persuasive theory of what the state is or how it operates has been offered by public finance. A rather unsophisticated model of a unitary entity imbued with the scientific method of decision making is presumed, but this model cannot withstand close scrutiny.

Third, the failure to provide an account of "communities" within the state is also a striking oversight of public finance. In fact, within the political bounds of the state, constituents find themselves routinely affiliated with multiple communities of interest. These communities compete for state largesse made possible by the process of taxation and redistribution.

Fourth, an emerging global community, generated by the free flow of capital and, to an increasing degree, labor, poses a direct threat to the unbridled process of taxation and redistribution and thus to the state itself. This is especially true to the extent that states engage in tax competition and lower entry barriers, which have the effect of weakening existing national communal affiliations and dependencies and depleting local sources of capital that sustain the impulse toward social welfare. However, majoritarian democracy can hardly be expected to modify these increasingly nonviable policies. A severe dichotomy thus emerges between

[1] For the public finance perspective, see, for example, Richard A. Musgrave and Alan T. Peacock, eds., *Classics in the Theory of Public Finance* (London: MacMillan, 1958), x. See also Richard A. Musgrave, "The Nature of the Fiscal State: The Roots of My Thinking," in James M. Buchanan and Richard A. Musgrave, *Public Finance and Public Choice: Two Contrasting Visions of the State* (Cambridge, MA: The MIT Press, 1999), 29–49.

political community on the one hand and economic and social communities on the other hand. Furthermore, latent contradictions in the social welfare and justice agenda surface as conflict and competition arise between the welfare of domestic dependents and the welfare of persons in need beyond the state's political bounds.

Fifth, the two philosophical underpinnings for modern redistributive states—utilitarianism and social welfare/social justice—suffer from the same shortcoming as does public finance: an unwillingness to inquire seriously into the state, its operation, and its interaction with constituents and their communities.

Finally, individuals organized into communities of special interest compete in the political marketplace made possible by the availability of private resources to bureaucratic and political agents. These bureaucratic and political agents make reduced tax burdens and redistributive transfers available at a price. This political-marketplace model calls into question the underlying premises and the attainability of the goals of public finance—social welfare and "justice" throughout the sovereign nation.

II. The Failure to Integrate the Allocation of Tax Burdens with the Provision of Public Goods and Redistributive Transfers

An ongoing debate in the United States over the appropriate tax structure, particularly with respect to the income tax, has been waged since the passage of the Sixteenth Amendment permitting an income tax. The debate has focused myopically on the allocation of the tax burden. There has been a striking disregard for the distributional side of the equation. This fixation with allocation has been so obsessive that it suggests a deeper significance than mere path dependence.

One explanation is that the allocation of the tax burden, the revenue-raising function, has been deemed to be distinct from the state's "obligation" to provide public goods and, more recently and controversially, to further the general social welfare through redistribution. The habit of conceiving of revenue raising and revenue spending as entirely distinct functions, deserving of discrete rather than integrated analysis, reflects a particular view of the state. This perspective, long unchallenged, beginning in the nineteenth century and continuing through the heyday of twentieth-century liberalism, might be characterized as "scientific." The state would apply principles from the discipline of public finance to ascertain the optimal allocation of the tax burden and, in like fashion, to allocate resources optimally for public goods and direct transfers for the greater good of all the constituents of the political community.[2] This

[2] See Musgrave and Peacock, eds., *Classics*, xi. Initially, the determination of public expenditures was regarded as a political matter (see ibid.). See also Adolf Wagner, "Three Extracts

scientific method, conceived in Europe, especially Germany, and then fostered in the United States in contemporary times by leading intellectuals like the Harvard economics professor Richard Musgrave,[3] rests on a central, but questionable, premise of an impartial, expert state in harmony with a unitary civil society. Despite the insistent and persistent assaults from various quarters, notably public choice scholars led by James Buchanan and his various coauthors,[4] this implicit bias persists in public finance.

As I observe in Section III below, communities take shape at every level of human social interaction. This does not preclude the possibility of a national community, but it does suggest that constituents have many other affiliations, any number of which may involve more significant interests and thicker loyalties.[5] The assumption of the harmonious coupling of the state's interests and the interests of its constituents, especially in a majoritarian democracy, is empirically unsustainable.

If individuals' primary allegiances are to communities other than that exemplified by the state, and if these are communities with quite divergent interests, then it will not be surprising that these communities of special interest will vie to be net gainers rather than net losers. It will also mean that differential treatment will be harder to justify on the basis of some social welfare function—such as the good of us all, when we are not really all in it together. If there is really not a "community" but rather a subset of communities competing within historically constructed political boundaries, then the pursuit of the utilitarian grail of the greatest aggregate good for the greatest number (or of social welfare, however defined)

on Public Finance," in Musgrave and Peacock, eds., *Classics*, 1, 5. This is not to say that contemporary public finance ignores the linkage between taxation and distribution. For example, optimal tax theory takes account of the effects of different tax-rate structures on individual utilities. It is a highly stylized mathematical approach. Thus, it, too, fails to take account of patterns of social-political behavior and self-interest that inevitably affect distributional decisions. For an excellent discussion of the optimal tax theory, see Lawrence Zelenak and Kemper Moreland, "Can the Graduated Income Tax Survive Optimal Tax Analysis?" *Tax Law Review* 53 (1999): 51.

[3] See note 1 above. Even Musgrave recognized the problem with an unquestioning faith in expertise. See Buchanan and Musgrave, *Public Finance and Public Choice,* 34. Nevertheless, according to Musgrave, the "vision of efficient government" is required as a standard by which performance can be measured. Furthermore, it should be regarded as attainable with the proper leadership. Musgrave emphasized that it is not "beyond the capacity of representatives and officials to seek the public interest" (ibid.).

[4] See, for example, James M. Buchanan, "Response," in Buchanan and Musgrave, *Public Finance and Public Choice,* 85–86. See also James M. Buchanan and Roger D. Congleton, *Politics by Principle, Not Interest: Toward Nondiscriminatory Democracy* (Cambridge: Cambridge University Press, 1998); James M. Buchanan and Gordon Tullock, *The Calculus of Consent: Logical Foundations of Constitutional Democracy* (Ann Arbor: University of Michigan Press, 1962); and Geoffrey Brennan and James M. Buchanan, "The Tax System as Social Overhead Capital: A Constitutional Perspective on Fiscal Norms," in Dieter Biehl et al., eds., *Public Finance and Economic Growth: Proceedings of the Thirty-seventh Congress of the International Institute of Public Finance, Tokyo, 1981* (Detroit: Wayne State University Press, 1983), 41.

[5] Charles Jones, "Patriotism, Morality, and Global Justice," in Ian Shapiro and Lea Brilmayer, eds., *NOMOS XLI: Global Justice* (New York: NYU Press, 1999), 125, 148.

is the pursuit of a chimera. For example, a state committed to impartiality will inevitably act, notwithstanding its rhetoric, in ways that benefit some at the expense of others, both in the short term and over the long term. The sociopolitical structure dictates this.

A focus on community would serve us well at present, if only because conceptions of political community are presently being challenged and promise to be challenged more strongly in the future. If capital and, to a substantial but lesser degree, labor are globalizing, they may actually be giving rise to dichotomous national-political and world-economic communities. The global economy, dominated by profit-maximizing private contractors, ignores national boundaries, while the political community strives to regulate economic relationships within those boundaries. The emerging cross-border linkages of individuals and groups weaken further the social welfare claims that support taking one person's property for the benefit of "the community." The closer affinities that individuals experience as members of communities formed at local and state levels enhance the legitimacy of these taxing authorities and generate ongoing struggles with competing units operating within a federal system. Thus, a progressive/redistributive public finance system at the national level is challenged by developing affiliations beyond the nation as well as intense, persistent affiliations with more geographically compact and responsive political units.

In theory, a net-benefits approach that accounts for outputs as well as inputs in an integrated fashion is more harmonious with social organizations, as well as superior from an economic-efficiency standpoint. Unfortunately, success at achieving a reliable accounting seems unattainable.[6] The tax law of the United States is itself so complex, and the affiliations of individuals with communities that benefit and lose are so numerous and varied in intensity over time, that no simple balance sheet could readily be constructed revealing a person's net gains or losses. Valuing an actual benefit or cost, short of a direct transfer, would appear to be a highly speculative venture. For example, no precise metric exists for valuing the benefit of a provision of a public good to a particular individual, especially when netted against other interests negatively affected. Interpersonal comparisons are even more complex and unreliable.[7] The task is further complicated by the numerous "community" affiliations of individuals, some of which communities may be in competition to varying degrees. Of course, the focus could be on measuring benefits to commu-

[6] There are other substantial problems with a net-benefits approach as well. These are discussed in Jeffrey Schoenblum, "Tax Fairness or Unfairness? A Consideration of the Philosophical Bases for Unequal Taxation of Individuals," *American Journal of Tax Policy* 12 (1995): 221, 225.

[7] See Lionel Roberts, "Interpersonal Comparisons of Utility," *Economic Journal* 48 (1938): 635, 637–40. See generally Stephen Utz, "Ability to Pay," *Whittier Law Review* 23 (2002): 867, 930.

nities, rather than to individuals, but even this departure from a traditional liberal focus on the individual would not make the measurement task any easier or yield more reliable outcomes.[8]

Still, a more realistic description and discussion of taxation/redistribution and its net beneficial consequences for particular individuals and communities would be helpful, despite the absence of absolute precision. For example, the contention that redistributive transfers have a net positive effect ought to be held up to a serious burden of proof before property is taken and redistributed. The inquiry might reveal that current policies, though intended sincerely as a tool for the achievement of the social betterment of the "community," actually do the opposite and create severe moral hazards,[9] or achieve their intended ends inefficiently, when weighed against the cost.

III. The Individual and the Community

A. *The formation and nature of communities*

Alone, each individual is inevitably self-centered and egoistic. *To be* must involve some concern with the self.[10] Although a person may survive alone, to be well and live a satisfactory existence, the individual needs others.[11] Indeed, even liberal thinkers have conceded the deficiency in their conception of pre-social individuals.[12] Inasmuch as each individual, nevertheless, also pursues his or her self-interest as a being with distinctive needs and preferences, there is the potential for conflict and exhaustion of common, but scarce, resources. A recurring mediation between unrestrained egoism and a more informed egoism through cooperation and contract defines social existence.

[8] One tax scholar has argued for a more communitarian approach to tax equity. See Reuven Avi-Yonah, "Why Tax the Rich? Efficiency, Equity, and Progressive Taxation," *Yale Law Journal* 111 (2002): 1391. However, the only community Avi-Yonah apparently sees is the mythic national community (ibid., 1402).

[9] Michael C. Dorf and Charles F. Sabel, "A Constitution of Democratic Experimentation," *Columbia Law Review* 98 (1998): 267, 341. A particularly intriguing discussion of this topic is presented in the context of the resistance to the private purchase of terrorism insurance. See Jeffrey Manns, "Insuring against Terror?" *Yale Law Journal* 112 (2003): 2542–43.

[10] Indeed, the argument has been made that the liberal conception of the unencumbered self is mistaken, that human nature is social, and that human beings necessarily define themselves in terms of their culture. In other words, association is not merely motivated by conscious pursuit of self-interest. See Michael Sandel, *Democracy's Discontent: America in Search of a Public Philosophy* (Cambridge, MA: Belknap Press of Harvard University Press, 1996).

[11] Daniel Bell, *Communitarianism and Its Critics* (Oxford: Clarendon Press, 1993), 31–39.

[12] See, e.g., Stephen Holmes, "The Structure of Antiliberal Thought," in Nancy L. Rosenblum, ed., *Liberalism and the Moral Life* (Cambridge, MA: Harvard University Press, 1989), 227, 228, where Holmes concedes "that concepts such as the pre-social self who enters civil society with a fully-formed identity were never meant to be metaphysical or ontological descriptions of psychological reality, but were instead mere rhetorical devices developed to demonstrate the injustice of certain political arrangements."

As social interactions multiply in pursuit of cooperative self-interest, a massive social network evolves. Associations, comprising this burgeoning network, are of varying intensity. Intensity may be influenced, for example, by the number of interactions over a concentrated or extended period of time, shared skills or beliefs, mutual financial gains to be had through exchange, physical attraction, and familial/biological bonds. The affinity an individual feels toward a particular other or others may oscillate over time and circumstance. Generally, the fewer the number of associates and the greater the extent or intimacy of the interaction, the greater the intensity and sense of "community" is likely to be.

Each of the social interactions a person has arguably constitutes a "community."[13] This is evidenced by legal and common parlance. For example, two people, a husband and wife, may own "community property." Persons refer to their neighborhood as "our community," thus also revealing their own attachment and stake by the use of the possessive pronoun. Persons who adhere to a particular religious faith may be viewed as a community, as in "the Jewish community," which may be segmented further, as in "the Reform Jewish community." Reference is often made to "the community of nations," wherein the attributes of individuals are projected onto nations, which are deemed to require some sort of social interaction to achieve their own individuated ends. Individuals, in contrast to nations, may belong to the "global community," which encompasses the idea of a bond among all human beings wherever they may reside. Those who approach ideas from a certain analytic viewpoint may be described as "a community of scholars."

Recognition of certain associative relationships can have important legal and tax consequences. For example, can a gay couple form a marital community under the laws as heterosexuals do, including the right to community property? Can that gay couple file joint tax returns, avoid taxable gain on transfers of appreciated property, or claim the marital deduction on the transfer of property at the death of a companion?[14]

B. The emergence of authority over the community

Although not all complex social relationships evolve in the same manner, a reasonable hypothesis is that at some point a "community" becomes too complex to rely exclusively on individual social interactions. Inter-

[13] See note 11 above. Daniel Bell refers to communities of place, communities of memory, and psychological communities.

[14] The Internal Revenue Code affords a number of tax benefits to married couples. By filing a joint return, they may be able to split income even when only one works and thus avoid some of the effects of progressive rates. They can also transfer wealth and gains between them, including by sale, without the recognition of income for taxation purposes. Finally, they can make unlimited transfers between them by gift or inheritance without gift tax or estate tax.

actions produce negative externalities. Investments require minimization of risk through a reliable system of predictable and uniformly applied rules of law. Overutilization of the commons must be regulated. Defense against outsiders and antisocial activity within the community must be provided. The demand for infrastructure must be answered so that further socioeconomic development will not be forestalled. Collective action problems, notably free-riding, discourage private provision of these goods and must be addressed by some other collective means.

A hierarchical structure with a leader having overall authority emerges. Commands are carried out by agents. Whether lords or bureaucrats, these agents transmit the commands across segments of the community. The number of agents and the extent of agents' powers affect private interactions of members of the community and eventually give rise to conflict, so that the friction at the margin of private and public is an inevitable theme in complex social interaction. In response, another set of intermediaries emerge: politicians, who translate from the leader to the community and from the community to the leader. The means by which the politicians are selected and their relative power vis-à-vis the leader differ from place to place, depending on culture, history, point in time in the evolution of the community, and the composition and size of the community.

The foregoing description of the emergence of hierarchical authority required to overcome collective action difficulties and assure common well-being differs from the Hobbesian model. That standard contractarian model begins with fearful individuals exhausted by their existence in a violent state of nature. They voluntarily submit to the coercive power of the state for their own security, contracting to surrender substantial autonomy in the process.

There does not, however, appear to be any compelling historical support for this Hobbesian account.[15] In fact, a more historically grounded account would support the view that there is no contract, explicit or implicit.[16] Rather, more formalized rule by a state over a community comes about through conquest by another community. This is followed by evolutionary accommodations and mixing of the conquering and conquered communities, yielding a hybrid set of communities. Again, this outcome is not the product of a voluntary contract at the initial point of conquest; nor does it appear to be the product of a voluntary contract among the members of subsequent generations. Even in those historically rare cases when the community describes its formal organization in contractarian terms, such as the founding of the United States or the French Republic, the rise of formal authority over the community is associated with the expulsion or suppression of large segments of the population

[15] Anthony de Jasay, *The State* (Oxford: Basil Blackwell, 1985), 42–43.

[16] Musgrave takes issue with contractarian accounts, but acknowledges their essential role in tax theory as a result of the inability to make reliable interpersonal utility comparisons. See Buchanan and Musgrave, *Public Finance and Public Choice*, 45–46.

who were previously regarded as an integral part of the community. Subsequent territorial expansion and consolidation typically follows the conquest model described above, as in the American experience.

The significance of the foregoing is that the authority to tax and redistribute is often justified by a disputable premise—that the constituents of the community have ceded a certain degree of autonomy and say over their property voluntarily and once and forever for mutual benefit via a social contract. Arguably, this may be true in certain unique instances and in certain limited respects. While these instances may be rare or nonexistent, their incorporation into a mythology serves the purpose of ameliorating concerns in a liberal state about state intrusions on liberty and differential treatment of its constituents.

The notion that individuals fear the state of nature and cannot associate profitably in it is also dubious. The contention is at least indirectly called into question by the interactions of nations, which have a long history of bilateral and multilateral relationships without any regulatory authority. While there have certainly been many instances of violence and coercion to achieve particular state interests, on the whole, nations have coexisted with each other and continue to do so. Nations have been prepared to surrender to a limited degree their sovereignty to a higher authority, such as the World Trade Organization (WTO). However, they have done so in a very measured way, while still preserving their autonomy and relatively cost-free exit options. Their complex interactions, involving trade, security, communications, and the rights of their respective citizens while on other nations' territory, suggest that individuals, too, could create a complex civil community in which at least some public goods would be produced without a strong state.

Assuming that there is some evidence that distinctive communities of persons—nations—enter into largely constructive bilateral and multilateral relationships without an overarching communal authority, the claim within a domestic political system that regulation of a variety of interpersonal relationships is necessary for the members to do better than they would without an intrusive, overarching authority deserves, at a minimum, careful scrutiny and a dose of skepticism. After all, the original purpose for establishing the overarching authority was to facilitate private interactions, not to supplant them.

C. *The state and the community*

The overarching authority previously referred to is commonly described as "the state." What precisely is the state? Strikingly, public finance has been uninterested in pursuing this line of inquiry. This reluctance to inquire into the nature of the state and its relationship to other participants in ongoing social interactions can be understood by reflecting upon the consequences for public finance if the state's neutrality, its independence, its wisdom, its synonymity with the community, and its contractarian origins, were called into question. If these premises were to be cast in doubt, the very "science" of public finance would be cast in doubt. Thus, the question of what the state is has vital consequences for public finance and its progeny—progressive taxation and redistributive policies.

There are any number of ways of regarding the state, and it may best be conceived in terms of some admixture of the following five models:

1. The standard public finance vision is of an unbiased, omniscient, independent actor that pursues enlightened, objective inquiry and policies to achieve net gains on behalf of the social welfare of the community. To secure these gains, it requires revenues, which must be derived from the private property of its constituents.[17]

2. This standard public finance account, however, is contested by a less sympathetic model of the state. It may be viewed as an organic, evolving entity that inevitably accumulates more and more authority over private resources and their selective redistribution. Pursuant to this model, the state invariably morphs from the benign facilitator of communal interactivity to an antagonist, its own existence increasingly dependent on the taking of private property from some in order to redistribute it to others, thereby purchasing the support that the state requires to survive.[18]

The state maintains its power under this model by a variety of techniques, depending on whether it is authoritarian or a majoritarian democracy. In either case, state takings and payoffs eventually become so prevalent that the constituents cannot ascertain whether they are net overall gainers or losers. The costs of rent-seeking are spread so broadly that there is little resistance. This process eventually produces constituents who are largely dependent on the state's tax, allocative, and redistributive schemes. Private transactions are squeezed out, and civil society shrinks in its significance in daily life.[19] The growing insecurity of private ownership shifts entrepreneurial energies and capital in substantial part to regulatory com-

[17] For Edgard Allix, a leading pre-World War II French public finance scholar and political economist, the foundation of the state's "right" to tax rests on its very sovereignty. The state is a historical necessity. It has a right, indeed obligation, to tax in order to secure its existence: "Le premier droit et le premier devoir de l'Etat est d'assurer son existence et son fonctionnement et, à cet effet, d'exiger de ceux qui vivent sous sa loi les moyens nécessares." ("The primary law and duty of the state is to secure its existence and its functioning and, with these purposes, to require from those who live under its law, the necessary means.") Edgard Allix, "La Condition de Etrangers au Point de Vue Fiscal," in Recueil des Cours, *Académie de Droit International de la Haye* 61 (1937): 545, 559. See also Rutsel Silvestre J. Martha, *The Jurisdiction to Tax in International Law: Theory and Practice of Legislative Fiscal Jurisdiction* (Deventer: Kluwer Law and Taxation Publishers, 1989), 18–22.

[18] See, for example, de Jasay, *The State*, 240–41, 247–48.

[19] See Robert D. Putnam, *Bowling Alone: The Collapse and Revival of American Community* (New York: Simon and Schuster, 2000). For a critique of civil society revivalists, see, e.g., Christopher L. Eisgruber, "Civic Virtue and the Limits of Constitutionalism," *Fordham Law Review* 69 (2001): 2131; and Linda C. McClain and James B. Fleming, "Some Questions for Civil Society Revivalists," *Chicago-Kent Law Review* 75 (2000): 30. However, even the critics acknowledge the decline of civil society.

pliance and special pleading, either for reduced tax burdens, beneficial allocations of resources, or direct transfers.

The foregoing model of the state, though perhaps extreme, suggests state action that is not always well-informed, benign, and successful, contrary to what the traditional public finance literature would suggest. To the extent that this second, more pessimistic model of the state is even a partly accurate one, it calls into question the assumption that the state's interests are harmonious with those of its constituent communities. If the state has an essence of its own, then its portrayal as a tool for achieving the worthy goals of social scientists seems mistaken. It cannot be relied upon to serve community interests—first, because there is no one community, and second, because even if there were one community united in its means and ends, these would not necessarily correspond to those of the state.

3. The state is the bureaucracy. The prior model of the state *in esse* is difficult to conceptualize once we get beyond the abstraction. The abstraction does not imagine action through persons. References are to the state "doing this" or "doing that," but the state is no personage. It cannot achieve its goals other than through agents. The principal agents of the modern state are the members of its bureaucracy. Through the individual acts of such agents, the identity and character of the state takes shape. Because they wield power in the name of the state, these agents are peculiarly positioned to capture the state and turn it to the service of their interests. And this bureaucratic community does have its own interests, a distinctive worldview, a definitive way of doing things, and a pronounced faith in its own expertise.[20] Various branches are well known for their willingness to collaborate with private special interest communities when there is a mutuality of interest. The bureaucracy has its own culture, and those who enter it sooner or later acculturate. The culture is evident worldwide, indicating community values that are distinct from affiliations with any national or local communities. Further, the bureaucracy has continuity, sizable membership, unique access to information, influence over those elected to govern, and a firm commitment to rational problem-solving.[21] Moreover, it is especially dependent on taxation for compensation and the accoutrements of employment.

If the bureaucracy has its own interests and biases, then the state, as the embodiment of its agents, cannot be expected to act for the general community. The bureaucracy has every interest in making dependency the social norm and promulgating regulations and rules that legitimize redis-

[20] Kenneth Minogue uses the term "philosopher bureaucrat." See Kenneth Minogue, "Ideal Communities and the Problem of Moral Identity," in John W. Chapman, ed., *NOMOS XXXV: Democratic Community* (New York: NYU Press, 1993), 41, 58.

[21] For the version of the bureaucracy as "experts" faithful to rules and rationality, see Max Weber, *Economy and Society: An Outline of Interpretive Sociology* (New York: Bedminster Press, 1968), 217–26, 956–1003.

tributive practices implemented under its watchful eye.[22] The complexity of the United States Tax Code, and the wealth of arcane accompanying treasury regulations and revenue rulings, all empower the tax bureaucracy from which favorable determinations must be sought.

The state as bureaucracy, however, may be an incomplete account. There are other agents besides bureaucrats, notably politicians. They are increasingly achieving, at least at the federal level in the United States, some modicum of the job security enjoyed by bureaucrats. Though they do not enjoy civil service protections as bureaucrats do, many legislators, especially those on the tax and budgeting committees, can achieve job security by selling tax loopholes, "public goods," and redistributive transfers.

In the end, the entire legislative body must vote. Even those who are not committee members can sell their support or engage in logrolling and other cooperative techniques with fellow legislators. No doubt some decisions by some politicians do rest on principle. Still, citizens grasp the susceptibility of politicians to "wheeling and dealing." This conduct is possible because these agents of the state can take private assets virtually without legal constraint by simply legislating taxes. Without that revenue, there would be much less to sell.[23]

Why does the politician participate? Simply put, politics is a business like other vocations. The politician needs to secure his or her position. He or she needs security to reap the rewards of office: remuneration, direct and indirect, present and future; community status; influence and the psychic rewards that come from receiving attention and praise; and even the sincere need to serve his or her represented community. The conception of a political marketplace is anathema to public finance, which depends on the purity of policymaking and the state's bureaucratic and political agents. But why assume that individuals in this business are more likely to surrender their self-interest than individuals in any other business? No evidence, in fact, has been presented that self-interested individuals abruptly abandon their self-interest upon being sworn into office or abandon it when exposed over the years to opportunities for substantial

[22] In the view of some administrative law scholars, and casting them in a more positive light, the "experts" are obligated to take into account the social morality of rulemaking. See Jerry L. Mashaw, "Small Things Like Reasons Are Put in a Jar: Reason and Legitimacy in the Administrative State," *Fordham Law Review* 70 (2001): 17, 33.

[23] Politicians may actually impose an expiration date on tax savings legislation and at each session may debate making the savings permanent so as to extract campaign contributions. One example is the debate in the U.S. over the repeal of the estate tax and the scheduled phase-out of tax benefits in 2010. See Linda Cohen, Edward J. McCaffery, and Fred S. McChesney, "Shakedown at Gucci Gulch: A Tale of Death, Money, and Taxes," USC-Caltech Center for the Study of Law and Politics, Working Paper No. 22, available at http://lawweb.usc.edu/cslp/papers/cslp-wp-022.pdf (accessed November 11, 2005). See generally Fred S. McChesney, *Money for Nothing: Politicians, Rent Extraction, and Political Extortion* (Cambridge, MA: Harvard University Press, 1997); and Elizabeth Garrett, "Harnessing Politics: The Dynamics of Offset Requirements in the Tax Legislative Process," *University of Chicago Law Review* 65 (1998): 501, 545–55.

personal gains. The very process of getting elected involves the need to finance a campaign. Financial support does not come in large part from selfless souls but from savvy, intensely self-interested, and not entirely altruistic constituents and their interest groups. In many instances, they seek through the democratic process to achieve gains to substitute for losses in the private market, and they regard both political activity and market activity as one seamless pursuit for the acquisition and preservation of gains.[24]

One might argue that a self-selection process is at work, whereby those who are most disinterested in gain, most unbiased, most committed to the social welfare, and most knowledgeable in the methods of achieving good for the community enter "public service" in each generation and at each level of government. However, this author is unaware of data that supports this proposition. There is considerable evidence, though, that these agents of the state are as biased, misinformed, and self-interested as are other individuals.

The reality of the political marketplace challenges the underlying assumptions of public finance. Not only do agents of the state act in their own self-interest rather than for all of us, but there is no independent actor capable of ascertaining the path to the general social welfare or the greatest good. A most fatuous conceit is that through committee hearings, the consideration of "expert" reports, and the commitment of the bureaucracy, the proper allocation of tax burden, investment in public goods, and redistribution can be accomplished. However, once the self-interest of the actors is appreciated, the rest is performance art.

4. There are a number of competitive states, not just "the state." Even if each state's agents could fit the public finance mold, the self-interest of their own states could clash and compete with each other, complicating the achievement of domestic welfare policy. In the federal system of the United States, for example, different political units compete with each other and in some cases reach accommodations as to the allocation of the spoils. In certain instances, efforts to appeal to the same voters result in overmining, resulting in particularly significant tax takings and redistributions in the aggregate.[25]

In addition to vertical national-state-local competition, states and localities compete with each other horizontally. These states and localities make efforts, based on expansive assertions of tax jurisdiction, to increase the tax base at the expense of their coequals. Compacts are entered into to allocate revenue among them. Nevertheless, vast concessions may also be granted to certain taxpayers because, unlike the federal government, the states lack a captured tax base. Taxpayers can choose to move to another

[24] Robert Dahl, "Why All Democratic Countries Have Mixed Economies," in Chapman, ed., *NOMOS XXXV: Democratic Community*, 259.

[25] Francis Edgeworth, "The Pure Theory of Taxation," in Musgrave and Peacock, eds., *Classics*, 119.

state.[26] Within a state, different branches of government and/or their agents engage in the same competition as do national and state units.

While, in some nations, the judiciary must fall into line behind the other state actors, in other countries such as the United States, this is considerably less true. Nevertheless, taxation has largely been removed from the domain of the judiciary in the U.S. The legitimacy of tax takings and differentiated tax burdens is simply not subject to serious legal challenge any longer. As for the executive and legislative branches, there are not so much institutional struggles for control between them as there are conflicts generated by capture of these branches by divergent special interests.

5. The "state" simply describes a process. The process contemplated is one already alluded to, in which special interest communities compete. At the heart of this process is majoritarian democracy. By purchasing majority support, a majority coalition of communities can accomplish its members' ends. Majority coalitions do not last. As coalitions constantly shift, gains enjoyed today may be lost tomorrow and vice versa. This cycling of benefits and losses emphasizes the need to stay in the game to be a net winner, and the importance of the game affords the state referees a continuous stream of product to sell. The game reaches its ultimate perfection in direct churning, whereby resources are taken from individuals and then redistributed back through public goods or direct transfers to those same persons, but only after the subtraction of administrative charges.

One example of how this process works is the current allocation of income tax burdens in the United States. Massive numbers of income earners have been relieved from any obligation to pay income tax at all. The top 1 percent of income earners in the United States were projected by the Congressional Budget Office to pay 21.5 percent of all federal tax liabilities in 2005, down slightly from actual payments of 22.7 percent in 2001. The top 10 percent of income earners were projected to pay 48.8 percent of federal tax liabilities in 2005. The top 20 percent were projected to pay 64.3 percent. Their share of income was projected to be approximately 52.4 percent.[27] The top 60 percent of income earners pay 96.3 percent of all federal income taxes. Middle income earners could have joined with the rich against the poor, but there would not have been as much revenue to siphon off as there is from siphoning off the income of the rich. Effectively, the lower half of income earners are enjoying the benefits of membership in the national political community at no income tax cost, while the other half bears those costs.[28]

[26] See Sheryll D. Cashin, "Federalism, Welfare Reform, and the Minority Poor: Accounting for the Tyranny of State Majorities," *Columbia Law Review* 99 (1999): 552, 598–99, 621–22.

[27] No figures on their share of total wealth are available.

[28] That is not to say that an intelligent defense of this situation cannot be mounted. See, e.g., Ramesh Ponnuru, "Tax Cuts for the Poor," *National Review Online*, May 20, 2005, available at http://www.nationalreview.com/ponnuru/ponnuru200505200751.asp. For example, gaps in income may be explained by life-cycle effects, so that nontaxpayers can be expected one day to age into taxpayers.

By no means do these statistics establish that all revenue raised is redistributed to the low income and lower middle income earners. That is hardly the case. As I have noted, there might be some direct churning going on. Moreover, not all upper, middle, and high income earners carry the burden. It is not distributed to achieve horizontal equity.

The state, conceived as a "process of redistribution," is limited, however mildly, by the vestigial protection accorded to private property in the United States.[29] In their work *The Myth of Ownership: Taxes and Justice*,[30] Liam Murphy and Thomas Nagel, professors at New York University Law School, urge the abandonment of this limiting principle to the extent that it impedes the raising of revenue for their preferred redistributive program. They urge a value shift so that social welfare and justice are allowed to trump private property. Yet the problem remains—who should be empowered to define "social welfare and justice," since this is a contestable proposition? Who determines which constituents are entitled to beneficence, and who determines the form it should take? Simply stated, Murphy and Nagel (or any other "neutral" academics) are no less suspect as disinterested "experts" than are the self-interested bureaucrats and politicians who will be called upon to legislate and implement the program. Indeed, there is no infallible and neutral process, just as there is no infallible and neutral state actor.

IV. The Emerging Global Community

As I have noted, an individual typically claims membership in a number of communities that command different levels of participation and allegiance. These communities might be comprised of spouses or companions, immediate family members, extended family members, ethnic or religious groups, business, professional, or labor organizations, or ideological and political associations.

In addition, there are also communal affinities primarily defined by geography. It is less costly and more efficient to interact with those closer by. Neighborhoods, villages, and towns are the centers of most individuals' daily lives. Not uncommonly, within these boundaries there thrives a civil society that is central to the identity and well-being of the individual.[31] The more distant the community, the less attachment typically exists. When one's property is taken to support the interests of distant or

[29] These vestigial protections may have been substantially narrowed by the recent U.S. Supreme Court decision in *Kelo v. City of New London*, 125 S.Ct. 2655 (2005) (holding that the state can take property from one private owner and redistribute it to another for a "public purpose"; the property need not be taken by the state for "public use").

[30] Liam Murphy and Thomas Nagel, *The Myth of Ownership: Taxes and Justice* (Oxford: Oxford University Press, 2002).

[31] But see, e.g., Putnam, *Bowling Alone*. Putnam raises doubts about the continuing vibrancy of civil society at the local level.

unknown members of an artificially constructed political community, alienation, resistance, and a determined interest in recouping losses may be stimulated. This often takes the form of a tax revolt.[32]

Historically and conceptually, the power to tax effectively stops at the nation's borders and is limited to persons and property over which the state exercises control. Yet why should the goal of social welfare or justice be denied to those who by the happenstance of birth or other contingency find themselves the nationals of one nation rather than another?[33]

If the argument is that the community enables those who are well-off to prosper and, thus, can demand of them a contribution (even a disproportionate one) to the general social welfare,[34] this does not end the inquiry. In our global economy, the well-being of even the poorest in the United States hinges in part on, and is made possible by, the efforts of even less well-off persons abroad.[35]

Not surprisingly, a number of scholars have made specific proposals for raising taxes globally and for the redistribution of resources.[36] For example, the political philosopher Thomas Pogge has proposed a global natural resources tax.[37] Other proponents of a global tax, such as Hillel Steiner, a professor at University of Manchester in the United Kingdom, while agreeing with the concept of a global tax, question its efficacy if only resources removed from the ground are taxable.[38] Other issues raised with respect to the proposal have included the need to expand the tax base to countries that are wealthy, though not as rich in natural resources, perhaps via a global tax on transfers of financial instruments (recently proposed by French president Jacques Chirac and Nobel Prize–winning economist James Tobin).[39] On the redistribution side of the equation, an

[32] In this regard, theories that hypothesize that the spreading of tax costs across the polity reduces opposition to redistribution are questionable. Constituents recognize the long-term threat to their wealth inherent in taxation and cannot be certain that they will recover (or have the time and resources to recover) it all by involvement in the redistributive political process. Each time the tax option is exercised, it confirms the state's potential to do it again.

[33] Thomas Pogge, *Realizing Rawls* (Ithaca, NY: Cornell University Press, 1989), 246. Pogge, indeed, takes Rawls to task for, first, emphasizing that only *persons* matter, but then recognizing, as a second principle, that on international matters, nations, not persons, would decide behind the veil of ignorance. Thomas Pogge, "An Egalitarian Law of Peoples," *Philosophy and Public Affairs* 23 (1994): 195–224. See John Rawls, *A Theory of Justice* (Cambridge, MA: Harvard University Press, 1971), 378.

[34] Thomas Hill Green, *Liberal Legislation and Freedom of Contract: A Lecture* (Oxford: Slatter and Rose, 1881).

[35] Even if this were not the case, there might be a superior "justice" claim of the poorest, which would have to be balanced against the "special claims" of those with whom we have the closer affiliations. See Samuel Scheffler, "The Conflict between Justice and Responsibility," in Shapiro and Brilmayer, eds., *NOMOS XLI: Global Justice*, 86, 95.

[36] See, for example, Charles Beitz, *Political Theory and International Relations* (Princeton, NJ: Princeton University Press, 1979), 143–53.

[37] See Pogge, *Realizing Rawls*.

[38] Hillel Steiner, "Just Taxation and International Redistribution," in Shapiro and Brilmayer, eds., *NOMOS XLI: Global Justice*, 171. Steiner has his own proposal of a global fund (ibid., 176).

[39] Ibid.

intense debate has raged over whether transfers should be made to the governments of developing nations or via some independent, nongovernmental agency, which would then distribute funds to individuals themselves, to communities to which they belong, or through public works projects. Moreover, an allocation formula has been urged so that the redistribution is not limited to certain countries or regions. Others have argued that nations should be the recipients, as they may have some claim to their constituents' resources in the same way that individuals have to their talents, or at least the enhancement of those talents for which they are responsible.[40]

The arguments for global taxation are not all altruistic. First, proponents argue that such taxation is in the developed world's interest. It could mollify foreign communities that otherwise could pose a mortal external or even internal threat. Second, it might actually generate demand for local production and open up new avenues for profitable foreign investment. Third, it represents a step forward in the cosmopolitan agenda to create institutions and a funding source for universal governance.

Nevertheless, proponents of the global tax overlook the weakness of the attachment of taxpayers to their membership in the global community. Unless symbols can be created to engender deeper commitment to their fellow human beings whom they do not know and who live in places they may be afraid to even visit, majoritarian support seems unlikely.[41] Constituents will question why their private wealth should be taxed for redistribution to an even more distant "state."[42] The domestic, voting poor will seek out allies to resist the threat to their own transfers.

The cosmopolitan who supports the global tax likely conceives of himself or herself as part of an international movement of enlightened elites, who have transcended arbitrary political boundaries often established by coercive means. He or she seeks out the Kantian ideal[43] and favors, at least to a certain extent, a world dominated by international organizations and nongovernmental organizations (NGOs) that accomplish what national states now do.

Cosmopolitan proponents of global taxation evidence the same abstract faith in the idea of the state (and in their own expertise in the name of the state to further the interests of the "universal" community) that the proponents of public finance do with respect to the "national" community. Overlooked by both are the thickness of political markets, the competition

[40] Ibid.

[41] Liam B. Murphy, "Comment on Scheffler's 'The Conflict between Justice and Responsibility'," in Shapiro and Brilmayer, eds., *NOMOS XLI: Global Justice*, 116–17. Murphy recognizes the problem but suggests that there is enough to go around by taking from the Western "rich." As to how much might be required, see Jeffrey Sachs, *The End of Poverty: Economic Possibilities for Our Time* (New York: The Penguin Group, 2005).

[42] Bell, *Communitarianism and Its Critics*, 150–51.

[43] Immanuel Kant, "Perpetual Peace: A Philosophical Sketch," in Kant, *Political Writings*, ed. Hans Reiss, trans. H. B. Nisbet (New York: Cambridge University Press, 1991).

of interest groups, the absence of a unitary national or international community, and the real-life inability of "experts" to identify what is proper redistribution and to successfully implement it. Without a clear connection between the global governors and the local taxpayers, and with too much distance between them for accountability, much of the revenue raised will inevitably go to the political and bureaucratic arbitrageurs and the most adept global rent-seekers. While the system of global regulation will not be pure majoritarian democracy, there will still be a marketplace that answers to the usual forces of supply and demand. Even if severe institutional constraints and oversight are imposed, as with the United Nations' oil-for-food program in Iraq, the opportunities for net gain will attract participants to the marketplace, even ones prepared to act illegally.

Despite the foregoing considerations, the cosmopolitan global intuition is not entirely off the mark. There *is* something going on internationally, but it is competitive in nature—specifically, tax competition. This phenomenon has always been present but has recently been accelerated by the enhanced mobility of capital and labor. Assume that profit is ordinarily derived from intangible capital assets, labor, and tangible immovable capital assets. With respect to intangible assets, the barriers to capital's free flow worldwide have now almost entirely fallen. A Tiebout-type phenomenon spurs the mobility of this capital.[44] Capital will seek out the situs from which the highest net return can be earned after accounting for taxation. Consistent with this thesis, intangible capital now flows routinely to low-tax or no-tax jurisdictions and then is reinvested in developed financial markets, which typically favor outsiders over their own citizens.[45] In this way, maximum returns can be earned at a minimum cost. For example, a resident of a European country may shift capital to an offshore tax haven and from there invest in the United States, which will not tax gains from sales of securities,[46] and, if assets are held in corporate form offshore, will not impose death taxes when the investor dies.[47] Other techniques are available for reducing taxation on foreign-source interest and dividends.[48] The identity of the investor is kept secret from the country of residence, which might otherwise tax him or her on the basis of residency, or assets may be owned through a layer of entities that

[44] Charles M. Tiebout, "A Pure Theory of Local Expenditures," *Journal of Political Economy* 64 (1956): 416. Tiebout was concerned with the efforts of competing municipalities to attract consumers of public goods, recognizing that consumers were limited to voting within their municipality, but could "vote with their feet" by physically moving to another municipality.

[45] David J. Hayton, ed., *Extending the Boundaries of Trusts and Similar Ring-fenced Funds* (The Hague: Kluwer Law International, 2002).

[46] Internal Revenue Code, section 865(a).

[47] *Fillman v. United States*, 355 F.2d 632 (Cl. Ct. 1966). See Jeffrey A. Schoenblum, *Multistate and Multinational Estate Planning*, vol. 2 (Gaithersburg, MD: Aspen Publishers, 1999), 151–52. There are a variety of ways that Europeans can avoid taxation in their home countries, some legal and some illegal but not effectively enforced (see ibid.).

[48] Joel D. Kurtz and Robert J. Peroni, *U.S. International Taxation* (Boston: Warren Gorham & Lamont, 2005), paragraph A2.03[1].

legally cuts off technical ownership for tax purposes in the home country. If this does not suffice, the investor can also adopt a residence in a low-tax or no-tax jurisdiction.[49] Of course, the investor retains ultimate economic control.

In response to this serious challenge to the sources of revenue for high-tax states with substantial social welfare obligations, the Organization for Economic Cooperation and Development (OECD) has coerced some tax havens into dropping their ring-fenced regimes whereby foreign investors are not taxed, but their own residents are. The OECD has also insisted on exchange of information. The outcome of this struggle for retention of capital and access to information is not yet finally settled. However, one emerging response of tax havens has been simply to impose the same low tax (or no tax) uniformly on locals and nonresidents.[50]

Many of the current tax havens have suffered from widespread poverty. The transfer of capital on account of tax competition has resulted in gains to members of those communities through service fees and employment.[51] This global redistribution through tax competition is, meanwhile, challenging the internal redistributive monopoly of welfare states.[52] The revenue loss from the exercise of the capital exit option is mirrored to a certain degree in the case of labor. Three facets of the topic stand out. First, highly compensated individuals are building new, global, professional communities, with more connectedness to their professional associates than to their fellow citizens. Pools of professional expertise are being assembled in certain preferred locales worldwide, and professionals are now able to cross borders freely to enter these pools on a temporary basis in order to maximize the return on their human capital. Multinational corporations have also accelerated this trend. Moreover, the exchange of information concerning cross-border opportunities is facilitated by low-cost global communications technology. Just as it has allowed for the free flow of capital efficiently, this technology sustains the creation of human capital networks worldwide.

The second facet is the availability of cheap, competent labor outside the national community. The uproar over outsourcing to India of various English-language customer service centers from the United States is rep-

[49] See, for example, William G. Hill, *The Passport Report*, 11th ed. (Hants, England: Scope International Ltd., 1996). Corporate-related techniques, such as transfer pricing and back-to-back loans, abound. See, e.g., Terrence R. Chorvat, "A Different Perspective on Tax Competition," *George Washington International Law Review* 35 (2003): 501, 510.

[50] Robert T. Kudrle and Lorraine Eden, "The Campaign against Tax Havens: Will It Last? Will It Work?" *Stanford Journal of Law, Business, and Finance* 9 (2003): 37.

[51] Reuven Avi-Yonah, "Globalization, Tax Competition, and the Fiscal Crisis of the Welfare State," *Harvard Law Review* 113 (2000): 1573. Of course, the gains may not be equitably or efficiently distributed among the populace of the tax haven.

[52] Ibid. Avi-Yonah argues that international tax competition has been a drain on welfare state resources and also claims that the low-tax or no-tax regimes of tax havens deprive their citizens of much-needed resources. Accordingly, on the basis of economic efficiency and equity grounds, he urges significant limitations on international tax competition.

resentative of this development. Again, communications technology assures provision of services at an increased profit by cutting overall labor costs. Not only does this pit foreign communities of laborers against each other, but it creates intensified fissures within the exporting nation, with consumers arrayed against the displaced labor. Again, the simplistic vision of public finance is exposed. Private market forces can no longer be contained once they skip beyond the political boundaries within which those making the decisions operate.

The third facet of the labor problem is the inflow of cheap labor from less developed countries. This inflow is a striking indication of the competitive nature of conflicting communities within the nation. The importation of foreign labor serves as a check on domestic laborers' wages, thus representing a distributive policy in favor of producers and consumers at the expense of the displaced labor. Tools outside the tax and redistributive policymaking system, such as lenient immigration policies, are employed. Not only does this reveal the immense difficulty in arriving at any final accounting of winners and losers within the society, but it also demonstrates the impossibility of any scientific approach to public finance that limits its concern to the design of an efficient or just tax system.

Of course, labor is not as mobile as capital.[53] Even within the United States, individuals often choose not to leave a high tax and regulatory state and move to a more favorable one. The affiliations with communities in the form of family, neighborhood, church, culture, or business opportunities contribute utility that may well overcome the lure of tax savings.

Immovables would at first appear to be safely within the control of the state as a tax resource. Real property cannot be transferred beyond political boundaries. It is not mobile. However, even here, clever strategies associated with equitable conversion can be employed. The real property is transferred by the owner to a corporation or limited liability company in exchange for equity ownership in the entity.[54] At least within the United States, this stratagem does not avoid taxation of rents; but impositions, such as death taxes, can largely be avoided if the true owner resides outside of the taxing jurisdiction.

The foregoing discussion of the globalization of capital and labor, though rudimentary, demonstrates the severe challenge confronting majoritarian democracies with heavy commitments to unequal tax and redistributionist policies. Tax and other price competition exacerbates the conflict of communities within the nation and between nations.

Essentially, those with resources who remain within the nation's political boundaries are called upon to fund the commitment to the nation's

[53] Janice R. Bellace, "Labor Law for the Post-Industrial Workplace: Breaking the New Deal Model," in Benjamin Aaron et al., eds., *Labor Law at the Crossroads: Changing Employment Relationships* (The Hague: Kluwer Law International, 1997), 22.

[54] Schoenblum, *Multistate and Multinational Estate Planning*, section 19.05[I].

multiplying dependents. This, in turn, encourages more capital and labor to exit in search of climes more respectful of private wealth. As dependents seek to influence policy through their natural advantage based on "one man, one vote," the state and/or its agents increasingly lose their ability to mediate among communities of rent-seekers. The state pursues increasingly contradictory and self-defeating policies. Labor is imported, but the savings are neutralized by the immigrants' own social welfare demands and those of displaced nationals and domestic interest groups. As immigrant communities grow, their affirmative welfare demands must be taken more seriously. The perception of national community weakens further.

The alternatives for the state and its agents are severely limited. They cannot cut back on redistributive policies, because that means the end of their power and the political market opportunities that it affords. Another more viable alternative is to eliminate tax competition. Yet, with a multitude of nations and the free flow of capital and labor to the most beneficial ones, this appears to be an unlikely source of long-term relief. In sum, the globalization of the economic community poses a direct challenge to the survivability of those Western social welfare states that continue to pursue progressive tax and redistributive policies. The fundamental tension between realistic economic communities and artificial political communities will have to be resolved, if only gradually.[55] Political communities will have to adjust their policies, an unlikely development, or face greater impoverishment and internal social conflict, a more likely prospect.

Some globalists, then, are not universalists. Rather, they are self-interested individuals who, in pursuit of their self-interest, challenge state claims to their capital by exercising the exit option. Other globalists may be of the previously described cosmopolitan type. They carry Western liberal thought to its logical end point. All persons, wherever situated and however talented, deserve at least a bare minimum decent existence precisely because they are human beings. The cosmopolitan, by insisting on faithfulness to the social welfare/justice ideology, exerts pressure on the public finance system (just as the global individualist does). However, the cosmopolitan's threat is principally an ethical challenge. The cosmopolitan exposes the parochialism of the social welfarist, whose concern for the needy stops with the needy within his or her own borders.

V. The Implications for Traditional Theories

Differentiated tax and redistributive policies are only sustainable by an untested faith in the ability of certain actors to arrive at sound decisions affecting the general welfare of an altruistic community whose members

[55] The divergence, more generally, was identified by Karl Marx in "On the Jewish Question," in Robert C. Tucker, ed., *The Marx-Engels Reader*, 2d ed. (New York: Norton, 1978).

have all bought in. Plausible theories are required to afford a rational and ethical basis for acting in favor of some constituents at the expense of others. Two theories in particular have provided the philosophical foundations for tax progressivity and redistribution—utilitarianism and social welfare limited by Rawlsian justice. Yet neither theory has seriously considered the nature and operation of the state or its communities.

A. Utilitarianism

Although there are numerous schools of utilitarian thought, the central premise is that state policies must seek the greatest good for the greatest number in the aggregate. For the utilitarian, the fact that a particular person suffers is unfortunate, but acceptable in view of the net gains that are achieved by the policies pursued.

While presented as a highly scientific and neutral theory for formulating and implementing tax and redistributionist policies, utilitarianism is built on quicksand. For example, tax burdens are allocated on the basis of ability to pay, which itself is determined by marginal utility analysis. Marginal utility analysis, in turn, requires the assignment of value in terms of utils (units of utility) to the preferences of each individual. These then would have to be summed up.

Importantly, there is no standard for valuing subjective preferences. The individual himself or herself does not know these values finally, except at the decision point. But who makes the valuations? Who has the skills and objectivity to do so? Absent the fiction of such an ultimate authority, the measurement called for simply cannot be made. Even if we assume that one additional dollar is more useful relatively to the poor person than to the rich person, that does not say anything about the absolute utility value of the dollar; nor does it permit us to make interpersonal comparisons at all.[56] It also tells us nothing of the public and private externalities that are the consequence of the attempt to implement the utilitarian program.[57]

Moreover, utilitarian theory generally ignores the question of the greatest good *for whom*. The concern could be, and perhaps ought to be, the greatest good for all mankind. If applied, this analysis would at some point leave the domestic poor to be taxed at the margin for the benefit of the even poorer elsewhere.

B. Social welfare theory limited by Rawlsian justice

This theory posits that policies pertaining to taxation burdens, the allocation of revenues for public goods, and redistribution should be employed

[56] See note 7.

[57] Frank Hahn, "On Some Difficulties of the Utilitarian Economist," in Amartya Sen and Bernard Williams, eds., *Utilitarianism and Beyond* (Cambridge: Cambridge University Press, 1982), 195.

to achieve general social welfare/justice. Again, the theory is commendable as long as the assumption is that an unbiased state and/or its agents are at the helm, guiding a unitary community toward a general welfare which is within the agents' expertise to identify and achieve. In this essay, I have challenged the component elements of that vision. If the vision is flawed, then the danger is that justice will not be done and the general social welfare will not be advanced. Rather, the parochial interests of certain individuals and communities, private and public, will be advanced.

A community in which altruism exists can certainly assist those in relative need on a private basis. Indeed, a considerable amount, in the range of $250 billion, is transferred annually through charitable intermediaries in the United States.[58] These transfers may reflect the limits of collective voluntary altruism, but it is also possible that charitable giving might be greater if tax burdens were lower. "Altruistic" transfers in the form of state-mandated taxation and redistribution constitute coercive transfers and should not necessarily be regarded as supported broadly by the community.

A number of political philosophers have sought to constrain the taxing and redistributive tendency. John Rawls is, of course, the preeminent example. His proposal that a just system should emerge from behind a veil of ignorance, while properly subject to much criticism, has an indisputably fair quality to it, since it is a principle of general application. However, his abandonment of Pareto optimality in favor of the difference principle[59] not only reveals his own bias, but again assumes a neutral, knowledgeable, efficient, and effective state apparatus reflective of shared values. The fact of a decision behind a veil of ignorance does not assure that the participants would believe that Rawlsian justice is feasible or desirable.

With respect to taxation, Rawls ultimately endorses proportionality, whereby taxpayers each pay tax in the same proportion to their respective incomes. However, as with most proponents of the social welfare approach, he focuses little attention on the link between the tax burden and redistributive sides of the equation. He also does not call into question the

[58] The precise figure is $248.52 billion for 2004. See Giving USA Foundation—AAFRC Trust for Philanthropy, *Giving USA* (Indiana University, 2005), with relevant data available online at http://aafrc.org/gusa/index.cfm?pg=giving.htm (pie charts), and http://aafrc.org/gusa/GUSA05_Press_Release.pdf (for a press release offering a detailed summary of the data).

[59] "Pareto optimality" embodies the principle that members of a collectivity enjoy maximum ophelimity (economic satisfaction), such that any small departure from that position "necessarily has the effect of increasing the ophelimity which certain individuals enjoy, and decreasing that which others enjoy, of being agreeable to some, and disagreeable to others." Vilfredo Pareto, *Manual of Political Economy* (1927), ed. Ann S. Schwier and Alfred N. Page, trans. Ann S. Schwier (New York: August M. Kelley Pub., 1971), 261. In contrast, the difference principle tolerates distributive gains to some in the collectivity at the expense of others if these gains enhance the condition of the worst off. See Rawls, *A Theory of Justice*, 76–83.

likelihood of successful implementation of efforts to achieve enhanced social welfare, notwithstanding much experience to the contrary.[60]

An alternative approach, recently presented by Murphy and Nagel, reflects an egalitarian take that dismisses the Rawlsian approach in preference for a frontal assault on private property.[61] Murphy and Nagel have fundamental faith in the attainability of the ends of the redistributive program and that these are the proper ends for the state to pursue. Of course, their very statement of ends with which not all would agree presupposes the existence of disputable ends. Their contribution is to acknowledge the ideological dispute, opening it to legitimate debate and escaping from the faulty premise of a "science" of public finance.

By persisting in the myth of the scientific state and refusing to come to grips with the messier version of the interaction among the individual, the state, and the community, public finance proponents need not confront the fundamental tensions that have already been highlighted in this essay. Clean models can be created that produce ideal outcomes. The experts/theorists can be mega-problem-solvers and can "discover" solutions. Complicating factors and reality-based data can simply be discarded as exogenous to the model.

Public finance rests on an unshakeable faith in the post-Enlightenment modern state. An elite "community" conceives and administers the programs. To doubt the public-finance proponent's neutrality and capacity to achieve results calls into question his or her work and the scientific nature and worth of the proponent's very professional activity.

There is no question that elementary models can prove critical in identifying issues and potential solutions. However, the complex interactions that occur in any community with a highly developed network of manifold and overlapping rights, obligations, contracts, and relationships cannot be easily modeled. At a minimum, more serious inquiries into individual, communal, and state behavior are needed, rather than placid assumptions.

VI. Defining the End Product

Even if the possibility of disinterested "expertise" were conceded, the "end product" tax policy problem would persist. The expert can design a program of redistribution but must first know what the end product is. Experts must know what end must be produced. A central question, then, is this: What is the proper application of tax revenues? There is no answer

[60] The deficiencies of the recipients may make failure in implementation inevitable. Joel F. Handler, "Discretion in Social Welfare: The Uneasy Position in the Rule of Law," *Yale Law Journal* 92 (1983): 1270, 1271–73; Jerry L. Mashaw, "Welfare Reform and Local Administration of Aid to Families with Dependent Children in Virginia," *Virginia Law Review* 57 (1971): 818, 833.

[61] See Murphy and Nagel, *The Myth of Ownership: Taxes and Justice.*

to this question that can be arrived at through rational analysis. The end sought is fundamentally a political and moral issue.[62]

The debate over taxation and redistribution that has raged since the nineteenth century leaves no doubt but that there are widely divergent viewpoints on how revenue collected via taxes should be expended. The answer does not rest in positive science because there is no agreement as to what the "public good" or "social welfare" means, or even what is the appropriate "community" or "communities" to be benefited. Thus, if we were to suspend disbelief and even grant the expertise of certain selfless public finance experts, we would still be at sea as far as the programmatic ends on which they would bring their expertise to bear.

Even assuming that the conceptualizers and the bureaucrats are pure and entirely capable, this would still leave the politicians. The actual design and implementation of the program would depend on them as well. Their fealty to neutral principles would be unlikely in light of the inherent nature of politics and the nonexistence of neutral principles. In short, the attainment of a "just redistribution," even if the outlines of the program and the conception of justice were universally agreed upon, would still prove impossible.

VII. Conclusion

The purpose of this essay has been to focus attention on shortcomings in the public finance approach to taxation. There are a number of reasons for the prevalence of this approach, including path dependence, the European traditions inherent in the discipline as it was transmitted to American scholars, the intellectual appeal of pristine conceptions that are easy to model, a liberal-modernist faith in the efficacy of the state and its capacity to represent the interests of the entire community, and the romantic vision of a just and unitary (or, perhaps, universal) community with "experts" leading the way.

This essay argues that a more realistic and nuanced portrayal of social-political-economic interactions must be the foundation of any attempt to explain and possibly improve the present public finance system. Unfortunately, these interactions make reform from within virtually impossible. Admittedly, one nascent force for reform is global tax competition. Whether or not it eventually does foster reform from within, or actually precipitates an outflow of capital and labor and eventual decay from within in those countries that choose to adhere to the public finance myth, remains to be seen. Either way, intense pressures are being exerted on the previously unquestioned "public" capture by the "state" of private property

[62] The early ability-to-pay theorists certainly regarded the determination of public expenditures as political in nature, rather than economic. See Musgrave and Peacock, eds., *Classics,* xi.

and its redistribution for the general welfare of the "community." In the end, unbiased expertise will not and cannot be found to save the day. Even if it could, the expert would still require guidance as to the ends to be produced. Those ends would be highly disputed by multifarious and shifting communities. The achievement of those ends against the backdrop of the political marketplace would be even more dubious. What all this should make clear is that taxation for the achievement of the "social welfare" is, indeed, a chimera.

Law, Vanderbilt University Law School

CHOICE, CATALLAXY, AND JUST TAXATION: CONTRASTING ARCHITECTONICS FOR FISCAL THEORIZING

By Richard E. Wagner

I. Introduction

As observers of society, we are inescapably prisoners in Plato's cave, where the sense we make of our observations is shaped by the mental maps we construct to order those observations. For the most part, fiscal theorists have worked with a mental map that treats government as a sentient being and assimilates fiscal phenomena to the choices of that being; if people write the first draft of the manuscript of social life through their market activities, the state is the editor who polishes and perfects the manuscript. The alternative mental map that I explore here treats government as a form of "catallaxy," where fiscal outcomes are emergent and not direct objects of choice; the relationship between state and market is coeval and not sequential.[1] This essay explores some of the contours of what might comprise a catallactical orientation toward fiscal phenomena, giving some attention in the process to how this catallactical orientation might be brought to bear on the relationship among taxation, prosperity, and justice.

The distinction between mental maps that I explore here contains both old and new sources of inspiration. The old sources pertain to a distinctly Continental orientation toward public finance that flourished alongside the Anglo-Saxon orientation until the late 1930s.[2] The new sources pertain to the growing interest in such intellectual constructions as complex adaptive systems and agent-based computational modeling.[3] These new sources offer ways of apprehending societal phenomena that arise not directly

[1] In volume 2 of *Law, Legislation, and Liberty* (Chicago: University of Chicago Press, 1976), esp. 107–20, F. A. Hayek distinguishes between an economy and a catallaxy. An "economy" refers to some individual unit that exercises choice, whereas a "catallaxy" refers to the entire nexus of economizing units, a nexus which itself is not a choosing, economizing unit.

[2] The contrast in orientations is presented in Jürgen G. Backhaus and Richard E. Wagner, "The Continental Tradition in the Theory of Public Finance: An Exercise in Mapping and Recovery," *Journal of Public Finance and Public Choice*, forthcoming; and in Jürgen G. Backhaus and Richard E. Wagner, "From Continental Public Finance to Public Choice: Mapping Continuity," *History of Political Economy* 37 (2005), annual supplement.

[3] For a crisp presentation of what can be done in this respect, see Joshua M. Epstein and Robert Axtell, *Growing Artificial Societies: Social Science from the Bottom Up* (Washington, DC: Brookings Institution, 1996). The pioneering effort within this genre is Thomas C. Schelling, *Micromotives and Macrobehavior* (New York: Norton, 1978).

from choice but through human interaction. A nice illustration of the distinction is provided by researcher Mitchel Resnick's computational model of a traffic jam.[4] Suppose initially that an endless line of cars is moving evenly spaced down a highway. This pattern is generated by having each driver follow two simple rules: (1) drive as fast as possible and (2) never get closer than, say, three car lengths to the car in front of you. These simple rules generate a steady stream of evenly spaced cars, until one driver suddenly slows down, at which time two things happen. One is the obvious: the following drivers slow down. The other is that the interaction among these individual choices generates a traffic jam that is shown by time-lapse photography to be moving backward.

If fiscal phenomena are assimilated to acts of ruler's choices, the traffic jam would have to be portrayed as a gigantic car that is moving backward. This is the approach taken by representative agent modeling, which has parsimony and tractability on its side, along with an obviously fictive character. In contrast, agent-based computational modeling is now starting to provide platforms for exploring the generation of such emergent outcomes as traffic jams and government budgets as objects in their own right. While the arrival of this analytical opportunity is relatively new, the underlying ideas are relatively old, going back at least to the spontaneous-order theorists of the Scottish Enlightenment of the eighteenth century.[5]

I begin this essay by contrasting the common, "disjunctive" approach to political economy with the alternative, "conjunctive" approach that I pursue here. Within a conjunctive political economy, government is a nexus of transactions and not some sentient creature, Leviathan or otherwise. Within this transactional nexus, a government's budget is treated as an aggregation across politically organized enterprises that themselves emerge in bottom-up fashion. Within a democratic polity, that budget is generated within a legislature that is conceptualized as a *peculiar* type of market forum. A society thus contains an ecology of enterprises, some privately organized and others politically organized, whose organizational rules and modes of operation generate both cooperation and conflict. This bivalent relationship between the two types of enterprise arises because politically established enterprises bear a parasitical relationship to market-based enterprises, due to the impossibility of economic calculation in a wholly collectivized economy. Following this sketch of a conjunctive political economy, I reconsider some traditional canons of taxation, for these were crafted originally in the context of a disjunctive political economy. In particular, fiscal sociology becomes the alternative point of orientation for the concerns that traditionally have been addressed by those canons.

[4] Mitchel Resnick, *Turtles, Termites, and Traffic Jams: Explorations in Massively Parallel Microworlds* (Cambridge, MA: MIT Press, 1994), 68–74.

[5] See, for instance, David Daiches, Peter Jones, and Jean Jones, *A Hotbed of Genius: The Scottish Enlightenment, 1730–1790* (Edinburgh: Edinburgh University Press, 1986).

II. Polity and Economy: Disjunctive or Conjunctive?

In his 1896 treatise on public finance, Knut Wicksell complained that the theory of public finance "seems to have retained the assumptions of its infancy, in the seventeenth and eighteenth centuries, when absolute power ruled almost all Europe."[6] The object of Wicksell's complaint was a model of political economy wherein individuals governed their private activities through market relationships, with the state intervening autonomously into the market economy. The historical record presents plenty of instances where this model of a disjunctive political economy would seem to be reasonably accurate. Louis XIV's oft-attributed assertion that "the state is me" is a limiting illustration of a model of disjunctive political economy, as is the contemporary literature on the welfare economics of optimal taxation set in motion by the British economists Francis Edgeworth (1845–1926) and Frank Ramsey (1903–30).[7] Raghbendra Jha's recent treatise on public finance is quite typical in this respect when it opens by asserting that "public economics [is] the study of government intervention in the marketplace."[8]

The alternative is a conjunctive political economy, which transforms public finance into the study of how people govern themselves. Government is conceptualized not as some sentient being that intervenes into the market, but rather as an institutionalized process or forum within which people interact with one another. This distinction between alternative conceptualizations of political economy corresponds, in turn, to distinct sociological circumstances to which the abstract terms "market" and "state" pertain.

For an absolutism of the form represented by a Louis XIV, it is quite reasonable to model subjects as relating to one another within a market economy, and to model rulers as intervening into the market economy on terms of their choosing. Kings could, of course, differ greatly in the choices they made, but fiscal phenomena would arise out of *their* choices in any case. One branch of choice-theoretic public finance, of which Edgeworth and Ramsey were the prime initiators, has sought to lay down norms for some relatively benevolent ruler, as illustrated by maxims to minimize the excess burden from taxation or to tax equals equally. In contrast, another branch of choice-theoretic public finance, of which the Italian economist Amilcare Puviani was the prime initiator (through his theory of fiscal illusion), has sought to portray maxims by which a ruler could

[6] Knut Wicksell, "A New Principle of Just Taxation" (1896), in Richard A. Musgrave and Alan T. Peacock, eds., *Classics in the Theory of Public Finance* (London: Macmillan, 1958), 82.

[7] F. Y. Edgeworth, "The Pure Theory of Taxation," *Economic Journal* 7 (1897): 46–70, 226–38, and 550–71; F. P. Ramsey, "A Contribution to the Theory of Taxation," *Economic Journal* 37 (1927): 47–61.

[8] Raghbendra Jha, *Modern Public Economics* (London: Routledge, 1998), xii.

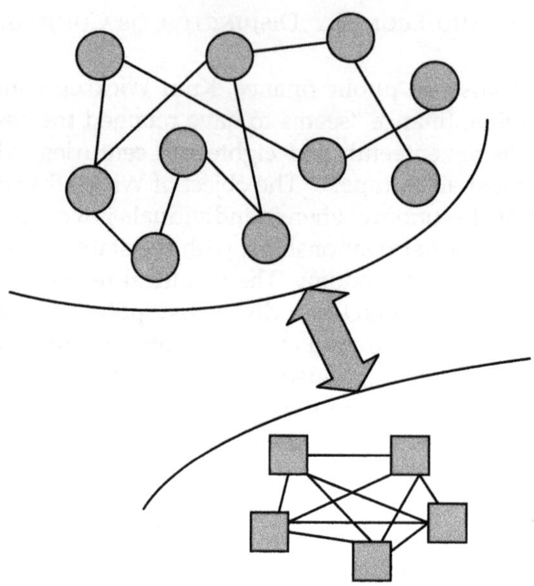

FIGURE 1. Disjunctive political economy

maximize the present value of his personal account.[9] In either case, the state is conceptualized as an autonomous entity that intervenes into market-based relationships as it chooses, with the only differences residing in the utility function that is ascribed to the ruler.

Figure 1 presents a simple graphical portrayal of a disjunctive political economy. The circles denote individual citizens and the squares denote members of a ruling cadre, or perhaps a royal family. In this figure, the members of the ruling cadre are fully connected, to indicate that they act as a single unit (or, equivalently, as an equilibrated collection of people). A king and his family would be a sociological instantiation of such an analytical construction. In contrast, the individual citizens who relate to one another within the market economy form an incompletely connected network, following economist Jason Potts's fecund formulation for modeling continuing processes of evolutionary development.[10] The double arrow denotes state intervention into the economy; one direction points to the ruler's demand for revenue while the other direction shows the subjects' compliance with that demand. This analytical model captures pretty

[9] Amilcare Puviani, *Teoria della illusione finanziaria* (Palermo: Sandron, 1903). Puviani has not been translated into English, but he is available in German: *Die Illusionen in der öffentlichen Finanzwirtschaft* (Berlin: Dunker and Humblot, 1960). A précis of Puviani's argument is presented in James M. Buchanan, *Public Finance in Democratic Process* (Chapel Hill: University of North Carolina Press, 1967).

[10] Jason Potts, *The New Evolutionary Microeconomics* (Hants, UK: Edward Elgar, 2000).

well the characteristic features of a hereditary monarchy. It likewise fits well with the predominant thrust of contemporary fiscal theorizing, where an exogenous state intervenes into market-generated arrangements.

Within a network-based analytical framework, economic or social transformation would be represented as a change in the connective geometry by which a society is described. As a hereditary monarchy gives way to some democratic or republican regime, a transformation occurs in the connective structure of the society. Royal families lose their lands and privileges, get jobs, and become relatively ordinary; the sociological disjunction between rulers and ruled erodes. The situation after this erosion has occurred is portrayed in figure 2, where the squares and circles in the disjunctive parts of figure 1 have commingled to produce the society represented by figure 2. In this alternative representation, government is no longer a creature that lords it over society, for it is a catallaxy and not an economy. It is, of course, always possible to aggregate over the activities of the various squares depicted in figure 2, and refer to this aggregate as indicating something called "government output." But this would be little different from aggregating over the circles and calling the result "market output."

The sociology of figure 1 implies a strong separation between rulers and ruled. The sociology of figure 2 implies a setting where some members of a family might staff political positions while others staff commercial and industrial positions. A brother may occupy a political node while a sister occupies a commercial node. Any particular classroom, clubhouse, or pew will contain members who are or will be found in both categories of position.

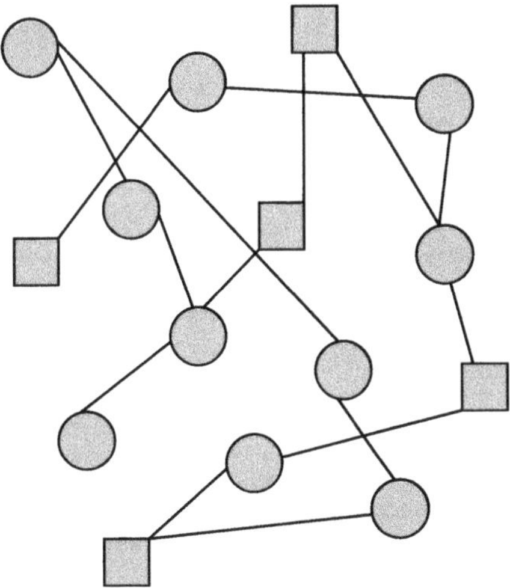

FIGURE 2. Conjunctive political economy

III. Crossing the Budgetary Bridge

For a disjunctive political economy, it is reasonable to consider taxation to be independent of expenditure. A ruler wants revenue for purposes that originate with him, and that revenue is to be extracted from his subjects. Rulership is the practice of intervention into society, as contrasted to participation in transactions within society. It is imaginable that a ruler would instruct his tax collectors to extract revenue in a horizontally equitable manner. The historical record would not seem to show much evidence for the realization of such products of the imagination.[11] With autocratic regimes divided between rulers and subjects, it is reasonable to examine the impact of taxation without regard to its place within some transactional nexus, because there is no transactional nexus.

The articulation of a conjunctive political economy requires us to recognize the underlying transactional character of state budgetary operations. In this recognition lies the chasm between rulers choosing to tax people and people choosing to tax themselves.[12] For a conjunctive political economy, there exists some form of transactional bridge that connects the taxing and spending sides of the budget. But how is this bridge to be built? What is the architecture according to which it is constructed? There are two snares that must be avoided in any such effort at bridging.

One snare is to embrace an *imposta grandine* assumption (literally a "hailstorm tax"). This assumption, which treats taxes as uncaused causes or external injections into society, was discussed extensively in the classic Italian literature that embraced a conjunctive political economy.[13] Autocratic rulers may blow hailstorms over society, but in a democracy taxes emerge from within society and have a transactional character. Even if this transactional character is acknowledged, another snare lies in waiting. This snare is to fuse taxing and spending wholly into one unified operation. Doing this would deny the compulsory character of taxation by treating government as just another firm within the market economy. A government is not just another firm, despite the transactional character of democratic politics, and yet taxation has a transactional cause.[14]

[11] For some relevant treatments, see Charles Adams, *For Good and Evil: The Impact of Taxes on the Course of Civilization* (London: Madison Books, 1993); and Carolyn Webber and Aaron Wildavsky, *A History of Taxation and Expenditure in the Western World* (New York: Simon and Schuster, 1986).

[12] In this particular regard, see Joel Slemrod and Jon Bakija, *Taxing Ourselves: A Citizen's Guide to the Great Debate over Tax Reform* (Cambridge, MA: MIT Press, 1996).

[13] For an extensive survey of the classic Italian literature, see James M. Buchanan, "'La Scienza delle finanze': The Italian Tradition in Fiscal Theory," in Buchanan, *Fiscal Theory and Political Economy* (Chapel Hill: University of North Carolina Press, 1960), 24–74. For an effort to relate that literature to the public choice scholarship that has developed since Buchanan wrote, see Richard E. Wagner, "Public Choice and the Diffusion of Classic Italian Public Finance," *Il pensiero economico italiano* 11 (2003): 271–82.

[14] The tension between these two snares is expressed crisply in Attilio da Empoli, *Lineamenti teorici dell'economia corporativa finanziaria* (Milano: Giuffrè, 1941), 91–136.

The snare of treating taxation as an uncaused cause is the typical treatment of taxation in the theory of public finance. Taxes are exogenous injections into a society, and fiscal analysis explores some of the consequences of those injections. One of those consequences is excess burden. The analysis of excess burden entails the claim that taxes impose a double burden on taxpayers: one is the direct burden of transferring resources to government; the other is an additional loss of utility (an excess burden) that arises out of tax-induced shifts in patterns of activity. In any case, a tax is equivalent to a hailstorm—recognizing, of course, that hailstorms can differ in the amount of damage they wreak.

Excess burden is a plausible tool for a disjunctive political economy when power resides with some relatively enlightened ruler. It may even be a useful tool for a less enlightened ruler who nonetheless felt it prudent to avoid skinning his flock while trying to shear them closely. Excess burden is of less significance within the context of a conjunctive political economy. Within this alternative context, a tax cannot simply be injected from outside a society, for it can only emerge from within the society. There are, moreover, two broad forms of such emergence. One is where fiscal outcomes reflect a broad consensus or concurrence among the affected parties, while the other is where fiscal outcomes reflect a domination of the victorious over the subdued, a situation that tends to undermine the transactional character of democratic budgeting if the domination becomes anything other than transitory and short-lived.

Suppose Prima, Secundo, and Terza inhabit a small town. They support a town enterprise to construct a project to eradicate mosquitoes from a nearby swamp. They agree that doing this represents a distinct improvement over the alternative. There are, of course, an indefinitely large number of ways the revenues could be collected. A simple one would be an equal per-capita assignment of liability: this would be a form of head tax for which conventionally there is no excess burden, because the tax would not induce any shift in market-based conduct. To allow for a standard excess burden, suppose a tax is imposed on the consumption of electricity. The tax would induce people to use less electricity, and it is this substitution away from electricity that is the source of the conventional excess burden. Yet the participants agreed to the entire fiscal operation, which means that they must have anticipated that they will be better off by having done so. (As to why they might have chosen to tax electricity and not create a head tax, several explanations are possible. A simple one is that the instrument to tax electricity was already in place, whereas a head tax would have required the creation of a new office to implement the tax.) While there is a clear burden associated with the tax, a burden which represents the resources necessary to construct the project, it is equally clear that there is no excess burden associated with the project. If anything, there is an excess benefit to the extent that the mosquito protection allows people to attain utility gains. The tax is simply one side of a transaction, and it cannot be reasonably appraised outside of the full transaction that caused the tax to appear.

An alternative to all participants agreeing to tax themselves is for a majority to impose some of the cost on an objecting minority. Prima and Secundo might own property in a low-lying area that is prone to flooding (and thus a breeding ground for mosquitoes), while Terza lives securely on higher ground. Rather than Prima and Secundo forming a joint venture to protect their property, they use their legislative majority to declare it a public project, thereby forcing Terza to contribute to the support of that project. It makes no sense to speak of the tax as possessing an excess burden for Prima and Secundo, for it is one side of a transaction by which they achieve a more highly desired state of affairs. Terza, of course, is helping to support a project that she would veto if she could, and so perhaps could be thought to bear an excess burden as she reduces her consumption of electricity in consequence of the tax. To claim that an excess burden exists in the aggregate, however, requires some presumption that utilities can be added across people. Such a claim also shifts analytical attention away from the fiscal process that generated the outcome and onto one hypothesized consequence of that process. About all that can really be said about the situation is that it improved the situation for Prima and Secundo while worsening it for Terza.

Once it is recognized that a tax arises from internally generated transactions and not from outside interventions, claims about excess burden would seem to lose a good deal of their significance, at least in the aggregate.[15] In a different but related vein, it is worth considering why we never speak of the excess burden of changes in market prices. About fifty years ago, American custom in restaurants placed tips at about 10 percent. That custom subsequently escalated into the 15 percent range, and in recent years there has been some momentum toward 20 percent. Why would it make sense to speak of the excess burden of a tax but not of a tip? It seems a bit disingenuous to distinguish the two by asserting that a tip is a voluntary choice. Conformity to custom is often not wholly voluntarily but nonetheless is a condition for getting along well in society, and can even verge on duress. In any event, it is surely the case that people will spend less on meals if they are expected to tip 20 percent than if that expectation is 10 percent. Thus, a rise in the customary rate of tip induces a substitution away from restaurant meals just as surely as would an increase in a tax on restaurant meals. We don't describe changes in market prices as imposing excess burdens because prices emerge through voluntary transactions. While taxes are clearly not voluntary, they do nonetheless have a transactional source and do not represent some hailstorm that wreaks its fury on a society.

[15] Richard E. Wagner, "Some Institutional Problematics of Excess Burden Analytics," *Public Finance Review* 30 (2002): 531–45.

A monarch or despot may stand outside the system over which he rules and into which he injects taxes as he chooses. Within a democratic polity, however, there is no such outside position from which taxes can be injected. Taxes emerge from within the polity, and must do so because the combination of less market output and more political output generates a higher level of utility for some people. Without doubt, taxation also generally involves a good number of people in paying for output they do not value, or value less than the sacrificed market output the tax makes necessary. Those people are burdened directly by the tax, and then burdened again as they rearrange their market conduct in response to the tax extractions imposed on them. To reduce this outcome to some measure of excess burden requires a problematical presumption about aggregation (on the one hand), and obscures the underlying character of the fiscal process that generated that outcome (on the other hand).

To be sure, one can leave a restaurant without tipping. Governments, in contrast, will not allow you to opt out of the tax system, though they do have procedures in place by which people can contest their assignments of tax liability. While taxes are part of the transactional nexus of governmental fiscal activity within a conjunctive political economy, they possess an involuntary character that distinguishes them from market prices. In his treatise on eminent domain, legal scholar Richard Epstein describes taxes as "forced exchanges."[16] Taxes are compulsory exactions and not voluntary contributions. Within democratic settings, the forced exaction is but one side of a transaction of a sort, with the other side denoting the receipt of valued services in return. While the term "forced exchange" might sound oxymoronic, it conveys an important truth. On the one hand, it recognizes that taxes are compulsory exactions. An effort to limit government to voluntary contributions would be hampered by free-riding. While a good deal of experimental evidence suggests that the extent of free-riding is less that what the economic logic of the situation would suggest, it also shows that free-riding is genuine nonetheless.[17]

On the other hand, the standard of a forced exchange holds that taxes should seek to mirror the voluntary payments that people would have made had they not engaged in free-riding. While there is no way to determine precisely what the terms of those unmade transactions would have been, there are some general principles that can be brought to bear in shedding some light onto the distinction between cases when taxes are plausibly one side of a forced exchange and when they are simply forced exactions imposed on political losers for the benefit of political winners. It is possible to claim that taxes are the prices we pay for civilization, but

[16] Richard A. Epstein, *Takings: Private Property and the Power of Eminent Domain* (Cambridge, MA: Harvard University Press, 1985).

[17] For one survey of this literature, see Thomas S. McCaleb and Richard E. Wagner, "The Experimental Search for Free Riders: Some Reflections and Observations," *Public Choice* 47, no. 3 (1985): 479–90.

this does not warrant that any and all taxes qualify as reasonable applications of the principle of forced exchange. To speak of taxes as prices is a simile that is both useful and corruptible. It is a useful simile because it expresses a truth about any claim that people genuinely choose to tax themselves, which they would only do if they valued the resulting public services more highly than they valued the options they sacrificed in exchange. It is a corruptible simile because it can be used to justify the imposition of force without concomitant exchange.

Earlier I noted two snares to be avoided when attempting to construct a bridge between the taxing and spending sides of the budget. The second snare is the assumption that the two sides of the budget are fused. To avoid this second snare while retaining the transactional character of democratic governance, democratic states are treated as ecologies of political enterprises and the legislatures that inhabit those states as *peculiar* market forums. This treatment corresponds to a conceptualization where taxation entails the assignment of obligations to stock the budgetary commons while appropriation entails the allotment of rights to graze that commons, and where the legislature serves as the arena wherein those various obligations and rights are articulated.[18]

IV. An Emergent Ecology of Political Enterprises

Suppose figure 2 above represents the enterprises within a society. The circles denote market-based enterprises and the squares denote politically-based enterprises. A government's budget is an aggregation over the set of politically-based enterprises. Likewise, the size of the market economy is gauged by aggregation over the set of market-based enterprises. The society itself is comprised of an emergent ecology of enterprises of the two forms, with each enterprise having various connections to other enterprises within the society. Within this ecology, some enterprises will expand while others contract; moreover, the patterns of connection among enterprises will change through time. The entire ecology constitutes an evolving, emergent order. Within this emergent framework, a government's budget emerges from the bottom, so to speak, and is not imposed from the top. Budgets are objects that are generated through various forms and processes of interaction, and are not products of some ruler's choice.

Markets and polities provide alternative forums within which enterprises can be organized. The abstract construction of the model of a market economy is based on the presumption that human relationships are governed by private property and freedom of contract and association. That institutional framework provides a catallactical forum within

[18] Richard E. Wagner, "Property, Taxation, and the Budgetary Commons," in Donald Racheter and Richard E. Wagner, eds., *Politics, Taxation, and the Rule of Law: The Power to Tax in Constitutional Perspective* (Norwell, MA: Kluwer Academic Publishers, 2002), 33–47.

which enterprises are created and operated. Polities, too, contain enterprises—only the forum within which those enterprises are created entails somewhat different rules from those created within the market forum. Nonetheless, the legislature provides an alternative forum for the organization of enterprises within an overall ecology of enterprises. In this vein, political scientist Vincent Ostrom describes how the organization of water supply involves both market-based and politically-based enterprises, in contrast to a formulation that would treat the provision of water as either a market-based or a politically-based activity.[19]

A legislature is like a *peculiar* market forum, in that it provides a venue wherein those who sponsor political enterprises seek support from citizens who have the means available to support those enterprises.[20] To the extent that there is complementarity between decisions about the support of enterprises and the ability of legislatures to generate revenue, there will necessarily exist a budgetary bridge, provided only that people who are attracted to operate within the legislative form of market forum prefer to do more business rather than to do less. There are some clear differences between legislatures and regular market forums. For one thing, there is no distribution of surplus within the legislature. The legislature is organized in nonprofit fashion. This does not mean that the legislative partners earn no profits, but only that profits are collected differently.

It is a truism to say that people who direct capital to political enterprises do so because they anticipate that they will receive a higher return than they would receive from an alternative use of that capital. It is also the case that political enterprises typically cannot compete on equal terms with market-based enterprises. At first glance, these two propositions might seem to conflict. This conflict is resolved once it is recognized that the people who direct capital to political enterprises do not direct capital from their personal accounts, but use capital from the accounts of other people, and do so through taxation. The creation of political enterprises allows the sponsors of those enterprises to leverage their own supply through their share of taxation with capital provided by other taxpayers who would not have chosen to invest in the political enterprise.

Political enterprises are created in the anticipation that they will generate returns to their controlling investors, and those investors comprise only a subset of the entire set of tax-induced investors. This brings into the foreground the nature of the returns that political enterprises gener-

[19] Vincent Ostrom, "The Water Economy and Its Organization," *Natural Resources Journal* 2 (1962): 55–73. For a review of Ostrom's contributions to polycentrism and the organization of self-governance, see Richard E. Wagner, "Self-Governance, Polycentrism, and Federalism: Recurring Themes in Vincent Ostrom's Scholarly Oeuvre," *Journal of Economic Behavior and Organization* 57 (June 2005): 173–88.

[20] To say that they have the means of support does not imply that they turn it over voluntarily, for if they did the state would be a regular market forum and not a *peculiar* one.

ate. They do not generate capital appreciation, as they do not operate with transferable ownership. Neither do they offer dividends, at least in any direct manner. There are, however, two types of indirect return that political enterprises offer to their controlling investors and supporters. One type of return takes the form of lower prices to favored customers. The other type of return accrues through higher factor prices paid to favored suppliers.

Whether the political enterprise is a school, a hospital, or a highway department, profits are appropriated in some fashion, as such appropriation is a necessary element in the generation of support for the enterprise. For market-based enterprises, the appropriation takes place directly through monetary payments and is simple to see. For political enterprises, the appropriation is indirect and can follow different particular channels in different cases. Consider, for instance, how a politically organized hospital can return profits to its supporters. One obvious question this raises is the identity of the hospital's supporters, both in the legislature and outside of it. Outside the legislature, that support can be divided between support among input suppliers and support among output demanders. On the demand side, the hospital might offer low-cost services to particular groups of demanders. That lower cost will be financed by imposing higher costs on some people. Much of that higher cost is imposed through taxation, which allows political enterprises to charge people who do not consume the enterprise's services, thereby making possible price reductions to those who do consume those services. As a result of this form of political price discrimination, political enterprises are able to gain standing in the commercial marketplace amid profit-seeking firms, as the Italian economist Giovanni Montemartini explained with particular insightfulness in 1900.[21]

Profits can also be appropriated on the factor supply side of the market, with the specific channels of appropriation again depending on details about the service in question. For a politically organized hospital, profits might be appropriated by the physicians who practice there. They could also be appropriated by the manufacturers of medical equipment who supply state-of-the-art equipment to the enterprise. Pharmaceutical manufacturers might gain also, through increased sales of patented drugs. The hospital might employ a unionized labor force, at least in some parts of its operation, with some of the returns to politically organized hospitals accruing in the form of supra-competitive wages. The central point in any case is that the appropriation of profit is not abolished by the creation of a political enterprise, for without profit to be appropriated there would not have been any interest in creating the enterprise. The shift from market-

[21] Giovanni Montemartini, "Le basi fondamentali della scienza finanziaria pura," *Giornale degli Economisti* 11 (1900): 55–76; English translation in Richard A. Musgrave and Alan T. Peacock, eds., *Classics in the Theory of Public Finance* (London: Macmillan, 1958), 137–51.

based to politically-based enterprise changes only the form that appropriation takes, and encases that appropriation in a fog of indirect transactions that would surely have made Amilcare Puviani proud of his articulation of fiscal illusion.

Within the legislative type of market forum, legislative participants seek to develop connections between people who have enterprises for which they are seeking support and people who have the means available to support political enterprises. Within ordinary market forums, all connections are crafted voluntarily. This is not the case with the legislative type of market forum. While the entrepreneurial creation of political enterprises arises voluntarily, the extraction of support for those enterprises typically involves a good deal of duress. Nonetheless, the legislature occupies an intermediary position within this transactional nexus, and it is out of this position that a good deal of the phenomena of public finance emerges in democratic polities. When we look at the aggregate of political enterprises, those enterprises obviously generate revenues sufficient to cover their costs of operation. If they failed to do so, political enterprises would be shrinking in the aggregate.

People who have ideas for enterprises have two forums through which they can seek to pursue those plans, a market forum and a political forum. A dichotomy between private and public goods seems to map directly and immediately into a dichotomy between markets and governments as methods of economic organization, with markets organizing the supply of private goods and governments organizing the supply of public goods. The effort to work with this dichotomy has spawned much analysis and disputation about the public or private character of numerous goods and services, most of it relatively inconclusive. There are numerous instances where similar enterprises are organized in both market-based and politically-based manners. Just as there are privately organized hospitals, so are there governmentally organized hospitals. There are tennis courts and golf courses organized by the private sector, and there are also golf courses and tennis courts organized through governmental arenas. It is the same for parks and other recreational facilities more generally, for libraries, and for educational services. There are governmentally sponsored enterprises that seek to help people learn foreign languages, and there are market-based enterprises that seek to accomplish the same thing. It is the same for the provision of security services. Indeed, private policing services may well exceed, in terms of both budgets and the number of people employed, the aggregate volume of policing services provided by governmental bodies. In short, the theory of public goods would seem to have relatively little to do with the phenomena of public finance. The dichotomy between public and private goods seems to map naturally into a disjunction between domains, with government providing public goods and market-based organizations providing private goods. This disjunction, however, does not conform at all well to reality.

V. Property, Taxation, and Parasitical Political Pricing

It is unlikely that the market and the political forums for the creation of enterprises will ever be fully harmonious, because their respective rules of operation are incongruent. Indeed, it is really inconsistent to conceptualize a market economy as operating according to the rules of private property and freedom of contract and association, while simultaneously treating the state as operating a form of fiscal commons that is layered with rules that assign various duties and privileges, because these two institutional arrangements and systems of governance will generate zones of conflict.[22] The economic theory of the market economy is predicated upon rules of private property and freedom of contract and association. Those are not the rules that characterize the formation of enterprises within the political forum. Just as the relationship among different market-based enterprises may be complementary or competitive, so may be the relationship among different politically-based enterprises. Furthermore, the same principles of complementarity and substitution can characterize relationships between market-based and politically-based enterprises. Politically-based and market-based enterprises interact with one another, and in myriad ways. Some of those interactions might produce widespread, general advantage. Others might provide advantage for some people at the expense of others, as manifestations of duress in the operation of political enterprises.

There is a well-elaborated economic theory of how an organized pattern of human relationships can emerge within the framework of private property, with market prices playing an important part in terms of the guidance they give to people throughout the range of their commercial activities. When we turn to the organization of a totally collectivized economy, we encounter a proposition about the impossibility of economic calculation because of the absence of prices that accompanies the absence of private property.[23] This situation was recognized by the Italian economist Maffeo Pantaleoni in 1911, when he articulated his claim that a system of politically generated prices could only exist parasitically upon a system of market pricing. One of the implications of Pantaleoni's formulation is the existence of a type of natural limit to the extent of political pricing within a society.[24]

[22] A related claim is advanced in Liam Murphy and Thomas Nagel, *The Myth of Ownership* (Oxford: Oxford University Press, 2002), but Murphy and Nagel conceptualize the state as a sentient, acting creature and not as an interactive process.

[23] See, for instance, the essays collected in F. A. Hayek, ed., *Collectivist Economic Planning* (London: Routledge, 1935). For more recent but complementary treatments, see Paul Craig Roberts, *Alienation and the Soviet Economy* (New York: Holmes and Meier, 1990); and Peter J. Boettke, *Why Perestroika Failed: The Politics and Economics of Socialist Transformation* (London: Routledge, 1993).

[24] Maffeo Pantaleoni, "Considerazioni sulle proprieta di un sistema di prezzi politici," *Giornale degli Economisti* 42 (1911): 9–29 and 114–33. Pantaleoni's argument is treated in

To be sure, there are various types of parasite-host relationships. In some cases there is a zone or range of mutual benefit, where the host is also better off because of the presence of the parasite. This mutual benefit comports with the classically liberal theory of the state, wherein the state supports a regime of private property. This zone of mutual benefit is one of concordant relationships among political and market enterprises. There will also be zones where the parasite's gain requires the host to lose. It is easy enough to imagine an urban transit industry that contains many different enterprises, all initially established through market arrangements. There can be political enterprises that are beneficial to the market-based enterprises: the various activities associated with traffic control are surely an example. Into this ecology of enterprises, inject a politically organized bus enterprise. This enterprise could be financed wholly by fares from riders. This approach would fuse the two sides of the budget, and would be unlikely to promote a successful political enterprise.

The ability to tax and appropriate brings a second pricing system into play, a political pricing system. The tax allows the bus enterprise to charge people who do not ride the bus, which in turn strengthens the competitive position of the bus enterprise because it can collect revenues both from riders and from taxpayers who are charged for not-riding. Furthermore, the political enterprise may be able to impose disabilities on competitive enterprises through regulation.[25] The competitive ability of a privately organized bus company might be degraded by requiring it to maintain routes and schedules that are not profitable. The competitive ability of the political enterprise might be strengthened by restricting the numbers of parking spaces that can be created within buildings located downtown, thereby increasing the demand for the services of the political enterprise.

There is an indefinitely large number of ways by which a government can use taxation and regulation to secure advantages for the enterprises it sponsors relative to other enterprises within a society. The parasitical nature of politically-based enterprises suggests that such enterprises will often seek to degrade the competitive ability of market-based enterprises located in their vicinity, and yet at the same time those political enterprises require the calculational guidance that only market-generated prices can offer. Furthermore, the transactional character of democratic government leads to the realization that there are also market-based enterprises that will gain from the activities of political enterprises. Within the emergent ecology of enterprises that constitutes a conjunctive political economy, there is no arena where political enterprises confront market

Richard E. Wagner, "Parasitical Political Pricing, Economic Calculation, and the Size of Government: Variations on a Theme by Maffeo Pantaleoni," *Journal of Public Finance and Public Choice* 15 (1997): 135–46.

[25] See, for instance, Daniel B. Klein, *Curb Rights: A Foundation for Free Enterprise in Urban Transit* (Washington, DC: American Enterprise Institute, 1997).

enterprises as general, opposed classes. For a political enterprise cannot inject itself into society from the outside, but rather emerges from inside society, which requires in turn that it possess supporters among some of the market-based enterprises.

VI. From Tax Canons to Fiscal Sociology

The history of fiscal theorizing contains numerous efforts to state principles of good or sound fiscal conduct. One of the most cited formulations occurs in Adam Smith's mini-treatise on public finance in the fifth book of *The Wealth of Nations*. There, Smith laid down four canons of good taxation: (1) taxes should be levied in proportion to property, (2) taxes should be certain and not arbitrary, (3) taxes should be convenient to pay, and (4) taxes should be economical to administer, for both the taxpayer and the government. Smith's canons have certainly been influential in subsequent fiscal scholarship, as they have been cited continuously in that scholarship. Whether those canons are effective in practice is a different matter, and one whose truth is not so easy to discern.

A few years before Smith, the cameralist scholar Johann Heinrich Gottlob von Justi presented six canons for taxation.[26] Justi's formulation of tax canons stated that (1) taxes should be in proportion to property, while bearing equally upon all those who possess the same amount of property, (2) tax obligations should be transparently clear to everyone, (3) taxes should be convenient and economical, for both taxpayers and the state, (4) a tax should not deprive a taxpayer of necessaries or cause him to reduce his capital to pay the tax, (5) a tax should neither harm the welfare of the state and its subjects nor violate the civil liberties of the subjects, and (6) a tax should be compatible with the form of government, as illustrated by tax farming (wherein a ruler would grant to such farmers the right to extract revenues on his behalf) being suitable only for absolute monarchies.

The first three of Justi's canons are similar to Smith's four canons, while Justi's final three canons cover territory not articulated by Smith. Justi's canons would seem clearly to place more constraints on the use of taxation than would Smith's. More than tax canons are involved, however, in a comparison between Smith and Justi. For Smith, taxation was ideally to be the exclusive source of state finance. Were Smith to have his way, the state would divest itself of such non-tax sources of revenue as lands and

[26] Johann Heinrich Gottlob von Justi, *Natur und Wesen der Staaten*, reprinted from the 1771 edition (Darmstadt: Scientia Verlag Aalen, 1969). Smith did not cite Justi, and it seems likely that the two formulations of tax canons were advanced independently of one another. The cameralists emerged around 1500 in Central Europe, and were influential into the early nineteenth century. For a brief treatment, with citations to the source literature, see Jürgen G. Backhaus and Richard E. Wagner, "The Cameralists: A Public Choice Perspective," *Public Choice* 3, no. 1 (1987): 3–20.

enterprises, and would rely wholly upon taxes imposed upon market-based commercial activity. In this formulation, the state was treated as existing and operating outside the framework of the market economy and intervening into the market economy to procure its revenues. The canons of taxation were to provide guidance for keeping the subsequent disturbances to the market economy in check.

In sharp contrast, Justi argued that ideally a state would not tax at all, because it should be able to derive all of its revenue from its operation of enterprises and the working of its lands. For Justi, a prince who resorted to taxation was verging on being a failure at his princely tasks. For Justi, the state was envisioned ideally as participating within the market economy on an equal basis with all other participants. To be sure, ideals are rarely found mirrored in practice. Yet the difference between Smith and Justi points to the divergent directions that different articulations of the theory of public finance might take, as illustrated by the earlier distinction between conjunctive and disjunctive visions of political economy.

There would surely be strong agreement that it would be wrong for two diners in a restaurant to force a third diner to pay part of their bill. But where does taxation play into this? Suppose we start with a uniform, broad-based tax. A measure that grants a tax credit to one particular person is equivalent to one diner sending part of his bill to the other diners in the restaurant. These things happen all the time in legislation. For instance, a tax credit might be offered to firms whose exports exceed $5 million annually. Alternatively, a credit might be offered for athletic arenas whose construction was finished during 1994 and which cost more than $50 million. Yet again, a credit might be offered for assisted living facilities that treat more than thirty dementia patients or, alternatively, less than ten. In all of these cases, and the myriad more like them, some people secure tax reductions that imply higher taxes for others, under the presumption that the total revenue generated by the broad-based tax is independent of the various exceptions and exemptions that are part of the structure of the tax.

There is, to be sure, a substantial literature that seeks to use equilibrium models to explain tax structure, including the domination of complexity over simplicity.[27] What is particularly interesting for an emergent and polycentric orientation toward fiscal phenomena, though, are the subsequent changes that are set in motion by the transformation of simplicity into complexity. This is the domain of fiscal sociology, which is a term that was coined by Rudolf Goldscheid in the course of his controversy with Joseph Schumpeter regarding the discharge of Austria's debt at the end of World War I.[28] In that controversy, Schumpeter took a Smith-like position

[27] This literature is examined in Walter Hettich and Stanley L. Winer, *Democratic Choice and Taxation* (Cambridge: Cambridge University Press, 1999).

[28] The relevant essays are collected in Rudolf Hickel, ed., *Die Finanzkrise des Steuerstaats: Beiträge zur politischen Ökonomie der Staatsfinanzen* (Frankfurt: Suhrkamp, 1976). For a recent

while Goldscheid took a Justi-like position. Schumpeter proposed to discharge the debt by levying an extraordinary tax to redeem the bonds. In contrast, Goldscheid argued for a recapitalization of the state that would give it the means to carry the debt.

Fiscal sociology entails a consideration of the relation between fiscal institutions and practices and the qualitative character of social relationships. For instance, compare a broad-based tax with a set of narrow-based taxes that raise the same revenue. The standard analysis of excess burden would focus on the greater excess burden associated with the set of narrow-based taxes. A fiscal sociology crafted for an emergent ecology of enterprises would focus on the changes in the pattern and character of societal relationships that evolve in response to different tax forms.[29] Narrower bases at higher rates will promote investment in various paraphernalia of avoidance and evasion. In response, state budgets will shift toward police forces, jails, inspectors, and the like. The relative importance of guns and nightsticks will expand in scope within the arena of human governance. The domain of trust will recede as stealth replaces openness in human relationships, for precautions must now be taken in light of the fact that the client who appears before you may be there not to do business with you but to entrap you.

Truly broad-based taxes on income or consumption conform more closely to reasonable notions of generality or uniformity in taxation than do narrow-based taxes, including broad-based taxes that have been narrowed through exemptions, exclusions, phase-ins, phase-outs, credits, grandfather clauses, and so on, all of which lead in the direction of each person's being assigned a unique tax liability. A centerpiece of democratic ideology is the belief that taxation is something we do to ourselves, in contrast to speaking of victors as imposing taxes on the vanquished. So long as taxes are generally or universally applicable, it is plausible to believe in the sentiment that we choose to tax ourselves. As taxes come increasingly to be used as rewards to supportive constituencies and as penalties for others, however, this belief that we are taxing ourselves for our common purposes would seem to become increasingly mythical. It is here, in such considerations as these concerning the evolving character of societies through time, that fiscal sociology comes potentially into play, as an emergent and evolutionary alternative to the standard constructions of Paretian welfare economics.

In thinking of taxation within the context of fiscal sociology, it would seem potentially instructive to ponder some similarities between govern-

survey of fiscal sociology, see Jürgen G. Backhaus, "Fiscal Sociology: What For?" in Jürgen G. Backhaus and Richard E. Wagner, eds., *Handbook of Public Finance* (Norwell, MA: Kluwer Academic Publishers, 2004), 521–41.

[29] A preliminary effort in this direction is set forth in Richard E. Wagner, "States and the Crafting of Souls: Mind, Society, and Fiscal Sociology," *Journal of Economic Behavior and Organization*, forthcoming.

ments and hotels that bear upon the fiscal sociology of taxation and politically organized enterprises.[30] Whether a hotel is plain or fancy, it has elevators, which are nothing but subways that run vertically, a form of public transportation. Hotels also provide such public services as security and refuse collection, and also typically provide various recreational opportunities, perhaps an exercise room, maybe a swimming pool, or perhaps even both, and possibly even more recreational options. Hotels, in other words, provide most or all of the services that we commonly associate with government. Yet hotels do not impose anything that looks like a tax; they are operated more like the cameralist principalities about which Justi wrote. Hotels provide services that people value, which makes people willing to pay room charges that are sufficient to cover the cost of those public-like services as well as the cost of the rooms.

A hotel is, of course, operated as a business. This is to say that it seeks to provide services that people are willing to buy. To the extent it does so, people support it and the hotel flourishes. A hotel exists in a world of open mobility and freedom of competition. People can take their meals inside the hotel or out. They can have their drinks inside the hotel or out. A hotel must attract residents, it cannot force them to stay and support the hotel. A well-working government should be attractive to people. This attractiveness will be reflected in the increased desires of people to locate within the boundaries of that government, which in turn translates into increased land values. Public services that make a government more desirable have the potential of paying for themselves, just as any profitable commercial enterprise pays for itself. Such considerations point toward a possible framework for injecting the entrepreneurial and commercial principles of service provision into the conduct of government, provided that competition, openness, and mobility can be maintained.[31]

VII. Conclusion

It is natural for a choice-theoretic orientation toward public finance to create a focus on pivotal choices, such as choices among forms of taxation, which, if made correctly, will lead to a better state of affairs, in keeping with the equilibrium methodology of comparative statics applied to a disjunctive political economy; for what is taking place is the simple replacement of one equilibrium with another. Nonetheless, within the context of a conjunctive political economy, some contours of which I have sketched here, there is no magical, singular choice to be made. Emphasis is shifted

[30] For an imaginative and constructive comparison of cities and hotels, see Spencer McCallum, *The Art of Community* (Menlo Park, CA: Institute for Humane Studies, 1970).

[31] In this regard, see, for instance, Fred E. Foldvary, "Public Revenue from Land Rent," in Backhaus and Wagner, eds., *Handbook of Public Finance*, 165–94; and the essays collected in Kenneth C. Wenzer, ed., *Land-Value Taxation: The Equitable and Efficient Source of Public Finance* (Armonk, NY: M. E. Sharpe, 1999).

to the *nexus* of relationships within which people govern themselves, and to our understanding of the operating features and characteristics of that nexus. It is the quality of the emergent nexus and not the quality of some ruler's choices that governs the quality of social life. Leonard E. Read's famous essay *I, Pencil* (1958) is worth pondering in this regard.[32] Read showed that no single individual could make even a simple pencil. The job was just too complicated. Pencils emerged out of a well-working network of relationships. The same is true of technical progress in the production of pencils. That, too, is a product of the nexus of relationships, for there is no singular point of insertion that generates progress. Some of the recent developments in the articulation of emergent systems of social order thus reaffirm in new ways some of the older insights that came to us from the Scottish Enlightenment, and the challenge for a theory of public finance is to recognize that government itself is a polycentric process embedded within an emergent network of human relationships, and is most certainly not some conductor that is orchestrating the activities of its citizens.

Economics, George Mason University

[32] This essay is available from the Foundation for Economic Education, http://www.fee.org, which Read established in 1946 and ran until his death in 1983.

GOVERNMENT AS INVESTOR: TAX POLICY AND THE STATE

By Jonathan R. Macey

I. Introduction

This is an essay about the relationship between taxation and liberty. Applying insights from constitutional economics[1] and corporate finance, I first make a descriptive observation about the role of government in its capacity as tax collector, and then move to a normative claim about how this description of government's relationship with taxpayers should inform constitutional economics and quotidian debate about tax policy.

As a descriptive matter, government, in its role as tax collector, should be viewed as an investor in all of the individuals and enterprises (firms) from which it collects revenues. Throughout this essay, I refer to the government as an "investor," despite the fact that, unlike private-sector investors, the government does not formally contribute capital in the form of debt or equity to the firms and individuals from which it collects taxes. Conceptualizing the government as an investor is meant to emphasize the fact that, like private-sector investors, government not only removes wealth from private-sector individuals and businesses (through taxes and regulation), but also can, in theory, contribute to the growth of the private sector by enforcing contracts and creating a stable business environment in which companies can operate.

Of course, not all entities that make claims on the cash flows of businesses and individuals are benign. Extortion rings and organized crime syndicates destroy more wealth than they create. Legitimate government investment crosses the line into illegitimate wealth appropriation when it ceases to be governed by constitutional rules of law.

However, at least in theory, the government does expend resources to supply goods and services such as contract enforcement, police protec-

[1] Constitutional economics applies economic analysis to constitutional principles. The phrase "constitutional economics" was first introduced into academic discourse at a Heritage Foundation conference by Richard B. McKenzie in 1982. The term applies to a field of research that has been described as "an integral, but distinguishable, part of the subdiscipline of public choice." The basic idea behind constitutional economics is that social interactions and economic productivity are determined not only by resource constraints, but also by the set of foundational rules (constitutional arrangements) that establish the "rules of the game" played during times of ordinary politics. See James M. Buchanan, "The Domain of Constitutional Economics," *Constitutional Political Economy* 1, no. 1 (Winter 1990): 1–18; Scott Gordon, "The New Contractarians," *Journal of Political Economy* 84, no. 3 (June 1976): 573–90; and Randall G. Holcombe, "Constitutions as Constraints: A Case Study of Three American Constitutions," *Constitutional Political Economy* 2, no. 3 (Fall 1991): 303–22.

tion, road construction and maintenance, the negotiation of trade agreements, and mail delivery, to mention only a few. A government invests in individuals by providing subsidized education, promoting research, and making similar investments that facilitate the development of human capital. I consider these expenditures by government to be analogous to the investments made by nongovernment investors, particularly since the quality of the government's provision of these services will have a direct effect on the government's revenues. In this way, the government displays many characteristics of an equity claimant (shareholder) and many characteristics of a fixed claimant (lender), but it has certain "rights" (legal privileges assumed as a matter of power) not shared with other claimants on a firm's cash flows.

This simple observation leads to a couple of useful normative insights about the ability of private citizens to successfully control the growth of the state during times of ordinary politics. For example, applying insights from constitutional economics to my "government as investor" framework leads to useful policy proposals about how the power of government can be restrained by constitutional rules regarding tax policy.

In particular, since government is a claimant on a firm's cash flows, it should not be able to engage in conduct that is prohibited to other investors. For example, just as private investors cannot make unilateral changes to the agreements they have reached with borrowers after their investment has been made, the government should have greater constraints on its ability to change its claims on the earnings and capital gains of people and firms after those entities have begun to pay taxes. More fundamentally, the role of the state as an investor in people and businesses should be formally recognized for what it is. Recognizing the state as an investor in businesses poses a fundamental challenge for democracy.

In its role as investor, the state, just like other investors, is justified in imposing constraints on people and businesses in order to protect its claims on the cash flows of the individuals and firms in which it invests. There are two problems, however, with this analogy between the state and private investors. First, while all investors can impose constraints as a condition on making an investment, in the private sector these constraints are the product of a consensual, noncoercive bargaining process. By contrast, the government can pass laws that affect the firms it taxes. These laws, of course, do not reflect arms-length bargaining between individuals and firms and the state. This distinction, however, is easy to overstate, as governments (particularly democracies) are constrained by competition for industry and capital, and by the desire to promote growth in order to remain in power.[2] In a system of optimal constitutional design, government actors will be constrained, and will be unable to impose

[2] Ian Ayres and Jonathan R. Macey, "Institutional and Evolutionary Failure and Economic Development in the Middle East," *Yale Journal of International Law* 30, no. 1 (2005): 398–429.

suboptimal or inefficient rules on people and businesses subject to their taxing authority. Basic rules, such as the rule that tax rules must be general, and not specifically targeted at firms and individuals, further limit government's capacity to act capriciously.

Second, in its role as the state, the government has obligations to protect its citizens and to enforce contracts. Clearly there is a conflict between the government's role as creditor and the government's role as neutral arbiter and protector of rights. This conflict should be resolved at the constitutional level.

In Section II, I discuss various arguments that have been put forward about the role of government in the collection of taxes, with particular emphasis on Ayn Rand and Robert Nozick. I examine the fundamental tension between the necessity of levying taxes to fund government and the elusive goal of creating a minimal state. I illustrate this problem by examining the history of taxation in the United States.

The discussion in Section II illustrates the fact that those in favor of a "night-watchman state" have not done a particularly credible job of explaining how such a state might fund itself. The problem of funding a night-watchman state is simply a variant on the perennial question of how to limit governmental power. It is an important variant, however, because it suggests an answer to the puzzle of why the government, once it has obtained the power to collect revenue by force in the form of its taxing authority, does not use that authority to take all of the revenues generated by the private sector. In other words, it is clear why the government's revenues are not zero: some money is necessary to fund even the minimal state. But if those funds can be collected by force, then why doesn't the government take everything? And what explains the cross-sectional variations over time and among countries with respect to levels of taxation and methodologies of taxation?

I continue in Section III with a discussion of the incentives that government, like other financial claimants on firms' cash flows, has to affect the behavior of the firms in which it is an investor. The key point here is that the interests of different claim-holders are both varied and conflicting. The precise nature of the claim held by a particular creditor will critically determine the nature of the incentives of that claim-holder. Employees' incentives and interests are different from those of shareholders, whose interests diverge from those of managers, suppliers, customers, and, of course, government. Among the various claimants to the cash flows of businesses, the nature of the government's claims has not been well specified in earlier work. One of the goals of this essay is to remedy that gap.

The critical attribute distinguishing government in its role as an investor from all other investors is that government has powers of observation (monitoring rights) and powers of coercion (access to criminal and civil sanctions) unavailable to ordinary investors. These differences are differences in degree, not in kind: all investors retain some ability to monitor and control the firms in which they invest. Along these lines, fraud committed against private investors is punishable with imprisonment, as is fraud against the government. It is, of course, true that private parties have to persuade the government to bring a criminal case, and that private parties do not operate their own prisons. An independent judiciary and independent prosecutors serve to mitigate this distinction.

The government's abilities to monitor and control are extensive, but, like other investors, the government does not enjoy plenary power in this regard (and even if it did, it would be limited by its own incompetence, as one routinely observes in the emergence of thriving black markets under even the most totalitarian governmental regimes).

In Section IV, I examine the possibility of making changes to the terms of government's legal claims on the cash flows of individuals and businesses in order to limit the power of government to intrude in people's lives. Here the argument turns to constitutional economics, in which constitutional provisions pertaining to the tax code are considered as a means to bolster other structural constitutional provisions that promote liberty.

II. Taxation and the Minimal State

The classic "night-watchman state" (what Robert Nozick calls a minimal state)[3] starts with the assumption that human beings have certain basic, "natural" rights, and that government can be justified only as a necessary instrument to protect those rights. An enduring question in political science, economics, law, and political philosophy is whether it is possible to create a government that is strong enough to protect people's rights, such as the right to contract for goods and services (including labor), without becoming so powerful that government itself is impossible to control.

The state and the various bureaucratic organs through which it operates have long been viewed as institutions with discrete, albeit complex, sets of preferences. The state enacts policies that reflect the goals of those in power, to be sure, but the goals of those in positions of power are influenced by the incentive structure of the institutional environment in which they find themselves. Thus, the public policies that we ultimately observe reflect the preferences of those holding policymaking positions within government. Before these preferences find expression in the form of regulation, however, they will have been influenced by the institutions in which the policymakers have been operating. The power of institutions to shape preferences is, of course, greatly enhanced by the fact that the individuals who rise to the most powerful positions in a bureaucracy are

[3] Robert Nozick, *Anarchy, State, and Utopia* (New York: Basic Books, 1974), ix.

those who are most successful in learning, and ultimately mastering, the institutional culture of the organization in which they work. In other words, for better or for worse, bureaucrats influence policy and shape the preferences of the agencies in which they operate.

A. The problem of taxation from the perspective of the minimal state

Public choice theorists such as James M. Buchanan and Gordon Tullock,[4] intellectual skeptics such as Michael Oakeshott,[5] and natural rights philosophers such as John Locke[6] and Robert Nozick[7] all advocate theories grounded in a healthy rejection of standard, unexamined assumptions about man's capacity to achieve nirvana through government intervention. These thinkers acknowledge the fact that humans have human failings that can be magnified exponentially when given access to the unchecked power of government, and these thinkers respond to this fact by restricting the range of legitimate government action to a very limited and discrete sphere. This sphere is limited to the establishment and maintenance of a legal order of rights, obligations, and duties that prevent conflict, enforce contracts, and allow individuals to be free in their quest for human flourishing in the private sphere.

Embracing in a disciplined fashion Thomas Hobbes's assumptions about the proclivities of man and the nature of the state requires one to recognize that government is the ultimate "necessary evil."[8] While Nozick maintained that civilized social interactions require what he described as a "dominant protective association," Oakeshott's telling response (consistent with the modern theory of public choice) was that this sort of institution, whether it is a government or a private protective association, inevitably "is occupied by men of the same make as the subjects they rule—men, that is to say, who have pervasive incentives when they attain governmental office, to go beyond the constitutional designs for limiting

[4] James M. Buchanan and Gordon Tullock, *The Calculus of Consent: Logical Foundations of Constitutional Democracy* (Ann Arbor: University of Michigan Press, 1962).

[5] Michael Oakeshott, *On Human Conduct* (Oxford: Oxford University Press, 1975); Michael Oakeshott, *The Politics of Faith and the Politics of Scepticism*, ed. Timothy Fuller (New Haven, CT, and London: Yale University Press, 1996).

[6] John Locke, *Two Treatises of Government*, ed. Peter Laslett (Cambridge: Cambridge University Press, 1988).

[7] Nozick, *Anarchy, State, and Utopia*, ix.

[8] Thomas Hobbes, *Leviathan*, ed. Edwin Curley (Indianapolis: Hacket Publishing Company, 1994). Hobbes was of the view that until man organizes a strong system of government, he will exist merely in a state of nature in which, in order to survive, each individual acts independently and autonomously, purely in his own self-interest. Absent the allocation of massive power to government, man lives in a "state of war," and life is "solitary, poor, nasty, brutish, and short" (ibid., book 1, p. 13). The only way out of the state of nature is through social contract: mutually beneficial agreements that require each individual to exchange his freedom of action for the security provided by a strong central government.

governmental power, and impose upon the community an 'order' particularly favorable to their own interests."[9]

One of the more perplexing problems in applying political philosophy to reality is how to pay for the work of the state. Even if, like Robert Nozick (and John Locke and Herbert Spencer before him), we confine the state to an institutional role in which it is organized exclusively to provide for "protection against force, theft, fraud, enforcement of contracts, and so on,"[10] we still must acknowledge that it is very costly to protect against force, theft, and fraud, not to mention the cost of enforcing contracts. This, of course, leads inexorably to the question of how to pay for these protections and services.

Nozick observes that, in the state of nature, people acting in their own rational self-interest would develop a voluntary association, indistinguishable for all intents and purposes from the modern state, which would exercise monopoly power over the use of force and afford protection of the rights of the people residing within its jurisdictional boundaries.[11] Whether the state "grows by an invisible-hand process and by morally permissible means, without anyone's rights being violated,"[12] or generates itself spontaneously in a "constitutional moment,"[13] hardly seems relevant, since either way the end result is the same: the emergence of the modern state.

Problems arise when one examines Nozick's conception of property rights a bit further. Nozick argues, rather convincingly I might add, that the state is not justified in engaging in the redistribution of wealth, so long as the initial allocation of property rights against which the state is acting was originally established through just transfer or just acquisition of property.[14] However, Nozick also argues, more problematically, that taxation is a violation of rights because it causes the government, unjustly, to be a "part owner" of the person taxed.[15] This means, among other things, that for Nozick at least, "taxation of earnings from labor is on a par with forced labor."[16]

The problem with this analysis is that if taxes are evil, there would appear to be no way to finance the many night-watchman functions

[9] Oakeshott, *The Politics of Faith and the Politics of Scepticism*, 33.

[10] Nozick, *Anarchy, State, and Utopia*, ix.

[11] Ibid., 115–19.

[12] Ibid., 115 (italics omitted).

[13] Bruce Ackerman, "Constitutional Politics, Constitutional Law," *Yale Law Journal* 99 (1989): 453–91; Bruce Ackerman, *We the People: Foundations* (Cambridge, MA: Harvard University Press, 1991); Bruce Ackerman, *We the People: Transformations* (Cambridge, MA: Harvard University Press, 1998).

[14] Nozick, *Anarchy, State, and Utopia*, 153.

[15] Ibid., 169–72.

[16] Ibid., 172. Of course, there are worse things than forced labor (or taxation, for that matter). See H. L. A. Hart, *Essays in Jurisprudence and Philosophy* (Oxford: Oxford University Press, 1974), 206 (arguing that it is not appropriate to "lump together" the taking of a man's income to save others from some great suffering, and killing him or taking one of his vital organs for the same purpose).

necessary to permit individuals to pursue their individual ideas of the good. Nozick's answer to the question of how to control the minimal state is that unfettered markets, voluntary associations, and private philanthropy produce sufficient pressure to protect private ordering. While Nozick's approach has the virtue of limiting (or eradicating) the state, in order for the approach to succeed, either coercion must ultimately be necessary, or else people will have to be a lot more cooperative and charitable than Hobbes—and experience—suggest is likely to be the case. In this way, Nozick's view of the world seems as naive as that of Ayn Rand, who, like Nozick, seems to think that government can be organized as a voluntary association without the power to coerce.

Rand thought that, in a just society, a contract between government and its citizens would specify that government has the sole right to use force. With the right to resort to force removed from human interaction, individuals would be free to exercise their rights to pursue the goals fashioned by their own reason. Government would be characterized by three institutions: a military to protect the citizenry against foreign invaders; police to maintain civil order; and a fair, objective court system to enforce the contractual agreements entered into in the private sector. Eschewing the notion of a state powerful enough to force the payment of taxes, Rand adopted a very optimistic view of how government would fund itself in her idealized world:

> In a fully free society, taxation—or, to be exact, payment for governmental services—would be *voluntary*. Since the proper services of a government—the police, the armed forces, the law courts—are demonstrably needed by individual citizens and affect their interests directly, the citizens would (and should) be willing to pay for such services, as they pay for insurance.[17]

Rand's view of human nature and the potential to limit government through good intentions seems impossibly romantic. From a rational choice perspective, the problems with the voluntary approaches to taxation suggested by Nozick and Rand seem almost too obvious to mention. One problem is estimating the amount that one should pay for government services. If payment is voluntary, people will tend to underpay. Another problem is massive free-riding. Why should individuals make voluntary payments to the government unless other people do so? Rational people

[17] Ayn Rand, "Government Financing in a Free Society," in Rand, *The Virtue of Selfishness* (New York: Signet, 1964), 116. Rand embraced the view that the ability to reason was the quintessential human attribute, and that the right to one's own life was the single most valuable right in a just society. According to Rand: "No individual or private group or private organization has the legal power to initiate the use of physical force against other individuals or groups and to compel them to act against their own voluntary choice." Ayn Rand, *Capitalism: The Unknown Ideal* (New York: Signet, 1967), 46.

will know that others are withholding payments and that they too can withhold payment without the system collapsing, because if only a small number of citizens withhold payment, the system will not suffer. Hoping that others will pay enough to fund government services, large numbers of people are likely to withhold payment.

While it is true that millions of people contribute to a myriad of charities, particularly in the United States, the total amount raised by government in taxes is orders of magnitude higher than that raised by charities and philanthropic organizations. For example, in 2004, total charitable giving was an all-time record $250 billion, an upturn of 5 percent over the previous year.[18] By contrast, the federal government collected $1.92 trillion in tax revenues during 2004.[19]

In other words, since the decision about whether to make or withhold contributions is not coerced or made under the threat of force, many individuals will elect to withhold payment or to pay only a token amount. Similarly, those who disagree with government policy (such as those against whom contracts are being enforced) are likely to decide not to pay.[20]

Putting aside the rather utopian idea of making taxes voluntary, the next best alternative would be to establish a simple system that imposed rules that caused as few distortions in the private sector of the economy as possible. From the perspective of those interested in devising legal rules that might be successful in controlling government, the flat tax is viewed as the most attractive method of organizing a mandatory tax system. The first sustained argument in favor of a flat tax was developed by F. A. Hayek.[21] Hayek believed that the tax rate for the highest income earners in society should be set at a flat rate equal to the overall level of taxation as a percentage of national income.[22] Subsequently, Milton Fried-

[18] See American Association of Fundraising Counsel, *Giving USA* (Bloomington: Indiana University Press, 2005).

[19] Office of Management and Budget, *Budget of the United States Government, Fiscal Year 2004*, historical tables, http://www.whitehouse.gov/omb/budget/fy2004/sheets/hist02z1.xls (accessed August 2, 2005). On the one hand, this data likely understates the difference between private philanthropy and government taxing authority, since it excludes state and local taxes, as well as sales tax and property tax revenues. On the other hand, if taxes went down, people would have more income, and would be less reliant on government largesse, so charitable giving would increase, in all likelihood.

[20] As Will Rogers famously observed, "The income tax has made more liars of men than the game of golf." Libertarians do not believe that contracts between private parties can be enforced without coercion; the claim that taxes can be collected without coercion is even more far-fetched. I am grateful to Eric Mack for this point.

[21] F. A. Hayek, "Progressive Taxation Reconsidered," in Mary Sennholz, ed., *On Freedom and Free Enterprise* (Princeton, NJ: D. van Nostrand, 1956), 265–84.

[22] National income is the total net value of all goods and services produced within a nation over a specified period (usually one year). A nation's national income will equal the sum of wages, profits, rents, interest and dividends, and pension payments to residents of the nation. Thus, for example, if national income were $10,000 trillion, and the government required $2,500 trillion, the top tax rate would be 25 percent, because the overall level of taxation ($2,500 trillion) is 25 percent of national income.

man adopted a similar view, asserting that, "[a]ll things considered, the personal income tax structure that seems to me best is a flat-rate tax on income above an exemption, with income defined very broadly and deductions allowed strictly for defined expenses of earning income."[23]

The government-as-investor approach trumpeted in this essay is in certain ways more radical and in certain ways more conservative than the flat-tax approach advocated by others. The flat-tax approach attempts to limit government's ability to treat similarly situated individuals differently. The government-as-investor approach is silent on this important issue.

Like the flat-tax concept, the government-as-investor approach recognizes the government's power to collect taxes by force, but attempts to simplify and limit this power. Moreover, like the flat-tax approach, the government-as-investor approach also endeavors to simplify the government's role, but in a much different way. The flat-tax approach is pragmatic: it posits that the flat tax is fairer and simpler to administer. The government-as-investor approach simply attempts to reconceptualize the relationship between the government and taxpayers in a more systematic way. This reconceptualization should lead to a better understanding of the nature of taxation and provide a more solid basis for limiting the government's interference in the economic privacy of its citizens.

The most widely accepted flat-tax proposal, offered by Robert E. Hall and Alvin Rabushka, recommends replacing the various personal federal marginal income tax rates in the U.S. (currently set at 10 percent, 15 percent, 25 percent, 28 percent, 33 percent, and 35 percent) with a 19 percent federal tax rate for both individuals and businesses.[24] The arguments for doing this are based on pragmatic concerns for simplicity, equity, and efficiency. A flat tax would contain no tax credits, deductions, or exemptions except for the personal, spousal, and child exemptions. Doing away with these deductions would make it easier for taxpayers to determine the amount of their taxable incomes, and would eliminate a great deal of complicated and time-consuming effort on the part of taxpayers, tax preparers, and bureaucrats.

In addition to lowering transaction costs and achieving greater simplicity, a flat tax would further the policy goal of creating an equitable tax system by better ensuring that people with similar incomes bear similar

[23] Milton Friedman, *Capitalism and Freedom* (Chicago: University of Chicago Press, 1962): 161–76. Friedman and Hayek had similar views in the sense that both favored a flat tax in the form of a proportional income tax, as opposed to a flat tax in the form of equal lump-sum payments for all. Both opposed modern progressive income taxes in which people pay higher percentages of their income in taxes as their income increases. For more analysis of the flat-tax idea, see the National Center for Policy Analysis Idea House website, http://www.ncpn.org/n/pi/taxes/flattax.html (accessed January 10, 2005); Robert E. Hall and Alvin Rabushka, *The Flat Tax*, 2d ed. (Stanford, CA: Hoover Institution Press, 1995); and Robert E. Hall and Alvin Rabushka, *Tax Notes* (August 4, 1995), at http://www-hoover.stanford.edu/PRESSWEBSITE/FlatTax/notes.html.

[24] See Hall and Rabushka, *The Flat Tax*.

tax burdens. A third benefit of the flat tax is that it would promote efficiency by eliminating the current tax system's distortion between consumption and investment. The current graduated income tax system distorts the decision whether to consume or to invest, by taxing income from investment but not taxing consumption. Eliminating this distortion, it is argued, will lead to greater incentives for people to work and to engage in entrepreneurial activity, thus resulting in greater capital formation, which in turn will lead to higher national income (GDP) and a higher standard of living.

As with the current "progressive" tax system, however, the flat-tax system advances no theory regarding what taxation itself illustrates about the relationship between the state (in its capacity as tax collector) and the citizens (who pay taxes). Absent such a theory, it is impossible to defend any particular system of taxation. The state-as-investor theory proposed in this essay fills this gap.

In his Nobel prize winning essay, Ronald Coase addressed the question of why some economic activity is organized across markets, while other activity is organized within firms. Across markets, market prices determine whether transactions will take place; within firms, however, transactions are made by entrepreneurial coordination. As the price of transacting across markets goes up (that is, as transaction costs increase), more economic activity will be organized within firms. As the cost of entrepreneurial coordination goes up (that is, as agency costs increase), more activity will be organized across markets.[25] Coase also observed that the firm should be conceptualized as a nexus, or a complex web of contractual relationships among its various constituencies.[26] Consistent with Coase's insight that the business organization is a nexus of contracts, the firm should not be viewed as an entity, but rather as a complex aggregate of various inputs (capital, labor, management, suppliers) that are coordinated by managers to produce goods or services. Fixed claimants (creditors) provide debt capital. Employees provide labor. Residual claimants (shareholders) provide equity. Management personnel (and boards of directors of corporations) monitor the various productive factors and execute the strategic plans of the firm.

If the state, like the firm, is simply a legal fiction representing the complex set of contractual relationships among the various inputs, it stands to reason that, following Coase, one should focus on the characteristics of the contracts that constitute the state in order to understand it fully. The government as tax collector resembles a contractual claimant on the cash flows of the people and firms it taxes. To the extent that a government's tax collections are morally defensible, they must be based

[25] Ronald H. Coase, "The Nature of the Firm," *Economica* 4 (1937): 386–405.
[26] Ibid., 401.

on some theory of express or implied consent; otherwise, taxation really is, as the saying goes, "theft."

However, regardless of the morality of taxation, government must be given the power to tax coercively if it is to survive. When this tax takes the form of an income tax, it gives the government a share of the profits of the individuals and firms subject to the government's taxing authority. This, in turn, places the government in the position of an investor with a stake in every person or firm in society.[27]

Government has not always played the role of an investor in the people and businesses it governs. A brief history of taxation in the United States illustrates this point.

B. Taxation in the United States

Income taxes were not made a "permanent fixture" of the U.S. tax system until 1913, when the Sixteenth Amendment to the Constitution, which settled the constitutional issue of whether Congress had the legal authority to tax income, came into effect. This constitutional amendment formally empowered the federal government to impose taxes on the incomes of both individuals and corporations.[28] By 1918, annual internal revenue collections passed the billion-dollar mark, rising to $5.4 billion by 1920.[29]

The United States was a tax haven in its early history. From 1791 to 1802, the United States government was supported by sales taxes levied on distilled spirits, carriages, refined sugar, tobacco and snuff, property sold at auction, corporate bonds, and slaves. The necessity of financing the War of 1812 led to new sales taxes on gold, silverware, jewelry, and watches. In 1817, Congress abolished these sales taxes and relied instead on tariffs on imported goods to provide sufficient funds for running the government.

In 1862, Congress enacted the nation's first income tax law in order to finance the Civil War. This income tax was eliminated in 1872 and renewed briefly in 1894. In 1895, the U.S. Supreme Court held that the income tax was unconstitutional because it was not apportioned among the states in conformity with the Constitution. In the same ruling, the Court also held that a tax on the income generated from property ownership was the same thing as a tax on the property itself.[30]

[27] See Sumeet Sagoo, "History of the Income Tax in the United States," http://print.infoplease.com/ipa/A0005921.html (accessed January 15, 2005).

[28] United States Constitution, Sixteenth Amendment, March 15, 1913.

[29] Sagoo, "History of the Income Tax in the United States."

[30] *Pollock v. Farmers' Loan and Trust Co.*, 158 U.S. 601 (1895). Though the Court held that the apportionment problem it identified was relevant only to income from property ownership, and not to labor or business income, the Court invalidated the entire income tax on the theory that the unconstitutional provisions were not severable from the provisions that were

The income tax of 1862 closely resembled the modern income tax system in several ways. First, the statute established the federal office of the Commissioner of Internal Revenue, which was given the authority possessed by that bureaucracy today. Specifically, the IRS had the authority to assess, levy, and collect taxes, and the right to enforce the tax laws through seizure of property and income, civil suits, and criminal prosecution and referrals. In addition, the income tax of 1862 was based on modern principles of graduated, or progressive, taxation and the principle of withholding income at the source. During the Civil War, a person earning from $6,000 to $10,000 per year paid tax at the rate of 3 percent. Those with incomes of more than $10,000 paid taxes at the rate of 5 percent. A $3,000 minimum threshold effectively limited the tax to the top 1 percent of the economic order.[31]

Sales and excise taxes were reintroduced and an inheritance tax also was enacted. By 1866, internal revenue collections reached more than $310 million, their highest point in the nation's ninety-year history. This figure was not reached again until 1911.[32]

The government's ability to use the coercive power of the state to impose taxes is by now well settled as a matter of law, if not of morality. One moral justification for giving government the power to tax is that such power is justified simply because the state needs revenue and the state is legitimate. As such, it is argued, the taxing power of the state is a straightforward aspect of the social contract that exists between citizens and the state. Under the terms of this contract, people cede to the state the power to coercively tax so that it may solve the collective action problems that plague any attempt to implement a voluntary system of tax collection.

Alternatively, one can claim that the state lacks the power to impose taxes under some natural rights theory. But as long as the state has the power to collect taxes in practice, this argument is purely theoretical and academic. To put it another way, governments compete for the right to control various land masses. States that lack the power to tax inevitably will fail in Darwinian competition for power and authority with rival states. For this reason alone, taxation will survive as a feature of civil life. This is troubling to those interested in controlling the power of government, not only for the obvious reasons that taxation creates distortions in the real economy and provides the state with sufficient resources to create a leviathan that can destroy fundamental rights and quash dissent, but also for other reasons.

---

constitutional. The Court's decision in *Pollock* also invalidated the imposition of a progressive federal tax on high incomes on the grounds that taxing higher incomes at a higher rate violated constitutional substantive due process protections for property rights.

[31] Akhil Amar, *America's Constitution: A Biography* (New York: Random House, 2005), 496; Act of October 3, 1913, 38 Stat. 166 (1913); Sharon Nantell, "A Cultural Perspective on American Tax Policy," *Chapman Law Review* 2, no. 1 (1999): 33–50.

[32] Sagoo, *History of the Income Tax in the United States.*

One such reason is that the power to tax creates new, powerful, and inexorable incentives for private-sector actors to withdraw from productive activity and divert their energy and resources to rent-seeking. This rent-seeking takes the form of petitioning government for various forms of support, including relief from the payment of existing taxes, the imposition of new or higher taxes on current competitors and potential competitors, and even forbearance from the imposition of new or higher taxes.[33] Perhaps the two most pernicious ways in which this rent-seeking aspect of the government's taxing authority reveals itself are the relentless pace of revisions to the tax code and the ever-increasing complications of the law. To examine recent history, we observe major tax law changes about every other year during the 1980s. The most important of these was President Ronald Reagan's tax cut of 1981, which effectuated a 25 percent across-the-board cut in personal marginal tax rates.

The Reagan tax cut revolution ended with President Bill Clinton's signing of the Revenue Reconciliation Act of 1993, which dramatically increased taxes on higher income recipients. In 1997, under pressure from congressional Democrats, Clinton signed another tax act, which cut taxes almost to the levels they had been before the 1993 Clinton tax increases. Additional tax laws were signed by President George W. Bush in 2001, 2002, and 2003. For example, the Job Creation and Workers Assistance Act of 2002 provided tax relief to businesses, a thirteen-week extension on unemployment insurance, and tax breaks for taxpayers affected by the September 11, 2001, terrorist attacks. The Jobs and Growth Tax Relief and Reconciliation Act of 2003, a ten-year, $350 billion tax package and the third-largest tax cut in U.S. history, temporarily reduced taxes on corporate dividend payments, reduced capital-gains taxes, and increased child credits for most taxpayers.

The point of this brief history has been to show that the government's role as income tax collector is rather recent in time, formally beginning only in 1913 with the passage of the Sixteenth Amendment to the Con-

[33] Richard L. Doernberg and Fred S. McChesney, "On the Accelerating Rate and Decreasing Durability of Tax Reform," *Minnesota Law Review* 71 (1987): 913; Richard L. Doernberg and Fred S. McChesney, "Doing Good or Doing Well? Congress and the Tax Reform Act of 1986," *New York University Law Review* 62 (1987): 891–915; Fred S. McChesney, "Rent Extraction and Rent Creation in the Economic Theory of Regulation," *Journal of Legal Studies* 16 (1987): 101–19. For a provocative critique of the economic theory of regulation as applied to tax policy, see Daniel N. Shaviro, "Beyond Public Choice and Public Interest: A Study of the Legislative Process as Illustrated by Tax Legislation in the 1980s," *University of Pennsylvania Law Review* 139 (1990): 6–7, 108 (describing public choice as a theory that predicts that regulation and legislation are products supplied to well-organized interest groups that are struggling to maximize the incomes of their members, often at the expense of the less well-organized). Thus, legal rules and public policy are, in effect, sold to the highest bidder, with bids being paid in the currency of votes, campaign contributions, and personal benefits such as honoraria. See also Timothy J. Conlan, Margaret T. Wrightson, and David R. Beam, *Taxing Choices: The Politics of Tax Reform* (Washington, DC: Congressional Quarterly Press, 1990); and Scott Gordon, "The New Contractarians," *Journal of Political Economy* 84, no. 3 (June 1976): 573–90.

stitution. Since then, the debate has been about the precise form that the income tax should take, rather than about how the imposition of the tax has changed the relationship between taxpayers and the state. In my view, two questions arise in the wake of the rather recent imposition of the income tax: (1) How can we better understand the nature of the claims that the state has on the income of people and firms in its jurisdiction? And (2) how can those claims best be controlled? These are the issues to which I turn in the remaining sections of this essay.

III. Understanding and Controlling Government's Claims on Private-Sector Cash Flows

A significant gap in the public choice and constitutional economics literature concerns the role of taxation in affecting the government's incentives to intervene in private-sector ordering. In its role as tax collector, government is the largest, most ubiquitous "residual claimant" on the cash flows of the firms in any economy. This simple observation suggests that scholars and policymakers can avail themselves of the rich and burgeoning literature in financial economics on the incentives that such residual claimants have to manage the cash flows associated with their investments.

A standard claim made by financial economists is that "[t]he state, thanks to its tax claim on cash flows, is de facto the largest minority shareholder in most corporations."[34] There is some truth in this assertion, but it is grossly oversimplified in three ways. First, of course, the government's power to tax is unilateral, removing the critical element of voluntarism that characterizes investments between private-sector actors. Second, the government can regulate, and therefore direct, the activities of the firms in which it invests, in ways that minority shareholders can only dream about. Finally, while it is accurate to characterize the government as an investor, in fact the government's financial interests in firms are more accurately described as a hybrid mix that has some of the characteristics of an equity claim and some of the characteristics of debt.[35]

[34] Mihir Desai, Alexander Dyck, and Luigi Zingales, "Theft and Taxes," ECGI Finance Paper 63/2004, SSRN paper 629350, http://papers.ssrn.com/sol3/papers.cfm?abstract_id=629350 (December 2004). Desai, Dyck, and Zingales have argued that as tax rates go up, insiders are more likely to divert cash to themselves at the expense of shareholders. In contrast, stricter enforcement of the tax code by the state reduces corporate insiders' ability to divert resources to themselves, and therefore can have the surprising effect of raising the value of investments in a company in spite of the increase in the tax burden. Thus, Desai, Dyck, and Zingales argue that when a corporate governance system is ineffective (i.e., when it is easy to engage in tax evasion), an increase in the tax rate can reduce tax revenues.

[35] Economist Alan Auerbach recently has claimed that the government has a significant ownership interest in the U.S. equity market "through its claim to future tax revenues." Auerbach recognizes the fact that there are some differences between pure equity claims and tax claims. For example, he recognizes that the government's equity claims do not apply selectively to particular companies and do not carry voting rights. Auerbach, however,

It is accurate to view the government as a claimant on the cash flows generated by the real economy, but its claims are rather unique in nature. Thus, the government-as-investor paradigm can be quite useful in constitutional economics, but only if the nature of the government's claims on people's earnings is understood with some reasonable level of precision and specificity. The government is a residual claimant in the sense that, like other residual claimants such as shareholders, the government receives more income when earnings rise (because people pay more taxes), less income when earnings decline, and no income when earnings fall to zero. However, unlike other residual claimants, the government's claim to distributions is periodic. In other words, a corporation's board of directors can determine, within reason, that distributions of dividends are not in the investors' best interests because reinvesting the funds in the firm would be more likely to maximize the value of the equity investors' stakes. Of course, the government does not permit taxpayers to make this determination. Thus, tax payments are not like dividend payments because, unlike dividend payments, tax payments are not within the discretion of the taxpayer.

In addition, ordinary residual claimants lack control rights. Shareholders have voting rights, but the power to control the corporation and to direct management lies exclusively within the purview of the board of directors.[36] Most important in this regard, perhaps, is the ability of managers of most firms to engage in "going private" transactions, under which they repurchase their outstanding equity at some premium over market price and then assume ownership free of the control of outside equity investors. Another way of conceptualizing the "going private" transaction is captured by the term "leveraged buyout," under which the management of some other group, using the assets of the business as collateral, borrows enough money to buy out the equity claims of the other shareholders. The result is a new "leveraged" capital structure in which the firm's debt burden is increased significantly, and the amount of its outstanding equity is concomitantly decreased. In this process, the proportionate equity ownership share of the buyout group (usually management) is greatly increased.

overlooks other important distinctions. In particular, his analysis ignores the fact that government requires that tax payments be made periodically and cannot be reinvested by taxpayers. However, the empirical result of Auerbach's analysis—that federal government revenue is very sensitive to stock market returns—is interesting and important, and suggests that the analysis presented in this essay, which models the government as an investor, is quite robust. See Alan Auerbach, "How Much Equity Does the Government Hold?" *American Economic Review* 94, no. 2 (2004): 155–64.

[36] For example, the Model Business Corporation Act (MBCA), in force in the majority of U.S. jurisdictions, provides that "[a]ll corporate powers shall be exercised by or under the authority of, and the business and affairs of the corporation managed by or under the direction of, its board of directors" (MBCA Section 8.01[b]). Section 141(a) of the General Corporate Law of Delaware provides that corporations are managed "by or under the direction of" their boards of directors.

Interestingly, it is not possible for firms to strike a deal with the government similar to the deal that management strikes with investors in the context of a leveraged buyout. It is impossible for a firm to "capitalize" the present value of its future tax obligations to the government, borrow that sum, and pay off the government in the current time period, thereby discharging its obligation to pay taxes in the future. This is surprising, in light of the fact that firms and the government (particularly incumbent politicians and bureaucrats) might benefit from engaging in this sort of financing.

Unlike other minority investors, the government has virtually unfettered power to impose rules that affect the behavior of corporations and individuals. Along these lines, it is particularly misleading to characterize the government as a "minority" shareholder, because minority shareholders generally do not even have the potential to direct the management of the firms in which they have invested, much less the actual power to do so. Thus, while it is true that the government is a residual claimant on the cash flows of the firms and individuals in an economy, these residual claims are not quite the same as the claims of other holders of equity stakes in firms. The government has more management rights and stronger rights to distributions (in the sense that boards of directors have less discretion in making tax payments to the government than in making dividend payments to shareholders).

Analyzing the government as an investor in the firms in which it owns claims (that is, all firms subject to its taxing authority) blurs the standard distinction between capitalism and socialism. Capitalism generally refers to legal and economic systems that are characterized by (1) the right of individuals and groups of individuals acting as "legal persons" (or corporations) to buy and sell capital goods such as land, labor, and money in free-market transactions and (2) a sharp separation between the public sphere and the private sphere. In these systems, people rely on government to enforce contracts, to defend private property rights, and otherwise to support a private system of exchange. Socialism is a catch-all phrase used to describe various theories that embrace governmental ownership and administration of the means of production and distribution of goods and services. Nevertheless, under capitalism, residual claimants are joint-owners of the firms in which they invest. Thus, in its capacity as tax collector, even the most free-market-oriented governmental system has significant socialist attributes from a financial perspective, because such a government is a residual claimant in all of the firms and individuals that pay taxes.

Unlike most residual claimants, the government lacks voting rights in firms, although the government is free to directly involve itself in firm management in myriad other ways, including passing laws and regulations that regulate the conduct of the firm. Similarly, equity investors are, by definition, last in line to receive distributions when the firms in which they have invested file for bankruptcy protection or liquidate their assets.

By contrast, the government generally enjoys a priority in bankruptcy more akin to that of a fixed claimant than an equity claimant. In bankruptcies in which the debtor company is liquidated (which are treated under Chapter 7 of the Bankruptcy Code), typically the debtor's liabilities far outweigh its assets, and the court distributes all available assets that are not given an exemption from creditors' claims under state law. As a practical matter, when an individual or a business is filing for bankruptcy, many tax claims will not be discharged, so the government can collect after the bankruptcy is finalized and the debtor's other debts are discharged.[37] However, where the entity filing for protection from creditors under Chapter 7 is a business, there often will be nothing left to collect after the proceeding is concluded.

Similarly, in a filing for corporate reorganization under Chapter 11 of the Bankruptcy Code (which allows companies, and some individuals, to postpone payments to creditors and earn operating revenue while obtaining necessary goods and services), the debtor will propose a plan of reorganization, which specifies how, and the extent to which, each class of creditor will be repaid, if at all. Most taxes that were incurred within three years of filing the petition for reorganization under Chapter 11 are not dischargeable and must be paid prior to the claims of shareholders or unsecured claimants.[38] The government's claims, however, are not first in order of priority; they rank eighth after certain administrative expenses such as attorney and accountant fees, newly assessed taxes (taxes incurred after the entity has filed its bankruptcy petition), and certain expenses considered necessary to keep the debtor's business functioning.[39] Tax claims also come behind secured debts, in which the creditor has filed

[37] Under certain extremely limited circumstances, tax obligations are dischargeable in bankruptcy. For example, a taxpayer can obtain a discharge where: (a) the tax owed is for a year for which a tax return is due more than three years prior to the filing of the bankruptcy petition; and (b) the taxes owed are taxes for which the debtor filed a tax return more than two years prior to the filing of the bankruptcy petition; and (c) the tax was assessed more than 240 days prior to the filing of the bankruptcy petition; and (d) the tax owed is not due to a fraudulent tax return; and (e) the taxpayer did not attempt to evade or defeat the tax; and (f) the tax was not assessable at the time of the filing of the bankruptcy petition; and (g) the tax was not secured by specific assets of the debtor.

[38] In Chapter 11, the debtor can pay these taxes over a period of six years from the date of assessment, including interest.

[39] Taxes that are not dischargeable in bankruptcy under Chapter 11 and must be paid include the following: (a) income taxes for tax years ending on or before the date of filing the bankruptcy petition, for which a return is due (including extensions) within three years of the filing of the bankruptcy petition; (b) income taxes assessed within 240 days before the date of filing the petition; (c) the employer's share of employment taxes on wages, salaries, or commissions (including vacation, severance, and sick leave pay) paid as priority claims under 11 U.S.C. 507(a)(3) or for which a return is due within three years of the filing of the bankruptcy petition, including a return for which an extension of the filing date was obtained; and (d) excise taxes on transactions occurring before the date of filing of the bankruptcy petition, for which a return, if required, is due (including extensions) within three years of the filing of the bankruptcy petition (if a return is not required, these excise taxes include only those on transactions occurring during the three years immediately before the date of filing the petition).

and "perfected" a security interest in property held by the debtor under Article 9 of the Uniform Commercial Code. Finally, under Section 507(a)(8) of the Bankruptcy Code, tax debts incurred within the three years preceding the filing of the bankruptcy petition must be paid. Unsecured claims are rarely paid in full, and unsecured creditors sometimes receive only a small percentage of the original claim.[40]

Equity claimants are never paid when companies are liquidated, but sometimes receive a new class of equity securities in the reorganized entity. Thus, another reason why it is inaccurate to characterize the government as a pure residual claimant is because the government's claims against bankrupt firms more closely resemble those of creditors than those of shareholders.

While generally the government enjoys greater advantage in relation to the people and firms in which it invests than other, nongovernment residual claimants, this is not universally true. Another important distinction between the government's claims on firms' profits and the claims of other residual claimants relates to the ability of nongovernment residual claimants to "alienate" or trade their claims in secondary markets, and otherwise to pick and choose among the firms in which they invest. Nongovernment investors can decline to invest in certain firms, can invest disproportionately in some firms rather than others, and can (should they object to the way their firms are being managed) sell their claims to other, more optimistic shareholders. Additionally, nongovernment equity investors can actively participate in the market for corporate control, thereby influencing how the firms in which they invest are managed through the operation of the capital markets. Individual investors can choose whether or not to diversify and can diversify internationally as well as domestically. Governments, by contrast, cannot do any of these things. They invest proportionately in all firms, and their claims are rather "lumpy" in the sense that they receive the same percentage of profits in all firms, at least in tax systems that are considered to be "just."

While it is true, of course, that firms and individuals who cannot and/or do not have any earnings do not pay any taxes (at least where there is no

[40] The recently enacted Bankruptcy Abuse and Fraud Prevention Act of 2005 (S-256) makes it much more difficult to eliminate (discharge) consumer debts through bankruptcy and is likely to reduce the number of bankruptcy filings and to increase the ability of creditors to collect unsecured debts. The specific provisions of the bankruptcy law discussed here were not affected by the new statute. Under the new act, filing bankruptcy requires more paperwork, more supporting documents, more court scrutiny, and, because of the increased complexity, more legal fees. The new law will be effective for bankruptcy petitions filed on or after October 17, 2005. The new law is the first significant revision to the bankruptcy laws in more than twenty-five years. Among its many changes, it dramatically alters the availability of bankruptcy for all individual debtors, creates new rules and procedures for cases involving "health care businesses" and "personal consumer information," sets limitations on a debtor's exclusive right to file a Chapter 11 plan of reorganization, and establishes stricter post-petition deposit requirements that a utility service can require from a debtor. Its impact is likely to be felt by individuals and businesses for years to come.

wealth tax), where these taxable entities have the potential to generate earnings, the government is still an investor. Its investment simply takes the form of a call option on the potential future earnings of the person or firm not currently earning money or paying taxes.

Thus, the differences between the government and other residual claimants are far more profound than is generally acknowledged in the finance literature, but this does not mean that there are no common features. Both government and individual investors enjoy "limited liability" in that their exposure to loss is limited to the amount of their investments. Most significantly, like shareholders and other residual claimants, the government benefits from increases in firms' net earnings (earnings after interest, depreciation, and amortization) in the form of increased revenues, and it suffers decreased revenues when firms' net earnings decline.

The government, like private equity investors, enjoys (or suffers the consequences of) the gains (or losses) resulting from the appreciation (or decline) in the value of the assets of the firms in which it has invested. When a firm increases in value by making positive present-value investments, shareholders and other equity investors benefit from increases in the value of the firm. This is a straightforward implication of the basic financial insight that equity values represent the present value to investors of the future earnings stream of the company. When a firm invests in a positive present-value project, the market will assess the value to investors of the future earnings to be realized from that project, will discount those future earnings to present value, and will adjust equity values accordingly. This explains why firms with no current earnings can trade at positive share prices. Such firms have projects that investors view favorably, and the share price reflects the present value of the future earnings of the firm. A critical function of the market, in other words, is to translate expected future profitability into high current share prices. In this way, current investors enjoy the benefits of current investments in projects that do not generate current revenue, and may not generate such revenue for a long time to come. The benefits of such investments are reflected immediately in firms' share prices. At the same time, of course, where the market is pessimistic about the long-term value of this sort of investment, current share prices will suffer from a firm's investment in such long-term projects.

The government also benefits from future investments, at least under certain circumstances. For example, when equity investors sell their shares for a capital gain, which reflects improvements in firms' investments, the government receives taxes on those capital gains. However, the government, unlike other equity claimants, does not benefit when a firm makes positive present-value investments absent a sale of shares by investors on which a capital gain is realized. This is a critical distinction because it means that the government, unlike other equity investors, is much more interested in short-term payouts rather than long-term payouts by the firms in which it has made investments. Where private-sector investors generally will prefer that firms reinvest earnings rather than make dividend payments, government tax policy is effectuated so as to require immediate "dividend" distributions in the form of taxes. In addition, when firms pay dividends, the government benefits from such dividend payments because it can collect taxes on such distributions. Likewise, when investors sell their investments, the government collects taxes on that transaction as well. By contrast, the government does not benefit when firms choose not to pay dividends and instead reinvest their earnings. The government does not benefit from reinvestment policy unless and until the investors in the firms making such reinvestments choose to sell their shares, which they are unlikely to do (if they can help it), in order to avoid sharing their gains with their fellow investor—the government.

Finally, while the government owns residual claims in all of the individuals and firms subject to its taxing authority, the government itself has no residual claimants on its income. Government officials cannot sell or bequeath their offices, nor can they sell their claims on future tax revenues after they have left office. This means that those in control of government must obtain all of the benefits of their investment policies immediately or forfeit them forever. One way for present-day government officials to obtain present benefits from future tax revenues, of course, is through deficit financing. Today's government borrowing is paid for out of future tax revenues. This provides strong incentives for incumbent politicians to authorize the issuance of debt.

For example, as Daniel N. Shaviro has pointed out, tax cuts, such as those implemented by the Bush administration between 2001 and 2003,

> seem to have been aimed at shrinking the size of government. The idea apparently was to force eventual spending discipline, even (or perhaps especially) with respect to Social Security and Medicare, by turning reduced tax revenues into a political fact on the ground that would be difficult to reverse. In fact, however, the idea that the tax cuts would make the government smaller seems to have rested on spending illusion, or confusion between the actual size of government, in terms of its allocative and distributional effects, and the observed dollar flows that are denominated "taxes" and "spending."[41]

Thus, borrowing by government appears to be "even more" rational than borrowing by private-sector market participants. This is so because when

[41] Daniel N. Shaviro, "The Bush Administration's Huge Tax Cuts: Steps Towards Bigger Government?" (September 2003), NYU Law School, Public Law Research Paper No. 67; and NYU Center for Law and Business Research Paper No. 03-17, http://ssrn.com/abstract=444201.

government borrows, it passes the chore of organizing repayment and living under the constraints of budget deficits to future generations of bureaucrats and politicians. Shaviro has argued, however, that there exists a "long-term budget constraint," which requires that government inflows and outlays "must ultimately be equal in present value."[42] This, in turn, means that any budget deficit (fiscal imbalance), whether it is caused by tax cuts, by spending increases, or by some combination of the two, is likely to be paid for with a mix of future tax increases and future cuts to the major social welfare programs in the federal budget—Social Security and Medicare.

Viewed through the government-as-investor framework of this essay, however, there appear to be two questionable assumptions in Shaviro's analysis. The first is the assumption that there is a "long-term budget constraint" on the government, which seems wrong for two reasons. The first reason is that governments, just like private firms, can default on their obligations and either decline to pay their obligations entirely or reach some agreement with their creditors in which the creditors accept a lower interest rate and extended payment terms in order to avoid complete default by the government to which they have extended credit. The second reason is that for governments, unlike private firms, these "reorganizations" can be accomplished informally, either by legislative fiat or by changing the terms of existing bargains with creditors by inflating the currency with which the government's obligations are repaid. However these reorganizations are accomplished, the result is that governments end up repaying less than what was required in the original bargain and sometimes pay nothing at all. Of course, in a world of perfect information, creditors will adjust the amount and the terms on which they extend credit to the government so as to compensate for the risk of insolvency by the state. But states are notoriously unpredictable.

A second questionable assumption made by Shaviro relates to his observation that tax cuts will not necessarily make the government smaller. In response to this, I would point out that deficits will constrain future government spending because rational creditors will be unwilling to lend to a highly leveraged government that may not be able to repay the funds. Thus, tax cuts combined with government borrowing ultimately will limit the growth of government.

Similarly, Shaviro's claim that future tax increases necessitated by present tax cuts are likely to make the government bigger both allocatively and distributionally seems wrong. While it is true that future tax increases will require the government to collect more money in the future from people (that is, to change the nature of the residual claims it holds against firms and individuals), if this money is simply channeled directly to the government's creditors, it will not necessarily lead to bigger government as

[42] Ibid.

Shaviro asserts. It also is the case that, to the extent that the government's debt burden leads the government to cut programs in order to be able to meet the principal and interest payments due on its debt obligations, current borrowing may in fact reduce the future size of government.

Shaviro is correct in his basic point that government borrowing can maintain the current size of government or even increase it during times of tax cuts, so that, in the present, tax cuts will not constrain the growth of government. Tax cuts today, however, are quite likely to constrain the growth of government in the future. From a public choice perspective, then, the government (like other firms) must choose whether to act in its role as investor or in its role as borrower in order to fund current projects. Since politicians have shorter-term time horizons than private-sector actors, politicians are likely to prefer paying for programs through borrowing. But is this also true for firms and individuals? They, too, are likely to prefer deficit spending. To the extent that low taxes and big government now mean high taxes in the future, firms will prefer deficit spending because such spending will impose barriers to entry on rival firms. As the government's claims on businesses increase, it is harder for new firms to justify entering existing markets, given the size of the government's claim on their future revenues. This serves as a barrier to entry to potential rivals that protects incumbent firms.

While it is true that when taxes rise, they rise for all firms both old and new, it also is the case that the early years of a new firm's business constitute the critical "make or break" period for a new firm. To see this point, simply imagine that there are two competing firms that are identical in every way except that firm "A" was able to organize, solicit initial capital investments, and enter the market under a low-tax regime, and firm "B" had to get its start under a high-tax regime. Firm A, the firm with the head start, is more likely to survive. More importantly, once firm A is underway, firm B will have a harder time getting started, because potential initial investors must compete with a rival investor—the government—that will have a higher priority for the cash flows of the business, so new equity will be "crowded out" by higher taxes. This means that the firm that got an early start under the lower-tax regime inevitably will face fewer rivals than it otherwise would have faced had taxes not been raised.

The government's claims on the profits of people and businesses bear a certain resemblance to equity claims, but in other respects more closely resemble debt. Thus, it is erroneous simply to call the government a minority shareholder in all firms.[43] It is more accurate to describe the government as a hybrid investor that has much in common with both types of investors. Like other investors, the government has a claim on the earnings of the firms in which it has invested. This, in turn, provides

[43] See Auerbach, "How Much Equity Does the Government Hold?," and the text accompanying note 35 above.

support for the view that the government is not a monolithic institution, but rather, like other firms, an entity made up of a nexus of contracts, an entity that can, and should, be constrained to act consistently with the parameters of its rights and obligations as a contracting party.

Tables 1, 2, and 3 provide an overview of the similarities and differences between the government and other sorts of investors, along with a quantitative analysis of these similarities and differences. Note that, when examined in appropriate detail, the nature of the government's residual claims on the earnings of individuals and firms differs from both the claims of equity claimants and those of fixed claimants. There are similarities between the government's claims and those of both fixed claimants and equity claimants, but significant differences remain.

IV. Constitutional Economics and Securities Design: Controlling the Power of the Government to Enforce Its Claims as an Investor

It seems clear that regardless of whether one views a modern market-based economic system as a spontaneously generated natural phenomenon, as a complex social contract among citizens, or as an economic institution created and sustained by rationally self-interested politicians and bureaucrats, the government cannot exist without taxes, and taxes cannot be collected without coercion. The notion of government sustaining itself through "voluntary" contributions by grateful citizens seems farcical. So too does the notion that the government's claims on the cash flows of the people and firms subject to its jurisdiction can simply be characterized as similar to the weak claims held by minority shareholders.

It is not helpful merely to hope that perhaps, some day, the Sixteenth Amendment will be repealed and the government will be transformed into a grateful recipient of voluntary largesse freely contributed to its coffers by private-sector participants. In this essay, my policy proposal is far more modest. I simply advocate a change in the way that we view the phenomenon of corporate and individual income tax as a conceptual matter. Instead of viewing taxation as some sort of *sui generis*, intellectually unique claim by the government on the earnings of people and businesses, I believe that the government's claims to remittances from the income of firms and individuals (taxes) should be viewed as returns on investments made by the government in society. The government's claims are legitimate only so long as it actually has made such investments. Otherwise, like the Mafia, the government's tax receipts represent simple extortion, from an ethical point of view.

The government, in other words, is a "stakeholder" in the economy. Specifically, it is a well-entrenched equity holder whose fortunes rise and fall with the fortunes of the economy it putatively "controls."

TABLE 1. *Characteristics of the government and other investors*

Characteristic	Government	Equity claimants (stockholders)	Equity claimants (partners)	Fixed claimants
Residual claim	Yes	Yes	Yes	No
Claims subject to taxation	No	Yes	Yes	Yes
Legal right to distributions	Yes (taxes)	No	No	Yes
Voting rights	No	Yes	Yes	No
Priority in liquidation or insolvency	Yes	No	No	Yes
Diversification (ability to eliminate firm-specific risk)	Yes	Yes	No	No
Rights to veto change in control	No	Yes	Yes	No
Ability to profit from change in control	No	Yes	Yes	No
Alienable/assignable/tradeable claim	No	Yes	No	Yes
Limited liability	Yes	Yes	No	Yes
Participation in gains/losses from increase/decrease in firm's net earnings	Yes	Yes	Yes	No
Participation in gains/losses from unrealized appreciation/decline in value of firm's assets	No	Yes	Yes	No

TABLE 2. *Number of common characteristics: Government and various equity and fixed claimants*

	Equity claimants (stockholders)	Equity claimants (partners)	Fixed claimants
Government	4 out of 12 (33 percent)	3 out of 12 (25 percent)	7 out of 12 (58 percent)

TABLE 3. *Number of common characteristics: Equity claimants and fixed claimants*

	Equity claimants (stockholders)	Equity claimants (partners)
Fixed claimants	3 out of 12 (25 percent)	2 out of 12 (17 percent)

It seems far more productive, not to mention accurate, to conceptualize the government as an entrenched equity claimant on all cash flows within the economy—a claimant that enjoys a unique constellation of rights to the cash flows of all income-generating entities within its borders (rights not shared by its private-sector counterparts). Thinking about the government in this way has a couple of advantages over the current, unspecified conception of the nature of taxation. First, viewing the government in this way is consistent with a contractarian conception of the government, in which the exercise of governmental power must be explained as consistent with individual rights and rationalized as furthering individual interests. The investor-firm relationship is much easier to conceptualize along contractarian lines than the government-firm relationship. Second, viewing the government as an investor makes it clear why it would be legitimate to limit the power of the government to collect its residual claims, and to limit its ability to make midstream changes to the nature of its residual claims.

This conceptualization also allows us to concentrate on what is important: how to create constitutional rules that restrict the government's apparently unconstrained ability to turn its "power to tax" into the "power to destroy."[44]

[44] *McCulloch v. Maryland*, 17 U.S. 316 (1819), 17 U.S. 316 (Wheat).

Constitutional economics, a subdiscipline of public choice, is a relatively new field.[45] Constitutional economics is the study of how constitutions (that is, the foundational, pre-parliamentary or pre-legislative rules) establish the rules of the game for future, ordinary lawmaking and otherwise regulate and limit the domain of government. For example, structural rules, including the U.S. system of checks and balances of which the separation-of-powers doctrine is a part, raise the decision costs of government, thereby thwarting the efforts of special interest groups to gain control of government. Utilizing the government-as-investor paradigm as a policy lever provides an additional tool for constraining the proclivity of government to usurp people's rights during times of ordinary politics. This method of governmental constraint is vaguely suggested by such things as the so-called Taxpayers' Bill of Rights, which was included in the Technical and Miscellaneous Revenue Act of 1988.[46]

The statute requires Internal Revenue Service (IRS) employees to explain and respect taxpayers' rights to privacy and confidentiality, and their right to know why the IRS is requesting information, how it will be used, and what will happen if the taxpayer refuses to provide the requested information. Recourse is available to taxpayers who are not treated in a professional, fair, and courteous manner. Taxpayers have the right to represent themselves or to designate an advocate (who must be an attorney, certified public accountant, or other person authorized by the IRS) to represent them before the IRS. Taxpayers also can make sound recordings of any meetings with IRS employees, and can avail themselves of the Taxpayer Advocate Service to help resolve problems with the IRS. Taxpayers also have the right to appeal adverse rulings about their taxes to a neutral arbiter, and the IRS can be held liable for negligently or intentionally breaching taxpayers' rights under the statute.

This law did not curb the government's ability to collect taxes, but it did curb the government's ability to abuse the rights of ordinary citizens during the tax collection process. However, taxpayers' bills of rights are, under the framework established in this essay, fundamentally misconceived, because they do not accurately reflect the relationship between the citizen and the government in the context of taxation.

The first and most important way to utilize the framework employed in this essay for public-regarding and liberty-preserving purposes is to formalize the framework by giving explicit recognition to the role of the government as an investor. In particular, formal recognition should be given to the fact that when the government is engaged in the collection of revenue, it is acting as an investor/creditor, rather than as an institution in possession of some sort of unarticulated, unquestionable, and unlim-

[45] See note 1 and the sources cited there for elaboration on the origins and meaning of constitutional economics.

[46] Public Law 104-168, 110 Stat. 1452, codified at 26 U.S.C. Section 7433 (2004).

ited fundamental right to the income of the people and entities being taxed. For example, as a matter of constitutional law, the government in pursuit of its claims against the earnings of citizens and firms should give formal, legal respect to the fact that people do—and should be encouraged to—make highly asset-specific and undiversifiable investments on the basis of the tax code then in effect. The government's taxing power, if unabated, can usurp the value of those investments. This not only provides a strong disincentive to make such investments in the first place, but it also constitutes a taking of the personal property rights of the people and firms whose investments are so taxed.

While the government's taxing authority (power) is not questioned here, the legitimacy of changes in tax policy is subject to doubt. Like other creditors' claims, the government's claims should not be subject to nonconsensual revision after investments have been made. Investment decisions, whether they are the capital-budgeting decisions of firms or the decisions of individuals to invest in their own human capital, should not be subject to ex-post expropriation by government. For example, once an individual has begun a specialized education program such as law school or vocational school, the government should not be able unilaterally to change the tax regime that governs the income earned by that person. Similarly, once a new firm is chartered, the terms of the government's claims against the earnings of that firm should be frozen in place. Otherwise, after an individual or firm has made an individual-specific or firm-specific investment in human capital or asset-specific capital, respectively, that investment would be subject to expropriation by government unless individuals and firms are protected by constitutional rules.[47]

The foregoing policy proposal is subject to the criticisms that it is both unrealistic and undemocratic because it prevents changes in tax policies that might either be desirable or, at least, favored by a majority of people. These criticisms are invalid for four reasons. First, the government is always free to lower people's taxes. Second, where a change in tax policy is proposed, and the result is uncertain, people should have the choice of "opting into" the new system or continuing under the previous system. This would give the government the flexibility to implement new tax policies, but only when such policies benefit taxpayers. Third, the clear advantages of this proposal in terms of fairness and predictability indicate that it is preferable to the alternative, which is the current system that allows the government to make even retroactive changes in tax policy and tax rates.

Finally, with respect to complexity, the current tax code is extremely complex, and the work of preparing taxes is done by professionals and with automated tax-preparation software. As such, it is not unrealistic to

[47] Constitutional rules are more difficult to change than ordinary rules and tend to be more durable.

think that taxpayers and the government could manage the complexity of introducing an option that gave taxpayers the choice of paying either under an "old" tax system or under a "new" tax system. Indeed, with the alternative minimum tax currently in effect, the government exercises an option to collect the higher of the alternative minimum tax or the amount owed under the traditional tax calculation with deductions included.[48]

In order to transform this idea into a specific policy recommendation, I suggest rewording some of the provisions of the Fifth Amendment to the Constitution. In its current form, the amendment provides that "[n]o person shall be ... deprived of life, liberty, or property, without due process of law; nor shall private property be taken for public use without just compensation." Here, in order to constrain the government's taxing authority, I would rewrite this section to read as follows:

> No person shall be ... deprived of life, liberty, or property, through any means of taxation or otherwise, without due process of law; nor shall private property, including intellectual property or human capital, gained through education or in any other manner, be taken by means of any tax increase or otherwise for any use without just compensation.

The reality that the government does, and should, have the authority to raise revenue through taxation is not being questioned here. However, the state should not be able to impose a tax increase of any sort unless it can meet the burden of justifying the increase, not on the basis of the government's "need" but on the basis of a quid pro quo received by every member of the group on whom the increase will be imposed. That is, the justification should be made on the basis of some improvement in the nature or quality of public services or protections (defense, for example) offered by the government, an improvement that is being produced in response to some changed circumstance that justifies the increase.

In his 1985 book *Takings*, Richard Epstein argues that the takings clause of the U.S. Constitution should be broadly interpreted to provide protection for the common-law property rights in place when the Constitution was promulgated, as those rights were articulated by William Blackstone.[49] At common law, every man had an "absolute right" to the "free use, enjoyment, and disposal of all his acquisitions."[50] Epstein proposes that

[48] For a discussion of the Alternative Minimum Tax (Tax Reform Act of 1969 [P.L. 91-172]), see U.S. General Accounting Office, "Alternative Minimum Tax: An Overview of Its Rationale and Impact on Individual Taxpayers," statement by James R. White, Director, Tax Issues, before the U.S. Senate Committee on Finance, document GAO-01-500T, March 8, 2001, available at http://www.gao.gov/.

[49] Richard A. Epstein, *Takings: Private Property and the Power of Eminent Domain* (Cambridge, MA, and London: Harvard University Press, 1985), 297–303.

[50] William Blackstone, *Commentaries on the Laws of England*, 4 vols. (Chicago: University of Chicago Press, 1979), vol. 2, p. 217.

this conception of the nature and extent of property rights should be used to inform judicial interpretations of the Fifth Amendment's takings clause ("nor shall private property be taken for public use, without just compensation"), since such a conception forms a vital link between the individual's bundle of rights and a government that is limited by those rights. Applying this theory to constitutional interpretation, Epstein argues that four questions must be addressed in evaluating any governmental action, including taxation: (1) Is there a taking? (2) Is there justification? (3) Is the taking for public use? (4) Was there just compensation?

Epstein maintains that if a taking is unjustified or not for public use, or if a justified taking is uncompensated, then the plaintiff is entitled to some recovery. Epstein argues that "[t]he modern effort to distance the takings clause from general laws cannot be maintained. All regulations, all taxes, and all modifications of liability rules are takings of private property prima facie compensable by the state."[51]

Epstein argues that many contemporary taxes, including windfall profit taxes, state severance taxes, estate and gift taxation, and the progressive income tax are unconstitutional. He also argues that the modern welfare state's massive framework of transfer payments—including welfare, Social Security, unemployment benefits, food stamps, and farm subsidies—is unconstitutional under his analysis. Following this radical diagnosis, Epstein favors a relatively modest treatment regime, which would include the reform of the tax system to eliminate progressivity, invalidation of the minimum wage, and elimination of zoning laws.

My approach is in the spirit of Epstein's and is broadly consistent with his theory. There are three important differences, however, between my approach to takings and Epstein's. First, I favor change through a constitutional amendment, rather than through an activist judiciary, both because implementing such radical changes without a constitutional amendment would be inconsistent with the Sixteenth Amendment and because judicial activism of this magnitude would provoke a confrontation between the judiciary and the Congress that the judiciary would be unlikely to win.

Second, while Epstein focuses on history and the common law to support his views on the takings clause, my approach focuses on the modern reality that returns on human capital have replaced income from property ownership as the paradigmatic source of wealth. Consequently, takings jurisprudence should be updated to reflect this modern reality.

Third, where Epstein examines taxes in general, my focus is on tax increases. The reason for this difference is that I am looking at taxation from the perspective of the incentives that people and firms have to make new investments in human capital and in other forms of productive enterprise. Such investments are made with knowledge of the current tax

[51] Epstein, *Takings*, 301.

system. Tax increases, therefore, reduce the value of people's investments and should be viewed more skeptically from a constitutional perspective than the taxes that were in place prior to such investments being made.

The same analysis does not apply to tax cuts. Under the government-as-investor analytical framework proposed here, of course, the government would be free to lower taxes at any time, just as any other investor could decide voluntarily to grant more liberal terms to a firm in which he or she invested.

Recognizing the government as an investor in business does not pose a fundamental challenge for democracy. It does, however, allow one to analyze the role of the government with more clarity and sharper focus and to understand the conflicts of interest that affect the government in its dual role as investor/tax collector and, simultaneously, as regulator of business.

In its role as investor, the government is justified in imposing constraints on people and businesses in order to protect its claims on cash flows. For example, once the government's role as tax collector is conceptualized as placing the government in the role of an investor, it follows logically that, since government is simply a claimant on firms' cash flows, it should not be able to engage in certain conduct, including collection activities that would be prohibited to other investors.

However, in its executive, legislative, and judicial roles, the government also has obligations to protect its citizens and to enforce contracts. There is a distinct conflict between the government's role as creditor and the government's role as neutral arbiter and protector of rights. For example, by denying or diminishing the claims of other creditors, either legislatively or judicially, the government is advancing its own private interests as an investor by increasing the resources available to satisfy its own claims.

The hope here is that people's conception of the phenomenon of taxation can be transformed from the current conception of taxation authority as a "state power" to a more refined conception of taxation authority as simply another aspect of the social contract that morally binds individuals to the state. It is to be hoped that the conceptual reassessment I am advocating here would be transformative from a policy perspective in two divergent ways. First, it would better legitimize the government's revenue collection function by providing a morally comprehensible basis for the government's claims on the earnings of firms and people. Second, it would provide citizens with a much stronger possibility of achieving the elusive goal of stability in tax policy. To better ensure stability, citizens and businesses should be given perfect buyout rights against the government's claims on their future cash flows. By this I mean that people should be able to choose whether they prefer to continue to meet their traditional periodic tax obligations to the government or whether they prefer to make a onetime lump-sum payment equal to the estimated present value of those future tax obligations.

Of course, estimating the present value of the future earnings of firms or individuals would be neither a simple nor a precise exercise. Such estimates, however, are necessarily and routinely performed by capital markets when securities are priced and when personal loans are made. Markets do it all the time. Here a sort of market constraint would work: If the government set the buyout price too high, one simply would not choose the buyout option. If the government set the buyout price too low, people would rush to invoke their buyout option (and the only consequence would be a shortfall in government revenue).

The buyout system proposed here, which flows logically from the concept of "government as investor," would permit individuals to "bet against" the government's statistical guess about their longevity and future earnings capacity. It also would enable people to obtain a binding commitment from the government against any future tax obligations. Of course, people would be able to borrow from private sources such as banks to obtain the payoff sums necessary to discharge all or part of their expected tax obligations. This buyout possibility should be viewed as a right, not a privilege.

V. Conclusion

This essay has advanced the descriptive assertion that the government's role as tax collector is that of an investor, or, to be more precise, that of a residual claimant on the earnings of all of the people and firms subject to the taxing power of the state. Building on this conceptual framework, I have made the normative claim that the role of the government as an investor in people and businesses should be formally recognized for what it is. Thus, the entire relationship between modern democracy and its citizens would be strengthened, as citizens could finally be viewed as equal contracting partners with the government, without jeopardizing the government's ability to collect the revenues it needs to provide for the protection of its citizens.

The core question in political theory is "What is the state?" The core question in political philosophy is "What ought the state to be?"[52] In this essay, I have attempted to contribute to the development of answers to both of these questions by constructing a new paradigm of the state as an investor. The advantage of this approach is that it permits elevating the taxpayer to the level of equal contracting party with the government to whom he or she pays taxes. This elevation in status alone, I believe, is sufficient to justify the intellectual exercise. There is an added payoff, however, in that the government-as-investor framework also suggests a

[52] See Buchanan and Tullock, *The Calculus of Consent,* 1: "Political theory has concerned itself with the question: What is the State? Political philosophy has extended this to: What ought the State to be? Political 'science' has asked: How is the State organized?"

number of tax policy improvements. In particular, this framework suggests limits on the government's ability to change people's tax status after they have already embarked on careers and made the sunken, nondiversifiable investments in human capital that such career training requires.

The framework advanced here also suggests that people should be able to make a once-in-a-lifetime payment in lieu of taxes to the government in order to discharge their tax liability. In these ways, the proposal here seems superior to the flat-tax proposal advocated most recently by Hall and Rabushka, and originally by Hayek and Friedman. This approach also seems superior to the utopian suggestion offered by Ayn Rand that taxation be voluntary, as well as to the unrealistic suggestion made by Nozick that income taxes violate man's natural rights.

Law, Yale University

INDEX